PENGUIN BOOKS

SIR PETER BLAKE

Alan Sefton is an experienced sports writer who manages Blakexpeditions, the company formed with Sir Peter Blake to operate the *Seamaster*. Sefton was chief executive of Team New Zealand during the 1999 America's Cup defence. Sefton has written several bestselling yachting books.

SIR PETER
BLAKE

AN AMAZING LIFE

THE AUTHORISED BIOGRAPHY

ALAN SEFTON

PENGUIN BOOKS

PENGUIN BOOKS

Published by the Penguin Group
Penguin Books Ltd, 80 Strand, London WC2R 0RL, England
Penguin Group (USA) Inc., 375 Hudson Street, New York, New York 10014, USA
Penguin Group (Canada), 90 Eglinton Avenue East, Suite 700, Toronto, Ontario, Canada M4P 2Y3
(a division of Pearson Penguin Canada Inc.)
Penguin Ireland, 25 St Stephen's Green, Dublin 2, Ireland (a division of Penguin Books Ltd)
Penguin Group (Australia), 250 Camberwell Road,
Camberwell, Victoria 3124, Australia (a division of Pearson Australia Group Pty Ltd)
Penguin Books India Pvt Ltd, 11 Community Centre,
Panchsheel Park, New Delhi – 110 017, India
Penguin Group (NZ), cnr Airborne and Rosedale Roads, Albany,
Auckland 1310, New Zealand (a division of Pearson New Zealand Ltd)
Penguin Books (South Africa) (Pty) Ltd, 24 Sturdee Avenue,
Rosebank, Johannesburg 2196, South Africa

Penguin Books Ltd, Registered Offices: 80 Strand, London WC2R 0RL, England

www.penguin.com

First published in New Zealand by Penguin Group (NZ) 2004
First published in Great Britain by Michael Joseph 2005
Published in Penguin Books 2006

1

Copyright © text Alan Sefton, 2005
Copyright © illustrations remains with individual copyright holders
All rights reserved

The moral right of the author has been asserted

Designed by Mary Egan
Set by Egan-Reid Ltd
Printed in England by Clays Ltd, St Ives plc

ISBN-13: 978-0-141-01929-1
ISBN-10: 0-141-01929-8

Contents

This work is dedicated to the memory of a very special New Zealander. I sincerely hope that it does him justice.

Introduction

When people talk of Sir Peter Blake's legacy, they often refer first to Auckland's downtown waterfront and the complete renovation that was achieved as a direct result of Team New Zealand winning the America's Cup. Impressive as it is, however, the completely refashioned Auckland waterfront is only a physical reminder of some of the enduring benefits the late, great sailor/adventurer left behind him.

Sir Peter's real legacy is the inspiration of a remarkable man and his equally remarkable life. It's the true tale of a young Kiwi who, from an absolutely normal and typical New Zealand upbringing, chose to aspire to and live out his dreams. In the process, he scaled the peaks of his profession, inspired those around him and gave his nation much to celebrate. He also changed the face of his sport, transformed the city in which he grew up, and then set out to save the planet.

Peter Blake was never constrained by horizons, whether at sea or in his own life. He was always seeking the next wind change, looking out for the next challenge, but only when the business at hand was completed. It took him 16 years and five attempts (three of them in his own boats) to win the Whitbread Round the World race. He then had to return to the fray after near-disaster to set a new record for sailing non-stop around the world. And then he picked up the pieces of three previous and unsuccessful New Zealand challenges to create the phoenix that was Team New Zealand,

9

with which he won one of sport's biggest prizes, the America's Cup.

I was fortunate enough to be a close friend of Peter Blake, to work with him on three of his Whitbread campaigns, to create with him Team New Zealand, and to be his business partner in blakexpeditions, through which he wanted to make people aware that we weren't taking very good care of Planet Earth. Like most others that were exposed to him, I can truly say that I am a better person for having known and worked with him, and that I have achieved a lot more in my life for being inspired by him.

Peter Blake was, in some ways, a complex person. On one hand, while pursuing his competitive goals, he was driven and frequently demanding. He would never, however, ask you to do something that he couldn't or wouldn't do himself. On the other hand, while with his family or friends, he sought only the simple pleasures in life, like playing board games with his children or hiking in the countryside. On both sides of the ledger, though, he was a thoroughly decent human being, with all of the right values – someone you were proud to call a friend.

This book hasn't been easy to write. Some of the memories of the man were still too vivid and real, and the spiritual scars of his senseless loss too raw. The further I tracked Sir Peter's remarkable life, however, the more I began to celebrate rather than grieve. He had an insatiable appetite for living, an infectious way of communicating his joy at being with us, and a stimulating determination to climb the next mountain.

I have not limited the recollections and the views expressed in the narrative to my own. That would have been self-serving and unfair to the man. He was too big a person, and he touched and was important to too many other lives, to make that a valid approach to his story. I have endeavoured to always be factual and to reveal the real man and the ups and downs, the thrills and spills, of his endeavours in life. I hope I have done him justice.

10

As I near the end of the undertaking, I keep going back to a piece of text that most fittingly sums up the spirit and being of the person who is the subject of this book. I wish it was my own.

> The spirit of adventure never dies.
> At its best it is born in the support
> and sharing of a family or friends.
> It can manifest itself in the work of the
> painter, the playing of music or even the
> laughter of children.
> It does not have to be competitively
> top gun, either with others or strangely
> enough, even oneself.
> It can be inherited through
> example but never imposed.
> And when the shouting dies away
> perhaps the greatest reward for
> any adventurer is to see it quietly
> growing in the next generation.

Alan Sefton, ONZM
October 2004
Auckland

CHAPTER One

Salt and Adventure in His Blood

IN September 1991 Peter Blake wrote in the foreword to *Wing of the Manukau: Capt. Thomas Wing: His Life and Harbour – 1810–1888* by T. B. Byrne: 'This book . . . reveals a man with whom I would have had much in common. His world was the sea – an environment which shaped his life and his family's, as indeed it did for a number of his descendants, including myself.' While exploring his genealogy, the then 43-year-old Blake would almost certainly have caught fleeting reflections in the mirror of time, for there were many similarities between the already legendary New Zealand ocean racer and his great-great-grandfather. In fact, if one was seeking a starting point to the people, events and influences that helped shape the person that his great-great-grandson became, Captain Wing could well be it.

Wing, from Blake's mother's side of the family, was a remarkable man. Born in Harwich (Essex) or Ipswich (Suffolk) – the records aren't quite clear – on 19 June 1810, Wing maintained family heritage by going to sea at age 14. His grandfather, a sailmaker, was also Thomas. His great-uncle, John Wing, owned a fishing smack which he sailed in the North Sea off Harwich in the 1700s. Shortly after his eighteenth birthday, in 1828, Wing signed on the *Ferguson*, which had been chartered to transport convicts from Dublin to Sydney. In the

15

northern spring of 1832, now aged 22, he again left the Old World, this time bound for New Zealand as first officer on the 132-ton schooner *Fortitude*. The voyage took four months, the *Fortitude* entering the Bay of Islands on 31 August 1832 to anchor off the Church Missionary Society station at Paihia. In the ensuing 50-odd years, Captain Wing was vitally involved in many of the pre-colonial and colonial events that became an integral part of New Zealand's early history.

Within a month of his arrival, Wing headed out from the Bay in the *Fortitude* on the first of six voyages across the Tasman Sea during the next two years. He was clearly a man of action, evidenced by an article in the *Sydney Gazette* on 16 March 1833: 'On Wednesday evening last, about 11pm, as Francoise Gabian, a prisoner of the Crown, of the cutter *Northumberland*, was on watch, looking overboard, by some accident his foot slipped and he fell overboard. The night being dark, he would have drowned, as he was evidently sinking, when Mr Wing, 1st officer of the schooner *Fortitude*, at the time in bed, jumped out overboard – and with great exertions succeeded in saving the unfortunate man, who was rapidly being borne away by the strong current. This was the 7th time this gentleman, at the great hazard of his life, has succeeded by his humane endeavours in saving human life, the late Emperor Alexander having presented him with a medal and a letter of thanks for doing the same kind act for a poor woman saved in the Volga, in 1827, during a hard frost. It is no little addition to this gentleman's merit, that he cannot swim a fathom's length. We are sorry to add, he feels severely from rheumatism, in consequence of his late endeavours.'

In 1834 the Church Missionary Society and the Wesleyan Mission both entered a new phase in their respective endeavours in New Zealand, embarking on an expansionary policy of finding suitable locations and establishing new stations south of the Bay of Islands and Hokianga. The *Fortitude*, with its 3.5-metre draft, was 'a vessel admirably suited for the coastal waters concerned' and was chartered at various times by both missions. Through these charter voyages, Wing came to know personally a number of New Zealand's early missionaries and also obtained first-hand knowledge of their southern ventures. Equally, the voyages added considerably to his expanding knowledge of New Zealand's coastline.

In 1835 Wing was made captain of the newly built schooner *Fanny* – 'of 41 tons, with a length of 14.3 metres and breadth of 4.3 metres' – and one of the earliest of 'those rare vessels which sailed under New Zealand's first national flag'. On 1 February that year, Wing, still only 24, set sail for Sydney in his new command. Wing and *Fanny* became synonymous, their subsequent voyages taking them up and down both coasts of the North Island.

Later that year Wing took the *Fanny* into Tauranga 'and completed the first known sketch chart of Tauranga Harbour'. Then, in January 1836, he sailed *Fanny* into the Kaipara and 'may have been the first European to have successfully sailed into that harbour'. Wing drew the first known survey chart of the complicated, sandbar-strewn entranceway to the Kaipara and, on the same voyage down the west coast, drew a survey sketch chart of the entranceway to the Manukau Harbour and surveyed and charted both the Kawhia and Whaingaroa (Raglan) harbours – all in the space of a month. He was also involved in the establishment, in 1837, of the first shore-based whaling stations at Poverty Bay and the Mahia Peninsula.

On that eventful, and productive, 1836 voyage, the *Fanny* was under charter to the Wesleyan Mission, transporting the Rev. William White and Thomas Mitchell, 'a member of a Sydney merchant family', to the Manukau where White intended to secure a site for the Wesleyan missionary establishment. As it transpired, White also had a 'decidedly non-secular motive for visiting the Manukau – a motive which was to result in a land grab of very considerable

17

dimensions'. At White's behest, Wing anchored *Fanny* off Puponga Point on the northern shore of the Manukau, where White and Mitchell met chief Te Kawau of the Ngati Whatua tribe. The stated objective was to secure a site for a Wesleyan mission station. The outcome of the visit, however, 'the purchase of a massive area of land by Thomas Mitchell, was a shameful piece of commercial knavery'. For the consideration of 1000 pounds of tobacco, 100 dozen pipes and six muskets, Mitchell acquired 'a portion of land on the North side of the before named River Manukau'. The acquired land included the site for the future city of Auckland. The deed of sale was signed on 11 January 1836, by Te Kawau and other Ngati Whatua chiefs – possibly on board the *Fanny* – and witnessed by W. White and Thomas Wing.

Then, in 1844, while the master of the 72-foot brigantine *Deborah*, Wing transported south a New Zealand Company expedition, led by 37-year-old civil engineer and surveyor Frederick Tucker, and helped decide a suitable location for the establishment of the settlement of New Edinburgh (known today as Dunedin).

On 18 March 1857 Wing was appointed pilot and harbourmaster of the Manukau, which the authorities were keen to develop as a west coast port for Auckland, despite its already feared bar entrance and sandbar-strewn channels. During his tenure, he and his eldest son Edward were central figures in New Zealand's worst maritime tragedy – the wreck of HMS *Orpheus* on the Manukau bar on 7 February 1863.

On a 'beautiful, fine New Zealand summer's day, with a nice fresh SW to SSW breeze with occasional slight squalls' the *Orpheus* hit the south spit of the main channel into the Manukau. She was overwhelmed by breaking seas, with the loss of 189 of the 259 souls aboard. The tragedy prompted a storm of controversy over who and what were responsible, and the official report laid the bulk of the blame on the shoulders of the Wings. Edward Wing, 'a young bearded man within a week of his 21st birthday', was in charge of the Manukau signal station on that fateful day.

However, T. B. Byrne's painstaking research pointed to different conclusions as to who and what were culpable. That research indicated that the *Orpheus* had proceeded to cross the bar entrance using outdated sailing directions and had come in under steam and full sail at about 8 knots. His conclusion was that the immediate cause of the *Orpheus* disaster was 'primarily the use of outdated sailing directions coupled with a combination of a lack of caution when entering a bar harbour known to have constantly shifting sandbanks at its entranceway; failure to comply with official corrective signals shown by the Manukau signal station; and an element of stubbornness and arrogance. Like many disasters, the cause of the *Orpheus* tragedy lay deeply rooted in the human factor.'

Captain Thomas Wing was harbourmaster of the Manukau for 30 years. His remarkable nautical career of over 60 years came to an abrupt end in 1887 following a stroke that left him partially paralysed. He died in August 1888. Blake observed of Wing: 'In addition to his wide range of experiences during the pre-colonial and early colonial periods, Wing witnessed the arrival and growing dominance of steam power in place of sails. I suspect, however, being a Wing, he was never more in his true element than when sailing across the vastness of the world's oceans.' The same could be argued of Peter Blake, and the similarities between Wing and his great-great-grandson did not end there.

In the introduction to his book, Byrne says: 'Wing was essentially a man of the sea. It was an environment which not only moulded the man but remained a constant influence throughout his entire life. A master mariner by the time he was in his mid-twenties, his skills of seamanship were held in the highest regard in maritime circles, as were his skills of designing and building boats. Like so many men of the sea, Wing was a man of action and considerable courage.

SALT AND ADVENTURE IN HIS BLOOD

Physically, he was well built, of above average height, with a kindly, frank face. Temperamentally, he was forceful and determined as well as being a strict disciplinarian who brooked no nonsense. Thomas Sharps, a contemporary of Wing's, who had worked for him for more than ten years, recalled him as being a "very temperate man (and) a typical John Bull – inclined to be hot tempered and peppery, quick to resent offence but equally quick to forgive and forget." '

With very little alteration, that character description could easily have been written of Peter Blake.

Researching the paternal side of the Blake family, the records allowed a look back only as far as Sir Peter's grandparents, Alfred and Elizabeth, but again there was a love of the sea in the Blake ancestry.

Alfred and Elizabeth lived in Southend-on-Sea, immediately to the east of London, and had four children – Noel, Don, Marjory and Brian. Alfred Blake was the manager of a small stockbroking firm in London, and Don Blake can remember his father leaving for the City early each morning, 'complete with top hat and gloves and, of course, invariably carrying his umbrella'. Brian Blake, Peter's father and the youngest of the children, was born on 18 November 1914, at the family home. According to Don Blake, the family were well dressed – 'I know, as I often got into trouble for getting my clothes dirty. We were not allowed out of the house without shoes on and inside had to wear slippers.'

On Sunday mornings a horse and carriage would pull up outside the Blake home and the family would climb in and head off to some fields about a mile away for a picnic. The children would be dressed in their Sunday best and were expected to behave themselves. During one of these picnics, they had barely got settled on the rug, eyeing the food, when the air-raid siren sounded and planes began taking

20

off in pairs from the nearby Rochford aerodrome. The Blakes watched as German bombers came over in perfect formation, headed for London. Southend is at the mouth of the Thames and the German planes followed the river to find their way to the city. The British fighters were invariably too late to intercept the raiders on the way in, but they would be in wait when the enemy planes returned down the river.

In 1919, with World War I over, the family moved to Sandown, on the Isle of Wight, where they lived for two months before the children 'were told the great news'. They would sail for New Zealand from Tilbury on 17 October 1919. Alfred Blake explained that there would always be wars in Europe so the family was moving to the other side of the world. Don Blake remembers that his father also wanted to get away from the class regime in England and believed that the Blake children would find their new country a much better place to grow up in. There are indications also that a successful wager on the horses might have swelled Alfred's purse sufficiently for him to take this bold step.

So, on 1 November 1919 (their ship was late), the Blakes boarded the 20,000-ton P&O liner *Orvieto* at Tilbury and set sail for New Zealand, via the Suez Canal and Australia. In Sydney, they transshipped to the much smaller *Maheno* for the final leg of the long journey to Auckland.

After installing his family first in a boarding house in Upper Queen Street and then in a flat in a large white house on the slopes of Mt Hobson, Alfred Blake travelled north. Two weeks went by before he returned with the news that he had bought a dairy farm near Whangarei. The Blakes again embarked on a ship, this time a small steamer called *Duchess*, and headed north out of the Waitemata Harbour. It was the southern winter of 1920. The rail link between Auckland and Whangarei would not be completed until some years later and the road would often be impassable in the winter months (teams of oxen had to be kept at critical points of the route to pull cars through).

The Blake farm comprised nearly 300 acres and was on a clay road running between Maungakaramea and Mangapai, nearly 12 miles south of Whangarei. 'I have often wondered how my parents coped with the very rugged conditions on the farm,' reflects Don Blake. 'In England they had lived a refined sort of life. They had a maid, part-time, to look after the children, shops close by and good entertainment. Now miles from civilisation (the nearest neighbour a mile away) and the children at the most basic of schools, Mother had to plan weeks ahead to keep us fed and Dad had to look after all the farm animals, and sometimes be midwife to an animal with a difficult birth. Worse still, he had to kill sheep and the occasional pig for our meat. A more drastic change in their living conditions is hard to imagine. Probably the greatest strain fell on my mother. She was city born and bred. The first three months must have been a nightmare for her, but she was a true Londoner and nothing would defeat her.'

The Blakes were nearly three years on the farm. Then, with prices for dairy products falling and Alfred near the end of his savings, the family sold up and moved to a cottage near the school at Mangapai. Alfred then got a job with the Public Works Department, with which went a staff house at Oakleigh, two miles down the road from Mangapai and on an inlet of the Whangarei Harbour. In the school holidays, Don and Brian (now nine years old) had the use of a small dinghy and would explore the mangroves and go down the river to Green Island.

They then moved south to Auckland where Don, finished with high school, 'joined the family in the construction camp at Purewa, just opposite the old St Thomas Church in Auckland'. Alfred secured a new job, doing costings for several large Ministry of Works projects. When the work on the Purewa railway tunnel and the waterfront

22

road (Tamaki Drive) started to wind down, Alfred decided to build a house in Nihill Crescent in the beach suburb of Mission Bay. The family moved in before the waterfront road was opened, so had to make the trek through Remuera and Newmarket in order to get to the city.

However, with New Zealand sliding slowly into the Great Depression, Alfred had to take work labouring on the Waitaki Power Station project on the Waitaki River in South Canterbury. Elizabeth went with him, leaving their four children to take care of the house in Mission Bay. When Elizabeth had to return to Auckland to care for an ailing Noel, Brian Blake joined his father working on the Waitaki hydro scheme. When the economy finally started to improve, Alfred and Brian were able to return to Auckland. Brian had been to Kohimarama Intermediate and then Auckland Grammar School. He had also studied at the Elam School of Art and this probably helped him land a job in advertising. Later, after he returned from World War II, he joined Goldberg Advertising Ltd and went on to become art director and associate director, working for the company for 25 years until his retirement in 1979.

While his parents were in the South Island, Don bought his first boat, a flush-decked 16-footer called *Lancia*. He got a real taste for sailing and joined the Tamaki Yacht Club which had just built a new clubhouse on Bastion Point on Auckland's waterfront drive. Looking to improve his chances racing, he sold *Lancia* and bought 'a smart little 18-footer called *Memutu*', which had been built as an M-Class but then converted into an Open V-Class. Brian Blake was part of the racing crew. Don, saving to get married, later sold *Memutu* and was boatless until he picked up old and abandoned 14-footer *Ramona* for a song and rebuilt her. By this time Brian Blake had also bought a 14-footer called *Eleanor*, and with his girlfriend Joyce (who was to become his wife), also used to race with the Tamaki Yacht Club fleet. But World War II was soon to intervene in all their lives.

23

Alfred Blake had little to say about the war. He had, after all, brought his family halfway around the world to get away from what was happening. Elizabeth Blake, however, on hearing Churchill's immortal 'We Shall Never Surrender' speech, declared that if someone would pay her fare, she would return home and 'if necessary go down on the beaches with an axe'.

Brian Blake joined up for the conflict in 1941, serving in the Royal New Zealand Navy Volunteer Reserve but attached to the Royal Navy and later the Royal New Zealand Air Force. He left New Zealand for England in April 1941 and, as Lieutenant Brian Blake, was based at Lowestoft and involved in anti-E-boat cover for east coast convoys, and offensive sweeps of enemy convoys off the Dutch coast. He then joined, as pilot, a 120-foot D-class gunboat, HMS *Midge*, before being given temporary command of *MGB 320* and *MGB 331*, again operating out of Lowestoft, protecting convoys against E-boat activity and making sweeps on enemy convoys in the North Sea. In July 1944 the flotilla shifted to Arramanches in Normandy where it patrolled against enemy convoys escaping out of Le Havre.

In October 1944 Brian returned to New Zealand for a long leave and a higher navigation course. Then, in January 1945, he was seconded to the RNZAF to take over a 63-foot air-sea rescue craft leased from the Americans and based at Emirau Island in the Bismarck Archipelago north of New Guinea. Awarded the 1939–45 Star and the Atlantic Star, he was demobbed in July 1945 but remained on the RNZNVR Supplementary List of Officers for another 20 years.

Before shipping out to Britain, Brian Blake married Joyce Hilda Wilson, daughter of James and Emily Wilson. The ceremony took place on 6 April 1940, at the Congregational Church in the Mt Eden suburb of Auckland, witnessed by Donald and Marjory Blake. Emily Wilson was a granddaughter of Captain Thomas Wing. Joyce was one of five children, the family living adjacent to the water in Pt Chevalier. Having frequently crewed for her brothers Alan and Lyndsay, she was more than familiar with sailing when, through work, she met Brian Blake. Joyce, like Brian, was a very good artist, so the pair had common interests in art and yachting when Brian first asked Joyce out for a sail.

While Brian was serving overseas, Joyce lived with her parents in Pt Chevalier. When he returned from the war, they moved into a rented house in Mairangi Bay, not far from where Brian's parents were now living. On 17 October 1945, Janet Blake was born – the only Blake child to arrive at the Mairangi Bay address. The other three Blake children were all born into 37 Beresford Street, Bayswater, the home that Brian and Joyce bought for £2000 in 1946 and which is still owned by the family today. Peter was the next addition to the family, arriving on 1 October 1948, followed by Tony on 29 March 1951, and Elizabeth on 20 June 1955.

With parents who were passionate about sailing, and living in a house the back garden of which sloped down into the harbour waters of the inner North Shore, it was almost inevitable that the younger Blakes would grow up messing about in boats. Tony Blake remembers that the family initially had a clinker-built dinghy, probably 9- or 10-feet long and 'white on the outside and varnished on the inside for some reason'. The Blake kids would spend hours after school, and in the holidays, rowing around the mangroves. Then Brian built a John Spencer design Frostply dinghy which was called *Japeto* – Ja for Janet, Pe for Peter and To for Tony. The Frostply was an all-purpose design which sailed well but could also be rowed or powered along by an outboard motor. A Seagull outboard was acquired for Blake family fishing trips. Two neighbours also built Frostplys, which led to friendly inter-family racing in the bay.

As the Blake boys became more interested in racing, Brian built Peter a P-Class, the classic 7-foot 6-inch sail trainer that is the nursery

SALT AND ADVENTURE IN HIS BLOOD

class for most of New Zealand's top sailors even today. The newcomer was called *Pee Bee* and Peter Blake started racing with the Takapuna Boating Club, which in those days was based in the now-protected clubhouse building at the water's edge in Bayswater. When Peter outgrew the P-Class, Brian bought the hull of a plywood Z-Class (Zeddy) and finished her off in the shed at home. She was called *Tango*. While Peter started to make a name for himself in the Zeddy, the younger Tony got to race *Pee Bee*. Peter had a liking for the colours orange and black, so *Tango*'s hull was black and her sails orange. Whenever it was blowing hard from the south-west and there wasn't a race on, the Blake brothers would slog the Zeddy across Auckland Harbour to the city's wharves, hoist a spinnaker in the lee of the wharves and then tear back across the harbour to Bayswater with everything hanging out. Usually they ended up capsizing in Shoal Bay and digging the top of the mast into the mud of the harbour bottom.

By now the Blakes also owned a keelboat – the *Ngarangi*. To make the purchase, they sold a section on the clifftop in Mairangi Bay that Joyce had bought during the war. *Ngarangi* was 30 feet long with a short waterline, sharp bow and counter stern. She didn't go well to windward at all, being heavy on the helm and not particularly well balanced, but she was the Blakes' introduction to the cruising delights of the Hauraki Gulf, and from then on family holidays took on a new dimension. The Blakes owned *Ngarangi* for only two seasons and the furthest they ventured was to Great Barrier and Kawau islands, on the outer fringes of the Gulf, and to Te Kouma Harbour on the Coromandel Peninsula. The seeds of keelboat racing and cruising had, however, been sewn in fertile ground.

Brian and Joyce then bought a boat called *Ladybird* from the deceased estate of a well-known Auckland yachtsman, G. 'Boy' Bellve. This was late 1962. *Ladybird* was a 34-foot Bert Woollacott ketch, designed and built for the inaugural Hobart–Auckland race in 1951. She won that race, and in the process did a 24-hour run of 212 miles, which was impressive stuff for a 34-footer. The Blakes had seen *Ladybird* in various anchorages around the Hauraki Gulf and greatly admired her. On one occasion, in Mansion House Bay (Kawau Island), *Ladybird* dragged her anchor and young Peter Blake quickly rowed across from *Ngarangi* and let out some more chain so that she was safe.

Martin Foster, a prominent member of the Devonport Yacht Club who was to become a close friend, recalls the first time he saw *Ladybird* under Blake family ownership. He was at anchor in his 22-foot Mullet boat *Patere*, in Mullet Bay on the eastern side of Motutapu Island, when *Ladybird* sailed in. Early the following morning Foster watched two boys on the deck of *Ladybird*, running around and enjoying themselves polishing brasswork. One was quite lanky with blond hair.

The following spring the Devonport Yacht Club had a race to Woody Bay on Rakino Island. *Ladybird* came in after the Devonport fleet and Foster, who was the vice commodore of the yacht club at the time, rowed across to introduce himself to Brian Blake and suggest that he might like to think about joining the club and taking part in its family cruising races. Foster was invited aboard for a cup of tea and met the then 15-year-old Peter Blake for the first time. That encounter was to be the start of a long and close friendship and one that was to be the source of some significant events in New Zealand yachting.

The adolescent Peter Blake had enjoyed a fairly typical New Zealand upbringing in a close-knit family that shared a love of the sea. All four Blake children followed the same schooling path – starting at Bayswater Primary, moving on to Belmont Intermediate and then on to Takapuna Grammar. But Peter Blake didn't really enjoy school, nor was he into the traditional team sports, rugby and cricket. 'Pete didn't really like school,' remembers Janet. 'He had a Mr Long as a maths teacher – he was known as Maths Long – who was also Pete's form teacher in, I think, the sixth form. He tended to be very sarcastic and I think he and Pete had a bust-up. Pete was more than likely the biggest boy in the class – he was already more than six foot tall when he started at Takapuna Grammar – and this could have become a focus for Maths Long's sarcasm. That would have really turned Peter off. Anyway, he did University Entrance and that was it. He passed UE and went to Auckland Technical Institute to do mechanical engineering – the New Zealand Certificate of Engineering, which was a technical rather than a university qualification. But Peter wasn't all that interested in what he was doing at school. Even in those formative years, he was very focused on what he wanted to do, and that was to sail boats. He didn't play rugby, he didn't play tennis or cricket or anything. It was just yachting – the Z-Class or *Ladybird*.'

He also used to sail a lot with Martin Foster who would telephone and ask simply: 'Want to go for a sail?' The answer would be an automatic 'Yes'. Foster noted one such occasion in the log of *Truant*, a 28-foot Woollacott design that replaced his 26-foot Mullet boat *Starlight*. It was a turbulent spring, and one stormy Sunday in 1967 he went around to the Blake home to see if Peter wanted to go for a spin. 'Oh yeah' was the response. They rowed out to *Truant*, which was anchored off Devonport, and managed to cast off under storm rig in a westerly gale. They reached at speed up the coastline of Auckland's North Shore to Long Bay where they anchored for lunch before reaching back down the coast and into the harbour.

'We were the only boat out there and Peter was in his element,' recalls Foster. 'He just loved it – thought it was fantastic.'

Certain traits that were later to be 'Blakey trademarks' had already begun to emerge. He was very intense when he stepped on a boat. Everything had to be done correctly. 'Don't forget, his father was a naval officer in the Second World War,' stresses Foster. 'His boats were always immaculately maintained and everything had to be just right, particularly on *Ladybird*. Brian was most pedantic in that, and Peter was the same. I don't think there's much doubt where he got it from. We put a new rig in *Truant* in 1975. Peter was then working for the mast manufacturer Yachtspars and had already done his first Whitbread race on *Burton Cutter*. He'd come out sailing with me and everything had to be spot on, even if you were only cruising – every sheet, every sail had to be checked and in its right place. I remember him telling me – "I hope you don't mind me running around like this, but I like things to be right".'

Janet Blake remembers how meticulous and particular her father was: 'He made lists of things and he kept logs beautifully. His car was always serviced well, and on the boat everything was done properly. The house was pretty good, but the boat was always better. Pete was always making lists too, just like Brian.'

The young Blake also held strong views about sailing, and this led to the odd 'meeting of the minds' when he raced with his father, according to Tony Blake. 'Our family always got along really well together. I can't remember any dissension at all, except when we were racing with Dad. Peter and I had both done quite a bit of racing by then, albeit in small boats, and used to make suggestions on where to go and what to do. I think we forgot that Dad had done a fair bit of racing himself. Anyway, I always remember him telling Peter to "pipe down, I'm the skipper" or, on the odd occasion, "I'm the skipper and what I say goes".'

The Blake brothers always pitched in on the maintenance of the family yachts, so it was no surprise when the now 18-year-old Peter decided to build his own boat. 'Peter was passionate about offshore racing, as was I,' remembers Tony. 'I think *Rainbow II* and her exploits would have really stirred us on in those days. I suspect that that was when Peter really decided what he wanted to do in life. That was the way he wanted to go. He wanted to go offshore racing. The entry level in those days was through the JOG (Junior Offshore Group) run by the Royal Akarana Yacht Club. So Pete decided to build *Bandit* and race her in the JOG.'

Bandit was a 23-foot hard chine, plywood design from Van de Stadt which had been featured in a *Yachting World* annual. Peter Blake mailed off for the plans and then set about building the boat in a shed at the front of the Blake home in Beresford Street – something that was quite normal in Auckland in those days, even if it is not quite so common a practice today.

In her first season racing with Royal Akarana in 1967–68, *Bandit* won the JOG championship. Peter was the skipper. Tony Blake and a close friend, Crawford Duncan, were the crew. *Bandit*, however, wasn't designed to any rating rule, and so wasn't optimised for JOG racing. Consequently, when boats designed with the rule in mind appeared on the scene in *Bandit*'s second season of competition, the Blake boat was not competitive. '*Bandit* didn't rate well,' says Tony. 'She wasn't designed as a rating boat at all. In our second season, Gil Hedges arrived with *Interlude*, a rule boat that was 31 feet long, with about a 9- or 10-foot beam. And Paul Whiting designed and built the first Reactor 25 and entered her. We reconfigured *Bandit*'s sail plan, cutting mainsail size and going for bigger genoas, but we still couldn't compete.' Blake's response was to build a boat that was designed with the rating rule in mind, and set about the construction, again in the shed at the front of the family home, of a Holman and Pye 26-footer – a rating boat with a stern-hung rudder. He got as far as completing hull and decks when he made the decision to go overseas. *Bandit* and the new boat, that was to be called *Oliver Twist*, were sold and the proceeds added to the Blake travel fund.

By this stage Peter Blake was already a very experienced yachtsman. He'd done the 1300-mile Auckland–Suva race in 1969 on the 50-foot double-ender (canoe stern) *Red Feather* with Doug Hazard, a family friend who had served in motor gunboats in the North Sea at the same time as Brian Blake. On that occasion, 20-year-old Blake became extremely frustrated when *Red Feather* ran out of wind two-thirds of the way to Suva and the boat's doctor decided to spice up happy hour by using a syringe to inject the ship's supply of oranges with gin. When the young Blake wanted intense trimming to ease *Red Feather* into a breeze line up ahead, there were no able-bodied takers to be found.

Then, in August of that year, he made a voyage on *Ladybird* that probably laid the very solid foundation on which his later legendary seamanship was built. Brian Blake had decided to take the trusty Woollacott design to the Pacific Islands. She was well suited for the task – built of inch-and-a-quarter-thick kauri with small portholes that could withstand the worst of seas coming aboard. Also, she was sea-kindly and could look after herself in rough weather. All of those assets would be put to the test on the journey that Brian had in mind. Father Brian, mother Joyce and 20-year-old son Peter would sail *Ladybird* to Tonga where she would be joined by Tony and Elizabeth, who were still at school (Janet was now married and living in Dunedin, so couldn't make this particular family cruise). The Blakes would then sail *Ladybird* to Fiji and cruise there until it was time for Tony and Liz to fly back to New Zealand. Brian, Joyce and Peter would then sail *Ladybird* home.

Two days out from New Zealand on the voyage north *Ladybird* ran into a severe gale. The Blakes were battened down and hove to for the 36 hours it took for the system to pass through and allow them to start sailing again. Martin Foster reckons that 'that's where his real seamanship came from – that first, tough ocean trip with a meticulous mariner like his father. Peter came back from that trip having ridden out a severe gale at sea and with the best part of another 3000 more ocean miles under his belt. He was a vastly more experienced yachtsman. I can imagine him with his father – the two of them. Peter had always been very good around a boat. He would have been doing all the for'ard-hand work. He could navigate too, using the sight-reduction table method. He taught himself, practising for hours in the garden at the back of the family home, with a bucket of water, on which he'd spread a film of oil, and a sextant. The water was his horizon and he'd use his sextant to bring down on to the water images of the planets, or major stars that would reflect in the water, to get his fix. He'd spend hours doing that and became very good at celestial navigation. The tables and sextant went with him everywhere after that, no matter what new navigation systems might be aboard the boats he was sailing.'

The *Ladybird* had other significant influences on the young Blake, like helping him to decide the rig configuration of the all-conquering *Steinlager 2* for the 1989–90 Whitbread Round the World race, and she etched herself indelibly into the hearts of all of the Blake family. Of the Woollacott design Peter Blake would later write: '*Ladybird* was a major influence in my life. My parents used every cent of their savings to buy her. She was just under 34 feet long with varnished timber spars and polished brass ventilators – a real beauty. We children were over the moon. As a youngster, I watched the large yachts out at sea while standing on a bluff near home. Now, I thought, *we* could do that. It was on *Ladybird* that I learned the 101 nuances of sailing a keelboat, experience that stood me in good stead in later years.'

Joyce Blake often told Martin Foster that the best thing she and husband Brian ever did for the family, particularly the boys, was to mortgage their home to buy *Ladybird*. When Brian Blake's health began to fail him in the mid-1990s, he and Joyce consulted the family about *Ladybird*'s future. At that stage neither Peter nor Tony was in a position to take over the family yacht, so Brian approached Foster about buying her. He knew that Foster would take good care of the vessel and that *Ladybird* would be in the best of hands. To begin with, Foster was hesitant to replace his own yacht *Truant* but Peter Blake finally managed to persuade him. Brian Blake died on 23 January 1998

– within two months of the hand over. Peter quietly visited Foster while he was working on *Ladybird*'s maintenance. 'He said "Martin, would you agree not to sell this boat without talking to me first?" ' recalls Foster. 'He wanted *Ladybird* for his retirement, because of everything she meant to him and the rest of the Blake family. That was last time I saw him in the flesh . . .'

CHAPTER Two

First Steps Up the Ladder

Englishman Les Williams facilitated the next step forward in Peter Blake's embryonic ocean-racing career. Outside of British sailing circles, Williams is probably less well known than contemporaries such as Sir Robin Knox-Johnston and Chay Blyth. Within the sport, however, he is recognised as one of those instrumental in changing sailing in the United Kingdom from a somewhat elitist recreation into a competitive sport accessible to everyone – provided they had the get-up-and-go to create their own opportunities. Williams certainly had plenty of that.

By his own admission, Williams had 'a fairly controversial' career in the Royal Navy. He joined in 1949, to be a pilot in the Fleet Air Arm, an artificer-pilot in fact, but the aircraft emerging soon after World War II were getting too complicated for such combined qualifications and Williams was made an artificer. He was aged 15, and having his dream of flying aeroplanes arbitrarily denied him by some navy selection board did not sit well. As he put it: 'I didn't want to mend the things. I wanted to fly them.' So he 'ran away' to become a pilot in the Royal Air Force.

The Royal Navy was not amused. Williams was brought back 'kicking and screaming', duly chastised and returned to his designated career of navy artificer. He decided there and then that if he had to be an artificer – and the navy was immovable on that subject – he would become the best-qualified artificer the navy had ever produced. He learned everything applicable about engineering and then did the same with air electronics and airfield radar. 'I was probably the most highly trained practical engineer in the country – no degrees, no certificated qualifications, but that didn't really matter,' he remarked. 'I was having a great time.'

By the time he was 26, Williams was the youngest-ever chief artificer in the navy. He was also 'by far the highest-paid chap of my age in any of the services'. But the Fleet Air Arm was, in modern parlance, downsizing and Williams had identified a new career path. 'I set up a thing called sail and expedition training, because I was very keen on sail training. Those were small beginnings, but today sail and expedition training is a ruddy great empire and is now a joint services deal.' Made a Special Duties Sub-Lieutenant, he seemed to escape the service system and used a fair bit of initiative to ensure that things stayed that way.

In 1964 he decided he wanted to do the first trans-Atlantic Tall Ships' race. He had managed to get his hands on a German prize of war that was built in the 1930s. Its wooden hull planks 'kept falling out' and it leaked like a sieve. But that didn't matter either. The start of the race was from Lisbon, in Portugal, and the enterprising Williams – with a complement of '16-year-olds that the navy had sent out to me without any money, without any clothes' – took aboard a film crew from the Independent Television Network (ITN) and, on a Friday evening, set sail for Lisbon. Just before casting off, he sent a signal to 'their Lordships' that read: 'Intend to sail Bermuda.' He knew that nobody in authority would get to read the signal until Monday morning and would have great trouble understanding what it meant. By that time, he would be long gone.

Williams recalls: 'When their Lordships found out what I was up to, they were going to bring me back from Lisbon and court-martial

SIR PETER BLAKE

me, but I had made friends with the vice president of Portugal who said: "No they're not. We want you to continue this race." Their Lordships had a problem. The ITN film was going out, making me a bit of a hero, sort of thing, while my bosses wanted my head. The vice president was as good as his word, though. The navy very reluctantly let me continue with the race and I was gone for the best part of a year.'

Williams' luck continued. HRH Prince Philip had become the patron of what was now the Sail Training Association and, according to the now Special Duties Sub-Lieutenant Williams, 'was thrilled with what I had done and sent for the boat to go up the Thames to London, to be at Tower Pier, with her crew, for the premiere of the film of the race'. Williams was introduced to His Highness and seems to have made a bit of an impression that was soon to be quite helpful.

When Williams decided his next venture would be the 1968 solo trans-Atlantic race, the navy refused to give him leave. He was, after all, an engineer, not a sailor, even though he had been running his sail and expedition training programme for four years by now. 'It just so happened that Prince Phillip came to a Fleet Arm anniversary dinner at Lee-on-Solent where I was stationed at the time. He walked towards me and said, "Bloody Williams", and we started talking. I told him I wanted to do the solo trans-Atlantic race, that I had the boat and had the sponsorship – but their Lordships wouldn't give me leave. He said, "By 10 a.m. tomorrow you'll have your leave." Sure enough, at 10 a.m. the next day, the captain sent for me and said, "Their Lordships have decided to grant the leave you have requested, but you will lose two years' seniority." I couldn't have given a toss about that. I was going to do the trans-Atlantic race.'

Williams left the navy, or the navy left him – he's still not quite sure which – in 1970, 'by which time I was already sailing *Ocean Spirit*, and their Lordships couldn't make up their minds whether I was out or in. I only discovered I was out when they stopped paying me.'

39

Ocean Spirit was a Van de Stadt design 70-foot ketch built in fibreglass by Southern Ocean Shipyards in Poole (Dorset). In her day she was one of the fastest long-distance sailing boats in the world and proved it by breaking a string of records. She was jointly owned by Williams and master mariner Robin Knox-Johnston, a former officer in Britain's merchant navy who had won the *Sunday Times* Golden Globe in 1968–69 for sailing solo, non-stop around the world in his ketch *Suhaili*. Almost first up, Williams and Knox-Johnston won the 1970 Round Britain race in *Ocean Spirit*, the only time it has been won by a monohull. They then did the 1970 Middle Sea race, after which *Ocean Spirit* was based in Malta for a while, being fitted out for future charter work. During the course of this work, there was a tap on the hull and Williams was confronted by this 'six-foot four-inch tall New Zealander, speaking a funny language'. It was Peter Blake.

Williams and Knox-Johnston vary in their telling of the event. Knox-Johnston recalls that Blake had written to them seeking a berth in the inaugural Cape Town–Rio race. This is also the somewhat vague recollection of Blake's elder sister Janet. But Williams remembers that Blake was 'backpacking' through the Mediterranean, saw there was a hive of activity on *Ocean Spirit* and offered his services.

First impressions? 'I liked him,' said Williams. 'He was pleasant and polite. He was willing to work. He was fit and strong and, as we were to find out, he knew a bit about sailing.' The pair got on well together, to the extent that Williams invited Blake to do the delivery voyage to Cape Town. Further impressed with what he saw, Williams extended the invitation to the inaugural Cape Town–Rio race which was to start in January 1971. The 3500-mile race from Cape Town to Rio de Janeiro is one of ocean racing's institutions. If the South Atlantic high pressure system plays ball, the race is traditionally a downwind slide in south-east trades with an exotic destination beckoning. Blake leapt at the opportunity.

Robin Knox-Johnston joined the boat in Cape Town and, with

Williams, began sorting out *Ocean Spirit*'s race crew. Williams had already formed a high opinion of Blake who had just turned 22 years of age. According to Knox-Johnston: 'Les reckoned Peter would make a good watch leader so we put him in. Once we got sailing it was obvious that we'd made the right choice. He was one of the youngest on board but he had authority, knew what he was doing and his watch very quickly respected him. He was also good to deal with – a guy you dragged into the consultations because he'd got good views to give.' *Ocean Spirit* was first to finish in Rio and Knox-Johnston, who had flown in for the race only, returned to Britain. He would soon be followed by Williams who had to deal with some pressing banking matters. Williams had no hesitation promoting Blake to delivery skipper and the young Kiwi was left in charge of getting the 70-footer back to her United Kingdom base.

With his first maxi delivery completed, Blake returned to Auckland where he started work for the mast manufacturer Yachtspars, checking masts against their design drawings (he worked there until 30 May 1977 when he flew back to Britain for the second Whitbread race). Blake stayed in contact with Williams, sourcing yachting products from New Zealand that might find a market in Britain – 'but we never made any money out of it', says Williams. Then Williams wrote to Blake to tell him he was building a boat for the inaugural Whitbread Round the World race in 1973–74: 'I think I finished the letter with "Do you want to come?" Quick as a flash, he was on his way.'

Blake had not been idle in New Zealand. He'd struck up a relationship with former JOG rival Gil Hedges, an ex-Royal Air Force officer who had immigrated to New Zealand where he resumed his love of offshore racing. Hedges and his wife Margaret built and raced first the successful JOG racer *Interlude* and then the highly competitive

41

One Tonner *Escapade*. Blake navigated on *Escapade* in the 1973 Auckland–Suva race and then, almost immediately, packed his bags for a return to England.

The boat that Williams was building for the inaugural Round the World race, an 80-foot John Sharp design to be called *Windward Spirit*, was already under construction in Poole, by a company that built aluminium industrial parts, but not boats. When the company ran into financial problems, Williams had to act quickly to rescue his project: 'Quite simply, the builders went bust and were taken over by an Arab who tried to screw us. We ended up sneaking the boat out of the shed in the dead of night and then had to all work like slaves just to get it ready. We were in such a state when we went to the start line. If it had been today, we would not have been allowed to race. The first time we'd ever connected the steering was as we were being towed out to the start. We didn't have any deck over the engine and there were no bunks in the boat.'

Very late in the piece, Williams secured sponsorship from the nationally known High Street tailor Burtons, and *Windward Spirit* became *Burton Cutter*. An even later addition to the programme was 18-year-old David Alan-Williams. His father was in the Royal Navy and got chatting to Williams, now ex-Royal Navy, to see whether there was an opportunity on *Burton Cutter* for his son who had just finished his A levels at school and was taking what the British call a gap year before resuming his education. The sum of £500 changed hands and David Alan-Williams became part of the *Burton Cutter* crew. He was allocated to the watch to be run by the now 25-year-old Peter Blake. The two were to become good friends and Alan-Williams was to be involved in many of the Blake triumphs that were still in the future. Alan-Williams recalls: 'The whole event (the first Whitbread) was an adventure. Nobody really knew what was going on, although a fair number of the crew – including Les and Peter – had a lot of miles under their belts. Pete's leadership qualities were already in evidence and it was clear that Les Williams had a lot of respect for him. That said a lot, because Les had a huge reputation. He'd done the solo trans-Atlantic, had been sailing a long time, and was fundamentally a really good seaman. He made Pete a watch leader over people who were older and actually more experienced in running a boat. But Peter took it all in his stride and was involved with detailing and setting up the rigging in addition to all of his other jobs.'

Blake wrote later: 'Building a round-the-world racer is a hectic business and there was many a last-minute improvisation on *Burton Cutter*. The food supplies for the first leg only arrived 24 hours before the start. We were still building the boat down below, putting in bunks and so on, and had nowhere to put all the cartons that were coming aboard so late in the piece. We ended up slinging a tennis net from the front to the back of the main saloon and dumped them all in that. Later we stowed all of the provisions in the bilge only to find, after a week at sea, that an unconnected toilet was discharging in amongst all of the food cartons. The decks hadn't been caulked so they leaked. One crew member had to sleep under a large black umbrella in his bunk. It was a real learning period.' Despite all the problems getting her ready, *Burton Cutter* proved to be surprisingly fast downwind. Her big rivals were the French blue-water racing hero Eric Tabarly, in his 73-foot André Mauric ketch *Pen Duick VI*, and former British paratrooper Chay Blyth in the 77-foot Alan Gurney ketch *Great Britain II*.

On a sunny morning in September 1973, solo circumnavigator Sir Alec Rose sent the 17-boat fleet, from seven nations, on its way. That fleet included two service entries from Britain – *British Soldier* (representing the army) and *Adventure* (representing the navy) – proof indeed of the progress made with the Les Williams-initiated sailing and expedition programme. The fleet enjoyed pleasant, if slow, conditions across the Bay of Biscay and through the Doldrums, but there were tougher times ahead. Williams used his knowledge of sailing to Cape Town (albeit from Malta) and, once south of the equator, *Burton Cutter* took the direct route to the Cape, as opposed to following the old sailing ship route around to the west of the South Atlantic High. This meant two weeks of bashing to windward in a boat that performed best downwind, but it was a winning ploy and became the 'must go' route in the next three Whitbreads (before the course was changed). *Burton Cutter* was first to finish, beating *Great Britain II* and her crew of British paratroopers into Cape Town by one and a half days. Alan-Williams described their victory: 'We were given a fantastic welcome (on Trafalgar Day). The whole of Cape Town was on the dock and we had the place all to ourselves. We were the heroes of the town and that probably gave us all a first taste of the grand success of winning. I've no doubt it was a factor in Peter wanting to go back and do more.'

Burton Cutter was to pay a heavy price for the bash to Cape Town, however. Her aluminium structure had been damaged by the continuous pounding into head seas, and when she struck the first gale of the second leg to Sydney, on the wind in the Agulhas Current, she started to break up. The longitudinal stringers (stiffeners) inside the hull broke away from the aluminium plate of the hull itself and the whole starboard side of the hull for'ard was panting in and out. The watertight bulkhead was secured to close off the bow sections from the rest of the boat, but those sections, lacking the right support, were now twisting in the heavy seas and the hull plate welds began to crack, letting in sea water. Despite continuous pumping, the front end of the boat began to fill. Williams had no choice but to withdraw from the leg and nurse his stricken boat to the safety of Port Elizabeth at the south-eastern tip of South Africa.

'I was tempted to go on,' Williams admits. 'If it had been sailing solo I would have gone on. But you can't risk other people's lives. The plates were starting to buckle further aft. They didn't actually split, thank God. The watertight bulkhead saved us. Fortunately, it was a port reach to Port Elizabeth or we might not have made it.'

Peter Blake had overseen the building of *Burton Cutter* (once she'd been 'rescued' from the original yard in Poole) and his knowledge of the boat's engineering came in very handy once the repair work started in Port Elizabeth. He launched into the task, with Williams intent on rejoining the second leg to Sydney just as soon as the repairs were complete. 'We got it (the hull) all welded up again, mainly on Pete's initiative, and got an inspector down to check the work,' recollects Alan-Williams. 'To our absolute horror, he found that the wrong welding rods had been used. The whole lot had to be repaired again. By that stage it was too late to have any chance of catching up with the fleet down to Australia, so we would have to cut our losses, go back to Cape Town, get the repair job done properly, and then sail across to Rio de Janeiro and rejoin the race there.'

Williams left *Burton Cutter* in Blake's care while he flew to Cape Town to organise repair facilities. While he was doing that, he got an urgent call to return to England: 'In the six weeks it took to do the first leg of the race, Britain experienced the biggest property slump and financial crisis ever. We just about still owned the boat when we arrived in Cape Town, but I had to go home in a hurry to do some sorting out.' So, Blake had to oversee a better repair of *Burton Cutter* and then take the boat across the South Atlantic to Brazil. He was now, for the first time in his career, in charge of a fully-blown (if poorly built) maxi ocean-racing yacht and was learning quickly about how and how not to campaign one.

These were early days in yachting sponsorship and Williams, in the vanguard, was walking a fine line in the marketplace. He didn't have much option other than to underpitch the worth of what he had to offer and, as a result, his programmes were undernourished in financial terms and doomed to never fulfil their true potential. Blake observed all of this first-hand and was almost certainly persuaded that it was better to cut your cloth to suit your purse. Rather than struggle

45

to build a full-on maxi with not enough money to campaign it properly, better to build a smaller yacht and do so within your budget, so that you had the wherewithal to achieve your objectives. It was a lesson that he would apply successfully when, in 1981–82, he finally got to skipper his own Whitbread boat. He would also have observed how difficult it was to get sponsorship for sailing, and the effort you had to put in to make sure your programme worked – for your sponsor as well as yourself. Together with the need to tightly control your budgets, these were more lessons that he would put to good use in later years.

For now though, he had a maxi to run and time to kill in South America before meeting up with the Whitbread fleet again. Alan-Williams and the rest of the crew were about to glimpse another side of the Blake character – the cruising person. In *race* mode, the Viking-like Blake, headband around his long blond hair, would urge his watch forward, out of the 'trenches' of the cockpit, to do battle with a sail change on the foredeck. In a manner reminiscent of a sergeant leading his troops over the top in World War I, he would yell 'GOW, GOW, GOW – aye!' (Gow sounding like Wow) at the top of his voice, and lead his 'troops' forward for another pounding and soaking, and more torn fingers from the piston hanks on the headsails, while frequently airborne on the pitching bow.

In *cruise* mode, however, 'the bridge club' was far more important than what was happening on deck, always provided that the watch up top had their minds on what they were supposed to be doing. 'It was Christmas time,' remembers Alan-Williams, 'and we were fully into the spirit of it as we crossed the South Atlantic to Buenos Aires in Argentina. Because she was going to be up for charter, *Burton Cutter* had a full three-piece suite, straight out of the furniture shop, in the main saloon. It was the only thing we did have in the boat. We might have lacked bunks and other such essentials, but we did have this leather, three-piece suite and it got a lot of use during the almost non-stop card games. We went first to Southern Brazil, and partied on the beaches there, then down to Uruguay and partied there, and then on to Buenos Aires where we had two weeks in which to celebrate before we started the Buenos Aires to Rio race. Pete was in the thick of it. In fact, you might say he showed another side to his fast-developing leadership skills.'

Burton Cutter raced into Rio de Janeiro a couple of days after the arrival of the Whitbread fleet on the leg from Sydney, and received first-hand the accounts of the tragic dramas that had been played out in their absence. Twelve days out of Cape Town, the wind was blowing 40 knots and gusting 50 knots plus. The Italian yacht *Tauranga*, a 55-foot yawl, broached violently in huge following seas. Crewman Paul Waterhouse clambered on deck to secure a spinnaker boom that had gone over the side and was threatening to punch a hole in the boat. He was lost overboard. His crewmates searched the raging seas for hours, but there was no sign of him.

Six days later disaster struck again. The crew of the 60-foot ketch *33 Export* was changing sails in a full gale when, without warning, the boat was swept by a breaking wave that washed three crew members down the deck. All were wearing safety harnesses but Dominique Guilett's harness broke and he disappeared over the side. A marker buoy was launched but building seas forced *33 Export* to bear off downwind, unable to conduct a search. Guilett was not seen again.

By the time the storm-lashed fleet reached Sydney, hardly a boat had escaped punishment and the reports of near-disastrous broaches, knockdowns, injury and damage were almost endless. The account of eventual race winner *Sayula II*, a very well-found 65-foot ketch, was typical. She had pitch-poled down the front of a huge wave and was all but overwhelmed. Crew went over the side but, fortunately, all had safety harnesses clipped on and were recovered. *Sayula*'s cabin filled with water and the crew below were sluiced around the interior like so much flotsam. Finally, the boat righted itself and the mess was sorted. *Sayula* was undamaged and her crew had suffered only injured limbs, ribs and backs. It could have been a lot worse.

There was more to come on the third leg when, as it headed towards the southern tip of New Zealand, the fleet was lashed by a violent frontal system in the Tasman Sea.

Pen Duick VI lost her mainmast and was forced back to Sydney. Farther east and at the head of the fleet, *Great Britain II* was stripped of her main and mizzen spinnakers before her crew could react to a particularly malevolent blast of wind and then, in Foveaux Strait, at the tip of the South Island of New Zealand, crewman Bernie Hosking was washed overboard and disappeared in conditions that made rescue almost an impossibility.

Peter Blake, already formulating plans to have his own entry next time around, had much to ponder as he prepared *Burton Cutter* for the final leg of the race. The Sharp 80-footer gave another hint of what might have been when she finished second across the finish line off Portsmouth. *Great Britain II* got the gun and the Mexican-owned *Sayula II* wrapped up handicap honours. The first Whitbread race had been a success and was on its way to becoming the pre-eminent open ocean race in the sport. It had also provided a sombre reminder of the dangers and challenges to be faced by those adventurous enough to tackle the world's great oceans in sailing boats.

None of this was lost on Blake as he contemplated, and not for the last time in his career, what was next. In the meantime, he had made a big impression on those directly involved with *Burton Cutter*. Les Williams summed up his performance thus far: 'Pete was by now my mate, in a nautical sense as well as personally. He had become my number one, and he remained number one until he finally left to do his own thing. He did run watches for me, but he was senior to everyone else on the boat, promoted quickly because he deserved it. He was quite outstanding really, and he worked so hard. He never got flustered and he had a fast-growing skill and knowledge base. I could trust him implicitly and that's a wonderful feeling – you can go to sleep and know everything is in very good hands. He was obviously ambitious but not to the point of pressing things. He seemed to be willing to learn a lot before he stepped out on his own, which was very wise. I still think that ultimately he stepped out on his own a bit too soon. If he had stayed with me a little bit longer . . .'

In his personal log, Blake wrote: 'For many, the Portsmouth finish meant the end of a fantastic eight months of racing. The hardships and privations experienced were overshadowed by the hospitality received in each of the ports of call and the numerous friends made by people from fourteen different nationalities. We said our farewells and wondered what on earth we could do that would not seem too dull or boring after such an adventure.'

The 'next' for Blake, and for Williams, was the 1974 Two-man Round Britain race – Plymouth to Plymouth, 1900 miles clockwise around Britain and Ireland with compulsory 48-hour stops at Cork (in Southern Ireland), Barra (in the Outer Hebrides), Lerwick (in the Shetland Islands) and Lowestoft (on the south-eastern coast of England). It would be a real challenge – two men sailing an 80-foot maxi that had required a crew of 14 in the Whitbread race, around a course that would take the fleet round the northern tip of the Outer Hebrides islands at 61 degrees North – further north than the feared Cape Horn is south (56 degrees South). For Blake, the race would also take him through the North Sea and English Channel waters patrolled by his father in World War II, and to Lowestoft where Brian Blake was based while seconded to the Royal Navy.

First up, though, *Burton Cutter* had to go back into the yard to properly repair the damage sustained in the Agulhas Current on leg two of the Whitbread. That work commenced, and with eight weeks to go before the Round Britain start, Blake flew home to New Zealand for a month's holiday, and to be best man at his brother Tony's wedding. He returned to England refreshed and hoping that the work on *Burton Cutter* would be nearly completed. No such luck, however. In his absence, it had been decided to replate the hull from the mainmast forward and to add many more frames and stringers to provide more support to the aluminium skin for'ard. So, it was another 'all hands' situation to get the work finished in time.

The Round Britain race was an interesting event for Blake, in that it allowed monohulls and multihulls to race on level terms in the same fleet. His total sailing experience to date had been in monohulls. Now he would get his first real exposure to the potential of multihulls, which at that time enjoyed a somewhat dubious reputation outside the ranks of those who raced them – certainly in terms of their ability to really go to sea and handle whatever Mother Nature might bring to the party. The record 67-boat fleet for the 1974 edition of the event comprised two-thirds monohulls and a third multihulls, of which Blake observed: 'I don't think such a wide and weird variety of craft had ever been assembled in such numbers in one place before. Just about every imaginable "boat" was there in Millbay Docks (Plymouth), ranging from the very potent looking *British Oxygen* (a 70-foot catamaran) and *Manureva* (a 68-foot trimaran), to the 80-foot *Burton Cutter* and down to several 24-foot keelers, including a Quarter Tonner, to the successful *Quarto* design, being sailed by two young Swiss lads.'

Burton Cutter was the fastest monohull around Britain, and by a comfortable margin. But she couldn't foot it with the multihulls. She sailed the course in just under 20 days – 1.5 days slower than *British Oxygen* which was skippered by Robin Knox-Johnston. Four other multihulls, including the 25-foot trimaran *Three Leggs of Mann*, were also faster than *Burton Cutter*. The point was not lost on Blake, who wrote: 'Will I be going back to have a go next time? If some kind owner offered the use of a large racing trimaran, I might be tempted.'

Les Williams had been presented with more reason to admire his 'mate', observing: 'We couldn't beat the multihulls but were miles in front of the other monos, and this was where Peter really came into his own. He was very strong and always willing. We didn't have modern gear – the winches were small and outdated, the headsails had to be hanked on, while the 500-square-foot spinnaker was a real handful for just two people. We both really had to work at it and Peter was absolutely magnificent.' By now, though, Blake had had enough of yacht racing and must have been unsure of the viability of making a career of his sport, for he returned to New Zealand, having decided 'it was time to look to my future, now that I'd "grown up"'. His problem was that he did not know what that future held and 20 years later admitted that he still didn't have the answer.

One of Peter Blake's first priorities when back home was to obtain a private pilot's licence. In England, Les Williams had let him take the controls of a low-winged, Japanese-built Fuji aircraft which was rated fully aerobatic. Williams had flown when in the navy – although unofficially – and judged Blake 'quite a natural, just like with everything else he did'. Blake recalled: 'I gave my instructor Carole Dennis a hell of a fright once when a sack of live crayfish I'd loaded on board came undone and they began to flap around beneath our seats.' But, on 9 December 1975, he was issued with Private Pilot Licence *10982 with no mention of crustaceans.

For a time he tried his hand as an industrial sales engineer – 'flogging valves and insulation, real death-of-a-salesman stuff' by his own testimony – but was probably more interested in racing and cruising with Jim Edmonds in the 48-foot *Quando* in which he did the 1974 Auckland–Gisborne race, some of the warm-up races before the trials to select New Zealand's first Admiral's Cup team, and then the

1975 Sydney–Hobart Classic and the Hobart–Auckland race back to New Zealand. He was to have navigated *Escapade* in the 1975 Whangarei–Noumea race but had to withdraw because of illness.

Not surprisingly the salesman's job didn't last long. Blake accepted an offer to skipper the *Dina*, a 72-foot luxury power yacht, owned by an Arab industrialist and based in Beirut. This wasn't to prove your normal commission, however. It was mid-1975 and political tensions within Lebanon were escalating. He told *New Zealand Herald* feature writer Susan Maxwell: 'I was skipper and engineer on this wealthy Arab's motor launch. It had everything that opened and shut. I had my own chauffeur and an Arab crew. They were pretty hopeless sailors so I had to learn to yell at them in Arabic. We cruised around Turkey, Greece and the eastern Mediterranean. Very hard work, yes!! The boat wasn't used that often and I spent half my time playing water polo and skin diving.'

The cruisy times came to an abrupt end when, in August, the Lebanese civil war broke out. Blake slept on board *Dina* with a knife under his pillow. The fuel tanks were kept topped up and the engines always ready to go. He and the crew could hear mortar fire from Beirut city at night. 'I wasn't quite sure if I should be there,' Blake said afterwards, 'but it was a bit of an adventure. Then, one day, we got a call from the owner to say we had six hours to take his two sons and get out.'

It was close. With Blake at the wheel, *Dina* roared out of the marina at 20 knots plus. Machine gunners arrived minutes after she dropped her lines and began strafing the multi-million-dollar line-up of luxury vessels behind her. Blake saw at least two boats holed and sinking as he fled, and heard later that one man had been killed on the marina. When safe in Limassol, Cyprus, eight hours later, he decided that he was now retired from the maritime jet set. Ocean racing, with its weeks in icy seas, showerless days and sleepless nights, was much more preferable.

Coincidentally, Les Williams and Robin Knox-Johnston were embarked on a second Whitbread race campaign and needed help with the construction of the yacht that was to be *Heath's Condor*. They contacted Blake to see whether he was available. He accepted their approach 'with indecent haste'. *Condor* was a 77-foot John Sharp design sloop being built in Honduras mahogany at the Bowman Yachts yard in Emsworth, which is on an arm of Chichester Harbour on the south coast of England. In the 1977–78 Whitbread race, Williams and Knox-Johnston would alternate as skipper – Williams on board for the Portsmouth–Cape Town and then Auckland–Rio de Janeiro legs, Knox-Johnston for the Cape Town–Auckland and Rio–Portsmouth legs. This was an unusual arrangement which only the British seemed to favour. Whatever their reasons for adopting this approach, the two pillars of British sailing wisely decided that, in the circumstances, they would need a constant on the boat, a man who would fully understand everything about the yacht and her performance and would provide continuity of authority for the crew. That man, they agreed, would be Blake.

Knox-Johnston described their reasoning: 'We decided that what we wanted was a bloody good mate who could be with us the whole race and someone we could both trust. We just looked at each other and said "Peter". So we sent him a telegram, which was the way you communicated in those days. It turned out that he'd just been approached by Claire Francis (the now successful novelist who skippered the 65-foot ketch *ADC Accutrac* in the second Whitbread), but he accepted us and came shooting over.' Alan-Williams explained how the arrangement worked in practice: 'Les and Robin intended switching around as skippers so they appointed Pete first mate, to be the ever-present. Basically, the other two were the nominated skippers but he was the head honcho and he ran the boat.'

The construction of *Condor* was already under way when Blake arrived in Emsworth, a delightful village in Hampshire which was steeped in its own maritime history and which was to become a focal point of Blake's life in the not-too-distant future. Knox-Johnston was living in Scotland, overseeing the construction of a new marina, while Williams spent most of his time in Devon where he was wrestling with business problems involving a boatyard. So Blake was left to coordinate the building process and liaise with the designer and race authorities. Two other Kiwis – Les Best and Alan Prior – were also working on the project and would be part of the race crew. The sponsor of the race campaign was going to be Heaths Insurance, the chief executive of which was Bob Bell. Having worked his way through the ranks of Heaths until he virtually owned the company, Bell would later provide another building block in the Blake career.

While Les Williams had sincerely explained to Blake that the *Condor* campaign would suffer none of the defects of the *Burton Cutter* endeavour, it didn't work out that way. There were problems in the design department. Williams and Knox-Johnston claimed they had paid for tank testing of the hull lines but were unable to access the results. Eventually, when the boat was trial sailing, they discovered, according to Knox-Johnston, a 'speed bump' in her performance at 14 knots: 'The stern was wrong. Had we known the results of the tank tests we would have had time to do something about it but he (John Sharp) didn't tell us. It was a design fault that we had to hump all the way around the world. You could drive the boat through the bump but you had to really push to do it.' Explained Williams: 'My brief to John Sharp was that I wanted a *Burton Cutter* with a refined bow, but the same stern. *Burton Cutter* had almost unlimited speed downwind. It didn't stop, didn't hit a brick wall at 20 knots or something. It kept on accelerating as long as the wind would blow and it held together. I didn't have time to spare during the construction of the boat, and when I saw what John had done I nearly cried. He'd gone for the (then) modern, trendy stern and it was a slow old boat. Everyone thought it was fast, but it wasn't. We had a rooster

54

tail out the back, just like a powerboat. It wasn't tidy and it wasn't particularly good in heavyish conditions. And it certainly wasn't *Burton Cutter*.'

Then there was *Condor*'s rig. Nobody seems to recall how or why the decision was made to take such a chance on new technology, but *Condor* went to the Whitbread start line with a big carbon fibre sloop rig which was highly innovative for its day but which, unfortunately, proved to be poorly engineered. It was to cost her any chance of victory.

After a fairly uneventful haul down the Atlantic to the equator, *Condor* was chasing Conny van Rietschoten's 65-foot Sparkman & Stephens ketch *Flyer* at the head of the fleet when she struck testing weather south of the Doldrums. Severe squalls lashed the boat and the crew noticed that above the top spreaders, the untested mast was beginning to act like a whip. The mainsail was reefed but that seemed to cause other problems and soon afterwards the spar snapped 20 feet or so above the deck. A replacement alloy spar was organised by Knox-Johnston, who was back in Britain, and *Condor* headed to Monrovia where the spar would be delivered. This was somewhat familiar territory for Williams and Blake who had put in there for fuel while en route to Cape Town in *Ocean Spirit*.

'Again, I had a choice to make,' explained Williams. 'I only had 20 feet of the mast left and we didn't know what was going to happen to that. I could have made a jury rig and struggled on with that to Cape Town, but felt that, in the best interests of the future, it was smarter to go to Monrovia and take delivery of a new mast which I was told had already been built. We could fly that mast to Monrovia, fit it and then try it out on the way down to Cape Town. That way, Robin (who would be skippering) and the crew could at least start the second leg with a known quantity. As it turned out, the mast had not already been built so we had quite a long wait in Monrovia.'

While the decision to ship in a new mast was being made, Blake

FIRST STEPS UP THE LADDER

explored what it would take to get to Cape Town under jury rig. He wasn't to know it at the time but, four years later, his efforts would be put to good use and in an almost identical part of the South Atlantic. When the replacement mast finally arrived, all the rigging and fittings had to be attached and then the rig had to be hoisted into the boat. Blake was in charge, and the facilities available were rudimentary to say the least. Finally, with everything about ready, he persuaded the skipper of an American rice ship to rig his two onboard cranes to perform the task of lifting Condor's new spar into place. 'We didn't realise until we came alongside the rice ship that there was a 2-foot rise and fall in the swell, even in the harbour,' recalls Alan-Williams. 'So it was quite a game lining up the rig and getting it in. Again, Peter was the person who was directing operations and instructing the cranes. He had it all planned out and everything worked just fine.'

Finally, Condor resumed her original course to Cape Town, now 12 days behind the fleet and effectively out of the race. She would continue in the event, however, and, like Burton Cutter before her, provide some hints of what might have been.

The second leg to Auckland was a thriller. After a couple of light days leaving Cape Town, Condor crossed tacks with race leader Flyer off the Agulhas Bank. That was encouraging. Then gale-force westerlies pushed the boats at breakneck speeds through the Southern Ocean, bound for Auckland, New Zealand, and there was the scare of a man overboard in the extreme conditions. With no safety harness clipped on, Condor crewman Bill Abram was flung over the side when a spinnaker lying on deck suddenly filled and flipped him overboard. A life-ring was tossed to him and he caught it. The sails were dropped and the engine started, but the folding propeller wouldn't unfold and the main had to be rehoisted. By this time, Abram was nowhere to be seen. Fortunately, a flock of albatross must have thought he looked like food and circled him, marking his position until the *Condor* crew could pull him back on board.

On *Great Britain II* a spinnaker brace whipped up off the deck as the sail filled, catching Nick Dunlop around the waist and Rob James around the legs. The full spinnaker began to squeeze the life out of Dunlop and sever the legs of James. By the time the brace was cut, all the blood vessels in Dunlop's eyes had burst and he couldn't be moved without screaming in pain. James couldn't walk. Fortunately, neither man was permanently injured.

Heath's Condor crossed the line first in Auckland's Waitemata Harbour on 25 November 1977, 31 hours ahead of the next boat, *Great Britain II*. Local boy Peter Blake was given a hero's welcome. 'Auckland was just huge,' recalls Alan-Williams, 'boats everywhere you looked and masses of excited people. That was the first time I heard the now famous voice of Peter Montgomery searing the airwaves. Marsden Wharf, where the fleet would be berthed, was jam-packed and the reception for Peter Blake was quite something. He wasn't officially the skipper, but he most definitely was the sailing master and his name was up in lights. He had the recognition he needed to do his own programme next time.'

Great Britain II took line honours in Rio de Janeiro, just a half-hour ahead of *Heath's Condor,* but *Condor* reversed that order at the finish in Portsmouth. For Blake, another 'if only' Whitbread race was over. He had, however, learned much about leading a crew and calling the shots on a maxi in the world's pre-eminent long-distance race, and was now even more determined to put everything he had learnt into practice.

Peter Blake's life and career were about to take some exciting new turns, one of which would lead to marriage, but there was also a slightly sad twist in his close friendship with Les Williams. While Blake would again sail with Knox-Johnston, his relationship with Williams would become more distant. 'Peter stayed in England, looking after what was now *Condor of Bermuda* for Bob Bell,' remembers Williams, 'and I was talking to him about a shared skippering arrangement. He would skipper one race, I would skipper the next. Then one day I went down to the boat and there was a meeting taking place between Peter and the designer John Sharp, on the redesign of *Condor*'s stern. I asked what was going on and Pete said, "I've been made skipper." I think he had presumed that I knew of this, but nobody had advised me. It was okay. I had about had enough of the *Condor* programme by then. But after that, while we continued to exchange pleasantries, Peter and I never again had a man-to-man chat.'

Interestingly, while noting that Blake's own first Whitbread boat, *Ceramco New Zealand*, had what he termed 'a *Burton Cutter* stern', Williams was puzzled by *Ceramco*'s size (or lack of it): 'I could not quite understand why she was so small.' He would race against the 68-foot *Ceramco* in the 1981–82 Whitbread, skippering his latest maxi *FCF Challenger* (an 80-foot Doug Peterson/David Alan-Williams design) and matter-of-factly bemoan the fact that 'again I didn't have enough sponsorship, so I had to try to sail without [the] sails I needed . . .'

CHAPTER Three

His Own Command

After the inaugural Whitbread race in 1973–74, the then
26-year-old Peter Blake had returned to his homeland
determined that next time around, in 1977–78, there should
be an all-New Zealand entry in the fleet, particularly as the second
port of call would be Auckland, New Zealand, instead of Sydney,
Australia. He went to see his good friend Martin Foster, then
Executive Secretary of the New Zealand Yachting Federation, who
was immediately receptive to the idea. The pair decided to form a
steering committee, which was the way of doing things in the very
regulated New Zealand of the 60s, 70s and 80s, and began formulating
their ideas.

The first Whitbread had been a gamble for the organisers, the
Royal Naval Sailing Association. The logistics were forbidding and
nobody knew whether it was feasible to race modern yachts hard
through the high latitudes of the Southern Ocean. But there were
plenty of adventurous souls prepared to try. The heavy-displacement,
upwind designs that dominated that first race fleet had proved almost
unmanageable in the huge following seas on the second and third
legs across the bottom of the world. In Blake's view, they were ill
suited for the task. For his own campaign, he wanted to build a
fractionally-rigged, light-displacement downwind machine that would

excel rather than struggle in the hard-running conditions of the Southern Ocean.

Wasting no time, Blake approached the Bruce Farr design office with his concept. Farr was then a young New Zealander who had made a reputation for himself designing the unrestricted 12-footer and 18-footer skiff classes that were favourites with the go-fast Kiwi and Aussie dinghy-racing sets. He'd also just won the Quarter Ton Cup in France with the radical keelboat *45 South*, and was in the process of revolutionising offshore racing with his light-displacement approach. Blake later wrote: 'I liked his boats and his fractional rigs. They made sense for an around-the-world race boat because of ease of handling and their readiness to surf quickly and maintain high speeds under complete control.'

Blake and Foster spent their own money on preliminary designs for a 65-footer from Farr. To build the boat, however, they would need a wealthy backer (or backers) or sponsorship from New Zealand's commercial sector. And while the emerging Blake and behind-the-scenes toiler Foster were known in yachting circles, they had little or no recognition in the marketplace. They quickly identified that they needed someone with a profile on board, and targeted the noted mountaineer/adventurer Peter Mulgrew.

Mulgrew, a former Royal New Zealand Navy chief petty officer whose speciality was communications, was the long-time friend and right-hand man of Everest conqueror Sir Edmund Hillary. He'd been with Hillary in 1957 and 1958 for what the media had dubbed 'The Last Great Journey in the World' – the race with Britain's Sir Vivian Fuchs to be the first to trek across Antarctica via the South Pole. The pair were together again in 1961 on a Hillary-led expedition to the Himalayas. The objectives of the expedition were to search for evidence of the existence of the yeti, the 'Abominable Snowman', and to climb the 27,790-foot mountain Makalu, the world's fifth highest peak, without oxygen in order to investigate the mysteries of high-altitude acclimatisation. During the ascent of Makalu, when just 400 feet from the summit, Mulgrew suffered a pulmonary oedema (a major blood clot) in his right lung. At that altitude, it probably should have killed him but somehow he survived the rescue off the mountain, in the process suffering severe frostbite to his feet and fingers. He was hospitalised in Khatmandu then returned home to New Zealand where both his legs had to be amputated six inches below the knees and replaced with prosthetics. Such was Mulgrew's spirit and determination that he overcame his addiction to painkillers, learned to walk again and, four years later, returned to the Himalayas with Hillary. He retired as a serving naval officer and moved on to excel in the business and sporting worlds – becoming the manager of a succession of large companies and a top-class ocean-racing yachtsman. Known affectionately by New Zealand's yachties as 'Old Tin Legs', he would jam himself in the cockpit of a boat and steer expertly. Sadly, on 28 November 1979, he was one of 257 souls who perished when Air New Zealand Flight 901, a DC10 on a sightseeing excursion from Auckland to Antarctica, ploughed into the slopes of Mt Erebus. Hillary and Mulgrew rotated as tour guides on these highly popular flights to the ice. It had been Hillary's turn, but he had to visit the United States on business and his good friend had stood in for him.

When approached by Blake and Foster in 1975, Mulgrew was probably at the peak of his new career and sporting paths. Somewhat ironically in hindsight, the primary sponsorship target became Air New Zealand. Blake was about to have his first serious encounter with the difficulties of securing sponsorships, and New Zealand's national carrier was to provide the experience. It was one that allows an early insight into the vision and determination that were to become trademarks of the young yachtsman. Decision day was 16 February 1976, when the airline had a full board meeting scheduled.

'There we were,' recalls Martin Foster, 'Peter Blake and I, sitting up there on the ninth floor waiting for a result, quite excited because we thought it was all on. The concept was fine and Air New Zealand was riding the crest of a wave. Finally, the door to the boardroom opened and Morrie Davies, the then chief executive, emerged. He came over to us and in a very bluff and abrupt manner said: "This airline sees no advantage whatsoever in being associated with a yachting project." Full stop. We left, probably in a state of shock.'

The pair caught the ferry back to Devonport, and walked along the waterfront to the upstairs bar of the Masonic Hotel to drown their sorrows. After several jugs of beer, Blake started regaling Foster with tales of the Two-man Round Britain race that he'd done in 1974 with Les Williams on *Burton Cutter*. Blake thought an event like that would be a go in New Zealand and Foster was quick on the uptake. A race around New Zealand (some 3000 miles) would be too long, however. People would not be able to take enough time off work. So it would be a race around the North Island, a sailing distance of around 1200 miles. They talked well into the night and the following day Foster wrote a complete Notice of Race for the event, based on his own experience of sailing around New Zealand in his yacht *Truant*. The inaugural race would be in 1977 and would coincide with the bicentenary of Captain Cook's third and final voyage to New Zealand. It would track counterclockwise around the North Island with three ports of call – Mangonui (in Doubtless Bay on the Northland coast), Picton (in Queen Charlotte Sound on the northern tip of New Zealand's South Island) and Gisborne (in Poverty Bay on the east coast of the North Island). All three stopping points had strong associations with Cook and his remarkable voyages of discovery in the South Pacific.

The next night there was a committee meeting of the Devonport Yacht Club, of which Foster was former commodore and a current committee member. He presented the proposal and the club hierarchy said 'Let's do it'. 'We had spent most of 1975 working on

64

our Whitbread proposal,' said Foster, 'talking about the race, modifying our thoughts. Now, here we were, not much more than 24 hours after having missed out on getting that one away, organising a major race around the coast of New Zealand.' Foster set up a four-man organising committee, comprising himself (chairman), Peter Blake (technical matters), Brian Blake (publications) and veteran yachtsman John Wollacott (trophies), and within nine months the race had been professionally set up. The Calliope Dry Dock in the Devonport Naval Base would be the pre-race assembly point, the Royal Yacht *Britannia* would act as flagship for the start off the Devonport Wharf, and the start gun would be fired by HRH Prince Philip, in the presence of HM Queen Elizabeth, on 22 February 1977.

The race was an outstanding success, attracting 44 entries and a host of the leading names in New Zealand sailing, including Blake who joined forces with Graham Eder to win line honours (fastest time) in the 42-foot Farr design sloop *Gerontius*.

Interestingly in this day and age, the entire event was unsponsored. The Devonport Yacht Club met all costs over and above those recovered from entry fees and from the proceeds of an impressive race publication.

Examination of the promotional and selling documents prepared by Blake and Foster for the abortive 1977 Whitbread entry shows just how far ahead of the field they were when it came to seeking sponsorships (a relatively new development at that level in New Zealand sailing at the time). The costings and budgeting are particularly interesting in these days of yachting campaigns costing hundreds of millions of dollars. The estimates show that Blake and Foster anticipated building the new boat for $190,800 (including design fee, rig, all deck fittings and sails). Their running expenses were forecast to be $22,500, including an allowance of $3 a day for 14 crew over the race period of eight months. In conclusion, the document stated: 'This challenge, which is the idea of Peter Blake, is to be an all-New Zealand

65

effort, mounted for the sole purpose of winning the 1977 Whitbread "Around the World" race. Commencing with the growing international reputation of Aucklander Bruce Farr, the design is assured of worldwide interest. To be built in Auckland by a local and well-known boat builder, wholly equipped and provisioned by New Zealand manufacturers and with a New Zealand sponsorship, it is a true New Zealand challenge without precedence in the history of New Zealand yachting. Highlighted by inclusion of Auckland as one of the three principal ports of call for the race, there are a number of firsts which must guarantee to the sponsor the tremendous amount of promotional publicity which can be further used for advantage. Unlike the normal sponsorships this project is a continuing one and will live for many years after the conclusion of the race in 1978.'

Although they almost certainly didn't realise it at the time, Blake and Foster were setting the standards for sponsorship in sailing, and not just in New Zealand, for many years to come. The inclusion in the sponsorship pitch of a powerful radio that would enable Blake to communicate with media and sponsors from any part of the world was a significant and far-seeing initiative. In the years ahead, frequent live reports by radio became a hallmark of the Blake approach to campaigning, to the delight of sponsors and public alike. Blake was later to observe: 'We were unsuccessful (in securing sponsorship) mainly, I think, because the Whitbread race had yet to make an impression on New Zealanders. The first race had visited Sydney and not Auckland, and Kiwi companies were unconvinced of the commercial merit of pouring a lot of money into a young man's pipedream.'

In late 1978, having successfully completed his second Whitbread race (this one on *Heath's Condor*), Blake committed himself to reviving his dream of an all-Kiwi 'Round the World' race entry. He was now the

66

skipper of the now *Condor of Bermuda* and had ongoing commitments to her owner Bob Bell that included racing the boat in the 1979 SORC (Southern Ocean Racing Conference) on the East Coast of the United States, and in the 1979 Fastnet Classic in England. He then had to deliver the vessel to Australia for the 1979 Sydney–Hobart Classic, and then on to Auckland where she would undergo a major refit at the McMullen & Wing yard on the Tamaki River.

Blake and Foster used the *Condor* delivery to Florida for the SORC to fine-tune their thinking for a Whitbread campaign, after which Foster flew back to New Zealand to announce the entry. As Foster jetted out, a young English lady by the name of Philippa (Pippa) Glanville arrived from London to join the *Condor* crew. Peter Blake's life and campaign style were about to change in the most fundamental ways.

The eldest of John and Judy Glanville's three children, Pippa was born in Portsmouth but had moved with the family to Emsworth when just six months old. John Glanville was a partner in the family law practice and had served as a Royal Navy officer in World War II. His wife Judy was from Guernsey in the Channel Islands. For both, the sea was part of their background and their lives, something they passed down to their daughter Pippa, son Charles and second daughter Louise. 'We always had dinghies as children,' recalls Pippa. 'I did my first sailing in a Heron and then a Firefly. But my sailing was definitely messing around in boats. I did a bit of racing with my brother Charles and various friends but I was definitely a fair-weather sailor at that time.'

Family holidays every year were in Guernsey where the Glanvilles had a converted lifeboat in which they did day trips to the islands of Herm and Sark. Back home in the south of England, the Emsworth Sailing Club was part of Pippa's growing up, and that's where she first met her husband-to-be, one Friday in August 1978. Blake had just finished the Whitbread on *Heath's Condor*. The boat had been built

67

in Emsworth and so was brought back to the same yard for a refit before heading across the Atlantic for the SORC.

At the time Pippa was working for the Arts Council of Great Britain at the Hayward Gallery in London, but most weekends would head home to Emsworth. On that fateful Friday, she arrived down in the early evening and, with brother Charles, headed for a drink at the sailing club. They hadn't been there long when 'in walked three guys, one of whom was Peter. I had never met anyone from the southern hemisphere before and I probably didn't get off to a very good start. I called him "cobber",' laughs Pippa. 'I came to realise that that was not the thing to do. It was an Australian term, not Kiwi. I remember being pretty smitten by Peter because he had these amazing, clear blue eyes and had the air of an adventurer. There was just something different about him, apart from his stature. He made quite an impression on me.' Pippa was 24 at the time. Peter was 30.

Charles Glanville had just left university with a law degree and was looking for something to do for the summer. He started chatting to Peter Blake, who was about to sail across the Atlantic, and it wasn't long before Charles was invited to join the delivery crew. 'Peter took to Charles,' says Pippa. 'But I also still have a feeling that he thought maybe chatting up the brother might provide an entrée to the sister. I have never had that confirmed, however.'

By December that year *Condor of Bermuda* was ready to leave for the Caribbean, and Pippa, who'd been meeting with Peter and 'the *Condor* lads' most weekends, was beginning to fret over the fact that 'he was going off across the sea and I might never see him again'. She decided to take matters into her own hands and, on the pretext of being unwell, took time off work so that she could stay in Emsworth and see her Kiwi every day. Out of the blue, Peter asked her if she would like to fly to the Caribbean after Christmas and meet up with him. 'I jumped at the chance,' says Pippa. 'I'd never dreamt of being asked anything like that. It was very exciting. Peter really captivated

68

me with his stories of the sea, of life at sea, stories of icebergs and the Aurora Australis, the birds, the wildlife, seals and dolphins. I had never heard anyone describing such things before. He was always a very positive person, always very polite and quite shy – he remained shy all his life, something people often mistook for aloofness.'

The 'Condor lads' warned Pippa not to hold out too much hope of 'landing' Peter who was 'cool' and who 'gets the girls just like that'. Gradually, however, the remarks about Peter's availability or otherwise became: 'Gosh, we've never seen him like this before.' Jokes emerged about the sound of violins. It was becoming clear that the young Kiwi skipper was as smitten with his English lass as she was with him. At her farewell party in London, her friends teased her about her English winter complexion, saying that by the time she got to America, Peter would have met some bronze Floridian beauty and that would be it. She decided to do something about that straight away: 'I went back to where I lived and switched on a sunlamp that we happened to have in the house. In those days, sunlamps didn't come with timers. I fell asleep under it and woke up probably two hours later with my face pretty badly burnt. I jumped in the car and drove straight down to my parents' home in Emsworth. They immediately took me to hospital. I wasn't kept in but the next morning when I woke up I couldn't open my eyes or my mouth, and the doctor who came to see me said that I might have to have plastic surgery. There I was then thinking, "Oh no, what have I done? I won't be able to go to Florida and the Caribbean. I'm never going to be able to see Peter again." It seemed like the end. I had visions of having to live the rest of my days with a black veil over my face.'

Unbeknown to Pippa, Judy Glanville managed to get a message to Peter – who was somewhat preoccupied skippering *Condor* in the St Petersburg–Fort Lauderdale race. Judy told him that Pippa had been seriously burned. He immediately sent Pippa a telegram to say he loved her. It was touch and go for while but, slowly, Pippa's face cleared up without scarring and she was finally able to catch a plane to join her man. 'Flying to meet him, in Bermuda by this time, was the most exciting thing I had done in my whole life,' reflects Pippa. 'I was so pale – straight out of a British winter – and everyone else was so brown. It didn't worry Peter, but the crew used to call me "the girl from the flour factory" and talked about my "pale Pommy pins".'

The next month was spent racing in the SORC programme. Pippa did her first overnight race – from Nassau to Miami – in rough conditions with *Condor of Bermuda* pounding into strong headwinds: 'I sat up all night eating roast beef sandwiches and three of us got through a bottle of port (things on racing yachts were a lot more relaxed in those days). I wasn't seasick. I loved it.' A short time later, on the marina in Miami, Peter proposed – 'I think I had passed his sailing test.' The surroundings weren't exactly romantic. The marina was 'pretty scungy and the parking lot was not a place where you were encouraged to walk at night', but Peter had phoned Pippa's parents to ask permission and the question was popped: 'My parents could not believe this was happening. They had only met Peter once or twice. He had long hair then and my father, being quite conservative, must have been wondering what on earth I was doing. We spent the next three months in the Caribbean – racing in events like the British Virgin Islands regatta and Antigua race week – and I saw waterspouts for the first time. It was simply wonderful being there with Peter and coming to realise that he was such a special person as well as a rather special yacht skipper. As always, he had a great group of people around him. It was a lot of fun.'

But it wasn't all play. Peter was *Condor*'s paid skipper and Pippa was now officially a member of the crew. So there were the usual lengthy lists of jobs that had to be done on a daily basis to keep a maxi yacht spic and span and in top racing condition. And, when the owner was aboard with guests, there was hosting and entertaining to do.

The newly engaged couple decided that they would marry on

August 25 that year – before Peter headed *Condor* south to Australia and the Sydney–Hobart Classic. So, while *Condor* was having her stern changed in Newport (Rhode Island) before the trans-Atlantic race from Newport to Cork, Pippa left for England to 'sort out the wedding'.

If the trans-Atlantic race in *Condor of Bermuda* was uneventful, the next race for the Blake-skippered maxi was anything but. It was the infamous 1979 Fastnet. The Fastnet, one of the world's blue-water classics, is raced every two years. It starts from Cowes, goes west down the English Channel and across the Irish Sea to Fastnet Rock off the south-eastern tip of Ireland, then back to the Channel via Bishop Rock (in the Scilly Islands) and on to the finish in Plymouth.

For *Condor* and her crew, the Fastnet race was another opportunity for a head-to-head battle with her old and formidable rival *Kialoa III*, the doyen of the world's maxi fleet. They had raced together in Antigua and in the trans-Atlantic – the honours going to *Kialoa* on each occasion. Bob Bell, *Condor*'s owner, was keen to redress that situation. There was also *Kialoa III's* Fastnet course record of 79 hours, 11 minutes and 48 seconds to have a crack at.

However, by the time the maxis at the head of the fleet reached the Fastnet Rock, that record looked well out of reach. The passage out from the Solent had been slow in light airs. *Kialoa* was first around at 1250 hours on the Monday, 46 hours and 20 minutes after leaving Cowes. At this time the smallest boats in the fleet, the Class V boats, were nearly 200 miles behind the maxis and just emerging from Mount's Bay to round Land's End. To beat her own record, *Kialoa* had to cover the remaining 251 miles to Plymouth in under 33 hours. This appeared out of the question in the light airs that persisted.

Condor was 1 hour and 7 minutes behind the leader at the Rock but skipper Blake was not dispirited. He knew that the American boat

71

had the edge in light winds, but was certain the shoe would be on the other foot if it blew hard. Stronger winds hadn't even been forecast at this stage but Blake had seen that there were low-pressure areas coming across the Atlantic. These would bring plenty of wind – if only they came in time. Blake also believed that the stronger winds, when they eventually arrived, would veer from the southerly Force 3 in which *Condor* rounded the Fastnet. So, instead of sailing close-hauled on the rhumb-line course to Bishop Rock, he had the crew set the No. 1 reacher with a genoa staysail and, with this double-head rig, reached off at maximum speed. *Condor*, therefore, was well into the return journey across the Irish Sea when the wind began to blow hard. Blake called for gradual reduction in the sail plan as the wind strength continued to climb. He knew from the sky before dark that this was no ordinary blow coming on, so he also made sure that all the storm gear was prepared, along with the emergency equipment.

The sails were progressively reduced until all that were set were the storm jib and a triple-reefed mainsail. *Condor* often had her lee rail under and was knocked flat on more than one occasion, but none of this caused Blake a great deal of anxiety. At times the sea conditions were worse than those of the Southern Ocean, but only because the waves were close together. By now it was clear that the Fastnet fleet was facing a severe storm. *Condor* was most definitely racing, travelling fast towards an unfriendly lee shore (Bishop Rock) with low visibility, but she was also already relaying distress calls from yachts caught by the full force of the storm while still headed for Fastnet Rock.

In his book *The Fastnet Disaster and After*, English yachting journalist Bob Fisher provides real insight into the levels of seamanship and racing expertise, along with fierce competitiveness, now evident in the emerging Blake: 'It is ninety nine miles from the Bishop Rock to the Fastnet finishing line off the breakwater at

Plymouth. By the time she was on this leg it was obvious to all on board *Condor* that the race record was going to tumble. But her crew had no idea of where *Kialoa* was. All they could do was race as hard as possible. And that is what they did.'

Once inside the shelter of the Lizard, Blake piled on the pressure. *Condor of Bermuda* was on a very broad reach in a north-westerly wind. It was still blowing Force 8 but, with a lee from the land close by to the north, the sea conditions were nowhere near as severe when Blake called for a spinnaker. Fisher writes: 'Up it went and *Condor* took off, surfing down the waves at speeds well in excess of 20 knots. It couldn't last, however, and it was certain that she would broach eventually. When she did she surprised everyone by the suddenness of the move and by the extent to which she went. Peter Blake later described it as a "three-point turn". *Condor* turned round through 180 degrees and the spinnaker was blown back on to the mast and spreaders. *Condor* started to make a stern board and Peter reversed the wheel and steered her out of the situation backwards. The boat spun round, faced her proper course, the spinnaker filled and *Condor* was on her way again. Not a manoeuvre to be recommended.'

The extra speed gained by hoisting the spinnaker was the telling factor in the *Condor* versus *Kialoa* duel. *Condor* pressed on through the driving rain and bad visibility and finally crossed the finishing line at 1355 hours on Tuesday, 28 minutes and 30 seconds ahead of *Kialoa*. Her elapsed time of 71 hours, 25 minutes and 23 seconds was 7 hours 45 minutes better than *Kialoa*'s record. And to rub salt further into the wounds, *Condor* also beat *Kialoa* on corrected time.

Of the 14 Class 0 yachts (42.1–79 feet in size), 13 finished. But behind them, the decimation caused by the worst storm in Fastnet history increased as the boat sizes decreased. The maxis had scooted home ahead of the real blow. Behind them, the fearsome conditions wreaked havoc and claimed 14 lives with five vessels 'lost believed sunk'. Another 15 yachts were abandoned but later recovered. Of the

303 yachts that started the race, only 85 finished. Among those to perish in the storm was Judy Glanville's cousin Peter Dorey, who was skippering his own boat in the race and who was lost overboard even though he was wearing a safety harness.

Pippa had driven down to Plymouth with her sister Louise for the finish. Their brother Charles was aboard *Condor* with Blake.

'There was a news flash on the car radio saying that people had been lost in the Fastnet race,' Pippa recounts. 'Every hour, more and more people had been lost at sea. I knew Peter and Charles were on a big boat, but it was still nerve-wracking. When we reached Plymouth, we headed straight for the marina where the boats would berth. I screamed out to someone on the gates, "Is *Condor* here?" To my huge relief, they answered that *Condor* was already in. They had won line honours and broken the race record but nobody was celebrating. They had been too far ahead to go back to specifically help anyone but they had done a lot of relaying of messages for boats in trouble.'

A week later Peter and Pippa were married at St James Church in Emsworth, after which they drove to Scotland for a three-day honeymoon. The first night was spent in a castle (complete with four-poster bed). The second night they were downgraded to an ordinary room. On the third night they stayed with Robin Knox-Johnston who was working in Scotland at the time.

Two days later they were back on the south coast, in a hyper-market in Havant, stocking up with supplies for seven men and one woman at sea for 90 days for the delivery to Sydney.

Martin Foster, meanwhile, had returned to New Zealand to pursue the intended entry in the 1981–82 Whitbread Round the World race, and had made real progress. His announcement of the entry in the New Zealand media prompted a telephone call from Warwick White, the then commodore of the Royal New Zealand Yacht Squadron, the country's most prestigious sailing establishment.

Throughout its long and somewhat introspective existence, the Squadron had been a male-only club that catered for the racing and social needs of its membership. Its event programme was extensive and featured divisions of keel yachts, determined mostly by size, racing in Auckland's spectacular harbour or to one of the many safe anchorages scattered around the Hauraki Gulf (which provides some of the finest racing and cruising grounds in the world). But the world outside was changing, and so were the ambitions of New Zealand's sailing fraternity. No longer content to excel on their own patch, they were straining at the leash to test their skills in designing, building and racing boats against international competition. Some of the newer breed of Squadron commodores recognised this and edged the club forward towards becoming the truly international establishment that it is today.

Commodore Bruce Marler probably led the way when, in 1968, he persuaded his fellow flags and committee members to back a challenge for ocean racing's One Ton Cup. This meant sending a 36-footer called *Rainbow II*, along with her skipper Chris Bouzaid and his crew, all the way to the small island of Heligoland to contest a five-race series in the North Sea. This was to prove one of the pivotal decisions in New Zealand's remarkable rise to world dominance in the sport of sailing in the second part of the twentieth century.

Rainbow II finished second on that occasion but Marler, the head of a prominent family footwear business in Auckland, wasn't to be deterred. With the backing of stalwart Squadron member Arnold Baldwin, the owner of a flourishing publishing business, he championed a follow-up challenge in Heligoland the next year. *Rainbow II* was revamped and reconfigured to be more competitive under the One Ton Cup measurement rule, and shipped back to Europe where she triumphed in the then Formula 1 event of offshore racing – clinching the series in the fourth race.

On that day in 1969 the *Auckland Star* newspaper's front page featured only two headlines and stories. One recorded Neil Armstrong's historic statement from the moon: 'One small step for man, one giant leap for mankind.' The other declared: 'Rainbow Wins Battle of Jutland.' *Rainbow*'s exploits, and those of her young skipper Bouzaid, had made a significant impression – not least on the even younger Peter Blake.

Like Marler and John McKenzie, another of the Squadron's more progressive commodores before him, Warwick White, a senior partner in a city law firm, wasn't content to spend his two years in office simply overseeing the club's traditional activities. He read of the Blake–Foster challenge for the Whitbread race and rang Foster, on behalf of the Squadron, to express his enthusiasm. It was agreed to join forces and mount a joint entry, forging what was, for those days, a highly unlikely relationship between the celebrated Royal New Zealand Yacht Squadron and the unpretentious Devonport Yacht Club. Another committee was organised with Squadron member Peter Cornes, well connected in the business community, recruited to join White and Foster in the bid to make a Whitbread challenge a reality. The first decision taken was to appoint Peter Blake the project manager. Then they concentrated on the big issue – funding.

Using the original material, albeit updated, from the unsuccessful 1975 foray into the sponsorship market, their initial efforts produced an immediate result and they were close to a deal with an international copying company, when the possibility of a New Zealand sponsor emerged. Enter Tom Clark (now Sir Tom Clark), then head of the Ceramco group of companies, who was to become a mentor to and a main backer of Peter Blake in the years ahead.

'We hadn't signed any documents,' says Foster, 'but we'd been to see the copying company and had more or less agreed a deal. Clarky (Tom Clark) got wind of it and, in a very cloak-and-dagger approach, cornered Peter Cornes in the Squadron car park and clearly wanted to be involved. To that stage, nobody had thought about Tom Clark and Ceramco as a sponsor.'

They met with Clark who told them: 'I can do a deal with you. My company will give you $250,000 cash and we will provide you with the equivalent of $100,000 in administration, support and a whole lot of other things. And you can get other sponsors.' The proposition was accepted immediately and a heads of agreement was drawn up on the spot.

'It became very difficult for Warwick and me,' concedes Foster. 'The copying company was not happy when we told them. We hadn't signed anything with them but we were accused of immoral behaviour. We did the right thing, however – for us and for New Zealand. It was the right call. Tom and Ceramco were a dream to work with and in the support and enthusiasm they brought to the project.'

Clark, then in his fifties and at the peak of his considerable business and motivational abilities, had been in business all his life. He had been a successful motor racing driver until a near-fatal crash had ended that pursuit and he'd turned his energies and competitiveness to sailing. He reflects on the sponsorship deal: 'I had just started the renaming of Ceramco from the old Amalgamated Brick and Pipe Company, Consolidated Brick and Pipe Investments and all that stuff. I emptied the whole thing out. I was the new broom and I was going to play merry hell with a big stick. In my wisdom, I decided that Ceramco was the new name and I was looking for a way to do something that was a bit dramatic to bring that name to everyone's attention. But how do you take something that is as old as the hills and give it a new life? Then the Whitbread entry presented itself as an opportunity and I decided it was the key, providing we could do a good job with it. So I met with White, Foster and Cornes and, without too much messing around, agreed to sign on the dotted line. But before I did so, we had a lot of discussion about the possible success of the venture which, I was certain, would be largely dependent on 1) the skipper and 2) the crew that the skipper could attract around him.' So, Clark met with Blake and 'as soon as I did, it was all over bar the shouting'.

'I played the hard man to convince,' Clark admits. 'He set about convincing me. And it didn't take very long before he had me convinced that it would all be a piece of cake, he would just blow the bastards apart. I wished I could have talked him into coming to work for me. I was immediately captivated by his imagination and his ability to sell.'

Clark tried to find flaws in Blake by 'flicking him this way and flicking him that way, to see whether he had a convenient memory about the way things happened, seeing if I could catch him out'. But what he saw and heard was what he got: 'Over the next three months, he came through smelling like a bloody rose and my confidence in him, from being very wary to start with, was 100 per cent. I have to say that in those same three months he was pretty wary of me, but he developed the same confidence in me that I had developed in him.'

The pair formed what, in effect, was an operating partnership, the key to which was keeping one another fully informed in a very matter-of-fact fashion. It was a relationship that would stand the test of time and grow into mutual admiration and genuine friendship.

Ceramco's commitment meant the project could begin immediately. But major additional funding still had to be obtained. White proposed an innovative solution – a public syndication scheme through which the people of New Zealand could become shareholders in the boat by purchasing $500 debentures. Through this initiative, the challenger would be truly a people's yacht and the project would command an automatic following nationwide. By this stage, Bruce Farr had been

78

confirmed as the designer and provided with a brief for a yacht that closely resembled the concept vessel he had produced for Blake and Foster in 1975, but with less emphasis on rating rule considerations.

'We didn't want hull-line distortion for rating purposes,' said Blake. 'My *Condor* experience told me distortion meant control problems in Southern Ocean seas. We wanted a fair, fast hull – a boat which could maintain high speeds readily and stay with the weather systems for longer without exhausting the crew. I was convinced that such a boat would sail to her rating, providing it wasn't cripplingly high, and have a royal chance of line honours as well. This would later help the resale value of the yacht as full-on rating boats tend to date quickly and are frequently difficult to quit.'

The only hitch in proceedings was that the Farr office had been approached by another group, from Europe, which wanted a 62-footer for the race. Blake and company didn't want another country in the race with a boat similar in pedigree, size and rating to their own. In Blake's view: 'It would tend to negate much of the edge we fully intended to gain from a close association with Farr and his team, and from the considerable input we had to offer.'

The solution was that the New Zealand group would have exclusivity within a 10-foot rating band – from 62 feet to 72 feet. The Farr office would not do anyone else a design in that range. To be completely confident of their position, the New Zealanders increased the overall length of their boat from 65 feet to 68 feet, which, Blake figured, was as big as they could go without the boat becoming a full-on maxi with all the attendant problems that would involve. It was also a hard fact that the budget could not be stretched any further than for a yacht 68 feet long.

The design requirements settled, Blake and the committee turned their attentions to construction. After a lot of deliberation, it was decided to build in aluminium, in the McMullen & Wing yard, which had already proved its capabilities with the One Tonners *Escapade* and

HIS OWN COMMAND

Wai-Aniwa, the 45-footer *Shockwave* and the 50-footers *Anticipation* and *Corinthian*. The yard had also done major underwater surgery on *Kialoa III* and so was fully conversant with big boat construction. Building was scheduled to start in January 1980 for an October 1980 launching.

While Blake returned to Britain to complete his commitments to Bob Bell and *Condor of Bermuda*, Messrs White, Foster, Cornes and Clark were busily enlisting the support of New Zealand industry and the public. Their efforts were coordinated by Alan Topham, from the Ceramco group, whom Clark essentially seconded to the yacht campaign to ensure that everything ran efficiently. Offers of equipment, materials and supplies came rolling in, and the concept of a people's syndicated boat promised to be a big success. By the time Blake brought *Condor* into Auckland Harbour in January 1980, everything was 'go'. Chris McMullen was lofting the boat, construction materials were on hand and the yard team was assembled.

'It was an exciting moment, to see everything beginning to come to fruition,' recalled Blake. 'But it was (a time) tinged with sadness too. Coming across the Tasman in *Condor* we'd struck a severe storm (the tail end of Cyclone David) which we rode out reasonably comfortably in a 78-footer. Behind us, the New Zealand team yachts returning from the Southern Cross Cup got a real hiding in 80-knot winds and huge seas. The One Tonner *Smackwater Jack*, with designer Paul Whiting and his wife Alison in the crew of four, was lost without trace. The Whiting family in Auckland is a boating institution and everyone shared their grief.'

The next 10 months flew by in a whirl of activity. The schedule was tight and *Ceramco* had to be in the water on time if she was to contest the 1980 Sydney–Hobart, a significant building block in her shakedown programme. It would provide the opportunity to check the yacht's potential against top opposition in one of the world's classic ocean races, and then Blake would have the opportunity to take

Ceramco down into the Southern Ocean on the way back to New Zealand, to give boat and crew a taste of things to come.

Ceramco took to the water in a blaze of publicity on 22 October 1980, with Dame Norma Holyoake, wife of the then Governor-General of New Zealand, Sir Keith Holyoake, doing the honours with the traditional bottle of bubbly in front of 600 invited guests, including all the shareholders and people who had backed the project. In the meantime, Blake had been struggling with the process of selecting his crew. It had been a long and involved undertaking. He'd sifted through the original 140 applicants, from all walks of life and the length and breadth of New Zealand, and whittled those down to 40, who were all interviewed by himself and Foster, and then down to a final squad of 18. He was left with a group of men with whom he would happily do the race, but he could take only 11 of them.

To help make his final determinations, in September 1980 Blake took the full squad of 18 on a three-day tramp around Lake Waikaremoana, 1920 feet above sea level and tucked away in the rugged Urewera National Park to the east of the centre of New Zealand's North Island. From this exercise he hoped to gain an insight into the people and personalities that would help him make his final selections. The long and often strenuous trek around the lake, and the cramped living quarters in the huts on the trail, might reveal idiosyncrasies that, in days on end of hard running in the Southern Ocean, could lead to personality clashes.

In his ultimate choices, he placed a lot of emphasis on compatibility, sometimes at the expense of proven experience. It was an approach that was to become one of the trademarks of his unique leadership style. The strong bond of friendship that remains to this day among all of his various crews and teams is testimony to the validity and success of that approach. Typical of the process was the selection of Simon Gundry. 'Simon had a bit of a reputation as a "larrikin", but he didn't put a foot wrong,' said Blake. 'He totally wanted to do the race, was always there when there was work to be done. He was experienced on boats of a similar size to *Ceramco* and was immensely powerful. He showed on the tramp that he would go until he dropped – which would be long after everyone else. He would be extremely valuable.' Blake would also later write: 'Simon had the last laugh on everyone who predicted he would foul up. He was totally dedicated and fully deserved his "Personality of the Race" award. He worked hard on his image and came out right on top.'

Gundry, from Auckland's North Shore and now a successful concreting contractor, says he was aware when he applied to join the *Ceramco* crew that 'Martin Foster had warned Blake to be careful with him – "he's got the reputation of being a larrikin, he could be trouble".' The 'larrikin' tag, he feels, came from 'just playing senior rugby here in Devonport and making a bit of noise every now and then with Chappy (Keith Chapman). There was never any malicious stuff. We never smashed things or beat up old ladies. But now and again we used to get a bit noisy. Peter saw through all of that – thank God. I believe he told Martin: "We'll probably need people like Gundry where we're going." '

Advising the successful applicants was a pleasant task. Not so telling those who had not made the cut, as Blake himself admitted: 'I explained everything to those who didn't make it and offered them help to get a ride on another Round the World boat if they wanted it. Only Grant Dalton took me up on that, and he went on to become a highly respected member of *Flyer*'s crew. I think I must have represented the biggest bastard in the world just then.'

He was right. Grant Dalton missed the cut for *Ceramco* but determinedly went on to carve out his own place in the annals of round-the-world racing, in monohulls and catamarans. He recalls: 'That (missing selection for *Ceramco*) nearly destroyed me. To this day nothing has ever hit me as hard as that, with the exception maybe of Perth (missing the cut for New Zealand's first America's Cup crew).

82

I still don't know how I got on *Flyer* but I believe what happened was because of Blakey – and, remember, at this stage I hated him with a passion. When I was trying out for *Ceramco*, he'd asked me to work at Lidgards, helping to build *Ceramco*'s sails, which I did. In the end, that's what got me on *Flyer*. They were looking for sailmakers. So Peter's fingers were in there, even if it was in a funny way.'

Dalton wasn't the only one with whom the *Ceramco* skipper was unpopular. 'There were criticisms around town of course,' acknowledged Blake. 'Auckland has a large but tight-knit yachting fraternity and by now the *Ceramco* New Zealand challenge had become national news. The boat and the crew were public property, almost like an All Blacks team. People asked, "Who the hell does Blake think he is, why is he skippering the boat?" My answer to that was that I was the one who had got off his chuff to start the wheels in motion. In more normal circumstances, you can dismiss the critics. If you are doing the race for a wealthy owner you can sit back and ignore them. But because *Ceramco* was public property, we were subject to a lot of pressure. The feeling that was generated became quite surprising, as were the lengths to which some people went in an effort to make their point.'

One leading Auckland skipper even tried to get the whole project stopped because Blake, he felt, was on an ego trip and the crew selected wasn't high-powered enough. He tried to meet with Tom Clark to emphasise his opposition, but Clark refused to see him.

All Blake could do was back his own judgement and get on with the job at hand, insisting that: 'In the main, the people who criticised the crew selection didn't have a clue of what was involved. If I'd stacked the boat with "heavies" we wouldn't have got further than the end of the dock without an argument. That was the last thing I needed. Ahead were 18 months of living in each other's pocket and it was absolutely essential that we got on well together.'

HIS OWN COMMAND

Blake was copping criticism from other directions too – according to some critics, *Ceramco*'s mast wasn't strong enough and he'd chosen the wrong sailmaker. He was beginning to wonder whether he'd created a monster. There was soon to be light at the end of that particular tunnel, however. *Ceramco* was about to cross the Tasman for the Sydney–Hobart Classic – a perfect opportunity to silence the doubters. Or, as Blake put it: 'If someone had written a Boy's Own adventure book script, they couldn't have improved on the actual events of December 1980 and January 1981.'

Ceramco had demonstrated her potential in a handful of local races before Blake set out for Sydney, but she'd lacked a yardstick of her own size. Across the Tasman waited the 66-foot Joe Adams design *Helsal II*, a stripped-out running and reaching machine which would really put the new Farr boat to the test.

At noon on Boxing Day 1980, in a lightish east-south-easterly, the Hobart race got away to its usual spectacular start. *Ceramco*, from a safe position down the line and away from the pin-end traffic jam, cleared her air and started to tramp down Sydney Harbour to the Heads and the Tasman. Close-hauled with the light No. 1 genoa (a full, baggy sail) and crew weight forward, she punched her way through waters churned up by a massive spectator fleet and was first out into the open ocean. Blake described the opening stages of the race: 'Once clear (of the Heads), we held out to sea. The former 12-metre *Gretel* skirted the cliffs on the down to Botany Bay to take time out of us. *Helsal* had been slow out of the blocks, but followed the same track as *Gretel* and she too closed in. Off Jervis Bay, some 70 miles later, the three of us were in line abreast.'

The breeze freshened that evening and shifted to the east. *Ceramco* and *Helsal* dropped *Gretel* astern as they reached down the coast of New South Wales. Early the next day, with the breeze shifting aft, Blake called for the 2.2-ounce, heavy flat kite with the pole right on the forestay. *Helsal* followed suit and there was nothing in it for speed.

By 1500 hours on the second day, the two were into Bass Strait with the breeze really starting to kick in. With 20 to 25 knots across the deck and right on the beam, *Ceramco* picked up her skirts and, by morning, after a sizzling ride across Bass Strait averaging 14 knots and surfing at 20 knots, *Ceramco* was on her own. *Helsal* was nowhere to be seen. Blake related: 'We roared on down the Tasmanian coast, the boat performing like it was on rails. *Helsal* reported her position eight miles astern. We found that *Ceramco* would flat run just like a big dinghy, lifting her bow out and riding on top of the seas as straight as an arrow. We were elated. No control problems and no broaches – just the characteristics we wanted for the Southern Ocean.'

Ceramco was on schedule to break the record for the 630-mile course (2 days, 14 hours, 36 minutes, 33 seconds set by the 79-foot *Kialoa III* in 1975) as she approached Tasman Island (at the south-eastern tip of Tasmania) and the turn into the aptly named Storm Bay. The bay was anything but stormy on this occasion, however, and *Ceramco* struggled in light air, covering only nine miles in seven hours. Finally she picked a light north-westerly and beat towards the Iron Pot at the entrance to the Derwent River. There, the wind then swung south-west and Blake went for the big spinnaker, shooter and full main for the blast up the river to the finish. *Ceramco* missed the record by 4 hours, 9 minutes, 7 seconds, reaching Hobart in 2 days, 18 hours, 45 minutes, 40 seconds. *Helsal* was 1 hour, 48 minutes, 51 seconds astern. Blake said of their triumph: 'We'd achieved our objective – line honours in our first major race, and confirmed too that *Ceramco New Zealand* was a thoroughbred downwind machine. She wasn't exactly slow upwind either.'

But that wasn't all. Astern of *Ceramco* and *Helsal*, the breeze died and then filtered in again from the south. The big fleet still at sea was slowed to a crawl and headed. One by one the challengers on rating missed their deadlines and *Ceramco* emerged handicap winner as well. 'The line and handicap double, first up. It was almost too good to be true,' enthused Blake. The double had been done only three times before in the 36-year history of the race – by Captain John Illingworth's *Rani* in 1945 (the inaugural Hobart race), by Ted Turner's *American Eagle* in 1972, and by Jim Kilroy's *Kialoa III* in 1977. *Ceramco* was already in august company.

There was little time to celebrate, however. There was a promotional schedule to be met back in New Zealand. So, on 3 January 1981, *Ceramco* slipped quietly out of Hobart for a dig down to 47 degrees South latitude on her way back across the Tasman to Milford Sound on the west coast of New Zealand's South Island. She left the Derwent in miserable weather and took it with her all the way to Milford Sound. In 40- to 45-knot south-westerlies, which built up big seas, she dashed the 1100 miles to Milford in four days, with noon runs of 260 and 270 miles, much of the time coasting with four reefs in the main and storm jib. 'I couldn't have been happier,' said Blake of *Ceramco*'s performance. 'I'd asked for a boat which would maintain consistently high speeds for lengthy periods without grinding the crew to a standstill, and I'd obviously got one.'

The Sydney–Hobart accomplishment had made a big impression back home. New Zealanders love nothing better than to beat their Tasman neighbours, the Australians, in the sporting arena, and the Hobart race, with all its media attention, is a particularly juicy prize. The crowds and media attention that the Sydney–Hobart winner attracted in a flag-flying tour of selected ports of call – Milford, Nelson, Wellington, Lyttelton and Gisborne – were as impressive as they were unique. Wellington was typical of their reception. *Ceramco* and her crew were a major attraction. It was calculated that the challenge fund was $26,000 the richer for their nine-hour stopover, many thousands of people paying $1 for a tour of the boat and shelling out more hard-earned money for *Ceramco* souvenirs such as mugs, posters and T-shirts.

Finally, *Ceramco* sailed back into the Hauraki Gulf on a beautiful summer's Saturday afternoon, the inner gulf and then the Waitemata Harbour crowded with racing and cruising boats. 'It was a big moment for the crew as we clipped close to Orakei Wharf to give the waterfront crowd a closer look and then sagged away across to the other side of the harbour to salute the Devonport Yacht Club,' rejoiced Blake. 'People were jostling for vantage points around Marsden Wharf as we dropped sail and motored in. If Blake's XI had any doubts as to what they were involved in, they were gone now. *Ceramco* and her crew were celebrities. We'd won respect and silenced the critics. The real business was yet to begin but the "Porcelain Rocketship" – a name given to the boat by our *Condor of Bermuda* mates back in the UK, in a congratulatory telegram to Hobart – had made a spectacular lift-off.'

CHAPTER Four

A Legend is Born

Hailing from the harbourside suburb of Devonport on Auckland's North Shore, the moustachioed Simon Gundry is your quintessential Kiwi – salt water in his veins and a rugby ball never far away. Gruff and faintly aggressive on the exterior, he's sensitive and generous when you get to know him and quotes Banjo Patterson and Robert Senior poetry verbatim. Gundry is one of the main organisers of the annual 'Mast Fall Down' gathering in Auckland, when Peter Blake crews get together over more than a few beers to recount tales of Whitbread yesteryears. He is a Blake devotee and declares unhesitatingly: 'If Peter Blake had said, "Come with me, there's a race around the moon" – I'd have gone with him, knowing that he would always get me back safely. A great leader.'

Gundry remembers clearly his first exposure to Blake's legendary loyalty to his people. *Ceramco New Zealand* had arrived in England for the start of the 1981–82 Whitbread race (shipped to the East Coast of the United States and then sailed across the Atlantic). Her crew had assembled at the Hamble (off the entrance to Southampton Water) where they would be based for the final work-up. Gundry, a self-confessed royalist, had been to London for the wedding of Prince Charles and Lady Diana, and had returned to the south coast to a very quiet crew house where he learnt that the next day there was going to be an in-house inquiry into an incident in Cowes on the Friday night, and that O. C. (Owen) Rutter was being sent home.

It appeared that Rutter and Geoff Stagg, one of *Ceramco's* two watch leaders and a noted offshore racing skipper in his own right, had been in the Three Crowns pub in Cowes and had 'got a bit lippy' with some of the locals who followed them out when they went to leave. Rutter and Stagg were outnumbered and, according to Gundry: 'It was obvious to O. C. that there were going to be punches thrown. So he (O. C.) figured he might as well have a go at them before they had a go at him.' The result – one of the locals went through the plate-glass window of the fruiterer's shop in the Cowes High Street. Rutter scarpered but Stagg, slower off the mark, was picked up by the police who mistakenly thought that he was the one who had thrown the punch. Stagg spent the night in the Newport cells before it was all sorted out.

Rutter subsequently appeared in the Newport Magistrates Court and was fined the considerable sum of £800. But it didn't end there. The story leaked into the New Zealand media and Rutter was judged to have brought New Zealand yachting into disrepute. The *Ceramco* committee (one of whom was the executive secretary of the New Zealand Yachting Federation) was staying in Cowes during the final work-up and was of the opinion that he should be sent home.

The in-house inquiry took place aboard *Ceramco*. She motored back and forth along the Cowes foreshore while the business was done. Gundry acted as Rutter's advocate and reminded the committee of All Black Keith Murdoch who had been sent home from a tour of Wales in 1972, after an incident involving a hotel security guard. 'I said to the committee: "You can look at this in two ways. Keith Murdoch was sent home in similar circumstances and was ostracised for life. A few years later, on another All Blacks tour, Brian Ford made a bit of a gash of himself in a nightclub, but it was dealt with internally and he stayed with the tour. He learned from it and it didn't ruin his life. Send O. C. home now and he will have to deal with that for the rest of his life. You'd better think long and hard about it."'

Despite Gundry's eloquence, things did not look good for Rutter until Blake suddenly stepped in and told the committee: 'OK, send O. C. home. But if you do, you'll have to sail *Ceramco* around the world yourselves, because we'll all be going home with him.'

'That finished it,' said Gundry. 'O. C. stayed, and thank God he did. He was one of the strengths in a great crew. That was my first exposure to Blake's loyalty to his crews, and I was impressed, to say the least.'

From Blake's perspective, there were more pressing matters to be dealt with as Whitbread start time approached – the first involving the anti-fouling application on *Ceramco*'s bottom, the second being salt water in her fresh-water holding tank. Gundry recalls: 'We'd spent three days sanding the bottom of the boat to get it perfectly smooth before new anti-fouling went on. Chappy (Keith Chapman, *Ceramco*'s other watch leader) was like a parrot the whole three days, chanting, "The faster we sand the faster we'll get to Cape Town" – if he said that once, he said it a thousand times. Then Staggy sprayed the boat and did a fabulous job.'

That night Blake received a telephone call from Trevor Geldard, then managing director of Epiglass New Zealand, who had supplied the anti-fouling. There had been a mistake. *Ceramco* had been sent the wrong application for her bottom paint job. It all had to come off again. 'We had to go down the next day and sand off all the newly sprayed anti-fouling while Epiglass air-freighted to us the paint we should have got in the first place. That was a little frustrating for the boys, I can tell you,' growls Gundry.

Salt water had contaminated the fresh-water holding tank through splits in *Ceramco*'s alloy plate hull. Vibration from the propeller shaft had caused the strut that supported the shaft to break free from the hull, causing cracks in the hull itself. It was a major problem that they didn't have time to fully resolve. So Blake decided they would do without the fresh-water holding tank and instead use a desalinator unit to produce their daily fresh-water requirements. There was no money in the campaign kitty so Blake bought the desalinator as a birthday present to himself. Stagg, who had built his own boats and so was highly resourceful when it came to fixing problems, filled up the water tank with expanding foam and sealed it off. Recalls Gundry: 'That little desalinator unit chugged away in the corner beautifully all through the race and we were soon to be very thankful to have it rather than rely on what was in the tank.'

In a four-race warm-up series that was part of the Cowes Week regatta, Blake was able to compare *Ceramco*'s performance against some of the world's circuit maxis, including *Kialoa III* and *Condor of Bermuda*, as well as three of her round-the-world race rivals – the new *Flyer*, *FCF Challenger* and *Licor 43*. With designer Bruce Farr aboard as well as sailmaker Jim Lidgard, the *Ceramco* crew played with trim, rig tensions and sheeting angles until *Ceramco*'s upwind performance was improved significantly. Her crew also became much more aware of where she did – and did not – like weight.

Blake's assessment: 'The conclusion was that only *Flyer* would pose a threat in the Whitbread. *Ceramco* was the fastest reaching boat, including *Kialoa* and *Condor*. But *Flyer* looked extra quick flat running. With her big masthead rig, she was a potent light airs performer and would take some holding in the Doldrums.'

Blake had a theory that the new breed of bigger boats in the 1981–82 fleet would be fast enough to stay with the weather systems for longer, and so sail away and leave the small boats to their own race astern. He was also convinced that Conny van Rietschoten, the owner-skipper of the new Frers maxi *Flyer*, had his sights on the line and handicap double.

Saturday, 29 August 1981 was cool and misty as *Ceramco* cast off her lines at the Camper & Nicholson marina in Gosport and headed out through Portsmouth's narrow harbour entrance to the start area in the Solent. The wind increased to a moderate easterly as the 1200 hours start time approached. That meant a dead beat to windward to Bembridge Ledge, at the eastern end of the Isle of Wight and the only mark of the course to Cape Town. The gun went at noon precisely and the 29-boat fleet, from 15 countries, was on its way with 6500 miles to go to the Cape of Good Hope. As the leaders rounded the Bembridge mark and headed out into the English Channel, *Flyer* was just ahead of *Ceramco*. *Kriter*, *Charles Heidsieck* and *Challenger* were immediately astern. The rest of the fleet was a long way back and the pattern for the race was already established.

For the next three weeks – out through the English Channel, across the Bay of Biscay, and down the North Atlantic to cross the equator almost due south of Sierra Leone, on the 'Bulge' of Africa – *Ceramco* paced the bigger *Flyer* at the head of the fleet.

On 21 September, 23 days into the race, the log recorded: 'Going like a rocket.' *Ceramco* was 105 miles to the north of Ascension Island in the South Atlantic and performing right up to expectations, averaging 9 to 10 knots, just cracked off with the No. 4 jib and one reef in the mainsail. *Flyer* was approximately 100 miles to the east and virtually the same distance south of the equator.

The log read:

'The wind swings SE and settles to 25 knots.

'0400hrs: No. 3 jib, 2 reefs. Lovely sailing.

'0600hrs: Sea tatapatchish, rocketing along.

'0800hrs: Wind 25 knots SE, sea lumpy. Fast sailing.'

Then . . .

'12.35hrs: Mast came down – fuck it.'

With a crack like a field gun, the lower intermediate shroud had parted at the bend over the lower spreaders. Unsupported, the

95

radically slender spar folded and broke at the middle spreader and then again at the bottom spreader. The whole top half went over the side. In a matter of seconds, Blake's dream of winning the 27,000-mile Whitbread race had turned into a nightmare. *Ceramco* was 2455 miles from the first stopping point of Cape Town, her race seemingly over. It was déjà vu for Blake who, in the previous Whitbread, had seen *Condor*'s mast go over the side only slightly north of where *Ceramco* had now come to grief.

The shocked crew reacted quickly. The first priority was to get the rig back on board before it punched a hole in the hull. The demanding and heartbreaking work took the rest of the day. The immediate problems dealt with, Blake assessed his options.

Monrovia was 800 miles to the north. It was familiar territory. He'd been there when *Heath's Condor* lost her mast. But to go back to Monrovia would mean the end of the race, just as it had for *Condor*. Cape Town was nearly 2500 miles upwind from *Ceramco*'s position – dauntingly far for a boat which had no chance of sailing an efficient course to windward under jury rig.

This left only the downwind route to Cape Town, the old sailing ship course around the western side of, and then underneath, the South Atlantic high-pressure system and its light airs and calms that block the middle of the South Atlantic to sailing vessels. It would be anything from 1000 to 1500 miles longer than the direct route but it held the promise of stronger, more favourable reaching and running conditions and might yet provide a way out of a seemingly hopeless mess.

There was one other choice – to withdraw from the leg, pick up fuel at Ascension Island and motor to Cape Town. But that was unthinkable. The downwind route it would be.

Blake gathered his tired crew in the cockpit to announce his decision. *Ceramco* was crawling south under trisail and No. 6 jib set on the bottom section of the mast, which was still in place, jutting

A young Peter aboard *Ladybird* with father Brian – '*Ladybird* was a major influence in my life.'

Joyce Blake launches *Bandit* with Brian at the bow and Peter in the cockpit.
The seven-metre (23 feet) Van de Stadt design was Blake's first keel boat.

Owner/skipper Peter Blake on the helm of *Bandit* in the Hauraki Gulf.

On the helm of the much loved *Ladybird* – 'My parents
used every cent of their savings to buy her.'

Peter Blake, age 22, on *Ocean Spirit*, one of the fastest long-distance race boats of her day.

His sextant was never far away – in use here on *Ocean Spirit*.

The 77-foot sloop *Heath's Condor* (also known as *Condor of Bermuda*), in which Blake won the storm-lashed 1979 Fastnet. Then 31, Blake is furthest aft in the crew on the starboard rail.

Blake's first Whitbread ride – the 70-foot Van de Stadt ketch *Burton Cutter* –
which was also Blake's first delivery as a skipper.

On the helm of *Condor of Bermuda*, with owner Bob Bell looking on.
Bob Fisher, Pickthall Picture Library

A quiet moment for Pippa and Peter Blake aboard *Ceramco New Zealand* in 1980. The Bruce Farr-designed *Ceramco* was Blake's first Whitbread Round the World race command.

Ceramco's 1980 Sydney–Hobart double celebration starts in Constitution Dock. *Ceramco* was only the fourth boat in Sydney–Hobart history to be first to finish and first on handicap, joining Captai John Illingworth's *Rani* (1945), Ted Turner's *American Eagle* (1972) and Jim Kilroy's *Kialoa* (1977).

Ceramco New Zealand heads for Cape Town under jury rig in October 1981 – one of the most remarkable feats of recovery in yacht-racing history. *Bob Fisher, Pickthall Picture Library*

On the helm of *Ceramco* in the southern Tasman in January 1981 – a taste of things to come in the 1981–82 Whitbread race. *Peter Montgomery*

Left: *Ceramco* closing on the Whitbread finish in Auckland after a record-breaking match race with *Flyer* through the Southern Ocean from Cape Town. *Bob Fisher, Pickthall Picture Library*
Below: Spinnaker drop on *Ceramco* – the skipper never asked you to do anything he wouldn't tackle himself.

16 feet above the deck. 'Tomorrow,' he told his crew, 'we set about hoisting the 45-foot top section into place and lashing it to the 16-foot stump so that we can get more sail on.'

Gundry recorded in his log: 'I was lying in my bunk reading when there was a sharp snap and a gentle crash. Somebody on deck cried out "Oh no!" Peter, who was standing in the navigatorium area aft, rushed on deck, looked up and yelled "Not again!" then "Everyone on deck – I'm afraid we've lost the rig!" I didn't seem to hurry from my bunk. I think it was a feeling of "I don't really want to see this . . ." God, I cried inside. A horrible sinking feeling came over me. After we'd got everything back on board and made it as safe as it could be, we had a crew meeting in the cockpit over a cup of coffee. Blakey came out with the classic statement: "Please, I don't want anybody to get demoralised. But if you do get demoralised, come and see me and we will get demoralised together." '

Left to his own thoughts, Blake reflected on the misfortune: 'We'd been level pegging it with *Flyer* down the South Atlantic and really beginning to look good on handicap. We felt that strategically we were in a good situation, but . . . Then there is the mast itself, slim in section and heavily tapered at the top. It caused a lot of comment when it was stepped in Auckland and there were any number of waterfront experts prepared to bet it would come down. Well, it has – but through no fault in the spar or its engineering. The problem was a rigging failure. It wouldn't have mattered what size mast we'd had – we could have been using a telegraph pole. When that particular piece of the rigging failed, whatever we'd been using would have come down . . . But there is little point in recriminations. Better now to devote all our thinking energy to getting out of this dilemma in the best possible shape, remembering always that there is still more than three-quarters of the race to run and a lot can happen to the opposition in more than 20,000 miles, particularly in the Southern Ocean where *Ceramco* has been designed and built to excel. Hopefully

97

we've now used up our ration of bad luck. For now, we're going back to what they used in Nelson's day. If we can rig the boat the way we intend, and get the same winds we've been having, we'll be doing 7 to 8 knots again. We won't be as hard on the wind as we'd like, but we will be able to steer a pretty good course and reach Cape Town not too far behind the others.' In the meantime Blake had put through a call to Foster's home in Devonport where the project committee was gathered. The group was deeply shocked by his news but decided, on the spot, to prepare and fly a replacement mast to Cape Town to await *Ceramco*'s arrival. There was no budget for the unexpected expense so the cost was funded by a bank overdraft personally guaranteed by Messrs White, Foster and Cornes – a commitment that was a big boost to crew moral.

By this time, *Ceramco* was under way again and heading more or less south with trisail and No. 6 jib set on the stump of the shattered mast. She was making 4 to 5 knots in the right direction but it was daunting to think how far she still had to go. Yet the 24 days that followed produced one of the most remarkable feats of recovery in yacht-racing history, along with a catalogue of ingenuity, seamanship and gut-determination that belongs in any archive of courage in the face of adversity. Blake's personal log recorded the voyage without a hint of self-pity and with large dollops of Kiwi humour.

First came the task of affecting a jury rig. A 7- to 8-foot swell didn't help with the job of hoisting the 45-foot top section vertical, alongside the stub of the original, as a new mainmast. There were a few anxious moments but the task was achieved with a fair amount of ingenuity plus the requisitioning of the cook's cherished kauri breadboard as a pad for the now deck-stepped spar. Shrouds, forestay and backstay were attached and the rig was now ready for some sail. The No. 6 headsail was fitted to the forestay, then the storm jib to the inner forestay, and *Ceramco* had power on. The trisail came next, hoisted to the top of the mast and sheeted to the quarter as a makeshift mainsail. The speedo shot up to 7.5 to 8 knots and everyone felt pretty pleased with their efforts in the first hours since the mast had come down.

Gundry noted in his log: 'Blake's leadership over the last few days has been magnificent – always leading from the front and never letting anything get him down during these trying circumstances. He's always positive about everything. He's probably eating up inside after all the effort that he personally has put into this project but, if he is, he's not showing it. If he showed deep depression, which he probably is entitled to do, I'm sure it would spread right through the boat like the proverbial bushfire. But he hasn't and the crew has responded likewise. I suppose that's the character he is and that's why we are all here in a lot of ways.'

The ship's log for 24 September read: 'We may look a bit like a Chinese laundry, but we can't complain about the results of our efforts – 198 miles to noon yesterday and then 209 miles to noon today. It looks as though we'll have this breeze for the next 1000 miles or so. The course we've chosen should give us the majority of wind on the beam or from aft of the beam and we already know we can really cover the ground if that's the case. But there are 3700 miles to go on our loop to Cape Town. How can we make the boat go faster still?'

The answer was to convert *Ceramco* into a ketch. The boat's two spinnaker poles were lashed together at their tops and hoisted into position as a bipod mizzen-mast over the helmsman's cockpit. A forestay and halyard completed the job. Sail was added and boat speed jumped up more than a knot. 'Necessity is quite definitely the mother of invention,' remarked Blake. 'We must look something akin to a rigged tuna trawler right now but who cares. Spirits on board have soared and we're not done yet.'

The plan was to continue to the south-west for another 870 miles before beginning to curve off south and then south-east and finally east at about latitude 38 or 39 degrees South, fetching up close to Tristan da Cunha. That meant 3200 miles to go to Cape Town, but that's the longest distance they would have to travel. If they could cut the corner a bit, they would reduce the amount of ground to cover.

Ceramco was really stepping out across the chart. Ascension Island was now more than 600 miles astern while the Trinidade and Martin Vaz Islands, some 550 miles to the east of Rio de Janeiro, weren't far ahead. Blake had been hoping to average between 7.5 and 8 knots under jury rig but Ceramco was doing better than that, hitting speeds of up to 11 knots. She should do even better in the Roaring Forties. As Blake expressed his aspirations: 'The big hope now is that the high moves east and slows down the boats that are going the direct route – Flyer, Charles Heidsieck, Kriter, etc. It's probably too much to hope for, but we face east and bow every now and then, just in case. Flyer has given a Cape Town ETA of 7 October. We figure we should be there on 15 October, sooner if we are lucky. There are limits on how fast we can go though.'

He was uncannily accurate in his assessment of likely progress. Even though she was held up by frustratingly light winds on the southern side of the South Atlantic High, Ceramco reached Cape Town at 1828 hours GMT on 15 October 1981 to a big reception from the crews of the 17 boats already finished, along with many hundreds of locals. She didn't limp in either – rather she approached Table Bay with a bone in her teeth trucking along in a 15- to 20-knot south-wester. Flyer was first to finish some 11 days earlier, reaching Cape Town in 36 days, 10 hours, 56 minutes, 37 seconds after leaving Portsmouth. Ceramco had been at sea for 47 days, 7 hours, 28 minutes and 5 seconds.

The Blake team had 16 days in which to step a new mast, carry out all the other routine maintenance, and then ready their yacht for the 7010-mile second leg to Auckland. The new mast had been flown to Cape Town in three pieces and had already been assembled and rigged by the shore team of Terry Gillespie and Jim Lidgard (with Pippa Blake lending a hand). This time, Blake was not taking any chances with new technology. The mast itself was an exact duplicate of the original but on this one all shrouds terminated at universal end-fittings on the spreaders, to eliminate possible stress areas.

Those were dark days in South African sport. Anti-apartheid feeling was gaining momentum around the world and sport, which was seen as particularly dear to the white South African heart, was being targeted. Sporting contacts with the beleaguered country were being severed as a means of bringing pressure to bear on those responsible for continuing with the abhorrent system of segregation. Only a few months earlier, the Springbok rugby team, the traditional arch-rival of the All Blacks, had received a torrid reception on its long tour of New Zealand. The anti-apartheid demonstrations were unprecedented in the 'Land of the Long White Cloud'. There was no support for apartheid but there was a strong body of opinion that neither was there a place for politics in sport. The country was virtually torn apart by the off-the-field conflicts.

Blake was being pressured to pull out of the Whitbread race as a continuance of the anti-apartheid protest in New Zealand, but he wasn't having a bar of it. In his log, he recorded: 'The HART (Halt All Racist Tours) movement back home want us to withdraw from the race because the fleet includes the South African entry *Xargo III*. I tore up HART's telegrams and threw them away.'

Clearly more interested in building bridges through sport, as opposed to tearing them down through protests, Blake asked himself: 'Why should we be singled out when all the big nations – the United States, Britain, France, Germany, Italy and so on – are doing nothing? Nobody in this race is condoning apartheid, but nor are they interested in the political situation. We are entered in a boat race. The multi-national crew on *Xargo III* are a great bunch of people who, like us, are intent only on the race in which the elements are the main opposition anyway.'

The now 26-boat fleet answered the start gun for leg two at 1500 hours local time on 31 October 1981. Ahead lay some of the roughest and most demanding ocean in the world – the Southern Ocean proper. Two men lost their lives when swept overboard by huge seas on this leg of the inaugural race in 1973–74.

Everywhere else around the globe, there are land masses to check the sea's progress. But down south, between the Antarctic ice shelf and the southernmost capes of South Africa, Australia, New Zealand and South America, the oceans roll unobstructed all the way around the world. Low-pressure systems sweep through these ocean wastes with a frequency and velocity that has led to the various high latitudes being dubbed the Roaring Forties, the Furious Fifties and the Screaming Sixties.

Blake's assessment was that: '*Ceramco New Zealand* was conceived, designed and built to excel in these waters, to take full advantage of the strong tail winds and long sea conditions that are to be "enjoyed" by taking yachts to the edge of the pack ice on a great circle course across the bottom of the world. But we are setting out with a new and untried mast, and with a crew that is bound to be a little gun shy after the mishap of the first leg. It is going to take a lot of personal discipline and dedication to push *Ceramco* to the prudent limits in a bid to beat the bigger *Flyer* into Auckland.'

The new mast appeared to be bending correctly as Blake took his boat to the line in Table Bay, under No. 2 genoa and full main in a fresh west-north-westerly and smooth seas. At dawn the next day, he could see 16 yachts. *Ceramco* was the windward boat. *Flyer* was to

102

leeward and about a quarter of a mile ahead. The race was on again.

The chart that Blake was using noted that in April 1928, many icebergs – some of them 100 feet high – were seen around *Ceramco's* current position and more big ones had been sighted close by in other years. Fortunately, not many had been seen recently and Blake was not expecting to encounter ice until *Ceramco* was well below 45 to 50 degrees South. Her planned course would take her almost due south towards Marion Island. They had started arcing down earlier than planned, to take advantage of a low-pressure system coming through from the west at 40 degrees South. It promised fresh westerlies and south-westerlies. Remarked Blake: 'That's what we're after and the quicker we get down into its path the better. The low means high-speed spinnaker stuff. *Flyer* is still holding up (to a more easterly course) while we slip through to leeward, sailing slightly cracked (yacht or crew?).'

That night, the barometer dropped three points and the breeze freshened as it swung north-east. But by 0500 hours it had died and swung west. *Ceramco* waffled through a string of sail changes before the breeze disappeared completely, and then came in with a bang at 20 to 25 knots from the south-south-west. They were off.

Blake noted in *Ceramco's* log: 'I was waiting for the afternoon weather map from Pretoria when I noticed a disturbing amount of water in the boat. We'd repacked the bottom rudder bearing in Cape Town but it obviously wasn't bedded down properly. Every time we surfed, the water poured in. Staggy was on the wheel and I asked him to keep the boat level while we sorted out the problem and tightened the nuts on the stern packing. This seemed to work for a while, but then we had a lot of water sloshing around the bilge again. The crew pumped manually while the electric pump was started up. The latter sucks up the power and isn't exactly fast, but it's a solid worker. We made no impression on the water level. The sea was coming in as fast as we could pump it out. By now, Vonny (*Ceramco's* cook) had grabbed a bucket and Staggy was getting more than a little frustrated, having to ease back the speed while he held the boat level. "What the hell, you guys," he shouted down, "we're racing up here." Vonny shot back: "You may be racing up there mate, but we're sinking down here." Then we found the cause of the problem. An exit pipe from one of the sink drains had ruptured, leaving a one-inch diameter hole open to the ocean. Vonny didn't know it, but the buckets he was emptying into that sink were sluicing right back into the bilge. We shut the outlet valve down and pumped for another 30 minutes before we had things under control. While all this was going on, *Challenger* slipped through to windward. Les Williams must have thought we were all drunk.'

The breeze faltered and played around that night but by 0600 hours the next morning it started to build from the east-south-east – and this time it was in earnest. As it rose to 30 knots, *Ceramco* reached off under No. 5 jib and three reefs in the main on a great circle course for the Kerguelen Islands, squirting to 16 knots in lumpy seas that already had that cold, green look of the Southern Ocean proper. So began one of the wildest match races in Whitbread history as *Ceramco* and *Flyer* charged through the Southern Ocean at record- and boat-breaking speeds.

On 6 November, Blake's log read: 'A mind-blowing 24-hour run of 316 miles – a Whitbread record, averaging more than 13 knots and verified by log and Satnav. The breeze freshened to full gale yesterday afternoon and kept at it all night. *Ceramco* blasted along in front of the gale under the big, heavy spinnaker (2.2 ounces) and one reef in the main. All yesterday afternoon she averaged better than 15 knots, bursting off the clock to an estimated 35 knots . . . tearing down the seas so fast that all the sails were aback. It was like being on a runaway train, except this one was totally under control. Not even a hint of a nosedive.'

The gale built to storm proportions, prompting the following

SIR PETER BLAKE

entry in the log of the usually eloquent Dr Trevor Agnew, one of New Zealand's pre-eminent cardiologists, who was 'enjoying' his first taste of the Southern Ocean: 'Bloody hell, what a time. Great tumbling, broken seas, screaming wind up our bum, the roaring of waves and the coldness are something very different. Up and down constantly. Nobody's had much sleep over the last 48 hours. The sail changes, from one reef and kite, to two reefs then three reefs, to storm jib then later poled out No. 6, have taken everyone's efforts. Had a few broaches when we tried to set a storm spinnaker, and subsequently tried to set a blast reacher in 50 knots of wind. A bloody lonely place to be in 50 knots.'

While chasing gale and storm systems with favourable tailwinds is one of the main reasons for digging deep into the high latitudes of the Southern Ocean, another plus for the round-the-world racer is that at 55 degrees South (for instance), 1 degree of longitude represents only 35 miles. The same degree of longitude a couple of hundred miles to the north represents 40 miles. Further north again it represents 60 miles. The reduction as you go south or north from the equator is a result of the earth's curvature as it tucks in towards the poles. The disadvantages are the severe cold and the fact that you can get on the wrong side of the low-pressure systems sweeping through and finish up with gale- or storm-force headwinds instead of tailwinds. It takes a lot of skill and experience to call the systems correctly.

Flyer had opened up an 80-mile lead in the lighter winds earlier on but was now less than 30 miles ahead. The Dutch maxi had broken her main boom during the storm. The breeze was down to 20 to 25 knots from the north-west, allowing a slight respite, but there looked to be more strong wind on the way with another low-pressure system coming through at about 52 degrees South.

The low came in with 35- to 40-knot south-south-west winds, enabling *Ceramco* to complete a 24-hour run of 275 miles – but not without problems, as Blake related: 'Chappy was caught by a vicious squall. The boat broached violently and lay on her side. The brace was run, the bow came up into the wind and wouldn't fall off again. The kite halyard was run – a mistake as the rope tail was too big for the sheave block at the top of the mast. It jammed. The spinnaker filled astern of the boat then dropped in the sea to act like a bloody great parachute scoop, trying to pull the rig out of the boat. The halyard, by now, was around the leech of the mainsail and under the main boom, the wire putting a couple of tears in the foot of the sail. The brace and sheets on the kite were flailing all around the place and wiped off one whip aerial and badly bent the other. If we weren't quick the mast would join the casualty list. We managed to grind the sheet back aboard and then, dropping the mainsail to stop the boat in the water, dragged the kite back on board without wrapping it around the steering gear or propeller . . . *Ceramco* shook and shuddered, staggered back to her feet and sat there quietly waiting to see what we had in mind for an encore . . . It was still snowing hard, the barometer steady at 1005. We had ice building up on the lifelines, up the sides of the mast and over the spreader fittings – plus snow all over the deck . . . We don't know where Conny is but his silence could mean we've got past him . . . At this incredible rate we'll be at the halfway mark in another three days or so.'

On day 12 of the leg (11 November), *Ceramco* did another violent, high-speed broach – this time with Geoff Stagg at the wheel. Blake was prompted to note in the log: 'I've had to do some firm talking, pointing out that to do well on this leg we first have to finish it, and in good shape. It would be worse than ridiculous if we pulled the rig out and had to retire, or damaged so much gear and wrecked so many sails we were no longer competitive. The desire to go for broke is understandable. We've learned that *Flyer* is 30 miles north and 15 miles east of us. At our lower latitude, the distance to Cape Reinga, on the north-western tip of New Zealand's North Island, is the same

– 3400 miles. We're neck and neck, but there are limits to how fast we can go and for how long – limits imposed by screaming winds and rough, confused seas. At the rate we are going, we will do some serious damage. So far we've been lucky.'

Ceramco wasn't the only one with problems however. *Flyer* had blown out a lot of spinnakers and was suffering from 'down time' – her big kites could not be put back together in a hurry. Van Rietschoten's voice on the radio indicated that he was feeling the strain. It was later learned that van Rietschoten had in fact suffered a heart attack while he and his crew drove themselves and their boat to the limit to keep the charging *Ceramco* at bay. He kept it a secret until the finish in Portsmouth but then revealed that the heart attack had happened seven days out of Cape Town. *Flyer*'s doctor, Julian Fuller, treated his skipper and was concerned enough to suggest heading for Perth or Adelaide. Van Rietschoten wouldn't hear of it and was later quoted as saying: 'If *Ceramco* had known about my health problem they might have pushed harder still, and how the hell would we have kept them down. We had to stay ahead and, so long as they didn't know anything, it was okay. If the worst had happened, and I had died at sea, then my crew would have put me over the side as is the tradition. Perhaps *Ceramco* would have seen me drifting by, but that would have been the only indication they would have had that all was not good with Conny.'

The duel between the two front runners continued all the way into Auckland, *Flyer* finally putting time on *Ceramco* upwind in rugged conditions in the Tasman to cross the finish line off Orakei Wharf 8 hours, 15 minutes ahead of her rival, breaking *Heath's Condor*'s record for the leg by 4 hours, 36 minutes in the process. Then the duel was on again for the 6000-mile leg from New Zealand to Cape Horn and on to Mar del Plata in Argentina.

The vantage points around one of the world's most beautiful natural harbours were packed with people and cars as the now 22-boat fleet went for the Auckland start line. On the water it was 'standing room only' as the spectator fleet swelled to thousands. They came in all shapes and sizes, from surfboats and canoes to large motor yachts and harbour ferries crammed with cheering schoolchildren. It was later estimated that there were an estimated 300,000 people on or around the harbour to see the fleet leave, and the departure was televised live nationwide.

Blake used all of his local knowledge of the New Zealand coast, along with his considerable skill, to stay ahead of the bigger *Flyer* for as long as possible, working *Ceramco* through the 'Hole in the Wall', a narrow, rocky passage inside the Mercury Islands in the Bay of Plenty, and then between East Cape and East Island, on the most eastern tip of the North Island, before heading out into the South Pacific and into the loneliest stretch of ocean in the world.

At East Cape he made the decision to take *Ceramco* south as quickly as possible. It meant sailing away from the next mark (Cape Horn), but his reading of the weather patterns dictated that it was the way to go. The following day, the breeze backed into the east-north-east and then into the north-east. The crew on *Ceramco* were all smiles as they eased away and picked up speed. Those smiles grew bigger when the breeze backed all the way into the north-north-west and started gusting 25 knots. *Ceramco* was off for the Horn, averaging 11 knots and shooting down long, easy seas. The wind slowly increased until, at noon on 30 December, it was gusting 35 knots from astern with the seas building. *Ceramco* was flying with three reefs in the main and the two-ply 2.2-ounce spinnaker. They ascertained from the fleet chat show that *Flyer* was 50 miles astern. Blake's call to head south as quickly as possible had paid handsome dividends.

Two days later Blake recorded: '*Flyer* has closed to within 20 miles of us. They must be driving their boat particularly hard and well because *Ceramco* isn't exactly hanging around.' The following day, *Flyer* was sighted approximately three or four miles away on the starboard bow. *Ceramco*'s log read: 'Here we are, 10 days and 2380 miles after the start, halfway across the loneliest stretch of water in the world, and *Flyer* is almost within shouting distance.' Blake had much to ponder when *Flyer* held up further to the north and disappeared from view, but he kept his nerve and *Ceramco* continued eastwards on a course approximately 55 to 56 degrees South, playing the low-pressure systems as they trucked through the Southern Ocean at about 60 degrees South. Who had got it right?

On 12 January, after 18 days at sea, they got the answer. *Ceramco*'s log read: 'At 1710 hours "Land ho", just forward of the port beam – the 600-foot high Isla del Fonso.' Then, at 2000 hours: '*Flyer* again in view – two to three miles ahead of port beam. Here we are, approaching the fabled Cape Horn after more than 4500 miles of racing through the Southern Ocean, and the opposition is in sight only a couple of miles ahead. Unbelievable.' *Ceramco* was already feeling the big swells for which Drake Passage, the relatively narrow stretch of water between Cape Horn and the Antarctic Peninsula, is either famous or infamous, and her crew didn't know whether to be relieved or disappointed that they should be making the most revered landfall in seafaring in such relatively calm conditions.

Cabo de Hornos – the very name has struck fear into the hearts of mariners for centuries. In his logs of the *Seamaster* expedition voyages in the early 2000s, Blake was to write of the most revered of capes: 'Why is the Horn so special in the minds of blue-water sailors, why has it earned such a reputation? Why is it the most famous (or infamous) landmark in the annals of the sea, commanding just as much respect (or striking just as much fear into the hearts of mariners) today as it has through the ages?'

The Horn's fearsome reputation is mostly the result of a unique combination of physical and geographical factors that combine to

109

produce almost continuous gales and storms, with accompanying horrendous sea conditions, in one of the most remote and desolate places on earth. Through most of its passage around the world, the Southern Ocean is unrestricted in its breadth and depth, averaging between 1200 and 1500 miles in width and 2000 fathoms (two miles) in depth. As this huge river of water approaches South America, abruptly it is faced with a gap of only 600 miles between Cape Horn, at the southernmost tip of South America, and the northern end of Graham Land, a peninsula protruding out from Antarctica. This gap is called Drake Passage, or simply 'The Drake', after Sir Francis Drake, the first man to sail through it, during his circumnavigation of 1582–85. Where the southernmost point of one continent (South America) coincides with the northernmost point of another (Antarctica), the water shallows to less than 100 fathoms. The water mass of the Southern Ocean, rolling unimpeded around the bottom of the world, suddenly finds that it has to squeeze through a gap one-twentieth its size. Inevitably it accelerates, and whenever waves from deep water run into a shallower patch they compress and their crests move closer to one another. The result – the wave faces get steeper, and that is precisely what happens at Cape Horn. Unpleasant seas can be expected in the area on these grounds alone. But the Horn also lies at 56 degrees South where stronger winds of up to storm and hurricane force can prevail. This compounds matters somewhat.

In sailing ship days, timing a voyage was of paramount importance and – with good reason – the preference was to round the Cape during the summer months (from November to March), thus avoiding the appalling winter storms from April to October. Beating around the Horn from east to west in winter, against the prevailing winds and currents, was a hazardous venture, to put it mildly. Captain Bligh chose to attempt to round the Horn in this manner, as a short cut to Tahiti, rather than taking the traditional downwind route around the Cape of Good Hope and under Australia and New

110

Zealand. The *Bounty* battled horrendous conditions for three months as she tried to beat through Drake Passage. Bligh is reputed to have chained his men to their posts. Finally, he had to concede, turn around and run with the conditions, across the South Atlantic, past the Cape of Good Hope, Australia and New Zealand and then up the Pacific to his destination.

The passage from west to east is easier as you are usually running before the winds. Even so, following seas can build up to extreme heights and yachts have been rolled end over end by larger than normal waves.

Ceramco New Zealand rounded Cape Horn at 0550 hours GMT – 0150 hours ship's time – on 13 January 1982, 30 minutes (or two to three miles) astern of *Flyer* whose masthead light was just visible ahead despite heavy rain. The winds were light and the seas slight.

The final 1100 miles to Mar del Plata (on the coast of Argentina and just to the south of the wide entrance to the River Plate), were sailed in frustratingly light headwinds. *Ceramco* and *Flyer* parted company as their skippers called different tactics. On 18 January *Ceramco*'s log read: 'We were hoping that Conny might have dipped out somewhere. We've neither seen nor heard from *Flyer* since the night of January 13. But we have just learnt, from Mar del Plata, that *Flyer* is 30 miles from the finish line. We've still got 70 to go. He's grabbed a jump of 40 miles, and there's no time or distance left to do anything about it.'

Flyer got the gun at 2021.56 hours that night (local time). *Ceramco* followed at 0339 hours the next morning, 7 hours, 17 minutes, 4 seconds behind her arch-rival but easily within time to beat the Dutchman on handicap. Additionally, *Ceramco* had won the Roaring Forties Trophy which goes to the boat with the best corrected time from Cape Town to Mar del Plata – and to be the fastest across the bottom of the world was one of the priority objectives of the campaign. Declared Blake: 'We'd covered 6000 miles from Auckland

111

in 24 days, 8 hours, 39 minutes, 24 seconds, averaging 10 knots. *Flyer*'s time was 24 days, 1 hour, 22 minutes, 20 seconds. We'd had each other in sight for the best part of 10 days for 2500 miles. The match race of all time.' *Ceramco* was now up to sixth on elapsed time, a remarkable recovery from eighteenth in Cape Town.

The final 6600-mile leg from Mar del Plata to the finish at Portsmouth was going to be a tactical battle, the outcome of which would depend on who did the best job of negotiating the Doldrums and the Azores high-pressure system. In golfing parlance, if Mar del Plata was the tee and the English Channel was the green, the Doldrums and the Azores High awaited like huge sand traps smack in the middle of the fairway which was the Atlantic Ocean.

The Whitbread fleet had been in Mar del Plata for nearly seven weeks, tied up in a huge basin of the Argentinian naval base which rubs shoulders with the swimming beach that is the summer 'annex' to the Buenos Aires-based Yacht Club Argentino. Across that wide basin were several World War Two vintage submarines. Unbeknown to the round-the-world racers, while they were relaxing and preparing their boats for the final leg of the race, the Argentinians were readying to invade the Falkland Islands and to go to war with Britain.

The restart was a shambles. The race committee had laid the line incorrectly, almost up and down the course, and the seaward end was the only place to be, so there was a considerable amount of barging and banging – and bad language – as *Challenger* shouldered her way in at the outer buoy. *Berge Viking* clipped *Flyer*, while *Disque D'Or* had to do an emergency tack to avoid being cut in two by *Xargo*. *Ceramco* kept her nose clean and by late evening was close-hauled on port tack, heading out into the South Atlantic with only *Flyer*, *Challenger* and *United Friendly* in sight. Blake kept his boat heading mostly east, in 15- to 25-knot headwinds, for more than 36 hours before he got the wind change he was banking on. It came on the third day at sea and quickly built to 30 to 35 knots from the east-south-east. Blake recorded: 'We're cracked off under the No. 5 jib and two reefs in the main, going like hell. But we need everything we can get. The fleet chat show tonight revealed that we have stood too far to the east and, for the moment, are down the pan. *Charles Heidsieck*, *Rollygo*, *Kriter* and *Disque D'Or* have gone up the shore at high speed on starboard tack in a completely different wind. They are now 60 miles ahead of us although a long way to leeward. This is, for now, a real kick in the bum but only time will tell whether we've got the bigger picture right. Everyone will have to make easting at some stage or another and the weather charts indicate that we should continue to get better winds than the yachts further inshore. For the moment we feel somewhat chastened but the coast of Brazil, near Rio de Janeiro, is notorious for light winds, so the opposition inshore had better watch out.'

Ceramco banged and crashed her way north, making solid if not spectacular progress on a course parallel to the Brazilian coast. On day nine at sea, Blake was able to note: 'We did 227 miles to noon yesterday but were down to 159 miles to noon today after a complete morning with the wind everywhere and heavy rain squalls. The conditions have really tried the crew's patience and resilience. Only *Flyer* and *United Friendly* are ahead. Most of the other yachts are now stuck inshore with light headwinds and pushing the strong south-flowing Brazil current. *Flyer* has a lead of 160 miles. *United Friendly* is 80 miles ahead but is also 120 miles inshore from us. She could soon begin to slow down in fickle winds close to the South American coast. Maybe our initial tactics weren't so wrong after all.'

With 800 miles to go to the equator, Blake began to position *Ceramco* for the negotiation of the first major sand trap – the Inter Tropical Convergence Zone (ITCZ) or, as it is better known, the Doldrums. The windless belt between the weather systems of the northern and southern hemispheres would play a big part in the outcome of the leg and, for some, the race itself.

Blake intended to work approximately 170 miles off the Brazilian coast on a course that would take *Ceramco* close to the Archipelago Fernando de Noronha. The routing charts showed a marked decrease in calm and variable conditions on this track and the hope was that *Ceramco* would sneak through the Doldrums without too many hold-ups and then get north as quickly as possible. It was too early to start worrying about the Azores High, but Blake noted that it was currently further south and west than normal, and as a consequence the lows were tracking east across the Atlantic further south than the norm: 'If this pattern persists, life is going to be most interesting. My view is that the boats that get the equator crossing right, and then make it past the Azores before the normal pattern re-establishes itself, will have the best chance of winning.'

Rata Island, in the Fernando de Noronha archipelago, was abeam at dawn on 12 March with squalls, heavy rain and high-energy electrical displays that could mean the Doldrums. A day later, at 1600 hours, *Ceramco* crossed the equator with indications that the Doldrums were now astern. Blake remarked: 'The signs continue to improve. The north-easterly piped up overnight to gust 30 knots with heavy rain, then the wind swung NNE and continued to blow hard. Tonight we're down to the No. 3 with one reef in the main, convinced that we are through the dreaded ITCZ and making a decisive break on the boats astern. The fleet is spread over an enormous distance, *Flyer* 200 miles ahead but well to the east, and some of the tail enders are as much as 1400 miles astern.'

The days clicked by with *Ceramco* making good time up the North Atlantic in winds of around 20 to 25 knots from the north-east to begin with and then from the east. *Flyer* continued to favour a more eastern track as did *Charles Heidsieck*. Only time would tell who had called it correctly. Blake was counting on the breeze continuing to swing through to the south, to enable *Ceramco* to hoist a spinnaker and make a high-speed dash past the Azores. If that happened, the easting being made by *Flyer* and *Heidsieck* would mean little.

The south-easterly wind change Blake was seeking clocked in early on 21 March. The 1.5-ounce spinnaker was hoisted and *Ceramco* set off downwind as though eager to finish her work. Runs of 242 and 258 miles in the next two days were good, but Blake and his crew wanted more. Portsmouth was 1850 miles away and the Azores 600 miles ahead. The weather maps showed a high-pressure system at 28 degrees North 19 West, drifting only slowly east. This was the Azores High – but further east than normal. There was also an unseasonal low coming in from the west at 28 degrees North. *Ceramco* was beginning to feel the funnelling effects as the isobars squeezed up between the two systems, running hard in a 25-knot south-south-easter. That was a bonus in an area where she could very well have been becalmed.

The blast continued for the next three days. On 23 March Blake recorded: 'Day's run 284 miles, and that was in 23 hours – the best sailing of the trip.' Heavy cloud added to the darkness at night and the helmsmen were working overtime to position the yacht for waves they couldn't see. To help protect their night vision, shades were rigged on all hatches and ports and torch use was cut to a minimum.

The morning of 22 March had produced one of the most magnificent sights of the race. Several large fin whales chased along behind *Ceramco*, criss-crossing her wake less than a couple of hundred metres astern. The second largest mammal on earth, the fin can reach lengths of 20 metres and weigh as much as 50 tons. The ones cavorting in *Ceramco*'s wake were acting more like playful dolphins, catching up with the yacht and blowing frequently as they surfed down the short, steep seas, clearly enjoying the chase.

As the wind increased to 40 knots, *Ceramco* was charging along, tight-reaching under storm spinnaker and two reefs in the main. Only the best heavy-weather helmsmen were used, and they were striving for every last ounce of speed with the crew trimming apace. The doctor noted in his log: 'What spectacular, crazy, race-winning sailing.

Not much sleep for the off-watch crew, blasting under spinnaker, no moon, cloudy sky and black horizon. Big waves coming on deck as *Ceramco* screams along through the seas. Communications difficult because of the wind.' The Azores island of Terceira was faintly visible, 15 miles away to port, the houses and hotels flashing white against the high, grey-green mountain backdrop as *Ceramco* slid by, but the 7800 foot peak of Pico had gone unnoticed earlier in the day.

The wind began to moderate as *Ceramco* closed to within 400 miles of the English Channel. There was a massive high-pressure system ahead, extending from Norway to Ireland. *Flyer* had been travelling fast too and was 140 miles almost dead ahead. The weatherfax showed another high approaching from the west, so the race was on to get this final leg over and done with before the newcomer joined the big high ahead and created one huge parking lot.

In a radio telephone conversation between Blake and van Rietschoten on 28 March – 30 days into the leg and 400 miles from the finish – the Dutchman said: 'Peter, if ever I do this race again I will do it differently – in a much bigger and faster yacht. I'm tired of looking over my shoulder to find you biting at my heels.' In the lighter winds, however, *Flyer* had been wriggling away from *Ceramco*, and Blake and his crew were striving to make some northing to take full advantage of a northerly wind change that was forecast in two days' time. In fact, the weather situation was changing quickly all around. While *Flyer* and *Ceramco* were oozing along quietly in smooth seas, somewhat frustrated with their lot, the yachts astern were battling 50- to 60-knot headwinds and extremely boisterous seas.

The breeze finally filled in again for the leaders late on the night of 28 March, light from the north-north-east at first but quickly swinging through the north and building. *Flyer* made short work of the English Channel and crossed the finish line off Portsmouth at 0747 hours GMT on the 29th. *Ceramco* was 18 miles south of Land's End at the time, blasting along under No. 4 genoa and one reef in

116

the main in 40-knot north-north-west squalls. She had 190 miles to go, and a deadline of 0338 hours on the 30th if she was to beat *Flyer* on handicap. The big tides in the Channel and Solent would turn against her just after 0100 hours the next morning, so she had to finish before that happened.

Blake took his boat in close to the shore on the English side of the Channel, to dodge as much adverse tide as possible going past Start Point at the western end of Lyme Bay. Boat speed across the ground dropped as she struggled in steep, wind-against-tide seas. With 110 miles to go, she had to average 9 knots in order to meet her deadline. But she now had the tidal flow with her and, if everything went according to plan, would shoot up the Solent on a spring flood and cross the line before the tide turned against her again.

Ceramco roared on past Portland Bill, then across Christchurch Bay and past Anvil Point to enter the Needles Channel, the western entrance to the Solent, at 10 minutes before midnight. Blake's luck was holding and *Ceramco* dashed on up the Solent, on a bitterly cold but clear night, to cross the finish line at 0056 hours GMT on Tuesday, 30 March 1982. She'd beaten *Flyer* on handicap by 2 hours, 41 minutes, 43 seconds.

Ceramco had raced the 6600 miles from Mar del Plata in 30 days, 6 hours, 56 minutes and 55 seconds. The 17 hours, 9 minutes, 8 seconds margin between Flyer and herself was arguably the furthest the two yachts had been apart since Cape Town. For Blake and his crew the great adventure was over. They would never race *Ceramco* again. She would eventually be sold to the United States and become *Winterhawk*, while the all-Kiwi crew that she had served so well went home to resume their lives.

In his summary of the race, Blake later wrote: '*Flyer* achieved what I always suspected that Conny had at the back of his mind – the line and handicap double (for the whole race). For us on *Ceramco*,

117

although we won that final leg and so finished on a high note, it was very much a case of what might have been and "If only . . ." We'd achieved much. In Auckland, we finished only 8 hours, 23 minutes astern of *Flyer* and won the leg on handicap. In Mar del Plata, we were 7 hours, 17 minutes astern of *Flyer* and finished sixth on handicap. In Portsmouth, we trailed *Flyer* by 17 hours, 9 minutes and won the leg on handicap.

'*Ceramco*, designed to excel in the Southern Ocean, won the Roaring Forties Trophy for the best handicap performance across the bottom of the world, from Cape Town to Auckland to Mar del Plata. Despite sailing 4000 miles under jury rig, we were third fastest yacht around the world and broke *Great Britain II*'s race record by two days.

'When the mast went over the side we were pacing *Flyer* to Cape Town and, the way the results went, would surely have placed in the top three. But . . . the mast came down – end of story. Conny won because his didn't, and because both *Flyer* and *Ceramco* were pushed to the limit in a manner none of us will ever forget. We set new standards for big ocean racers. The Whitbread race will be the better and more exciting for it.

'Looking back, there are few things I would change in the situation that prevailed, least of all the crew. It was significant that *Ceramco* and *Outward Bound* (the two all-New Zealand entries) were the only two boats to do the race without a change of crew whatsoever. That says a lot for character and commitment.

'Will we do it again? I can only speak for myself. On this, my third Whitbread, I frequently said it would be my last. I have to settle down sometime, particularly as Pippa and I want children. But there lingers this feeling of unfinished business. Most of my convictions about this race, manifested in *Ceramco* and her crew, were proved correct. I know what should be done to progress a step further again and so the temptation will be there.

'Our race with *Flyer* will be a hard act to follow however, and I'm

118

not sure that Conny will find the motivation to put another boat and campaign together. He will be pushing 61 years of age by the time the 1985–86 race comes around. But there is no fiercer competitor in deep-water ocean racing . . . so, who knows? With his sort of determination, Conny could be back too for what would be the 1985–86 edition of the great race. If this proves to be the case, there will again be no limit – to the adventure or the fun.'

Van Rietschoten, in his foreword to the book *Blake's Odyssey – the Round the World Race with* Ceramco New Zealand, wrote: 'When *Ceramco* . . . lost her mast in the South Atlantic, three things happened aboard *Flyer*. The first reaction was one of sadness – that such bad luck had befallen our number one competitor. At the same time we realised that with *Ceramco* out of the first leg our chances of taking line honours in the race were enhanced, if we could keep our show together. So we immediately steered off 10 degrees to lessen the strain on our mast and rigging as we punched into the south-east trades.

'The crew of *Ceramco* soon had a jury rig set and we all began to appreciate the excellent leadership qualities and seamanship of Peter Blake. He and his crew continued to race to Cape Town so that they could go on to prove themselves over the next three legs of the race, which they did.

'On *Flyer*, we did not always enjoy having *Ceramco* breathing down our neck nor, for that matter, ahead of us. But it inspired both crews to push the boats well beyond their limits. At the same time, it strengthened the appreciation and friendship among the two crews, which is what the race, mainly, is all about. The exhilarating match racing between our two boats set new trends and paved the way for a maxi division in the 1985–86 Round the World race.

I sincerely hope that, in future, others will be fortunate enough to experience the excitement and good sportsmanship that we on *Flyer* and *Ceramco* New Zealand have shared.'

Van Rietschoten did not race around the world again. The tough and meticulous Dutchman who helped set new standards for long-distance ocean racing is now living in retirement in Portugal, where these days he derives great pleasure from fishing from a small dinghy.

CHAPTER Five

One Step Backwards

The decision to go to the Ron Holland design office for a full-on maxi to contest the 1985–86 Whitbread was a contradiction in the logical progression that was Peter Blake's climb to pre-eminence in the world of blue-water ocean racing. The Farr design *Ceramco New Zealand* had embodied pretty much everything that Blake regarded as required for the event. True, she was skitterish in the way of a big dinghy when flat running in heavy winds and big seas, and the long main boom that came with a fractional rig was a worry, dragging through the water when hard reaching and running. But she was light displacement, easy to drive with a small crew, extremely fast, and mostly well behaved downwind in the Southern Ocean. She was also competitive enough upwind to hang on to a full-blown, masthead-rigged maxi like *Flyer* in all but the light and heavy ends of the wind scale. In other words, the Farr design and her campaign had met most of Blake's convictions about the race and what was needed to win it – an impressive outcome given that *Ceramco* was a significant departure from the norms of ocean racing at the time and that she was the first bigger boat produced by the Farr office.

In that context, the boat that became *Lion New Zealand* was anything but a progression. She was a complete departure. *Lion* was a masthead maxi, the heaviest displacement yacht in the fleet, and she needed a crew of 22 to muscle her through. With the benefit of hindsight, it seems fair to say that Blake did not back his own instincts and better judgement. Instead, he allowed himself to be persuaded in favour of a design office that, while extremely well credentialled, was eager to please, rather than persevere with one that he perceived to be, and frequently was, difficult to deal with. There was a lot of history in that fateful decision, along with some arrogance, personality clashes and campaign immaturity. Not that you couldn't have made a strong case for the Holland office.

Holland was another product of the sailing-mad Auckland of the 1960s and 1970s. Not quite a contemporary of Blake's, he trod a similar path to international renown but in a different direction. Born in 1947, on leaving school Holland became an apprentice boat builder in the Atkinson yard at Browns Bay on Auckland's North Shore. Of even more importance to this account, the Atkinson yard was next door to the John Spencer boatyard.

An avid racer, Holland took night-school courses in yacht design before going overseas to seek more experience and opportunity. After a spell in California (a hothouse of yacht design at the time), he hung out his own design shingle near the tiny village of Crosshaven, on an arm of Cork Harbour in Southern Ireland and a stone's throw away from the oldest sailing establishment in the world, the Royal Cork Yacht Club. After successes in the Quarter, Half and One Ton classes, he moved up into bigger yachts until ultimately securing what, in those days, was almost the royal commission in yacht design – a new maxi (*Kialoa IV*) for Jim Kilroy. On the back of the Kilroy order was a near-sister ship (*Condor*) for Bob Bell. *Condor* and *Kialoa* became the new glamour maxis in the world fleet in the early 1980s, and on this basis alone the Holland office was a logical consideration when thinking of a maxi for the 1985–86 Whitbread.

The charismatic Holland – a consummate salesman – was very

124

adept at working the upper echelons of the international sailing scene, while also never losing the common touch. But he was more of a conformist, designing boats that were mainstream under the measurement rules of the time. Farr was almost the opposite. He never forsook his light-displacement approach to yacht racing and remained true to his beliefs through a succession of measurement rule changes and interpretations that looked suspiciously like they were aimed at thwarting his burgeoning success.

Farr prevailed and went on to become arguably the world's most successful designer. Early in the process, however, and with some justification, he became suspicious of the offshore racing establishment and its politics, and at one stage seemed prepared to turn his back altogether on designing boats to the measurement rules. Rightly or wrongly, he and partner Russell Bowler acquired a reputation for being arrogant and difficult to deal with. There could be no denying their success, however. Even while the rule makers appeared to be doing their level best to eliminate Farr-style boats from offshore racing – and many of those influencing the rule changes were in fact design rivals of the Farr office – Farr boats began to almost completely dominate the sport in the 1970s, winning just about every major event in sight.

It was no coincidence either that many of the successes were achieved by New Zealand owners and crews racing the downwind-orientated, light-displacement Farr machines that provided the kind of sailing experiences they loved. Sure, these craft might have been less comfortable and required bums on the rail, night and/or day, to help stability, and they might have needed constant trimming to keep them in the groove – but, hell, they were exciting, particularly when you got them to the top mark and started hoisting spinnakers.

But by the end of the constant rule changes of the 1970s, the Farr office was showing signs of having had enough of the rule makers, and this coincided with a slight lull in the ambition of New Zealand's offshore racing contingent who, for the previous decade, had journeyed to the far corners of the world in pursuit of success. So the commission from Blake to design what became the 68-foot *Ceramco New Zealand* appeared, to some Kiwis at least, like a lifeline to Farr and Bowler. It was the biggest race boat they had been asked to design and the commission had come from a young skipper who had already done the Whitbread race twice and who enjoyed a growing reputation in the sport, even if there were those in his home town Auckland who considered Blake more of an ocean walloper than a highly skilled racer.

Although *Ceramco* lost her mast and became an also-ran in terms of official results in the 1981–82 Whitbread, hers was unarguably a memorable performance and one that fully demonstrated the potential of what Farr and Bowler had to offer. It was natural to assume, then, that if Blake did the race again it would be in a Farr boat. There were, however, other forces at work. Simon Gundry recalls that, in the midst of the major party that followed *Ceramco*'s finish in Portsmouth, Ron Holland was in deep conversation with Blake and Tom Clark. Clark knew Holland from when he built boats, including the revolutionary Spencer design *Infidel*, at the John Spencer yard next door to where Holland was apprenticed. Probably more to the point, Clark was still smarting from what he considered a difficult experience with the Farr office when the *Ceramco* design was negotiated. And probably even more to the point, Clark privately blamed the Farr office for the rigging failure that brought down *Ceramco*'s mast.

Clark argued his case thus: 'When it looked like we would get the money together for another go (at the Whitbread) in 1985, I started talking to Peter about a designer. I was still annoyed with *Ceramco* losing that race basically because of that rigging failure. To this day, I'm not sure whether Farr knew about it or not. But if he didn't, he should have. He should never have allowed it – that old

126

bend-the-wire bit, no toggles. It still makes me mad when I think about it.' He had lost a forestay in mid-Tasman in the maxi *Buccaneer* through a similar rigging set-up where he had toggles to take care of fore and aft movement by the stay, but not sideways movement: 'That bloody piece of stainless steel, which was about 2 inches by 0.5 inches, just snapped off like a carrot – so I had very definite ideas about toggles!' Clark also claims that he was ignorant of the lack of toggles in *Ceramco*'s rig: 'The whole thing was all taped up so you couldn't see what the hell was underneath. If I had seen that rig without toggles, I would have jumped up and down – and I'm sure Peter would have listened to me.'

Yet somehow this claim doesn't ring quite true, even with the passing of time. Clark had, and still has, a very keen eye for detail on boats and took more than a passing interest in *Ceramco*'s construction. He was also on the wheel – earning himself the nickname 'Captain Araldite' – when *Ceramco* broached badly off Kawau on her delivery trip across the Tasman for the 1980 Sydney–Hobart race. That broach was so violent that Blake was prompted to observe that if *Ceramco*'s rig was ever going to fail, it would have been then. So the detail of her rig would have been discussed at some length after that broach. Also, Clark's insistence that the Farr office should not have allowed the rig set-up that brought about *Ceramco*'s downfall is unfair. The rigging system used was not exactly new to the sport and incorporated the latest technology, aimed at cutting down windage (drag) in the rig. If anyone should have had reservations about its reliability, it should have been Peter Blake who had considerable experience with rigs, having worked for Yachtspars in Auckland from late 1974 to May 1977.

While this debate may not be particularly relevant nearly 25 years on, it most certainly was relevant in 1983 and 1984 when the design decisions for Blake's next Whitbread boat were being made, as Clark attests: 'So we talked about designers and I'm still pissed off to the

127

nth degree about Farr. But I said to Peter, "See what you can do." So Peter started negotiations with Farr, and instead of recognising the fact that we had a limited budget and it was going to be tight, tough and hard, we couldn't get any concession out of him (Farr) at all. We would have to pay the going European rate for a design and it was going to cost a fortune. Peter came back with all this information and I did my nana. I said, "Stuff him", and Peter said he felt much the same way. So I said let's go off in another direction, let's give Ron Holland a go. We had discussions with Ron and he was just wonderful to get on with, whereas Farr was prickly and difficult. I could never really get on the same wavelength with him, couldn't warm to him at all. Ron was just the opposite. I go to Cork and I'm treated like royalty.'

From all of these assertions, it is clear that the very forceful Clark was a major influence in the decision to run with Holland and not Farr. What is not clear, and now never will be, is why the equally strong-willed Blake did not back his own deeply held convictions on what was needed to race around the world. For, despite Holland's undoubted design credentials, the Farr approach to yacht design was a much closer fit with Blake's own instincts and beliefs.

Later on in his career, it would become clear to those close to him that Blake did not enjoy personal confrontation. The decision-making process and the ultimate determination not to stick with Farr, even though that might have been the more logical option, was perhaps the first real sign of this trait. The choice to go with Holland could also have been indicative that Blake was still going through his own learning curve and was not yet prepared to go head to head with his sponsor – something that would change in later years.

Tom Clark, meanwhile, was busily putting together the sponsorship package to raise the $NZ2 million that would be needed to build and campaign the new boat. The decision to campaign a full-blown maxi in 1985–86 meant that the cost spiralled proportionally and the price tag was beyond the marketing and promotional budgets of New

Zealand's handful of major corporates to whom the opportunity might appear of benefit. So Clark carved up his cake into more digestible portions. To fund the building of the boat, he would go for $NZ500,000 from a naming rights sponsor and $NZ100,000 each from 12 subsidiary sponsors. Then he would solicit public support to pay for the campaign itself.

Clark arranged a meeting between himself, Blake and Douglas Myers, the new managing director of Lion Breweries Ltd which was the largest player in New Zealand's liquor industry and a public company listed among the country's 12 largest enterprises. It was to prove a pivotal encounter in the life and career of Blake, for Myers, one of the 'Young Turks' who were reshaping New Zealand business, had the financial muscle and connections to open the campaign doors that Blake was now approaching. Importantly, Myers, in the New Zealand vernacular, also had the balls to back his instincts and possessed a vision for New Zealand and what it could achieve if it concentrated on what it was good at.

Then 45, Myers had just taken over the brewery and was making sweeping changes to streamline the business. He acknowledges that not everyone in the company liked what he was doing: 'I had just come into Lion and they didn't like me being there. Like all institutions in New Zealand, they didn't want to change, and the company was faced with the need for very significant change. I always used to say that, other than the abattoirs, we were probably the oldest industry in New Zealand and the unions involved in that industry had the most entrenched positions. Management was the most defunct and, therefore, the need to change mindsets was great. Like all old institutions in New Zealand, we were locked in the past. I thought, therefore, that getting involved in something dynamic and dramatic, and having access to people who were adventurous, not business people, seemed to offer an opportunity to talk about positive things rather than what the staff probably considered negatives – like change.'

Myers did not like yachting – indeed, had rarely set foot on a yacht. He felt that the people who sailed boats were missing the whole point of being on the sea: 'All they did was sail on top of it. I've never met a yachtie, other than Peter, who liked fishing or diving, although I am sure there are plenty that do.' But it was obvious to him that New Zealanders were good at yachting and he liked what he saw in Blake: 'He was very tall, had a very nice manner, didn't talk too much and seemed to be admirable. Or maybe I just picked up a projection of an outstanding person. I don't know. I think I maybe sensed something special in Peter.'

These were, in Myers' terms, 'pre Roger Douglas days when New Zealand seemed extraordinarily gloomy and incapable of seeing its way through to its position in the world' and there were 'those few of us who felt that New Zealand was capable of better'. In short, the proposal to do a Whitbread race campaign with Blake was something tangible for the brewery and the country to invest in.

'I wasn't doing it because I was interested in yachting,' Myers emphasises. 'I was doing it because I was interested in the company and I was interested in the country. I was interested in them both being involved with success. But it wasn't that I was backing a winner at that stage. I don't think Peter had won anything so I wasn't consciously going with a winner at all. A potential winner – yes. I was really taking a punt on his ability to do the things that until then he had not done. He had certainly shown tenacity, which was admirable, and the fact that he was continuing after not winning was absolutely the way the world is. Most people, most of the time, don't win first up.'

Myers didn't refer the proposal to his board or consult with anyone. He backed his instincts on the spot and Blake's next Whitbread boat became *Lion New Zealand*. Interestingly, Myers recalls that decision as 'the deal with Peter'.

The big one secured, Clark was able to concentrate on the 12 support sponsors he was seeking, and in time signed up Air New Zealand, Atlas Corporation, Auckland Coin & Bullion Exchange Ltd, Chase Corporation Ltd, Construction Machinery Ltd, Fay, Richwhite and Company, Mogal Corporation, Healing Industries Ltd, McConnell Dowell Corporation, John W. Andrew Ford Ltd, Newmans Coach Lines and New Zealand Shipping Corporation – all among the country's most progressive corporations and companies. 'I leaned on everyone heavily,' he recalls, 'made myself unpopular with a lot of my friends – but I stitched the package together.'

It was now July 1983 and Blake, who had made his home in Emsworth in the south of England, was captain of the 1983 New Zealand team for the famed Admiral's Cup and was in Cowes, Isle of Wight, preparing to skipper the Frers 46-footer *Lady B* in that contest. The clinching decision of who would design his Whitbread boat had still not been taken at this stage, and he was scheduled to make a final visit to the Holland office in Ireland for more talks with the expatriate designer.

Also in Cowes myself at the time, covering the regatta for the *Auckland Star* newspaper and *New Zealand Yachting* magazine, I was aware, through Blake, that there were apparently difficulties in dealings with the Farr office and that a Holland design was under serious consideration. Nevertheless, knowing Blake's enthusiasm for *Ceramco*, I found it hard to believe that any stumbling blocks in the dealings with Farr would not be overcome. On the night of the New Zealand team's official cocktail party at the Royal Corinthian Yacht Club, Blake had just returned from Ireland and I was late arriving at the function because of copy deadlines. When I walked into the function venue, Blake spotted me and steered me to a corner. He had, he said, made his decision and his designer would be Holland. Somewhat surprised, I discussed with him the different philosophies

131

of the two design offices. Wasn't he forsaking his own beliefs, I asked. Blake acknowledged that it might appear a change of approach on his part, but insisted it wasn't. He had given a precise set of design criteria to Holland who had assured him that those criteria would be met. Holland's success with *Kialoa* and *Condor*, he added, were strong influences on his decision.

Holland recalled later: 'Peter's visit was certainly inspired by the maxi boat situation with both *Kialoa* and *Condor* racing in Cowes. I was impressed with the concept of *Ceramco* – lighter and more downwind-oriented was certainly the correct way to go for the Round the World race. And Peter was keen to know what could be achieved if the *Kialoa/Condor* approach was modified to what would be required for the Whitbread. *Kialoa* and *Condor* showed a big performance advantage over the existing maxi fleet and there was a logic that if you could take that performance and orient it to round-the-world racing, you'd be really state of the art.'

Blake's design brief to Holland involved some vital differences from the *Ceramco* approach. This time he wanted a masthead rig. He was, he said, concerned about having to gybe a maxi fractional rig, with less permanent support, in rugged conditions in the Southern Ocean, and he wasn't too enamoured by the prospect of dragging a fractional rig's longer main boom through those same oceans either. He also planned to race with a large crew to keep driving the boat at optimum speed 24 hours a day for weeks on end. The combination of a lightish boat and a large crew would not have been possible in previous races. The weight of food and water for larger numbers of people would have been prohibitive. It was now, however, entirely feasible due to the advances made with freeze-dried foods and onboard fresh-water makers. Blake explained: 'What I was really seeking was a boat with abilities and characteristics not too far removed from those of *Ceramco*. With the benefit of experience and hindsight, however, we wanted performance gains in some areas and

132

better handling qualities in others. If we couldn't get exclusivity on that approach from Farr, we'd seek it from Holland, provided he was confident that he could design and engineer the boat we wanted in the first place.'

There were those who thought Clark and Blake made too big an issue of exclusivity, and the Farr office has disputed the Clark–Blake version of events. But the pair firmly believed that the experience, input and information they had to offer a designer was significant and hard-earned, in terms of both effort and expense. They didn't want that contribution available to anyone else who could come up with a design fee and commission the same design office.

The Farr office tried to accommodate Clark and Blake by proposing an exclusivity fee that would compensate the design office if it had to walk away from other Whitbread maxi (above 65-foot rating) commissions. The opening proposal was an upfront fee of US$220,000. Clark and Blake considered that sum exorbitant and didn't bother to negotiate further.

Holland, on the other hand, gave Blake and Clark the assurances they were seeking – both in terms of meeting their design criteria and of exclusivity – and the deal was done. Holland would later claim that he could see no reason why Blake would not have gone back to the Farr office for his next boat except that he recalled a 'sense of being let down'. He did not know whether that was 'truly related' to the mast failure or whether it had to do with 'subsequent communications with the Farr office related to exclusivity'. 'I would say, however,' Holland added, 'that Peter was influenced by Tom who, remember, was a very strong and imposing person.' He also recalls that the two things Blake was really adamant about in his design brief were: 1) not getting too extreme in any particular direction of the boat (what yachties call 'hitting the corners'); and 2) the boat must not break – 'He was really quite vocal about that.'

While he admired the Farr concept for *Ceramco* and wanted to design a narrower boat because of his experience aboard the famous Bill Lee design Transpac boat *Merlin*, Holland was reluctant to trade off displacement. *Condor* was, after all, slightly longer and heavier than *Kialoa*, with plenty of sail to compensate for that, and could always beat her near-sister ship downwind. So *Lion* was designed 'a little lighter, a little shorter and a little narrower' than *Condor* and *Kialoa*.

The Blake campaign for 1985–86 was now committed to a boat that would prove to struggle to compete against her rivals from the Farr design board, but not so much because of her pedigree and concept – she was just too heavy. Neither did Clark and Blake get the exclusivity they thought they had achieved, because the Holland office had already designed a similar boat to the one they were seeking – for noted British offshore skipper Rob James and to be called *Colt Cars*. Blake would address this issue later, saying: 'Some people thought we contradicted ourselves by commissioning Holland who had already done a boat for Rob James which wasn't that far from our thinking. The difference was that the Farr office would not even give us an assurance that they would work on no other Whitbread boat once they'd received our submissions and ideas and produced a design for us. This was the least we would accept if we were to feel sure that nobody else would benefit from what we had to offer.'

The first real confirmation of *Lion*'s weight problems came at dawn on 4 November 1984, when, minus mast, she was slipped into the water for a pre-launch check at the McMullen & Wing launching facility on Auckland's downtown waterfront. Holland was there and recalls: 'I'll never forget that she floated beautifully level, but she was where she should have been with the rig in. I just looked and thought, "Oh my God". She was down (on her lines) more than what we had imagined.'

Later that morning *Lion* was officially launched by Lady Tait, wife of Admiral Sir Gordon Tait, the patron of the New Zealand International Yacht Racing Trust, in front of a huge crowd at Auckland's Princes Wharf passenger terminal. She was suspended from the hook of the Auckland Harbour Board's floating crane *Hikenu*, which included in its equipment a load cell to accurately weigh the items it was lifting. Roy Mason, who had helped build the boat and who would be on *Lion*'s crew, turned to the crane driver to ask what she weighed. The reply came back: 'Thirty-seven going on 38 ton.' Mason gulped. *Lion* was supposed to weigh five tons less than that. Close by, John Newton, who had raced with Blake on *Ceramco*, was watching the launch with Auckland boat builder/designer Chris Robertson, who, on seeing how far down on her lines *Lion* was, issued a prolonged 'Ohhhh shhhhiit'.

Blake would have known immediately that Lion had a weight problem that would be, at the very least, difficult to overcome in terms of performance. But he never let on. While looking for answers and solutions internally, he maintained an external air of confidence. As *Lion* underwent sea trials and was put through the measurement process for rating, however, his concerns grew and he communicated these to the Holland office. On 3 December 1984, he telexed Holland to say: 'Thanks for telex re *Lion* rating. Please give this your utmost attention as I do not plan to race in the Whitbread on a 66-foot or even a 69.3-foot rating. As the hull construction was strengthened (extra Kevlar in bottom, inside and out) and then two tons of lead were added to the keel, all this weight [is] extra to original design. I feel you should have known we would rate low. I wanted a maxi, not something approaching that figure. Thoughts please.'

Holland responded with: 'Understand your concern and we are working on studies that can be finalised after we examine the first rating certificate. I was aware we would be 5000 pounds overweight but the additional 2500 to 3000 pounds was a surprise. I felt we had enough in hand when we reinforced the bottom. Our experience suggests the additional keel weight will prove correct even though we will have to cut holes in the top of the keel to get back to original weight. We need some guidance from (boat builder) Tim (Gurr) on this and I will have a final proposal when in New Zealand at the end of January.'

How *Lion* ended up so much overweight is known. She was quite simply overbuilt, possibly in response to Blake and Clark making it clear to everyone that the boat must not break. But why there was not greater attention paid to the final weight factor is more difficult to pin down or explain.

Holland offers one explanation: 'With *Kialoa* and *Condor* we had opted to have an internal aluminium space frame to take the rig and keel loads. The philosophy was that we would do the hull and the decks really on the edge of being too light but we would stiffen the boats with the space frame. Why we did not do that with *Lion* I am not sure. We probably thought that if we made the shell of the boat strong enough to hit an iceberg, then that hull would be stiff enough anyway. That was a big departure – not following the space frame concept. Without the alloy structure, you had to put material back into the hull itself to get the stiffness and that contributed to the boat being overweight. I'm conscious that there was disappointment on Peter's and Tom's part, that the boat wasn't as fast as it should have been, didn't win, couldn't win. She was just heavier than we had hoped and that, I think, was due to layer upon layer of conservatism. Peter probably started that [process] with his stipulation that the boat couldn't break – he'd lost it last time because of a breakage and was not going to have it happen again. So we designed him something that wasn't going to break and then I think Tim Gurr and his team, probably following the same philosophy, made things just a little bit stronger. So, every step of the way we were all at fault, if you like, in covering our arses against having Tom breathing down our necks – you could just hear him.'

136

Roy Mason agrees with Holland: 'A lot of extra cloth and resin went in that wasn't actually necessary. It was probably inexperience at the time, erring on the cautious side through that inexperience. Remember, *Lion* was the first maxi built in New Zealand and because it was such a big boat a lot of people probably thought it could handle a bit of extra. Plus, there was a lot of talk at the time about having a good-looking boat to enhance its resale value. A lot of extra material went into fairing the inside of the hull. This is never a consideration when you are building a race boat these days.'

Tom Clark elaborates: 'As the boat progressed, the crew had a lot of say in what was going to be done and how it was going to be done, and nobody was watching the weight and saying, "Yes, you can have this but you are going to have to give up that". Little by little the additions came on and the boat finished up too heavy. It was built like 16 brick shithouses. That was okay in the Hobart race, which was a very rough trip. We didn't have a single breakage and that gave the guys a lot of confidence in terms of what might be to come in the Southern Ocean. But of course, the Southern Ocean for the 1985–86 Whitbread was absolutely wonderful the whole way around, with a very small amount of shitty weather.'

Because she was heavy, *Lion* came in well below the 70-foot maxi rating (she did the Whitbread with a rating of 68.6 feet) – hence Blake's telexed comments to Holland that he was not going to race a 66-foot rating 'maxi'. A new keel was built and fitted to the boat just prior to the Whitbread race start, in an attempt to improve rating and performance. While this helped, it was too little too late. Holland reflected: 'I have thought since that we could have dramatically changed things by putting a bulbed keel on, but our heads just weren't there then, it just wasn't right enough at the time. We were into those triangular-styled International Offshore Rule (IOR) keels which, when you look back at them now, were so draggy. If we had put what we now regard as a modern keel on the boat, she would

137

have been back up to displacement, to rating, and had a lot less drag.'

There was to be an interesting sidelight to the new keel story. An almost identical keel had been fitted to the British maxi *Drum England* (*Lion*'s near-sister ship that had started life as *Colt Cars*) that was now owned by pop idol Simon Le Bon (of Duran Duran fame) and was also entered in the Whitbread. As a final warm-up race before the Whitbread start, *Drum* was contesting the 1985 Fastnet Classic when, on the second day out, while beating close to the English Channel coast near Falmouth, her keel literally fell off and she capsized. A terrible tragedy was avoided only because *Drum* couldn't have picked a better time or place to perform what could have been a death roll. She was in full view of the shore, just a couple of miles off, and being watched by two coastguard observers taking their lunch break. They immediately raised the alarm and within 10 minutes a helicopter from nearby Culdrose air-sea rescue base was hovering overhead and winching down a survival expert.

As *Drum* rolled, with almost slow deliberation, two of her crew – one of them designer Ron Holland's brother, Phil – had the survival instinct to walk around the hull and take up secure positions near the rudder. From there they were able to haul their crewmates up the impossibly smooth underwater sections of the upturned maxi using the straps of two lifejackets as a lifeline. Most of *Drum*'s crew had been thrown into the water when they couldn't find a grip on the slippery topsides. They made it back to the boat and found some security by standing on the top (now bottom) guardrail and gripping the boat's toe rail. Even so, they had to snatch deep breaths and hang on for dear life as *Drum* wallowed in the swells.

The 16 people in the water were soon hauled to what was only the relative safety of the upturned hull where they were now subjected to the problem of hypothermia. Six others, including Le Bon, were still inside the boat, one of them trapped in his bunk and in danger of drowning as the water level rose. These six

138

were brought to the surface by the chopper's diver and the operation of winching everyone to safety commenced. The chopper made quick dashes to the nearby shore to unload and return for more. By the time this operation began, several of the half-clad people, who had been off watch below when the boat rolled, were very cold and shivering violently. If help hadn't been so close at hand – everyone was ashore within half an hour of the boat's rolling – who knows what the outcome would have been. What if *Drum* had turned turtle out in the middle of the ocean in the Whitbread, or even if it had happened where it did, but at night and unobserved? *Drum*'s keel had snapped off at the hull when welds in the upper keel frame structure failed. The new keel on *Lion* was similarly attached. Was it also suspect?

It was determined that *Drum*'s keel had flexed from side to side and finally snapped off, leaving the keel bolts still in the hull. It seemed that the welding work had not been done to specifications. The Woolfson Unit at Southampton University, in an independent investigation into the mishap, found that the all-important welds were porous and had insufficient penetration, or none at all. The welding on *Lion*'s keel had been faithfully carried out and the welds carefully inspected and X-rayed, so there was no concern in the Blake camp. But Roy Mason went to look at the *Drum* keel to satisfy his own curiosity: 'I wanted to see for myself exactly what happened because there were a lot of people back home hoping to hell that *Lion*'s keel was not going to fall off. The way the keel was constructed, there was lead ballast in the bottom and then an aluminium can about four feet deep above that. This was welded to a 20-millimetre alloy plate which was bolted through the hull. The welding on the alloy can to the top plate was like birdshit. There was just no penetration in the metal and the whole thing fell off. I built *Lion*'s can and top plate, and when you know a little bit about metal you can see what's going on in the molten pool as you're welding. If the metal is the wrong temperature

139

it will form like bubbles on a dry surface. You know when you've got a good penetrating weld.'

Like *Ceramco* before her, *Lion* would do the Sydney–Hobart race and then undertake a promotional tour of New Zealand before leaving for the race start in England. Blake had picked his crew of 21 and was confident he had the right blend of 'big boat experience, small boat enthusiasm and character'. *Lion* was going to be a totally different proposition to *Ceramco*. With a masthead rig and twice the sail area, she would impose brutish demands on the people who sailed her.

One of the first to sign on was Grant Dalton, who had missed the cut for *Ceramco* but made a big impression in the crew of *Flyer*, and of whom Blake said: 'Dalts came to me very early in the piece and asked to be considered not only for the project but also as a watch leader. I wasn't sure how Dalts would handle people but decided to give him the chance he was after. There's nothing like being thrown in at the deep end to bring out the best, or the worst, in a man.'

As it turned out, *Lion* would bring out the best in Dalton and equip him further for his own journey to international renown as one of the outstanding blue-water racing skippers of his day. There were times, however, when his hard-driving approach on the wheel would cause friction with Blake. 'There was a complete contrast in the personalities of Pete and Dalts,' said Roy Mason. 'With Dalts, the more sail you put up the faster you are going to go, but that's not always the case. Normally, when he came on watch, he'd shake reefs out or go for bigger headsails, or whatever.'

Dalton has a slightly different take on the personality clash: 'I'm not sure to this day that he (Blake) would have ever decided that making me watch captain was a very good idea. We all know that *Lion* was a bit of a cock-up. And although I learned a lot from him, I didn't have respect for him at that stage because I thought he didn't

140

push hard enough. I was 26 at this stage and probably I was pushing too hard. He said that he wasn't sure that I knew when to button off, which maybe was true to a point. But *Lion* was such a pig, you had to push her or nothing happened.'

The 1300-mile crossing of the Tasman for the 1984 Sydney–Hobart was notable only for a bit of a dusting a couple of days off the New South Wales coast when *Lion* was reefed down to her smallest gear in 50 knots but still jumping out of big waves. Blake used the opportunity for a hove-to drill. That blow was a portent of things to come.

On paper, the course for the 630-mile Hobart race looks more of a coastal contest than a blue-water classic. The course involves a hard right-turn at Sydney Heads then tracks down the New South Wales coast and across Bass Strait on to the eastern coastline of Tasmania. Another hard right-turn, this time at Tasman Island and across Storm Bay, and then there's a short sprint up the Derwent River to the finish off Hobart's Wrest Point Casino. No problems.

But the simplicity of the track belies the difficulty it can present when the elements are unfavourable. The New South Wales coast, with its unpredictable currents, can be rugged enough when it is blowing hard from the southern quarter. Bass Strait can be something else again – a funnel for winds and currents as the Indian Ocean squeezes between mainland Australia and Tasmania to enter the Tasman Sea, where it meets the East Australian current coming down the coast of New South Wales. The Aussies call Bass Strait 'The Paddock' – more often than not it is a deeply ploughed field. The coast of Tasmania is tactically tricky, but frequently the best, or worst, is yet to come. Tasman Island is one of the great maritime landmarks although it is further off the beaten track of the old trade routes than, say, the Cape of Good Hope and Cape Horn. It juts out from the southern tip of the Tasman Peninsula, its stark cliffs sculpted into memorable designs and shapes by centuries of winds and seas conjured up in the Antarctic, not that far to the south, and marks the turn into the aptly named Storm Bay where many a good yacht's race has come unstuck. Then there's the Derwent. It can be blowing old boots 'outside' yet be as calm as a millpond in the river. There are generations of yachtsmen with good reason to wish that the Hobart race finish was off the Iron Pot, at the mouth of the Derwent, rather than 10 miles upstream off the city of Hobart itself.

The line-up for the 1984 classic comprised 152 boats. Among them were the Holland design *Condor*, the 76-foot Lexcen design *Apollo*, the 80-foot Frers design *Ragamuffin*, and the 77-foot Tasker design *Vengeance*. All four were previous line honours winners of the race – *Condor* in 1983, *Vengeance* in 1981, *Ragamuffin* (as *Bumblebee IV*) in 1979, and *Apollo* in 1978. They would provide a valuable yardstick to *Lion*'s potential.

The wind for the traditional Boxing Day start was from the south and freshening – a tight reach down the harbour before hardening up through the Heads for a beat down the New South Wales coast. *Condor* was first through the Heads and into a Tasman that was already large and lumpy as well as churned white by the hundreds of launches and runabouts that were determined to get a close look at the maxis before having to turn back to shelter. The weather forecast that morning had not been promising – gale-force south-westerlies later in the day. *Lion* and the other bigger yachts in the fleet chased *Condor* down the coast, hard on the wind in the building gale. They beat on into the night not knowing that the first casualties were already on their way back to Sydney or seeking help. In the next 36 hours the fleet would be decimated.

Condor was among the first group of casualties, losing her steering gear when a turning block tore away from the hull. As she turned back to Sydney in difficult seas, she was one of 31 yachts already in trouble. Four boats had been dismasted during the night. The other 27 reported varying problems, from critical rig or hull damage to chronic

142

seasickness. *Ragamuffin* and *Apollo* were also among the retired, the former with a broken main boom gooseneck fitting and a seriously injured crewman, the latter with a shredded sail wardrobe and injured crew. *Lion* and *Vengeance* were now the only big boats left in the race. So far, the only problem on the New Zealand yacht was seasickness.

By now the wind was gusting 45 knots from the south-south-west and *Lion* had almost dealt a permanent blow to the well-known voice of radio commentator Peter Montgomery who was covering the race as part of her crew. Montgomery had been trying to get some sleep lying on the floor alongside the navigatorium. The boat jumped out of a wave and Blake's brass parallel rollers were flung off the navigation table into Montgomery's throat. With blood running down his chest, the injured broadcaster sought the help of *Lion*'s doctor, Fraser Maxwell, who was comatose in his bunk with a rather severe case of *mal de mer*. The only response Montgomery got was, 'Yes, you've cut your throat.' Not knowing the extent of his injury, Montgomery turned to Blake who was lacking sleep after a night of plotting *Lion* through the building gale. His bedside manner was as accommodating as the stricken doctor's but he did, on Maxwell's grumbled advice, clean and dress Montgomery's wound, closing the cut with strips of plaster. The only problem was, Blake used the backing strips instead of the plasters themselves and Maxwell finally had to get out of his bunk for long enough to do the job properly.

By that evening the casualty list had reached 70 and later that night came the shocking news that 70-year-old Wally Russell had been lost overboard from the 38-foot Hank Kaufman design *Yahoo II*. Three huge waves had swept over the yacht, capsizing it and washing Russell, a veteran of 15 previous Hobart races, over the side. The yacht was on its ear, completely engulfed by water. When she righted herself, Russell was 30 metres away waving to attract attention. His crewmates frantically started the engine, which ran for only 10 seconds before cutting out. It took two minutes to manoeuvre

Yahoo II back to Russell's position. By then he was face down in the water and drifting away from help. *Yahoo II*'s crew risked their own lives in huge seas, trying to find Russell again. Finally, they had to look to their own safety and headed for shelter in Jervis Bay. The Hobart race had claimed its first victim in its 39-year history.

Deputy race officer Gordon Marshall issued a warning to yachts still racing. It read: 'In the light of forecasts please assess the ability of your boat and crew in proceeding across Bass Strait. A conscious decision should be made on each yacht before continuing across.' By 0700 hours the next day the casualty list was 78 boats. The barometer was dropping again and the forecast was for south to south-west winds of 30–40 knots with very rough seas.

A further 53 miles down the track than anyone else and entering Bass Strait, Blake and his crew could vouch for the accuracy of the weatherman's predictions. *Lion* was getting hammered but taking it all in her stride, with Montgomery informing his listeners in New Zealand that it was 'like driving a 10-ton truck off the top of a three-storey building, every couple of minutes'. A laconic Blake remarked: 'We didn't need to nurse *Lion*, but it was prudent to hold her back a bit. You can't keep dropping a big boat off 25- and 30-foot seas all the time without doing some damage.'

By 0600 hours the following morning, the retirement total was 101 boats. As far as could be ascertained, only 36 of the survivors were still racing. The rest were sheltering in ports on the southern New South Wales coast, waiting for the weather to abate before continuing. The weatherman was still forecasting south to south-west winds of 30–40 knots, but in Bass Strait it had swung to the south-east and was beginning to drop. *Lion* was starting to ease away down the eastern coast of Tasmania. With 170 miles still to go, her closest rival on the water was *Vengeance*, 95 miles astern. The pressure for handicap honours was coming from the 40-foot Farr design *Indian Pacific* which had gone well out to sea the first night out, and had

144

experienced little of the punishment that had been meted out closer inshore. In addition to this, she had clocked into a south-easterly change as she entered Bass Strait and was rocketing towards Tasman Island with a breeze that had kept shifting through to the north-east.

Lion dashed across Storm Bay, averaging 13 knots with a 30-knot north-easter on the beam. The final 10 miles up the Derwent were mostly a drift in light headwinds and she struggled across the finish line 30 minutes after midnight on the fourth day of the race, 12.5 hours ahead of *Vengeance*. The slow start and fast finish of the race had put paid to any chance of repeating *Ceramco*'s line and handicap double but *Lion* had been put to the test in rugged conditions and had come through with flying colours. She had spent the best part of three days punching into 40-knot headwinds and big seas in the toughest Hobart race on record (only 46 of the 152 starters reached the finish) and she had left highly respectable opposition in her wake.

In the weeks that followed, *Lion* recrossed the Tasman to Milford Sound and undertook an exhausting promotional tour of 14 ports of call around the coast of New Zealand. The reception she received surprised even those who had done a smaller version of the same exercise with *Ceramco* after the previous race. The scene was set in Bluff, at the southernmost tip of the 'mainland' South Island, where the queues of people lined up to see through the boat were several hundred metres long despite cold, rainy weather. The hospitality and generosity were almost overwhelming. In the space of just over three weeks more than 40,000 people were shown through the boat, parting with in excess of $300,000 for a look-through and for a whole range of souvenirs, prompting Blake to observe: 'It was tough on the crew, but in the tougher months to come, maybe in the middle of a bad night in the Southern Ocean, they would remember the little old ladies from the country areas of New Zealand who travelled far and handed over hard-earned dollars to see what those young fellas from Auckland were up to this time and to do their bit to help.'

CHAPTER
Six
A Weighty Problem

Sarah-Jane (SJ) Blake, Peter and Pippa's first child, was born in Emsworth, England, on 2 May 1983. Her second birthday was celebrated aboard a 78-foot ocean-racing maxi yacht in miserable conditions in the middle of the South Pacific between New Zealand and Easter Island. With her parents, she was part of the crew delivering *Lion New Zealand* to Britain for the 1985–86 Whitbread race. Some of the most important items loaded aboard just before *Lion*'s 14 April departure from Auckland's Marsden Wharf were 700 disposable nappies. The usual last-minute items brought aboard included lemons and fresh bread; the unusual items included a potty trainer and seat, a blackboard, a washing machine and a blender – the last for the adults (to make banana daiquiris).

Although the addition of family made his objectives more difficult to achieve, Peter Blake had determined that his wife and child (and, later, children) would be as directly involved in his life as possible, and that included delivery voyages. That had seemed perfectly natural when his young fiancée and then wife became a part of the *Condor of Bermuda* crew, but when he stepped ashore to take hands-on control of the *Ceramco New Zealand* programme there were hiccups.

The Blakes had rented a property on Stanley Point on the northern side of Auckland Harbour and it was, in Pippa's words, 'our

149

first sample of real married life in a proper house'. Apart from the *Condor* crew, however, she knew hardly a soul in New Zealand, and all of a sudden her husband was going out to work and keeping 'office hours' at the builder's yard. Pippa was left at home with a lot of time on her hands, and she wasn't happy. Quickly realising this, Peter chatted things through with his wife and it was decided that everything would be much better if Pippa became directly involved in what he was doing. So he started taking her everywhere, business or social. When he went to the yard, Pippa went too. When he gave promotional talks to yacht clubs around the country, Pippa was there to lend support. It raised a few eyebrows, but Blake turned a Nelsonian eye and the pair became inseparable.

One who apparently didn't approve (at least to begin with) was *Ceramco* sponsor Tom Clark. Pippa recalls that, a couple of nights before *Ceramco* was due to head for Sydney for the Hobart race, Blake got a telephone call from Warwick White saying that if she was on board for the journey, Clark said he would not be. Pippa recalls: 'Peter told them that if I wasn't on board, he wouldn't be the skipper. So we set out with both Tom and me aboard and Tom did this amazing broach off Kawau. It was complete chaos down below – water and food everywhere. When Tom saw that I wasn't going to burst into tears and that I helped just as much as anyone else to clean up the mess, I think he began to change his mind about me. By the time we got to Sydney, we were good mates and Tom paid for Peter and me to stay ashore at the Travelodge Motel rather than on the boat.'

When Sarah-Jane arrived on the scene, Blake took it all in his stride and it quickly became obvious that wherever he went, Pippa and now SJ went too. 'He was a very chuffed father,' says Pippa, 'and SJ became part of the action, part of the package. A few weeks after we arrived in New Zealand, I got appendicitis and ended up in hospital. SJ was only 10 months old at the time and Peter's parents were away. No problem. He just took SJ to the yard in Poland Road every day until I was back on my feet again.'

Even so, the Blakes had second (and probably third) thoughts about taking their still-not-two daughter on a three-month voyage halfway around the world in a racing yacht. The week before they were due to leave, they admitted to each other that they were very apprehensive. They were worried about SJ's safety and 'Plan B' – Pippa flying back to Britain with SJ – was discussed. Blake, however, was a cautious person, especially when it came to the sea, and he had complete confidence in his own abilities. Also, there would be a doctor (Fraser Maxwell) on board as well as a registered nurse (crewman Martin Ford's wife Ginny). So the decision was made to proceed as planned. SJ and Pippa would join the delivery crew.

As it transpired, SJ thrived on the trip and the only problems encountered were in the education department. The crew went to great lengths, with utmost patience, to teach her to say things like 'Chill out, Granny' when she met Pippa's mother in England. There were some unusual incidents when the socially precocious two-year-old went ashore, however, like when *Lion* arrived at the Royal Cork Yacht Club, in Southern Ireland, after crossing the Atlantic. SJ wanted to go to the loo and there were no qualms when one of the crew simply took her off to the gents, much to the bemusement of some of the local ladies.

Pippa reflected on their daughter's unconventional experience: 'SJ spent three months on the boat with 11 adults. It was a wonderful trip, and particularly brilliant for potty-training. Any time it looked like she was going to have a little accident, or do something on the sails (which were the racing sails being carried to England), the boys would yell at her and she would do the right thing in the right place. By the time we reached England, she'd already visited Easter Island, the Galapagos Islands, the Panama Canal, Nassau, Bermuda and Ireland. And she was fully potty-trained to boot. Not bad for a two-year-old.'

Blake wrote later: 'To see the delight on her face with every new experience was enchanting. With the patience and indulgence of the crew, she had developed much more quickly than a child of equal years ashore. And she had an amazing recall of where she had been and what she had done – remembering clearly the statues on Easter Island, the seals at the Galapagos, swimming in the Gatun Lakes in the Panama Canal, and taking her first bubble bath at Peter Comes' house in Bermuda. I certainly would not have wanted to do the trip without SJ and clearly the experience had done much for her.'

Only five of *Lion*'s racing crew made the delivery trip. The remainder flew to England to join the vessel when she reached her UK base at Port Hamble marina, near the Solent, and there was much to be done before the Whitbread start on 28 September. The top priority was to replace *Lion*'s keel with a new one that was more refined in shape and, most importantly, was 1.5 tons lighter than the original, with the lead ballast in the bottom of the structure so that *Lion* displaced less but retained the same stability as before.

Blake used the Seahorse Maxi Series, which included the 200-mile Channel Race and the 605-mile Fastnet Classic, as a final warm-up series. This gave the *Lion* crew a first look at some of the opposition they would encounter in the Whitbread, including the Farr maxis *Atlantic Privateer* and *UBS Switzerland*, her near-sister ship *Drum England*, and the circuit maxi *Condor*. While *Lion* was fully competitive in lighter airs, she lacked the speed of the Farr boats reaching and running and Blake got his first premonitions that, despite the new keel, it was going to be a long Whitbread race. He wrote: '*Lion* achieved mixed results. She won a light airs race easily but in the fresher stuff that predominated during the three weeks of racing, culminating in a gale-swept Fastnet Classic, we began to fear that she lacked the legs against the Farr boats downwind.'

152

The Farr boats, in fact, were quick on all points of sailing. Even inshore, the masthead-rig *Atlantic Privateer*, owned and skippered by South African-born but United States resident Padda Kuttel, was a close match for the circuit maxis. In the Fastnet, which was predominantly a two-sail reach in mostly gale conditions, she chased the state-of-the-art 83-footer *Nirvana* all the way around the course to finish only 31 seconds astern. As did *Lion*, the fractionally-rigged *UBS Switzerland* skippered by Pierre Fehlmann pulled out of the Fastnet with mainsail problems, but she'd shown some devastating reaching speed in the lead-up races.

If Blake had his own reservations about *Lion*'s competitiveness, he kept them to himself, as Roy Mason commented: 'A few people realised that the extra weight was hurting *Lion*'s performance, particularly relative to the Farr boats. But at the same time, most of the crew were so young, those details were not embedded, because they didn't have the experience to sort that out for themselves. And Peter would never mention anything like that.'

'Peter never let on that he wasn't completely happy with *Lion*,' said Pippa Blake. 'He always dealt on the positive side of things, never the negative. He was always optimistic.' And Blake himself acknowledged: 'Although *Lion* was a couple of feet shorter than the boat I originally had in mind – 78 feet instead of 80 feet overall – and rated 1.4 feet under the maxi limit of 70 feet, we had the utmost faith in her ability even though the Farr boats might have the legs on her in fresh downwind conditions. She was a real powerhouse to windward, in all conditions, and fast on all points of sail in the lighter stuff. What was just as important, however, was that she was built to finish the Whitbread, and that wasn't necessarily true of her opposition. In the quest for lightness they had, in my view, cut corners which would prove their undoing if the 1985–86 race was anything like the previous three Whitbreads. There was already evidence of this, with frames cracking and hulls flexing even in the relatively sheltered English Channel. What would happen if the Southern Ocean really turned it on?'

Blake's observations, about the opposition and the prospects for the fleet in rough weather, were to prove remarkably prescient.

A fleet of 15 yachts went to the start line off Portsmouth on 28 September 1985. This was a month later than previously in the hope of better weather in the Southern Ocean. The South Atlantic was to prove the major test, however.

Blake briefed his crew on the way to the start area. *Lion* had been labelled 'too heavy' and 'off the pace' following the Seahorse series and he wanted to put that into perspective. *Lion* was a maxi which, in this fleet, wasn't quite a maxi, so there would be times when length was the determining factor, when she would lack the legs against the longer Farr boats. She was also heavier, and Blake now discussed this openly with his team: 'I have never said that publicly, but we've weighed the boat and I know the figures.' He added: 'But *Lion* has also been built and geared up to withstand the rigours of the Whitbread race. Barring something over which we have no control, she will be there at the finish, no matter what the elements and the major oceans of the world decide to deal to her. I suspect that some of our opponents will not.' There would, Blake told the crew, be times when *Lion* would need all the help they could give her, if she was to keep up. There would be times when they would be grateful for her pedigree and her integrity. She was the strongest boat in the race with the best crew. All he could ask was for everyone's best shot. For the rest of it, nature would take its course.

Drum got the best of the light airs start and was first out into the English Channel by a handy margin. By the time *Lion* reached the Needles at the western entrance to the Solent, she was hard on the stern of her New Zealand rival, the fractional Farr maxi *NZI Enterprise*.

154

There was a brief skirmish with *NZI* defending her position, but her spinnaker unclipped from the pole and *Lion* slid through her lee and set out after *Drum* and *Atlantic Privateer*. Blake noted in the log: 'The crew were still chuckling about the preliminaries to our little dice with *NZI*. As we moved in to within 100 metres of her port quarter, her supporters' boat camped right in front of us and fed us its propeller wash. We waved at them for several minutes, asking them to get out of the way, but they ignored us. I blew my cool and whipped down below to grab *Lion*'s Very pistol, a mean-looking 38-millimetre bore job. When the *NZI* supporter group saw me coming back on deck cocking the pistol and making my intentions absolutely clear, they got the message in a hurry and scooted clear. The pistol wasn't loaded, of course, but I must have been pretty convincing. The *Lion* guys thought I'd gone mad and promptly nicknamed me "Rambo".'

Blake celebrated his thirty-seventh birthday on 1 October by tacking *Lion* out to sea in a 25-knot southerly in the Bay of Biscay. He was heading for a frontal system coming in from the Atlantic that he thought looked promising. There were still only about eight miles separating the maxis and this was his first opportunity to try something 'smart'. At about 0400 hours he got the westerly change he was hoping for and tacked back on to starboard, laying course down the Atlantic with a nice windward advantage on his rivals. As it transpired, *UBS Switzerland* had done the same but held on to port longer to make an even greater gain on the fleet.

By 3 October *Atlantic Privateer* and *NZI Enterprise* were 60 miles astern, with *Drum* 25 miles behind. But there was lighter weather in the offing with the Canary Islands just ahead and the Doldrums beckoning. *Lion* was second both on the water and on corrected time – with *UBS* leading both categories. Morale on deck was high, evidenced by an entry on 7 October that read: '*Lion* barrelling along in 20-knot tailwinds and closing on *UBS*. The deck watch is trimming by animal noises. Two dog barks meant shooter sheet in, one bark

155

meant shooter sheet stop. A moo signalled shooter halyard up and a baa meant spinnaker sheet in. And so it went for hours, the boat cutting a real dash while the whole crew was in hysterics.'

The fleet chat show became terse as the windless belt approached. Much would depend on who got it right and who got it wrong. *Lion* had been holding her own downwind against the Farr boats and that was encouraging, but *UBS* still had a jump of 123 miles as *Lion* passed abeam of Dakar on the western extremity of the Bulge of Africa. *Atlantic Privateer* was cutting the corner, and was nearly abeam to the east and on a more direct course closer to the African coast. *Drum* was 75 miles astern of *Lion* and about 60 miles further inshore. *UBS* had gone inshore too, leaving *Lion* the most westerly boat in the fleet. The positioning for the Doldrums had started, and for the time being Blake was quite happy with the situation. *Lion* was matching her rivals for downwind speed and the upwind bash through the south-east trades was to come – once through the Doldrums.

After four days of constant sail changes to match the mood of the windless belt, the fleet plot showed six maxis spread out in a line across the ocean with not much difference in the distances they had to travel to Cape Town. Who had got it right? *Lion* was still furthest to the west, following a more traditional route to the Cape. *Atlantic Privateer* was furthest to the east, closer to the coast of Africa. The answer was that the east would pay. *Lion* struggled in patchy conditions while the boats closer to the coast enjoyed more consistent breeze. Blake noted: 'On the night of 23 October, after 25 days at sea, we ran into 12 hours of almost complete calm. The breeze had been switching crazily from the north-west to the south-east, and then it died almost completely. It was worse than the Doldrums, and I had an awful feeling that it was a private parking lot. The next day we listened gloomily to the radio to find that some of the other boats had done 100 miles more than us in the last 24 hours. *Atlantic Privateer* was now 120 miles closer to Cape Town, although still well to the east. While we were struggling to make 105 miles to the south, *Cote D'Or*, which was now heading due south down the Atlantic, had covered 200 miles. *Drum* had caught and passed us, and *UBS* had gained 35–40 miles on *Lion*. It was a really low blow. The only solace was that we'd sighted *NZI* on the 24th. She'd been 20 miles ahead according to the position reports on the 23rd, but we'd pulled him in all through the night until by dawn we had him in sight.'

On 26 October the log noted: 'There's a funny sea running now, big swell with chop running in opposite direction. Hard to steer. There is something going on ahead of us that is pushing up a big sea in our path.' Over the next 36 hours, the wind gained slowly in strength until, by late on the 28th, *Lion* had 30 knots across the deck and the sea was 'tatapatchish'. Blake tacked on to starboard and *Lion* was headed straight for Cape Town where, according to the radio, it was blowing 60 knots plus. The *Lion* crew now knew where the unusual sea conditions were coming from. They were out of all proportion to the wind strength and *Lion*, close-hauled and doing 8 knots under No. 5 jib and two reefs in the main, had already leapt out of two particularly big and backless waves to land with a crash on the other side. The weather maps showed that the South Atlantic High was much lower down and further east than usual and was piling up the isobars against the southern African continent near Cape Town. Gale-force southerlies were being spun off into the path of the maxis. These were blowing across the prevailing south-westerly ground swell from the Southern Ocean to produce an evil, steep sea for up to 1000 miles off the coast. This combination proved disastrous for the Whitbread leaders.

Drum, 600 miles from the finish, was the first to succumb. The continuous pounding on starboard tack proved too much for her construction and she began to delaminate through a lengthy strip of her for'ard port sections. She squared away downwind, reduced sail and headed for Lüderitz in Namibia, 480 miles up the coast from Cape

157

Town, to assess the full extent of the damage. *Cote D'Or* was next, reporting that she too was delaminating in the port sections forward of the mast, the area of the boat that was taking most of the punishment as she came out of the waves and landed in the troughs. Eric Tabarly had tacked on to port and headed almost due south while he took stock of his predicament. Meanwhile, *NZI Enterprise* had lost her main halyard and torn her mainsail but was continuing after her riggers had courageously spent a torturous time at the top of the mast reeving a new halyard so that the spare Kevlar main could be hoisted.

That night in Cape Town, race director Rear Admiral Charles Williams alerted the South African Navy and other race yachts in the vicinity that he had three maxis with problems, two of them serious. There was no relief. It was blowing so hard in Cape Town that people were having to use ropes to cross intersections in the downtown part of the city. The fleet at sea was now copping winds of greater strength and even more vicious seas.

Atlantic Privateer, just a day from the finish and with a big lead on her rivals, was the next to go, with Kuttel radioing in to report that part of his starboard rigging had failed and the mast had gone overboard. Like *Drum*, he was running with the now full gale and heading for Lüderitz. *NZI* struck more trouble soon afterwards. Her port cap shroud tore away from the mast and, unsupported, the top of the spar had kinked and was leaning over to port at an alarming angle. This left just two – *UBS* and *Lion* – still racing, and *UBS* had her problems. She was down to trisail and small jib, Fehlmann nursing his boat through the seas. He couldn't reef his mainsail deeply enough to get rid of sufficient area in the blow so he'd taken it down. Now he faced the problem of getting it up again if the wind eased. Not an easy task in the seas that were running.

Lion was down to No. 5 jib and three reefs in the main, still going strong. Her crew had nicknamed her 'The Urban Wave Destroyer' because she just kept on charging in seas so steep it seemed she must

158

slide back down the face of them. Yet apart from some very heavy landings when she jumped out of backless waves, the only serious concern aboard was on the weather rail where the smokers in the crew were in dire straits. Desperately low on matches, they resorted to keeping one cigarette alight 24 hours a day – not an easy task the way *Lion* was chucking the water about.

Blake wrote: 'We pounded on into what should have been our last night at sea on this leg, and a wonderfully wild and moonlit night it was. I was enjoying a spell on the wheel when the Doc pointed to the mainsail. He could see the moon through the cloth. Before we could do anything, the sail split right across. We sounded the emergency alarm to summon all hands for a mainsail change. By this stage the flogging and torn mainsail had really given up the ghost, tearing right up the seam between the Dacron cloth and the Kevlar. With a great deal of care, because *Lion* was still doing 8 knots through 25-foot breaking seas, we lowered the main boom to the deck and rolled the now-ruined sail into a manageable unit. There was nothing else to do but dump it over the side once we'd salvaged the battens and any fittings that would be useful again. It wasn't an easy decision. A replacement would cost $30,000. But the sailmakers were adamant that the Kevlar had had it and the sail was irreparable. So we cut it from the boom and eased it overboard. Within 70 minutes of the Doc noticing the start of our problem, we were pedal to the metal again with the replacement Dacron main triple-reefed and *Lion* back up to 9 knots.'

The gale abated a lot faster than it had developed, leaving *Lion* to struggle the remaining miles into Table Bay amid light and variable winds and frustrating patches of calm. She finally crossed the finish line at 0706 hours local time on 2 November – 34 days, 17 hours, 46 minutes after leaving Portsmouth and second to finish. *UBS* had beaten her by 16 hours, 7 minutes.

'The Royal Naval Sailing Association would have had much food for thought as the fleet struggled in,' wrote Blake. 'The Whitbread dock, near the Royal Cape Yacht Club, resembled the pit area after a stockcar demolition derby. One maxi, *Atlantic Privateer*, had been dismasted. Another had a bend in its mast that was severe enough to render the rig useless. Two others were in need of major construcstional repair after being in danger of breaking up. That represented a casualty rate of 60 per cent among the maxis, and there were serious doubts whether three of the big boats could continue the race. The smaller yachts had not encountered conditions anything like those which had decimated the big guns, but there was no reason to believe that they would have escaped a similarly alarming damage list if they had. Yet the truth of the matter was that a well-found Round the World race fleet should have taken the four-day gale in its stride. Sure, it had been nasty and some of the seas were amongst the worst one would like to encounter. But it wasn't severe enough to wreak the havoc that it did among boats which had supposedly been purposebuilt to handle such weather conditions.'

Not surprisingly, there were no jibes about Lion being 'off the pace' or 'too heavy' and Blake was left to wonder what the outcome would have been had the gale lasted another day.

The difference in weather patterns as a consequence of being later into the Southern Ocean than in previous races was revealed early on in leg two. The systems gave no clear indication as to the way to go and the tactics of the various boats reflected this, with some going south early while others held to a more northerly route. Blake played the middle in the early stages, and paid for it. *UBS* and *Atlantic Privateer* headed south and were quickly 50 miles ahead of *Lion*. *Cote D'Or*, to the north, made a similar break. Blake cut his losses and headed south, planning to go down to 55 degrees before levelling off and playing the weather systems at that latitude. The price to be paid was significantly colder temperatures – water down to 2.3 degrees Celsius and the air no warmer. It started to snow on 12 December and *L'Esprit D'Equipe*, quite some way to the north of *Lion*, reported sighting a 300-metre-long iceberg.

By late on 14 December, *Lion* was at 53 degrees 36 minutes South, and it looked like Blake's decision was going to pay handsome dividends. *Lion* was 'honking' under her chicken chute (heavy, flat-cut running spinnaker) in 30 knots of wind. Blake had a spell on the wheel and got a burst of 21.6 knots (*Lion*'s best yet) in long, easy seas that were ideal for surfing. The opposition was reeled in with only *Atlantic Privateer* matching *Lion*'s pace. By 17 December, with 3900 miles to go to Auckland, *Lion* was furthest south in the fleet with air and water temperatures hovering around zero. She was travelling less distance, being the furthest south, but around her the situation was changing, and over the next four or five days her position began to become a negative. *NZI*, *Atlantic Privateer*, *UBS* and *Drum* all found more consistent winds and drove straight over the top of *Lion*'s track. The boats astern were reporting little or no wind in the middle of a slow-moving low that was coming through. Blake started to head north-east to escape but the move came too late. The Farr boats, with *Drum* just managing to hang on to their coat-tails, were spinnaker reaching at high speed while *Lion* was still two-sail reaching in a different breeze.

Atlantic Privateer and *NZI Enterprise* led the fleet around the northern capes and on to the north-east coast of New Zealand. *Lion* was around 180 miles astern and Blake could only listen with envy as Peter Montgomery, on Radio New Zealand, described an emotion-charged, incredibly close finish between the two big Farr boats – *Atlantic Privateer* snuck across the Orakei finish line just 7 minutes, 20 seconds ahead of *NZI* after 7010 miles of racing through the Southern Ocean. *UBS* followed them in, 1 hour, 54 minutes later, with another nine hours back to *Drum*. Blake and *Lion* had to make do with a distant fifth but were still greeted by a packed waterfront and crowded Princes Wharf.

'We were stunned,' said Blake. 'The welcome was so over-whelming and spontaneous, making us awfully proud to be New Zealanders.'

There were more than 7000 boats on the water and an estimated 300,000 people lining the shoreline as New Zealand's Prime Minister David Lange fired the start gun for leg three to Punta del Este in Uruguay. The 6215-mile leg around Cape Horn was to again show the Southern Ocean in a different mood and once more favour the swift downwind Farr machines.

Hard on the wind in a shifty breeze all the way out to the Colville Channel, *Lion* was second only to *Cote D'Or*. The fleet then reached across the Bay of Plenty in almost perfect sailing conditions – if you were on a Farr boat that is. *UBS* caught and passed *Lion*. *NZI* had already eased through her lee, and even *Drum*, now with Simon Le Bon aboard for the last two legs, had slipped by. In these conditions, Lion was paying dearly for her weight and lack of sailing length. Blake determined that he had to virtually ignore his rivals and sail his own course to the Horn – not something the ocean-racing textbooks would recommend – conceding that 'the truth of the matter is that the Farr boats, and maybe *Cote D'Or*, are quicker than Lion reaching, so it is no use following them. We don't want to be taking any radical fliers, but we need to do something different if we are to steal a march on them. Right now they seem to be heading south at more of an angle than we are. I can't see any reason for that on the weather maps, so am quite happy to let them go.'

To lighten ship, Blake had left most of *Lion*'s spare sails behind in Auckland – it was a gamble that might cost him if his main wardrobe didn't hang together. He comforted himself with the knowledge that he had a good sailmaking team on board and the boat seemed to be going quite a bit faster without the extra weight.

Less than three days out from the restart, *NZI*'s mast collapsed when a diagonal supporting rod broke. She headed for the Chatham Islands, out of the race. The rest of the fleet eased on down into a surprisingly docile Southern Ocean with Blake using all of his considerable knowledge and skill to keep *Lion* in touch with her rivals. In predominantly fresh reaching conditions, however, the remaining Farr boats, *UBS* and *Atlantic Privateer*, along with *Cote D'Or*, utilised their length and speed to pull slowly away, leaving *Lion* to vainly try and make a race of it with *Drum*.

Lion was becalmed 40 miles to the west of Cape Horn early on 5 March but finally had the Cabo close abeam at 1025 hours. The good news was that while she had been becalmed, *Atlantic Privateer* and *Drum* had experienced similar problems in the Straits de Le Maire, between the south-eastern tip of Tierra del Fuego and Staten Island. First to round the Horn, *UBS* had taken off up the eastern coast of Argentina with a beautiful reaching breeze.

With perhaps an eye on the future, Blake wrote in his log: 'There was little snow to be seen as we worked our way north-eastwards from the Cape along the coast of Tierra del Fuego, even though some of the closer mountains were between 3000 and 4000 feet and others further away were at least 8000 feet. But it was still a coastline of intrigue, the islands and bays looking most enticing, and I would love to go back there one day, with more time, and take a good look around.' For now, though, he had the Straits de Le Maire to contend with and they needed all of his attention. *Lion* was hard on the wind, doing 9 knots, with 4 to 5 knots of tide running under her. So she was tearing along at 14-odd knots over the ground less than 400 metres from a lee shore which Blake and his crew could not see because it was too dark. 'It was rough,' said Blake, 'with *Lion* crashing through big, steep, phosphorescent waves in what seemed a total blackout. But we were going like a rocket and things would have been a lot worse if that current had been against us. We put a lot of time on *Drum* but I heaved a big sigh of relief once we were through.'

Still hard on the wind to the west of the Falkland Islands, with 26 knots of breeze and a nasty short, steep sea, *Lion* was 93 miles behind *Drum*, 110 miles behind *Atlantic Privateer*, 160 miles behind *Cote D'Or* and 277 miles behind *UBS*. The on-deck crew were spending a lot of time on the weather rail with all of this windward work but they had a bonus attraction to keep them sane. Halley's Comet was perfectly visible when the frontal cloud cleared. To celebrate, 'special' drinks were ordered from the galley and it was amazing just who had a small bottle of something stashed away in his bunk for a nip on a cold night.

Lion crossed the line in Punta del Este 1 day, 8 hours behind the leader *UBS*. *Drum*, which had done an impressive job in the tactically testing leg up the Argentinian coast, was second, 9 hours, 19 minutes later, followed by *Atlantic Privateer* and *Cote D'Or*. *Lion* was now 2 days, 14 hours behind *UBS* so, mishaps apart, the race for line honours around the world was all but run. But *Lion* still had 18 hours, 7 minutes up her sleeve on *Drum* with just one leg of the race to go.

Looking back on the Southern Ocean, Blake wrote: 'It was plainly evident that altering the start time of the Whitbread had changed the character of the race, and the feeling of having been cheated was only heightened by leg three. We'd had a maximum of three days of the hard downwind running for which the race had become famous. If we hadn't sighted icebergs and seen Cape Horn in daylight, it would have been difficult to believe that we had been in the Southern Ocean at all. My crew was asking: "Who wrote the brochure?", and they weren't the only ones complaining. Padda Kuttel, bemoaning the fact that *Atlantic Privateer* had had to beat for eight days to reach the Horn from down south, when the chances of a north-easterly in those waters at that time of the year were only one per cent, commented: "The race is being held at the wrong time. It is too late in the year – the winds are too light and too fickle. The Whitbread should be about heavy weather running, and lots of it." *UBS Switzerland* hadn't broken anything, not even a halyard, and Pierre Fehlmann confessed that their hardest sailing had been between the Straits de Le Maire and the finish in Punta del Este and that had been tactically hard as opposed to physically demanding.'

In the first few days of the leg to the Portsmouth finish, Blake noted down two of *Lion*'s log entries that were to prove highly interesting when considered some years further down the track. The first recorded the fact that *Lion* had hit another whale: 'Only a slight bump this time. It has been quite noticeable that there are a lot more Jonahs this trip, so maybe the conservationists are winning their fight to save these giants of the oceans. Not that *Lion* is doing her bit on their behalf. The log records: "*Lion* NZ (three whales, two sunfish) five, Whales and Sunfish (one rudder) one". Someone suggested that we should stick little transfers on the bow as the fighter pilots in World War II did to record their "kills". But somebody else observed that maybe there were a couple of whales swimming around with *Lion* transfers on their heads.' The second entry noted that Grant Dalton had won the 'Dick of the Day' award. When Kevin Shoebridge remarked that Dalton looked a lot like *Kialoa* owner-skipper Jim Kilroy, Dalton had retorted: 'Yeah, you're looking at a legend in the making.'

Lion and *Drum* paced one another through the Doldrums and up the North Atlantic, consumed by their own private duel, and the wind continued to be fickle, both in strength and direction. After one more calm patch, the *Lion* log reflected on this situation: 'Hughie (the New Zealand yachtsman's wind god) is a malicious, cantankerous, conniving, cunning, malevolent bastard – but he certainly is a funny sod.'

After passing the Azores, *UBS Switzerland* was sailing her own race, well out in front, but *Drum*, *Lion*, *Cote D'Or* and *Atlantic Privateer* formed a line across the ocean at right-angles to the course to the English Channel. *Drum* was to the north-west, then *Lion*, then *Cote D'Or* to the south-east of her, and then *Atlantic Privateer* coming back into contention after taking a real punt to the east. It was going to be a sprint to the finish for the minor places.

Drum found a better slant of breeze to the north of *Lion* and it looked as though that might prove decisive. But the breeze went south-west and increased to 25 to 30 knots, enabling *Lion* to roar through the Western Approaches and into the English Channel at almost optimum speed. *Drum* crossed the line 5 hours, 44 minutes ahead of *Lion* but on overall elapsed time, *Lion was* 12 hours, 22 minutes faster around the world. Only *UBS Switzerland* was quicker.

Blake's final log entry reflected: 'Second fastest around the world – on this occasion, no mean effort. I have no doubt that I had the best crew in the race. I am only sad that the boat we sailed wasn't quite as highly capable. Deep down, and as a group, we had accepted this a long time before. We had our suspicions during the pre-race build-up in Britain. Those suspicions were confirmed in leg two when we found that there was nothing we could do to keep *Lion* up with the Farr boats when they took off downwind in the fresher stuff. But *Lion* was the boat we had and *Lion* was the boat we would sail to the maximum. We pushed her as hard as possible to see if the rest could sustain the same sort of pressure. The outcome might have been different had the conditions been more Whitbread-normal, but they weren't – and that, as they say, is yacht racing.'

Blake also pondered what might have been, and he couldn't help feeling 'a little disappointed' with the Ron Holland design office, even though the ultimate responsibility for *Lion New Zealand* was his. He'd gone to Holland for the pre-eminent Whitbread maxi, a boat that would be as light as the Farrs but a lot stiffer with a lot more sail. *Lion* wasn't that boat, even though the Holland office had assured him that they could achieve the design features and figures specified. Having said that, however, *Lion* was a lot more competitive in the final leg when more gear had been removed to make her lighter, and a new mainsail, built by Tom Dodson and his team at the North Sails loft in Auckland, had been added to the sail inventory. That mainsail made a significant difference to a lightened *Lion's* performance.

Of *Lion's* heaviness, Blake later wrote: 'Instead of being 31 tons actual weight, *Lion* was close to 38 tons. The keel was about right (in weight) and so was the rig, so nearly all of that extra weight was in the hull, deck, the internal stiffening bulkheads and space frame and fittings – which meant that the hull and deck were approximately 50 to 60 per cent overweight. The result was a yacht which, all-up, was 20 per cent heavier than what we were seeking, with a righting moment which was the lowest of the maxis, when we had set out to achieve the highest. To cap it all, the rating came in at 67.4 feet IOR instead of the maximum 70 feet IOR. We were handing the opposition performance and handling advantages even before we started, and all we had to offset this was a boat which, we were understandably sure, wouldn't break.'

Typically, Blake added to his observations: 'Still, *Lion* was potentially a good yacht, as she proved in the last leg going up the Atlantic, and there were times, particularly in the blow going to Cape Town, when we were thankful for her constructional integrity. In some ways she was the right boat for the wrong race. Or maybe it was the wrong race for the right boat. Whatever the case, crew and boat had given it their best shot and, in the process, had been tremendous ambassadors for New Zealand. On this occasion, second fastest around the world had to be good enough. But next time . . .'

CHAPTER Seven

The Trilogy

While Blake was putting a positive spin on *Lion's* Whitbread performance, and whereas second fastest around the world would have made creditable reading in the curriculum vitae of most skippers, in the Peter Blake CV it would always be a paradox. It never quite fitted.

Simon Gundry, who did the first two legs of the 1985–86 race on *Lion* before family reasons forced him to quit, summarises the campaign with typical Kiwi yachtie candour: 'Blakey didn't make many cock-ups, but *Lion* was one of them. What Peter should have done is told Farr, "Give us an *Atlantic Privateer*, give us a big, fast Farr boat and I'll have the crew to make it a winner." But Tom (Clark) stepped in and said "Bugger it".'

Grant Dalton, who was a watch captain on *Lion* for the whole journey, is just as candid: '*Lion* was a pig. I think I've heard all the reasons why Pete went to Holland instead of Farr, and it wasn't as wild a call as it would be, say, if you did it today, but there is no denying that it was a cock-up – almost like a page in the book that doesn't fit. You want to tear it out. Having said that, look what came out of it. The crew that Peter put together to race *Lion* became the backbone of New Zealand yachting and remains so even today. That campaign was the basis for a lot of relationships that exist to this day.

'Building on his *Ceramco* crew, he created a family of yachtsmen who became the heart of New Zealand sailing. There are certain other groups that have developed outside of that family, but it is still the heart and has taken New Zealand yachting through a wonderful 20-odd years. There are no obvious reasons why it worked so well when it could have blown to pieces. There was nothing obvious that Peter did to hold it all together. But it was a magical mix and an absolute credit to him. We were all quite young, all on an adventure, and he was the glue that made it all work.'

Blake had shown with the *Ceramco* campaign that he had his own very definite ideas on what was required in a crew for a long campaign. He put a lot of emphasis on character, temperament and compatibility – often ahead of skill and experience. He had a definite ability to bring out the best in people and he was very strong on accountability and loyalty. The *Lion* campaign only enhanced his reputation for having 'a good eye for horseflesh'.

People like Gundry were also noticing changes in the Blake style of running his campaigns and managing his people. On *Ceramco* he had tried to do everything himself – the classic mistake made by just about every young skipper in total charge for the first time. Gundry recalls that only Blake took *Ceramco* off the dock or put her back on it, even though there were several others in the crew who were more than capable of doing so. With *Lion*, though, he had begun to delegate responsibility a lot more, as Gundry experienced at first hand: 'I guess you can understand it. *Ceramco* was his baby, from concept to fruition, and he was the only one, at the time, who had done a Whitbread race. We were new and young and he was conservative. The *Lion* group was much bigger and the campaign more complex, but Pete was also growing up, if you like, in terms of running major campaigns. He worked out that you couldn't do everything yourself so he began to give more responsibility to others, and it was very interesting to see how people responded. He gave us all self-belief. I don't know

172

how he did that. I would be making up words if I tried. But he did.'

That Blake's people had something special quickly became evident in New Zealand's first campaign for the America's Cup, in Fremantle in 1986–87. Eight of the *Lion* crew went straight from Portsmouth to Fremantle to join the already established New Zealand camp. Five of those – Mike Quilter, Kevin Shoebridge, Tony Rae, Andrew Taylor and Ed Danby – established themselves as prized hands on the race boat *KZ7* (*Kiwi Magic*). A sixth – Grant Dalton – missed the cut but considerably enhanced his reputation through the way he undertook the somewhat unrecognised role of captain of the back-up boat. That *KZ7* campaign, headed by (now Sir) Michael Fay came closer than most people realise to winning yachting's biggest prize first time up, and the extra maturity, experience and commitment that the Blake people added to the campaign played no small part in that extraordinary effort.

Blake, meanwhile, had returned to his home in Emsworth where he began fine-tuning his thoughts for the future. 'He never was one to just let things lie,' says Pippa Blake, 'and it was obvious that he wasn't going to retire from yachting. There was still a lot more that he wanted to do in sailing. He always asked for my view first and I always said yes.' A large percentage of that 'lot more' was embodied in Blake's next project (or parcel of projects) which was bold even by his adventurous standards. Another Whitbread was almost inevitable in his thought processes. The race was still 'unfinished business' and, despite his trials and tribulations with *Lion*, with four Whitbreads on his CV, he was one of the most experienced blue-water ocean racers in the world. Plus, while he had tasted certain successes in the race, he still hadn't knocked the bastard off. At the back of his mind for some time, however, had been a different race around the world – non-stop in a vessel unencumbered by rule considerations, that would be as fast as state-of-the-art design and construction, plus his own experience and intuition, could make it.

In the depths of the English winter of 1986–87, he decided to link the two together and see whether he could find a sponsor to match his vision. For good measure, and probably to expand his own knowledge of multihulls (an obvious option for maximum speed potential around the world), he tacked on the front end a trimaran entry in the upcoming Two-man Round Australia race that was being organised as part of the celebrations of the bicentenary of the 'Great Arid Land'. It was an audacious plan, particularly for the mid-1980s, but Blake made up his mind that it was do-able and that support from the commercial sector was achievable.

Before he could get stuck into finding the sponsorship needed, he became a father for the second time – Pippa giving birth to James John Blake in St Mary's Hospital, Portsmouth, on 31 December 1986. Young James was welcomed with the same all-consuming enthusiasm as Sarah-Jane Blake had been in May 1983, according to his mother: 'Peter was over the moon about his daughter, and when James came along it was just the same. Peter always made sure that the children had the team clothing and that we were always considered a part of whatever he might be doing. We were both very pleased that we had a daughter and now a son, and decided that we would stick at having just the two children. He was always thrilled to have both children on a boat with him.'

Blake did not have to look far to find the project backing he was seeking. Lion Breweries, oblivious to *Lion New Zealand*'s weight problems, was more than satisfied with its exposure from the 1985–86 Whitbread, and managing director Douglas Myers was even more impressed by the lengths to which Blake had gone to ensure that his sponsor got the required return on investment. Blake's proposed trilogy of blue-water events would become 'The Steinlager Challenge', with Myers convinced that success against 'the outside world' represented a way to help curb what he termed New Zealand's divisiveness, and to encourage New Zealanders to measure themselves against world

174

standards: 'It became much more a nationalistic thing for me. I felt it was good for the company to be involved, and on a basis probably not as commercial as one would be today. It seemed like a positive for big companies to try and break this negativity in New Zealand by being involved with success on the international stage.'

In retrospect, Myers is unsure that such involvements made the difference he was hoping for: 'It didn't, of itself, totally change things. But it did engender some success. It gave a lot of people a lot of pleasure and some time in the future, maybe, people will look back and say that for a while there we did do things differently. Through big companies getting involved we did, after all, win the Whitbread and then the America's Cup. We were competitive on a world stage.' While Lion Breweries also had ambitions in Australia, which made the Round Australia race proposal attractive, Myers admits he was personally backing Peter Blake: 'When he came to me with this idea of three events – that's when I probably started to view him as an adventurer on a world basis, and not just a yachtie. It all sounded good stuff, but it was more just supporting him really, because in the *Lion New Zealand* campaign he had bent over backwards to be very supportive of us and was doing great things.'

Blake's approach to Myers could not have been better timed. Lion Breweries had just merged with another New Zealand liquor industry 'heavy' L. D. Nathan and the whole basis of the company had changed, along with the board. Myers had made up his mind that total reliance on commercial activity in New Zealand was a cul de sac. The focus had to be on the outside world. As a result, Lion was negotiating to take over the Alan Bond brewing empire in Australia. All of this paved the way for an external focus in sponsorship, backing sports at which New Zealand could succeed internationally. Increasingly, this meant yachting and/or rugby.

For Myers, the logic of this approach was supplied by the Harvard Business School which had had a team in New Zealand examining

175

its ability to compete internationally. Their conclusion was that the only areas in which New Zealand enjoyed a potential competitive advantage were in yachting and rugby. While making a business case for rugby was problematic, it was not so for yachting with its support industry. The proposition wasn't new to Myers but it was confirmed in a more coherent manner. If you wanted to be involved with external success, yachting and rugby were the vehicles. From there on, Lion Breweries increased its involvement with yachting, principally through Blake projects, and with the All Blacks. Together with similar initiatives by the Fay Richwhite merchant bank and the whiteware manufacturer Fisher & Paykel, along with some less obvious players, this backing provided the support that was to underpin the development of a viable boat-building industry in New Zealand. With his later achievements, and with further support from Lion Breweries and a second wave of the more visionary companies, Blake would play a leading role in helping to facilitate further significant development of that industry into a major export earner.

By the time he did his first Whitbread race, with Blake on *Lion New Zealand*, the 31-year-old Mike Quilter had already done two Admiral's Cups in England, three Pan Am Clipper Cups in Hawaii, and two Southern Cross Cups in Australia. He had also been on the sailmaking team for *Australia II*'s historic America's Cup win in Newport (Rhode Island) in 1983. He had raced in the same New Zealand team as Blake – on Neville Crichton's *Shockwave* in the 1983 Admiral's Cup.

Quilter applied to join the *Lion New Zealand* crew 'only because you couldn't shut the *Ceramco* guys up. Every time you went to a party they would always be telling *Ceramco* stories, they would never stop talking about *Ceramco*. I decided that anything that had that much effect on their lives must be a good thing to do. So I went to see Blakey.' That was the beginning of a relationship which saw Quilter – or 'Lowlife' as he is known internationally – become Blake's most trusted man on a boat. He quickly became a watch captain on *Lion*, crewed with Blake on *Steinlager 1* in the Two-man Round Australia race, was navigator on *Steinlager 2* in the 1989–90 Whitbread race, and later became a key man in the weather programmes for the Blake-led America's Cup win in 1995 and successful defence in 2000. Speaking of this relationship, Quilter said: 'So I did the *Lion* race, and once you'd sailed with Pete – I don't know what it was – you'd always go around with him again. You'd never say no. He'd say, "Come on" and you would say, "Yep I'm off, I'm with you". And you knew he'd be completely loyal, just as his crews were always very loyal to him. Still are.'

Quilter was one of the eight crew who stepped off *Lion New Zealand* at the finish in Portsmouth and flew direct to Fremantle to join New Zealand's America's Cup team. Not long after he arrived in the New Zealand camp, he volunteered to be a navigator: 'I became a navigator in Fremantle mainly because there weren't any navigators in those days. That was at the start of computers on boats – we had a big desktop computer and screen down below loaded with navigational and tactical programs. Terrible stuff by today's standards, but it worked really well. Nobody else was interested in it so I put up my hand. Then Blakey comes over for a visit. He walks up, pulls out this rough drawing of a trimaran (which was to become *Steinlager 1*) and says, "What about doing this Round Australia race with me?" Then, "OK, you can also navigate around the world (on *Steinlager 2*)." Apparently, if you can find your way around a three-mile track in an America's Cup boat, all of a sudden that qualifies you to navigate around the world for some reason.'

Blake clearly didn't just happen to drop in to Fremantle. He had the green light from Douglas Myers, his trilogy of campaigns was go, and he was recruiting the best talent available. The casualness of his approach was a typically understated reflection of his respect for Quilter, as a navigator as well as a top yachtsman. Before he left

177

Australian shores, he had the commitment to the Steinlager Challenge of a small but elite group of New Zealand sailors, most of whom were his 'people' anyway.

During the 1985–86 Whitbread, the *Lion* crew formed an alliance they called 'The Whitbread Lifeline', a pact among the crew that, if anyone felt tempted to do the next Whitbread in four years' time, he could ring up his mates and they would dissuade him with tales of cold, wet, windy nights in the Southern Ocean. Obviously the phone lines were down when Blake made his Fremantle house call.

For the 1989 Two-man Round Australia race, Blake had decided on a 60-foot trimaran designed by his *Burton Cutter* and *Condor* friend David Alan-Williams. Alan-Williams had taken a course in yacht design at Southampton University at the end of the 1977–78 Whitbread race, and although not yet well known globally, he had a growing reputation in Britain. Most importantly, he was experienced with multihulls and had Blake's respect.

Alan-Williams produced for Blake a futuristic tri, 60 feet long and 52 feet wide, with a huge wing mast. To be built entirely of carbon fibre and Kevlar, pre-impregnated with the correct amounts of resin, she was extremely radical for New Zealand at the time. She would be light and fast, but also strong if she was to withstand 7000 miles of racing around the biggest island in the world. Quilter recalls: '*Steinlager 1* was a completely different sort of trimaran and, remember, multihulls didn't have a very good reputation in those days, particularly down this end of the world. But Pete was always a bit ahead of his time. In fact, he wasn't a bit ahead of his time, he was miles ahead of his time to build a 60-foot tri like that in New Zealand. There was nothing like it in Australasia.'

While *Steinlager 1* was building, *Steinlager 2* was in the planning stages. While *Steinlager 1* was racing, *Steinlager 2* would be building.

178

It was a management and logistical challenge of some magnitude and complexity, and Blake used it to demonstrate that he had come a long way in both departments. It was almost as though everything that had gone before was simply a learning experience. He hand-picked his people with care, gave them autonomy in their various areas of expertise, and turned them loose on the two projects while he adopted the role of CEO and got on with matters strategic and financial, as well as provided that unique, but difficult to define, Blake glue that bonded everyone and everything into one powerful entity.

Blake also showed that he could take his lumps, for he had no hesitation in returning to the Farr office for the design of *Steinlager 2*. There would be no issues over exclusivity on this occasion. The much sought-after Farr office had organised to cater for the demands on its services by initiating a research and development programme to which the four customers seeking its designs would subscribe on an equal basis. At a specific point in that research programme, those doing the commissioning would enter into confidential discussion with the Farr office and customise the R&D findings to their own interpretations of what it would take to win.

The Whitbread course, meanwhile, had undergone changes required by the political situation surrounding South Africa and to cater for the addition of extra ports of call. The traditional 'sailing ship route' around the world, with stops in Cape Town, Auckland and South America, had been replaced by a course that would be Southampton (England) to Punta del Este (Uruguay), to Fremantle (Western Australia), to Auckland (New Zealand), to Punta del Este, to Fort Lauderdale (USA), to Southampton. The new course would require a downwind-oriented yacht as, in particular, the close-hauled bash from the Doldrums to Cape Town had been eliminated. In effect, the skippers for the 1989–90 Whitbread were going to their designers with a clean sheet of paper and much would depend on their own interpretations of what the new course would mean in terms of performance.

At the appropriate time, Blake set out for Annapolis, on the eastern seaboard of the United States, where the Farr organisation was based. With him he took his right-hand man Quilter, who recalls: 'Conceptually, we wanted a long boat, the longest boat we could possibly get. We wanted the rudder as far aft as possible so that we could steer the thing in big waves in the Southern Ocean. We went there [to Annapolis] looking for a fractional sloop, because of the performance of *UBS Switzerland* in the previous race. But there was no big beat into Cape Town, it was a downwind race, and Blakey, keen to explore alternatives, asked about a ketch, even though there hadn't been a successful ketch in ocean racing since Jim Kilroy's *Kialoa III* in the mid-1970s. At that stage we didn't know that Dalts (Grant Dalton, who was mounting his own Whitbread campaign, backed by Fisher & Paykel), was looking at a ketch and Farr didn't mention any names either. He just said one other person had asked that question. Farr then pulled out this maxi ketch, ran it through the computer and, lo and behold, yes – it was faster around the world.'

Quilter was referring to the means by which designers assess designs and their potential. Using sophisticated programs, the parameters of a design are inputted into a computer which then generates what is called a Velocity Prediction Program (VPP) for that design. This is a computer prediction of how fast a design will sail in given sets of conditions, upwind and down. The next step is to computer-sail the VPP of that design through the course and predicted weather in which it is intended to race. In this way, various designs can be tested against the course and weather as well as against one another.

'We went through this process,' recollects Quilter, 'and arrived at a masthead ketch design that, in retrospect, looked very similar to *F&P*. Everybody seemed happy – except Blakey. Acting on another of his gut feelings, he was pushing Farr to investigate a ketch with a

180

fractional rig. Bruce resisted. He didn't think the idea had much merit and held out until a couple of hours before Pete and I were due to head to the airport. He finally consented to run the fractional ketch through the computer, probably just to get Blakey off his back, and a rocket ship emerged. All of a sudden the boat was getting longer and the masts were jumping up in height as Bruce raced to give us an answer before we had to leave. He penned the basis of the *Steinlager 2* design as we ran out the door.'

Blake's gut feel about a fractional ketch originated from the family's Woollacott design *Ladybird*. She was a fractional ketch and he favoured that configuration because it produced a bigger main and smaller headsails. You could let the mainsail traveller down further and so get the mizzen working in freer air. With a masthead rig, you've always got the traveller up further, and the mizzen doesn't work as well.

Mike Quilter witnessed the result of Blake's hunch: 'Bruce drew up essentially the same size hull as the masthead ketch we'd arrived at and just turned it into a fractional ketch. He put it through the VPP and it came out rating about 6 feet under the maximum. Then he started playing with the concept. He put the mainmast up a metre, the mizzen-mast up a metre and made the boat a metre longer. When he put it through his computer again, it was still about 3 feet under the maximum rating. So he made the boat another metre longer, and the masts another metre higher and tested that. As the boat got bigger and heavier it fell into the Mark IIIA element of the rule that was intended to help heavy boats be more competitive. The rating went down again. He was struggling to get the boat up to maximum rating, and we had a plane to catch, so he gave us a basic drawing of a boat that was 85 feet long, a huge boat with huge main and huge mizzen. We grabbed that piece of paper, raced out the door and headed back to New Zealand, excited that we had something special through a concept that, it was obvious, nobody else had pursued.'

Blake and Quilter had every right to be excited. Through Blake's gut-feel insistence, they had a boat that, once it had been fleshed out and maximised by the Farr team, was to create Whitbread history.

As it transpired, Grant Dalton was the Farr customer who had first asked for the ketch rig option – albeit masthead – to be explored. He readily admits that he did so almost by accident: 'I went there (to the Farr office) to talk fractional sloops and I just stumbled into ketches. I asked a simple question that was prompted by something I'd overheard at a barbecue in Annapolis just before I was due to meet with Farr. I was standing in the corner talking to someone when I overheard this guy from the Farr office mention the word "ketch". My radar went up immediately. I thought, "Something's going on here." When I met Bruce the next day, I popped the question, asked him, "What about a ketch?" That's how the whole ketch thing started for me. What Blakey was able to do was get Farr to run a fractional. To a point, this was luck, but he pushed them further than I did. And his boat just got bigger and bigger and bigger. Now that I know Bruce a lot better, he would have had a philosophical problem with the Mark IIIA thing and the role that more weight played. He likes light displacement. He is determined to win the America's Cup with a lighter displacement boat come hell or high water. With me, it was my first boat and I didn't understand anyway. So it would have been easier to mould me to his thinking than it would Blakey. I ended up with *Fisher & Paykel* which was probably as far as Bruce instinctively wanted to go.'

Back in Auckland, the enthusiasm of Blake and Quilter for their massive fractional ketch initially wasn't shared by the rest of the core Steinlager Challenge group. They were expecting to build a middle-of-the-road fractional sloop, a development of the highly successful

UBS Switzerland. Instead, they were presented with an 85-foot fractional ketch that would weigh in at around 35 tons. As they were taken through the VPP process, however, and saw for themselves the projected comparative performances of the various options, they were won over and, as a group, enthusiastically got stuck into ensuring that everything about their new yacht would be completely optimised for the job at hand.

The objective was a completely stripped-out racing machine with little consideration for creature comfort, and none whatsoever for resale value. The priorities were to keep the boat as light as possible, the bunks dry and comfortable, and the galley capable of producing hot food in any conditions. If the boat was fast, and the crew could sleep and eat well, the rest didn't matter. Deck openings were restricted to an absolute minimum, to keep water out of the interior when driving through the Southern Ocean, while a heater was considered but, for weight considerations, rejected. These were decisions that would later bear re-examination when the interior of *Steinlager 2* stifled in the tropics and froze in the sub-Antarctic. The Blake team was shaping a boat that was 'teased out' in every detail by people who had the background and experience to know exactly what was required, working for a skipper who had complete faith in their considerable abilities and expertise.

The trimaran project, while important in its own right, also turned out to be a fruitful test platform for systems and techniques that would later prove invaluable on *Steinlager 2*. The computerised navigational and performance programs, along with all the other electronic devices used in modern-day ocean racing, were a case in point. Invariably it takes a long time to debug the computer software and successfully interface all the various systems. In the Steinlager Challenge programme, all of this work was done on the exhaustingly fast *Steinlager 1* so that, when she hit the water, *Steinlager 2* was effectively a year ahead of her opposition getting these vital systems up and running. Yet despite all this attention to detail, not everything went exactly to plan.

While Brad Butterworth and Kevin Shoebridge remained in Auckland to keep a close eye on the construction of *Steinlager 2*, Blake and Quilter, with a support team comprising Tony Rae, Godfrey Cray and Ross Field, together with David Alan-Williams, headed for Sydney for the start of the Two-man Round Australia race. Blake and Quilter would race *Steinlager 1*. The support team would pace them around the Australian coast in a couple of four-wheel drive vehicles packed with spares and stores. Then, just three days before the start, Blake had to scurry back to Auckland. Butterworth and Shoebridge had notified him that there had been a fatal delamination problem in the construction of *Steinlager 2*'s hull. It was a complete write-off, as were the moulds on which it had been built. These had been demolished as they were extracted from the new hull. It was a catastrophe that threatened the whole Whitbread aspect of the Steinlager Challenge.

Blake called a hasty meeting with the chairman of the Steinlager Challenge trust, John Lusk, and the managing director of Lion Breweries, Ron Endley. The building process would have to begin again. There was (barely) the time, but was there the money (the hull failure cost an estimated $NZ1 million)? Endley didn't hesitate – start again. It was a decision that received the full support of Lion chairman Douglas Myers: 'Peter came to see me at my Victoria Avenue home. Over dinner, he said that there had been a million-dollar meltdown. I think he was expecting the worst, that it was maybe the end. I told him, "No, build a new one." These things sometimes happen and if you are going to back someone you've got to back them. My confidence in Peter by this stage was absolute.'

Tim Gurr and his boat-building team started straight away on the task of cutting up the ruined hull and building new moulds. It was heartbreaking work, but they would perform brilliantly and produce a new hull and deck for *Steinlager 2* in just 17 weeks. Blake, meanwhile,

184

flew back to Sydney, able to concentrate on *Steinlager 1*, which pretty soon would require all his attention.

Turning north from Sydney Heads after the 8 August start of the Two-man Round Australia race, *Steinlager 1* found herself battling severe conditions with a 55-knot southerly, against the southerly set of the current, whipping up big seas. 'We twice nearly lost her,' reported Blake. 'We weren't all that sure what she could take and, while getting sail down, we landed sideways on top of a big sea with both starboard float and main hull out of the water at an angle of about 30 degrees. For a moment we hung there not knowing if she would capsize or flop back into the water again. Fortunately she came down the right way up.'

'The first night was pretty horrendous,' remembers Quilter, 'but I was there with the right man. It was blowing very fresh from the south and we were running up the coast against the current. The seas were huge and we took some big hits. That's the only time in my life that I've chundered through nervousness. I wasn't nervous that I was going to die or anything, but nervous that we might flip the boat, or drop the rig and not win the race, nervous that we might stuff up this beautiful boat on the first night at sea.' Reflecting on the experience, Quilter says: 'In hindsight, I don't think we nearly flipped. You don't know how close you are to flipping until you actually flip. It was, though, a pretty tense experience. If I'd been by myself I would have been bloody apprehensive. But Pete was such a big rooster, so calm and so strong. There was a guy washed overboard and lost the first night, then, later on, one trimaran got flipped and two monohulls sank on the way around – one up north and one near Melbourne, completely lost – it was a tough old race.'

The 7000-mile course took the fleet counterclockwise around the Australian coast with stops at Mooloolaba and Cairns (in Queensland), Darwin (in Northern Territory), Fremantle (in Western Australia), Adelaide (in South Australia), Hobart (in Tasmania), and Southport (in Victoria) to finish in Sydney. In reality, the rest of the Round Australia fleet was no match for the state-of-the-art *Steinlager*. Blake recalled: 'We sailed this fantastic machine at speeds of up to 33 knots, adrenalin-pumping, knife-edge sailing at its best.'

The true opposition was the elements while the real challenge was to successfully race the big trimaran counterclockwise around Australia in a wide variety of conditions, which Quilter described: 'It was a good race with a bit of everything – beautiful sailing through the Great Barrier Reef, around the top of Australia through the calms and the heat of the Gulf of Carpentaria and the Timor Sea, then down that desolate coast of Western Australia. Once around Cape Leeuwin, we had these big black fronts coming through. And it blew 60 knots for days on end across the Great Australian Bight and around the bottom of Tasmania. Then it was up the east coasts of Tasmania and New South Wales to the finish in Sydney. We were the only boat to come through all of that unscathed and undamaged.'

Steinlager's wing mast, while a problem when the boat was at anchor or tied up to the dock (the vessel wanted to sail away), proved a real success at sea. In the open ocean, *Steinlager 1* would sail more than adequately under wing mast only. If the weather got too willing, the mast could be stalled or rotated as the squalls went through. In fact, *Steinlager 1* made her departure from Hobart under wing mast only. It continued to blow so hard that she sailed all the way up the eastern coast of Tasmania and halfway across Bass Strait to Southport under wing mast alone.

The motion of the boat, however, was so violent that Blake and Quilter built a bunk under the cockpit that was suspended from the underside of the deck rather than attached to the hull. They acquired pillows from stopover hotels to jam themselves in the berth and rigged a line which the off-watch crew would tie to their big toe. If the man on deck needed help, he would yank on the line. Quilter recalls: 'We were going around Cape Leeuwin and knew that there was a front coming. I was on deck while Blakey was asleep. I saw this huge black front roaring up behind, so I yanked the string. Blakey stuck his head out the hatch and I said, "Here comes the front." He said, "Yep, that's it", closed the hatch and went back to bed, leaving me to it. I thought, "Bloody hell, I'd hoped for a bit of a hand up here."

'He knew when to do that though,' grants Quilter. 'I remember, on *Lion*, the first night it blew. We were going down the Atlantic and the wind built to 30 knots. *Lion* was quite a handful in that stuff. I was the watch captain but I'd never sailed a maxi in that sort of breeze before. It was pretty hairy so I decided that I had better get Blakey on deck. I went down below and woke him, saying, "It's pretty willing outside." He said, "Oh, good", rolled over and went back to sleep again. I was a bit put out at the time but when I thought about it later I realised he was testing me. If he had come up and taken over, I would never have assumed the responsibility that went with my job on board. Everything worked out fine and I passed his little test. It was the same sort of thing on *Steinlager 1* going around Cape Leeuwin.'

If there was a plus side to the delamination of the first *Steinlager 2* hull, it was that the second hull was better for the lessons learnt. The fact that she would be a fractional ketch was kept secret for as long as possible. The Blake team were convinced they had a winner and, as far as they knew, only one other skipper, Grant Dalton presumably, had also investigated the ketch option.

The rivalry between the two New Zealand camps became intense while the two yachts went through their final work-up programmes before being shipped to England. First in the water, *Fisher & Paykel* beat the newly launched *Steinlager 2* in the 1989 Balokovic Cup, one

187

of the classics in the Auckland race programme. But brief trialling between the two yachts – with both teams agreeing to confidentiality on the outcome – proved inconclusive.

What was evident, however, was the degree of professionalism in both teams. Much had been learned from previous Whitbreads and, more particularly, from the America's Cup campaign in Fremantle. While still something of an adventure, the Whitbread was now very much a full-on race, and this was reflected in the thorough preparation of both Kiwi campaigns. When they got to England for the race start, it was clear that they were a big step ahead of their rivals in this department at least.

The first real comparison of performance against Whitbread competition came in the 605-mile Fastnet Classic. *Steinlager* had already won the 180-mile Channel Race, on line and handicap, but she was the only Whitbread maxi entered. In the Fastnet she would meet not only the masthead ketch *Fisher & Paykel*, but the two new Farr fractional sloops *Merit*, skippered by 1985–86 winner Pierre Fehlmann, and *Rothmans*, skippered by the hard-driving Lawrie Smith. Determined to make the test as meaningful as possible, Blake and his team decided to race *Steinlager* in full Whitbread trim. They did, however, use their practice sails, preferring to preserve *Steinlager*'s race wardrobe.

After a tactical battle down the English Channel, followed by a beat across the Irish Sea to Fastnet Rock, *F&P* and *Steinlager* were first and second. *F&P* had been particularly impressive upwind and led her Kiwi rival by a good five miles, while *Rothmans* and *Merit* were snapping at *Steinlager*'s stern as they rounded the Rock and headed off on a spinnaker reach to Bishop Rock. With *Steinlager* slowly winding in *F&P*, the two ketches eased away from the sloops. As they rounded the reefs off Bishops Rock, the race for line honours was now a private duel and the *Steinlager* crew could readily make out the instrument lights glowing in *F&P*'s cockpit.

For the next 65 miles to Plymouth Sound, *Steinlager* sought a way

188

past but Dalton and his crew defended grimly. Finally, *Steinlager* got her chance and slipped into the lead. It was Dalton's turn to attack and he launched a gybing duel all the way to the finish line off Plymouth Hoe. *Steinlager* clung to her slim advantage and crossed the line 2 minutes, 50 seconds ahead.

The jury was still out on the relative merits of fractional as opposed to masthead ketches, but both were clearly very fast downwind, and were more than competitive upwind too. 'The sloops,' says Quilter, 'had much to ponder. That Fastnet race must have put the fear of God into them. We went upwind across the Irish Sea with them and rounded Fastnet Rock a boatlength ahead of them, albeit a long way behind Dalts. Downwind on the way back to Plymouth, they couldn't foot it. The indications already were that the ketch-rigged maxi was the right boat for the Whitbread. Whether fractional ketch was faster than masthead ketch, we would have to wait and see.'

CHAPTER
Eight
The Big Red Rocket

As the eighties drew to a close, two New Zealand campaigns, one led by Peter Blake and the other spear-headed by Grant Dalton, were readying themselves to tackle the 1989–90 Whitbread Round the World race. Only a little more than 10 years earlier, a 20-year-old Dalton had stood on Auckland's waterfront and watched *Heath's Condor* lead the Whitbread fleet around North Head and into the Waitemata Harbour. He remembers vividly her huge yellow spinnaker with a black vulture image spread right across it. Dalton, an 18-foot-skiff sailor, was excited. Here was a sophisticated race yacht, the likes of which he'd never seen, coming in from the depths of the Southern Ocean. He'd read in the newspapers that her sailing master was a Kiwi by the name of Peter Blake. He hurried down to Marsden Wharf to catch a glimpse of Blake who turned out to be a tall, bronzed fellow with long, blond hair. Even in the crowd of similarly clad *Condor* crew, Blake stood out. There was something about him. Dalton determined almost there and then that he too wanted to race big yachts around the world.

Although Dalton wasn't to know it, a dozen years and three Whitbread races later, the pair would square off across the steering wheels of two giant maxis for what would be one of the greatest long-distance races of all time. For Blake had opened a door to inter-

193

THE BIG RED ROCKET

national sailing opportunity that a small army of talented Kiwis would march through. His competitive ambition inspired others to follow, and his success with commercial sponsorship had made it possible for them to do so. Michael Fay had launched New Zealand's first America's Cup challenge. Mostly the same army of Kiwi sailors had discovered more great battles to win and their sport had developed from an enthusiastic amateur pastime into a lucrative professional occupation.

What might readily be called the 'Blake Era' – the 20 years from 1980 to 2000 – was in fact the second wave of New Zealand success in international offshore racing that was out of all proportion to the nation's size and resource base. The first wave began in the mid-sixties when Jim Davern took the pencil-slim 60-footer *Fidelis* to Sydney to win line honours in the Sydney–Hobart Classic, and Chris Bouzaid took *Rainbow II* to Heligoland to win the One Ton Cup. There followed 10 years of remarkable success in the Quarter, Half and One Ton Cups, and in the Admiral's Cup, the Southern Cross Cup and the Kenwood Cup. Kiwis weren't just racing their boats successfully either. They were mostly designing, building and rigging them too. But the pace and cost of international competition, and the speed of the rule changes of the mid-to-late seventies, took their toll and Kiwi ambition flagged. Almost coincidentally, Blake arrived on the scene, added a vital new dimension to the ambition and showed the way to achieving objectives that were, at that point in time, beyond the personal pocket of most.

Dalton was part of the second wave and, to a degree, a protégé of Blake in that he tried out for the crew of *Ceramco* and was a watch captain on *Lion*. Blake and Dalton, however, could not have been more different. One was tall and reserved with an unmistakeable air of authority about him. The other was shortish and brash, and, in those days, still growing up both as a person and a competitor. Each

194

man, however, was amply endowed with ambition, commitment and determination, if in different ways.

Today Dalton looks back and reflects: 'We were chalk and cheese really. Pete was a seaman. I've never been a seaman in my life. Pete could navigate and was extremely good at it. I can't navigate. He was a complete yachtsman in that respect. I have never been one at all. Pete was interested in and could identify birds and sea life. I couldn't give a shit. Birds have got wings and whales are things that you'll run into if you're not careful. They'll bugger your race. Pete loved the sea. I don't. It's cold and wet and you can't get much sleep. It just happens to be my chosen arena for competition. That was true of Peter too, but he was much more at peace in that environment. I just want to get in there and out of there as quickly as I can. Pete loved cruising. I hate cruising – haven't been cruising in my life, wouldn't buy a boat if it was the last vehicle on the planet. So we differed completely in our philosophies. He was a much more rounded person, his whole personality was more complete, and I admired him for it. Having said all that, put us both in a one-man Laser dinghy and I reckon I'd kick his arse.'

Athough he had already been involved with Blake campaigns on two occasions, Dalton, as he put the *Fisher & Paykel* project together for the 1989–90 Whitbread race project, did not fully respect his former skipper: 'I had learned a lot from him but at that stage I didn't have respect for him because I thought that he didn't push hard enough. I was 26 and probably was pushing too hard. Pete said later he wasn't sure that I knew when to button off, which maybe was true up to a point.'

Quilter does not agree that Blake was too careful: 'I remember one time on *Steinlager 1* in the early days. We were going pretty fast and I would have backed off, but Blakey didn't back off. I suggested we should toss in a reef or something. He said, "No, we might as well find out if it is going to break, we may as well test this thing," and we just blasted on for hour after hour, fully pressed. He could push it along, for sure. But he was seamanlike cautious too. He could push it with anyone, but he also knew when you did have to chop back.'

In the space of the upcoming 1989–90 Whitbread, Dalton's view of Blake would change completely. He would not only come to admire the man, but also respect him and seek his advice. But their differences in temperament and in campaign experience were also evident in the way the two put their Whitbread challenges together. While Blake was approaching the zenith of his leadership, management and communication skills, Dalton was just setting out on the journey and he would make some of the same mistakes that Blake had made before him, including trying to run a whole campaign himself. Nevertheless, while the rivalry between the *Steinlager 2* and *F&P* camps was intense, it was put aside in the final weeks before the start as they joined forces to fight an orchestrated attack on the rule legitimacy of the Kiwi ketches. The opposition, worried about the size and speed of *Steinlager* and *F&P*, set out to undermine their eligibility.

Rothmans skipper Lawrie Smith and *NCB Ireland* advisor Harold Cudmore, senior members of the British racing contingent, led the charge and seemed to be getting more support than was appropriate from Royal Ocean Racing Club measurer and Whitbread Race Committee member (later to be race chairman) Ian Bailey-Wilmot who, perhaps coincidentally, also happened to be British. For openers, Smith and Cudmore challenged the way in which the mizzen forestays of the ketches were attached to the deck. They also wanted the New Zealand yachts remeasured, to check the rating statistics achieved when the process was carried out in Auckland before the yachts were shipped to the UK.

The forestay set-up on both boats was exactly as designed by Bruce Farr, so its legality had never been questioned by the Blake or Dalton teams. They got wind, however, of the fact that their legality was being questioned and instigated discussions with the race committee and the English measurers in an endeavour to sort it all out. Unable to obtain answers, they sought a ruling from Ken Weller, the American head of the IOR committee. Weller's decision was hand-delivered to *Steinlager* by Bailey-Wilmot, waving it angrily and accusing the Kiwis of trying to put one over him while muttering that 'the bloody mizzen is going to fall down anyway'. Bailey-Wilmot probably wasn't aware of how close he came to physical harm that day. Not only did the *Steinlager* crew take great exception to being accused of cheating, but the New Zealanders had gone to great lengths to ensure that they were squeaky clean when it came to rule compliance.

With a minimum of fuss, the mizzen support set-up on the ketches was quickly changed to one approved by the measurers, but Smith and Cudmore persisted and the ketches were ordered to be remeasured, even though the vital figures that determined the boats' rating (handicap) had already been checked and rechecked no less than six times by fully qualified measurers in New Zealand. The outcome – the ratings of both boats in fact reduced, which meant that, if they wanted to, Blake and Dalton could add even more to their already massive spreads of sail.

The Smith/Cudmore efforts tailed off significantly after this backfire, even if Smith remained perplexed and suspicious about how the Kiwis had managed to achieve such big and potent boats. But if the opposition had something to worry about before the start, they most certainly did by the time the fleet reached the first port of call, Punta del Este, 6281 miles down the North and South Atlantic. But that was in the future.

The Duchess of York sent the 23-boat fleet from 12 nations on its way from Southampton on 2 September 1989. *Steinlager* powered away

197

from the start in a 15-knot northerly, five-sail reaching down the Solent at 13 knots with *F&P* chasing up a couple of minutes astern. By dusk, *F&P* was still there, about a mile back, but their sloop-rigged rivals were falling off the early pace, as was the stock Farr design masthead ketch *The Card* from Sweden.

That night, Blake and Quilter plotted *Steinlager* through the narrow channel off Ushant, on the north-western tip of France, that forms the tidal gate between the English Channel and the Bay of Biscay. Get it wrong and you can be parked there for hours until the tide starts to run in your favour. But *Steinlager* had 6 knots of current under her and she whipped through in light airs and boiling tide. Not that it did much good. Come the morning, *Rothmans, Merit* and *Union Bank of Finland* (*UBF*) had done a number on the New Zealand ketches by sailing closer to the French coast and led them by five miles. It wasn't the first time, nor would it be the last, when the Europeans would use local knowledge to steal a march on their 'Downunder' competitors.

Once clear of the coast, *Steinlager* graduated to her big red spinnaker and mizzen staysail and trucked across the Bay of Biscay in perfect conditions. The sloops were soon astern again and even *F&P* was struggling to stay in touch. However, the idyll was rudely interrupted the third night at sea when, off Cape Finisterre on the north-west corner of Spain, the Portuguese trades quickly built to 40 knots from astern with confused seas. *Steinlager* teetered on the edge of control at 19 knots under a full-size main spinnaker and a small heavy-duty mizzen spinnaker, until helmsman Ross Field was able to convey his need for a smaller, more manageable extra with reefed mainsail.

At daybreak, *Rothmans* was spotted on a converging course to *Steinlager*, which had continued out to sea overnight on starboard gybe. *Rothmans*, on port gybe, crossed just two boatlengths astern. The two maxis, at close quarters in the open ocean and surfing at more then 20 knots, must have made a spectacular sight. But Blake and Quilter weren't taking in the view, impressive as it must have been. They were down below plotting what would prove to be the big break of the leg and, in fact, of the race. Their facsimile weather maps and computerised routing program agreed with their instinctive view that a westerly course was the way to go. The orders were given and *Steinlager* headed out into the Atlantic. Of her maxi rivals, only *Merit* followed suit, the rest opting to work close to the Portuguese coast. *Steinlager* found herself threading her way down what was almost like a river of wind that appeared to be the only breeze around.

Those were nervous times. No racing yachtsman is comfortable parting company with his opposition in such a fashion. He will usually gybe back to cover what the others are doing. There were those on *Steinlager*, including navigator Quilter, who wanted to do just that. But Blake said, 'No.' Quilter recalls: 'We'd made the gain, we were ahead and it was looking good. So I was all for gybing and getting back across in front of the fleet. But Blakey said, "Bugger it. Let's go for it. All your planning says go that way. All the work we did with NIWA (New Zealand's National Institute of Water and Atmospheric Research) says go that way." So go that way we did. Blakey had enough balls to say, "No – let's do it. It's logical and it's right, so let's stick to our guns." '

The courage of Blake's convictions bore immediate fruit, *Steinlager* recording a Whitbread record 343-mile day, averaging 14.3 knots. And then Blake's call really began to pay dividends. While *Steinlager* continued to break records in stronger winds out to the west, the boats to the east were stuck in a dying breeze. *Steinlager*'s log noted: 'The gale abated by day six and we were once more sailing downwind in light-to-moderate airs. *Merit* was 30 miles astern and there was a huge gap back to the rest of the maxis. If the moderate running continues, with *Steinlager* further out to the west with a better angle of attack, we'd ease away from *Merit* as we headed on south and built up a huge lead over the boats languishing in lighter airs inshore.'

It was the ocean racer's dream break on the fleet and it was the more satisfying because, while it had been facilitated by painstaking weather research and modern technology, it also involved a strong element of seaman's intuition and, finally, had relied on the skipper's courage to back that intuition.

Steinlager's charmed run continued. By the end of the first week at sea she had sailed 1900 miles under spinnaker and was well to the south-west of the Canary Islands where, at 26 degrees North, she started to pick up developing trade winds. First into steady trades (and by a big margin), *Steinlager*'s situation just kept getting better and she continued to build on her lead. By day nine she was 80 miles ahead of *Merit*. *F&P* was a daunting 205 miles astern, prompting Dalton to ask Blake, on the inter-fleet chat show, what the weather was like in the tropics, claiming that on *F&P* they were still wearing their snow suits 'up north'. The next day, *Steinlager* was finally headed and reaching headsails were hoisted. By this stage, *F&P* was 270 miles astern.

But the following day, as if as a reminder that there was still a long way to go and a lot still to happen, the breeze swung through to the south and died completely. *Steinlager* was becalmed at 11 degrees 30 minutes North, in her own private parking lot (courtesy of the infant Hurricane Hugo). While she sat motionless, her opposition, including *Merit*, continued on down the track at 10 knots and, by the noon radio sched, the Swiss maxi sloop was within 40 miles of the lead. The tables turned again, however, and a fairly painless transit of the Doldrums saw *Steinlager* slowly rebuilding her lead until, by day 18, she was 7 degrees South with *Merit* tucked away about 100 miles astern and *F&P* nearly 200 miles behind.

A burst of RF (radio frequency) energy sent *Steinlager*'s sophisticated satellite navigation equipment on the blink for a couple of days but the skipper's ever-present sextant was immediately in use and

200

Blake happily spent the next two days and nights taking sun and star shots by which to navigate *Steinlager*, until the satnav problem was diagnosed and the equipment reprogrammed. By the beginning of the fourth week at sea, *Steinlager* was well to the east of Rio de Janeiro in freshening northerlies – again almost exactly what Blake and his crew would have ordered. With less than 1000 miles to go to Punta del Este, and with the wind increasing to 35 knots from astern, *Steinlager* was reeling off the miles, surfing down the waves at 22 knots and sending huge bow waves creaming back either side of the boat.

But with 600 miles to go to the mouth of the River Plate, the weather gods decided to make life a touch more difficult. A depression forming off the coast of Uruguay spun freshening southerlies into *Steinlager*'s path so that Punta del Este was now 600 miles dead upwind. Within hours, the wind was up to 35 knots and *Steinlager* was down to No. 5 genoa and triple-reefed main, with the mizzen down completely. The seas continued to build and the boat was making sickening noises as she crashed off backless waves. With such a big margin on the fleet, there was no point risking serious damage so Blake made the call to drop the headsail and slow the boat down – another wise decision.

A long way astern, *Rothmans* was pushing too hard into the gale and crashed particularly violently off a wave, cracking the deck beside the running backstay winch. They had no option but to ease off. Then it was *Steinlager*'s turn, even though she was being nursed through the worst of it. The mainsail detached itself from the headboard car that pulled it up and down the mast. In near impossible conditions, Godfrey Cray and Kevin Shoebridge went up the rig, equipped with the boat-hook taped to a length of sail batten, to try and retrieve the headboard car and reconnect it to the mainsail. Almost miraculously, they succeeded at the first attempt. The mainsail was rehoisted and *Steinlager* was on her way again.

Unbeknown to the *Steinlager* crew, arch-rival *F&P* had lost her mizzen-mast in the strong tailwinds off Rio de Janeiro. So in Punta

201

del Este, *Merit* was the closest opposition to the big red ketch from Auckland, albeit 80 miles – or 11.5 hours – behind. *F&P* was 32 hours off *Steinlager*'s pace. After the first 6281 miles of the journey, Blake and his crew had already established a winning lead.

Rothmans skipper Lawrie Smith flew back to England during the Punta del Este stopover, claiming that all the yachts should be remeasured. By this time, Blake had had enough and moved quickly to defend his yacht and crew. He told London's *Times* newspaper that *Steinlager*'s winning performance on the first leg was due to her design and crew: 'I don't know what more we can do,' he remonstrated. 'You don't win this kind of race by fiddling the yacht's rating. You win with good tactics and a well-fed and motivated crew.'

Blake pointed out that *Steinlager* had undergone two full machine measurements of the hull before it left New Zealand, using the same type of machine as used in England. Two separate measurers then evaluated *Steinlager* by hand, to double-check the machine. Additionally, she had been re-inclined seven times (to check the yacht's stability), with the freeboards (flotation) also checked. The last set of checks, on stability and freeboard, had been made by Commander Ian Bailey-Wilmot, a member of the Whitbread Race Committee and a measurer from the Royal Ocean Racing Club, and were made in perfect conditions at Southampton's Ocean Village just before the start. They had led to a slight drop in *Steinlager*'s rating, from 70 feet to 69.97 feet. The yacht's sail inventory had also been remeasured.

Blake's statements were confirmed by the race chairman, Rear Admiral Charles Williams, and Smith was left to complain that nobody had seen *Steinlager 2* out of the water, although Blake wasn't quite sure what he expected to see. Smith would later claim that there was nothing personal in his allegations. *Steinlager* was the opposition and he was simply trying to wind up his opponents. If he was, he didn't get the reaction he was hoping for. Blake and his crew had set out from day one to ensure that *Steinlager* was completely rule compliant, as was the way in which they sailed her. The bottom line was that Smith was accusing them of cheating, even though all the evidence declared otherwise. Their response was to put as much distance as possible between *Steinlager* and *Rothmans* and leave Smith to stew in his own baseless complaints – which he was forced to do in ever-diminishing company.

Leg two of the race – 7650 miles from Uruguay, across the bottom of the world, to Fremantle in Western Australia – would present *Steinlager* with a whole new set of challenges. For a start, the Blake boat was the heaviest in the fleet. So – on paper at least – the opposition maxis, including *F&P*, should all be faster in Southern Ocean conditions that would, in the main, prevent the ketches from using their extra horsepower (sail area) to advantage. Mike Quilter has a much more basic way of describing the situation: 'We were slow in the Southern Ocean. *Steinlager* was such a huge, big, fat, heavy boat. It was tough, and we broke a lot of gear down there.' Dalton adds (mischievously): 'It's one of the great arguments of all time on the weather rail. *F&P* was quicker on the first Southern Ocean leg – no doubt about it – and I reckon that was because we were tougher and pushed harder, and didn't give a shit.'

On a great circle course – the shortest route to Fremantle – *Steinlager* would head south-east from Punta and maintain that general heading for about a week before levelling out in the Southern Ocean at a latitude not too affected by Antarctic ice. She would then head almost due east for two weeks until clear of the Kerguelen Islands, when she would start to arc north-eastwards towards Fremantle. The final challenge would be to negotiate the large area of high pressure that is usually to be found off the south-west coast of Australia.

Blake and Brad Butterworth, a top match-racing helmsman/

THE BIG RED ROCKET

tactician in more regular guise, got *Steinlager* away to another good start and she led the fleet south and east away from Punta in a rapidly freshening breeze. By nightfall the wind had swung aft and the fleet was rocketing along under spinnaker at speeds in excess of 20 knots.

Racing yachtsmen, particularly tacticians, frequently talk of being in phase with the shifts – and the principles are the same whether you are short-tacking around a harbour course in a day race or playing the low-pressure systems roaring through the wastes of the Southern Ocean. The wind is never absolutely constant in direction but shifts back and forth. The trick is to be in phase so that you always position your boat to take advantage of the breeze when it is lifting. For the first week at sea, while *Fisher & Paykel*, *Merit* and *Rothmans* were completely in synch with the conditions, *Steinlager* most definitely was not, and as a result she was steadily losing ground to her rivals.

By the end of that week, the weather had cooled dramatically. The water temperature was down to 3 degrees Celsius and the air temperature was no warmer. In addition to not fitting fans for the tropical legs, it had been decided not to fit a diesel heater for the Southern legs, in order to save not only on the weight of the heater but also the fuel that would be required to run it. As the interior temperature of the boat dropped to around freezing and the stark white bulkheads and deckheads gave off the ambience of a refrigerator, the *Steinlager* crew were beginning to question their earlier bravado. Even *F&P*, whose sponsor manufactured, among other things, a leading range of refrigerators, had a heating system on board.

Some 1700 miles after leaving Punta, there was no improvement in the situation. *Steinlager* was still behind the leading three boats, who were enjoying more wind to the south of her. Having lost 30 miles to Dalton in a 12-hour period, Blake called a meeting of his three watch captains and navigator. The decision to be made was whether to continue on the present course in lighter winds, and face the risk

204

of losing more miles, or bite the bullet, gybe across on to starboard and head south in search of the fresher winds that her rivals were benefiting from. The discussion was brief and the decision unanimous – gybe over and head south. It meant handing F&P 20 miles on a plate while on the unfavoured starboard gybe, but that was deemed to be short-term pain for longer-term gain.

Confirmation of the wisdom of this decision was almost instantaneous. The next day *Rothmans* was spotted through fog, three miles astern, and the next fleet sched revealed that *Merit* and *UBF* were off *Steinlager*'s port beam. *F&P* had made the expected gain but Blake and his team were back in the hunt.

A large low-pressure system to the south of *Steinlager* produced a few days of variables, but the wind then began to build from the west and kept coming. The ride got faster and faster as the wind reached gale force and the seas built accordingly. *Steinlager* didn't like it. Hard running in fact proved to be one of her Achilles heels. The sloops did, however. Considerably lighter, they quickly overhauled *Steinlager* and sped away to lead her by more than 50 miles. At the head of the fleet *F&P* also picked up her skirts and romped away to a lead of more than 100 miles.

Driving the heavier *Steinlager* through the unrelenting gale then began to take its toll on equipment. First to go were the spinnaker halyard blocks. As a result, the wire halyards themselves were badly damaged, and while one of the blocks was thrashing around in the rig it tore a hole in the mainsail, which had to be lowered to the deck for two hours for repairs. To add insult to injury, the track, to which the inboard end of the spinnaker pole attached, shattered. Then to cap it all off, the hydraulic main boom vang broke as the boom was dragged through the freezing seas.

Blake and Barry McKay effected a repair in which Blake had so much confidence that he declared he would 'walk home naked if it broke again' – which it did, the very next day, leading to considerable

205

debate about the skipper's impending promenade. Not to be beaten, Blake and McKay went to work again, this time using a length of galvanised anchor chain for the repair. It looked somewhat out of place on a sophisticated multi-million-dollar race yacht, but it did the trick.

It was still blowing gale force and, with so many breakages and the resultant down time for repairs, the decision was made to nurse the boat through the worst of it rather than risk terminal damage. Decks covered in snow and ice and freezing temperatures were adding to the hazards of driving hard in 50-knot tailwinds. *Steinlager* was by no means the only boat suffering, either. That evening's radio sched revealed that *F&P* had pulled a spinnaker halyard winch clean out of the deck while *NCB Ireland* had broken her main boom and a spinnaker pole and blown out a spinnaker. The 80-foot cruising division entry *Creightons Naturally* had lost two men over the side in a violent broach. Both were recovered but efforts to revive Anthony Phillips failed and he was buried at sea three days later.

The gale finally abated as the low-pressure system that had fuelled it sped off eastwards. The lighter conditions that ensued came as a welcome relief aboard the biggest and heaviest boat in the fleet. Over the next few days *Steinlager* closed right in on the sloops and to within 40 miles of *F&P*, which clearly had had even lighter conditions up front. Just ahead were the Kerguelen Islands, lonely and weather-swept outposts of France at nearly 50 degrees South in the wastes of the Southern Ocean. Smack in the path of the race boats, these islands were to prove the undoing of *F&P* on this leg.

As *Steinlager* made her approach, in company with *Merit* and *Rothmans* which were out of sight in thick fog, the wind freshened and swung aft. Further to the north, *F&P* was forced to gybe on to port and ended up close-hauled as she skirted the rocks, sometimes so close inshore that she was ploughing through seaweed as she wriggled around the northern side of the rather formidable obstacles blocking her course. 'We were unlucky getting that shift when we did, but it was still a cock-up on our part,' Dalton admitted later. 'We should have put the helm down earlier in our approach and driven off to pass to the south of the islands. But the damned things seemed to be sucking us in.'

Further south and still making her approach, Steinlager was able to take that option and break from F&P in the process. As a bonus, the wind swung through all the way into the north-west at precisely the right time and she was able to gybe on to port and start making some northing. As she did so, sheets of ice from the rig and sails crashed down to the deck, almost like a signal that it was time to head for warmer latitudes after three weeks of cold, snow and ice and almost perpetual gales. Fremantle was now 2000 miles ahead – three Sydney–Hobarts – with a large high-pressure system to negotiate. The trick would be to avoid the clutches of the high for as long as possible. While the temptation was to race arch-rival F&P, Steinlager's real focus had to be Merit which was only 11.5 miles behind overall at the beginning of the leg.

Quilter and his routing programs agreed that Steinlager should get north as quickly as possible, to break into a new band of breeze. With 1150 miles to go to the finish, there were seven boats spread within 50 miles of the lead and it looked like F&P would be first to the new breeze. But Steinlager's impressive light airs abilities were starting to make a difference. In very light winds, she remorselessly chased and passed her rivals and then eased away to lead F&P and the sloops by five miles as she neared Rottnest Island which guards the entrance to Gage Roads and the approach to Fremantle. These were 1987 America's Cup waters and so familiar territory to the KZ7 contingent aboard Steinlager, which was being nursed along with all the skill and concentration of a boat and crew completing the last leg of an America's Cup race rather than finishing a 7000-mile leg of a round-the-world race.

On a pitch-black night, in light and flukey winds, the four leaders

THE BIG RED ROCKET

approached Rottnest from different points of the compass and nobody was able to identify which set of navigation lights was which as they headed into the final 14 miles. *Steinlager*'s crew were literally in the dark until their boat was suddenly bathed in the lights of media and spectator boats. She was in the lead and there was now no catching her. She crossed the finish line 93 minutes ahead of *Merit* and *Rothmans*, who match-raced to the finish, and three hours clear of *F&P*.

Two legs sailed, two guns and two handicap wins so far. Now came the important one – the 3272-mile 'sprint' to home port Auckland. The 23 December restart meant that the race crews would celebrate Christmas at sea. *Steinlager* and *F&P* must have decided on their own form of celebrations because they would turn on a spectacular shindig through the Great Australian Bight.

The morning of the start of the third leg produced the first rainfall of the stopover. It was accompanied by a fresh westerly airflow in place of the usual south-westerly sea breeze which the locals refer to as the 'Fremantle Doctor'. This meant a very fast reach through Gage Roads and on down the coast with the wind on the beam. *Steinlager* and *Merit* led the way, *F&P* and *Rothmans* 300 metres astern, with the wind building to 35 knots. At dark, *Merit* angled off to leeward leaving *F&P* camped just 200 metres astern of *Steinlager*, where she remained all night, her navigation lights resembling a pursuing pair of red and green eyes.

Dawn revealed *Merit* in front and to leeward. *F&P* was still behind, but only just. The wind was up and the seas had built even more, making for extremely fast sailing. *Steinlager* and *F&P* roared off across the Bight, locked in what would be a 3000-mile match race to be first in to Auckland. The lead swapped back and forth throughout the morning as the boat behind attacked and the boat in front defended. *F&P* first broke through on a spectacular surf, no more than 50 metres to windward of *Steinlager*. In the pale light, both crews were treated to the inspirational sight of 35-ton maxis with five sails set, surfing down the face of grey seas at more than 20 knots and tossing water everywhere as they charged forward.

On the helm of *Steinlager*, Kevin Shoebridge did not enjoy being passed. With both the duty and standby watches on deck, he counter-attacked and went searching for every wave that would help gain back precious metres. Again and again *Steinlager* scorched down the seas to within a couple of metres of *F&P*'s stern before being forced to hurriedly bear away to avoid a collision. The two crews were constantly trimming their five-sail wardrobes and the spray being churned up cut visibility to almost zero. Finally, Shoebridge found the one elusive wave he was searching for and, in a blast of more spray, it was *Steinlager*'s turn to cream on by and into the lead. Unable to hold the duelling Kiwis, *Merit* and *Rothmans* slowly disappeared over the horizon astern.

Four days and nights later the pair were still toe to toe, their crews having one of the wettest, wildest, most exhilarating and demanding rides of their lives. Ross Field was on the helm when the two big ketches converged yet again. *Steinlager* was blazing down the front of a large wave when *F&P*'s illuminated transom appeared out of the spray only metres dead ahead. Field took evasive action and disaster was avoided, but that one had been too close for comfort. It was, after all, a big piece of ocean, so why not put a little more distance between the charging giants?

It was almost a relief when, the next day – New Year's Eve – the wind and seas finally moderated. Frenchman Alain Gabbay, an old friend from the 1981–82 race, had blasted *Charles Jourdan* into the lead while the breeze was still up. But his moment of glory was short-lived. The maxi ketches had too much power and length in the lighter winds on the approach to Tasmania and *F&P* led into the Tasman by 7 miles

THE BIG RED ROCKET

from her arch-rival. *Rothmans* had hung on as best as possible and was 25 miles astern of the Kiwis. *Merit*, nursing a damaged steering system, was another 60 miles back.

The first sched of the New Year revealed that *Steinlager*'s devastating light airs speed was going to be a telling factor yet again. In 12 hours overnight, she had turned a seven-mile deficit into a seven-mile lead. Cape Reinga was 800 miles away to the north-east and the Tasman in between was dominated by a large high-pressure system. Approaching Cape Reinga early on the morning of day 13, *F&P* closed to within 200 metres before *Steinlager* picked up a wind shift and stretched her lead back out to three miles. The two crews got a shock when they were finally able to make out what was going on at the Cape itself. Local fishermen were out in force while hundreds of people lined the tops of the high cliffs to get a glimpse of the epic duel unfolding below them.

Sailing across the top of New Zealand to North Cape, the watch system on *Steinlager* was cancelled. Auckland was only 200 miles away and it was going to require all hands to keep *F&P* at bay. Once around North Cape, the wind was astern again for the sprint down the Northland coast. Throughout that night the *Steinlager* crew defended their lead jealously and, gybe after gybe, they covered every move that *F&P* made. The Bay of Islands slipped by during darkness, but there at dawn were the dramatic Whangarei Heads. These were home waters to the Kiwi yachtsmen and the adrenalin levels reached new heights with a hefty boost of emotion. Blake took the helm where, with Butterworth calling the tactical shots, he would stay until the finish. Everyone else concentrated on extracting every last ounce of speed from their big red machine. This was another finish that was going right down to the wire and it was being played out in front of the home crowd, live television and all.

The spectator boats were out in force as the duo roared on past Flat Rock, off Kawau, with *F&P* carrying a freshening breeze down to *Steinlager* and narrowing the gap between them to just one mile. Dalton and his crew were every bit as charged up as Blake and his team and giving this one everything they had. Up ahead, the sky over Auckland was starting to look ominous, sending Quilter scurrying to his nav station to listen for any updated weather reports on the radio. Almost immediately, on the talkback station Newstalk 1ZB, he heard a listener from Titirangi, on the western side of the Auckland isthmus, saying a southerly front had just passed through.

Blake's response to the information was instantaneous. A small genoa was made ready and the crew went on standby for a crash spinnaker drop. There was a major and sudden change approaching. Immediately he saw signs of that change on the water a mile ahead, Blake screamed 'Get rid of it!' The crew's reaction was instantaneous and *Steinlager's* spinnaker and mizzen staysail dropped from view with not a moment to spare as the southerly switch slammed in from dead ahead.

F&P was caught still charging after *Steinlager* with everything set and was immediately in trouble as her crew struggled to get rid of the downwind sails and hoist the upwind wardrobe she now desperately required. Quilter's vigilance and Blake's instincts had facilitated a vital break which prompted a highly satisfied 'Got the bastards!' from the steering department. With the initial fury of the squall past, *Steinlager* was again one mile ahead of her rival and there was no way Dalton and his team were going to overcome that deficit in the 16 or so miles left to travel to the Orakei finish.

The welcome, on the water and ashore, was huge and emotional as *Steinlager* crossed the line 6 minutes, 4 seconds ahead, and it was as much for the valiant *F&P* and her crew as it was for the victorious Blake and his team on *Steinlager*. It was a dream finish for the home crowd and the pride and passion were inescapable. *Rothmans* and *Merit*, in that order, were also given a warm welcome an hour later, by which time the party was already well under way. Halfway around the world and *Steinlager*'s record was now three wins, on line and on handicap, in three legs – an unprecedented success.

SIR PETER BLAKE

CHAPTER Nine

Game, Set, Match and Glory

The start of the 6255-mile leg four, around Cape Horn to Punta del Este, was spectacular. Auckland was crowded with visitors and in carnival mood for the double attractions, on successive days, of the closing ceremony of the highly successful 1990 XIVth Commonwealth Games and the restart of the Whitbread. The waterfront was packed with cheering Kiwis and the harbour was wall to wall with boats.

Steinlager's departure, however, was inauspicious. She was back from the line in light airs and slow away. Swede Magnus Olson, on *The Card*, would have been wishing for something similar. He took his big ketch into the spectator fleet at the port end of the line, thinking he could thread his way through the jam of boats, and snagged *The Card*'s mizzen-mast on the rig of one yacht that could not get out of the way in time. The result – one spectacular mizzen dismasting and a hasty return to port for the Swedes.

Blake wore a path between *Steinlager*'s twin steering wheels as he nursed his 35-ton giant through the crush and strove to identify the first turning mark, off Auckland's East Coast Bays, among what seemed a solid barrier of spectator boats. Slowly, the armada of well-wishers dropped behind and the Whitbread skippers and crews could concentrate on the business at hand as they headed out across the

215

Firth of Thames and through the Colville Channel, between Great Barrier Island and the Coromandel Peninsula, and into the Bay of Plenty. These were waters that Blake's great-grandfather Thomas Wing would have sailed many times, but never with the level of interest in his endeavours attracted by his popular descendant and his state-of-the-art racing machine.

By day four the now-familiar pecking order had been established at the front of the fleet, with *Merit*, *F&P*, *Steinlager 2* and *Rothmans* leading the way, and by day 10, *Steinlager* and *F&P* were again locked in their personal match race, with just five miles between them as they slid past numerous icebergs and dug deep into the loneliest stretch of ocean in the world, heading for its most revered, and feared, maritime landmark, still 2000 miles away at this point.

Approaching Cape Horn on their nineteenth night at sea, *Steinlager* was 20 miles ahead of *F&P* with *Merit* and *Rothmans* more than 100 miles astern. But she was struggling in light and variable winds accompanied by heavy drizzle, and her radar seemed to be on the blink. An uncharacteristically strong blip on the screen, five miles astern, had the Blake team puzzled. The signal looked too powerful to be *F&P* so they assumed it to be a large fishing boat. At dawn, they were shocked to see that the radar was actually working fine. The blip was *F&P* which had brought up new breeze and closed right in while *Steinlager* had been flopping around, becalmed in the rain.

While rounding the Horn in light tailwinds, Blake read a short service and prayer before scattering the ashes of an old Cape Horner and former Devonport Yacht Club member, Frederick Chapman. The only witnesses were a few albatross, but the *Steinlager* crew were sure that the old mariner would have approved. The interlude was brief because *F&P* was only four miles astern and the notorious Straits de Le Maire tidal gate on the south-east tip of South America was just ahead.

Once through the Straits and on to the Argentinian coast, Blake decided it was time to introduce *Steinlager*'s secret weapon – a pair of brightly coloured ski socks. It had become tradition in the Blake household that Pippa would give Peter a pair of such socks before the start of a race. They were Pete's 'Lucky Socks', which he would wear whenever it appeared that boat speed and sailing skill might not be enough to prevail – such as in the intensely close finishes with *F&P*. On this occasion, the socks were green and the Steinlager crew were prepared to believe that their worth as a source of good luck far outweighed their smell. (Later in his career, Blake's 'Lucky Red Socks' would become a national rallying symbol for New Zealand's 1995 America's Cup campaign and have the country's knitting mills working 24 hours a day to meet public demand for them.)

The two big ketches managed to escape the clutches of a stationary high-pressure system that trapped their sloop rivals, and approached the mouth of the River Plate with *Steinlager* navigator Quilter confidently predicting that they would have no more than 25 knots of wind for the last 100 miles to the finish. Twenty-five knots of boat speed would have been closer to the mark. The wind kicked in to 55 knots from astern and pushed up a punishing seaway in the 12-metre-deep water. With *F&P* a comfortable 12 miles astern and under control, the decision was made to ease back to minimise the risk of serious damage. It was a prudent call, but it almost proved costly.

As *Steinlager* closed to within 10 miles of Punta, the rain squalls cleared to reveal *F&P*'s spinnaker looming out of the mist astern. Dalton and his crew had not slackened off but had pushed on relentlessly to close to within four miles of their rival.

Steinlager scrambled across the finish line just 21 minutes ahead in another incredibly close finish. Had Blakey's 'Lucky Socks' done the trick again? Two legs to go, and *Steinlager* still had a perfect record to defend, doubling her lead over the Swiss sloop *Merit* in the process.

The fifth leg – 5475 miles from Uruguay to Fort Lauderdale, just to the north of Miami in Florida – saw another tussle with the Doldrums. The atmosphere on board *Steinlager* was altogether different to when she left Punta five months earlier, headed for the Southern Ocean. The prospect of watches in T-shirts and shorts was a lot more appealing than that of taking 20 minutes to struggle into layers of warm and foul weather gear before venturing out on deck. Thunderstorms and torrential rain the first night were followed by moderate tailwinds the second day. *Steinlager* eased away from her opposition under her big red main and mizzen spinnakers, and by day three was 11 miles ahead of *F&P* and *The Card*. *Merit* was 20 miles astern with *Rothmans* a further 10 miles behind.

It appeared that Lawrie Smith on *Rothmans* had decided there was no point in trailing *Steinlager*. As long as they followed they would never make up the 50 hours that separated the two boats on corrected time (handicap). So immediately after clearing Punta, *Rothmans* spiralled off on a course well to the east of the rhumb-line. Blake and Quilter opted for a middle track in order to keep close tabs on *Steinlager*'s more immediate rivals, *Merit* and *F&P*.

However, the 'outside route' paid immediate dividends. While in the first 48 hours *Rothmans* paid for the easting she needed to make, she then picked up the breeze that Smith was looking for and turned an 81-mile deficit into a 25-mile lead. *Steinlager*, committed to her cover of *Merit* and *F&P*, could only watch as, over the next few days, *Rothmans* continued to march away across the chart, extending her lead to a hefty 80 miles. There was no panic aboard the big red boat just yet, as 50 hours was a lot of time for Smith to make up and the Doldrums were just ahead. Of greater concern was the fact that no one had remembered to put sea-water shampoo or soap on board in Punta. In the freezing Southern Ocean you could learn to live without washing, but in the steamy tropics it was important to wash occasionally to get rid of the perspiration build-up.

218

Reaching around the north-east corner of Brazil, the wind was so steady that sail changes were rare and, true to 'Sod's Law of the Sea', what few there were invariably occurred during the standby watch's meal-time, prompting the observation from Godfrey Cray that it was like going for a quick three-kilometre run between the main course and dessert during an evening meal at home.

By day 11 the weather maps and satellite pictures showed the Doldrums to be dead ahead. It is a natural phenomenon that the windless belt is narrower on the Brazilian side of the Atlantic than the African, and so the likelihood of getting caught out badly is a little less than it is further out into the Atlantic. As *Steinlager* closed in on the Doldrums, a 'window' appeared in the towering cumulonimbus clouds that dominated on the weather satellite receiver. *Steinlager* altered course and headed straight for this potential escape route and, with Blake's lucky socks not even out of their bag, the big red boat slid right on through, hindered by only one night of heavy rain squalls.

Further to the east *Rothmans* slowed to a crawl in light or no breeze, while to the west and close in on the Brazilian coast, *Merit* and *F & P* had the best of it all and wriggled through into the lead. In one brief period of fickle Doldrums weather the tables had been completely turned – *Merit* was 26 miles ahead of *F&P* and *Steinlager*, while *Rothmans* was back in the familiar position of trailing the Kiwi ketches, this time by six miles. The race to Lauderdale had restarted and, to Smith's chagrin, the north-east trades were well established to the north of the Doldrums. The ketches were able to bring their big mizzen spinnakers into play and their crews relaxed and enjoyed the ride while the sloops disappeared over the horizon astern.

Sailing past the mouth of the Amazon River, albeit 200 miles out to sea, *Steinlager* experienced some peculiar waves, similar to a river in flood, which, it was determined, were caused by a deep-flowing counter-current that surfaced periodically to hinder her progress. Had anyone aboard been blessed with clairvoyance, the strange turbulence in otherwise perfect sailing conditions might have sent a shiver down their spine.

The heat was unrelenting. Sailing downwind, little air made its way below, particularly with *Steinlager*'s minimal deck openings. No surprise then that there was little sympathy felt for the Italian crew of *Gatorade* when they revealed on the fleet chat show that their ice-cream maker had broken down. Sailing around the eastern side of the Caribbean islands, still 1000 miles from Fort Lauderdale, the two ketches held the breeze and did nasty things to the sloops, which were now struggling with light tailwinds in an extended calm patch. In one 24-hour period, *Steinlager* and *F&P* put a whopping 156 miles on their rivals. The tension was building as another close finish loomed large – and now it was time for Blake's lucky socks to make a reappearance. The radio scheds became all-important as the *Steinlager* crew kept close tabs on *F&P*'s progress.

Then, only a little over 200 miles from the finish, *Steinlager* found herself becalmed off the coast of Eleuthera, one of the Bahama Islands. At nightfall, *F&P* was only just over the horizon astern and there were anxious moments the next dawn when a ketch was spotted on the horizon ahead. The relief was almost palpable when it turned out to be a big cruising ketch and *F&P* was picked out, barely visible, still on the horizon astern. The sail through Providence Channel, which separates the Bahama Islands, was almost idyllic as *Steinlager* slid downwind with big mizzen spinnaker set, gybing periodically to take advantage of the wind shifts. Nevertheless, *F&P* carried a freshening breeze and closed to within seven miles as night fell, and with the demanding Gulf Stream still to be negotiated, the Blake team most definitely had a race on its hands.

Like all major ocean currents, the Gulf Stream is a river in the sea. Its warm waters initially flow north-westwards out of the tropics and through the Caribbean until the shape of the coastline of North

America directs the water north-east, up the eastern seaboard of the United States, and then east across the North Atlantic to exert its major warming influence on the climate of Western Europe. Sailing south into the Stream can be a punishing experience, particularly if the wind is from the north and against the huge flow of water. *Steinlager*, however, was spinnaker running north-west, both wind and current mostly with her. With every inch of sail set, she charged down the steep seas in 30 knots of wind and driving rain, pedal to the metal, and conscious that on the hotly pursuing *F&P* they would be doing exactly the same.

Quilter called the lay-line perfectly and *Steinlager* roared on, right on target, to the finish line off Port Everglades. There was a moment of panic when the finishing boat announced on the radio that it had both yachts (*Steinlager* and *F&P*) on radar, three miles from the finish, but Brad Butterworth had been constantly monitoring the radar and reassured everyone that the information could not be right. There was no way that *F&P* could have caught up. Butterworth was correct, and *Steinlager* surfed across the finish line at 0430 hours, doing 15 knots through torrential rain, with *F&P* still eight miles adrift.

Meanwhile, the fresh tailwinds were a bonus for the sloops. They picked them up 150 miles from the finish and rode them all the way in, closing the gap on the ketches considerably. *Rothmans* arrived in Fort Lauderdale five hours behind *Steinlager* with *Merit* another 13 hours back. *Steinlager* was now just one leg away from the perfect result – winning all legs on line and handicap – and the New Zealand ketches were running first and second.

With just 3800 miles across the North Atlantic to go, Blake wasn't taking any chances. The crew went through *Steinlager* with a fine-tooth comb to ensure that she was in a perfect state of readiness for the final leg. The boat was moved to the Derektor Gunnel boatyard in Fort Lauderdale to have the rigs pulled out and checked once more. Then she was slipped so that the keel could be repainted and fine-sanded to a perfect finish. Every single item of equipment was checked and rechecked for the slightest sign of potential problems. Nothing, but nothing, was left to chance.

Even so, just 10 days before the restart, Blake was quietly going through the whole boat, checking it for himself, and spotted a hairline crack in one of the titanium chainplates that anchored the main shrouds that hold up the mainmast. He had a basic distrust of titanium, which was fantastically strong and light but which tended to hide or disguise any flaws that might be developing. The faulty plates were consigned to the yard's recycle bin while replacements were ordered from Southern Spars in Auckland.

By the time all the work was done and *Steinlager* was again back in racing trim, there wasn't much opportunity for rest and recreation, but some of the crew still managed a trip down to the Florida Keys and also to Cape Canaveral where they witnessed a spectacular space shuttle launch.

Much of Blake's pre-leg briefing was taken up with how *Steinlager* would be raced these final miles. The obvious priority was to finish in one piece, but the opposition would not allow a conservative cruise and there was also the tantalising prospect of an unprecedented grand slam. The line between ensuring a finish and maintaining *Steinlager*'s winning ways would be a fine one, but it would have to be sailed. The day before the start, Blake and Quilter took a flight in a chartered helicopter to get a bird's-eye view of the Gulf Stream – which would be a serious consideration during the earlier parts of the final leg.

The Card got the best of the start and led *Steinlager* by a boatlength as they rounded the inshore turning mark and headed once more out into the Atlantic. *F&P* and *Merit* were 200 metres astern, engaged in their own private duel. However, any hopes of an easy ride were dashed the next day when the breeze swung through to the north-

222

west to put the fleet on the wind. The fresh trade winds blowing against the 4-knot current of the Gulf Stream kicked up a nasty seaway and *Steinlager* found herself crashing to windward under double-reefed mainsail and No. 4 jib. Damage was almost inevitable given the combination of fresh winds against strong current, and the evening radio sched produced the first casualty. *Gatorade* informed the fleet that she had rig problems after losing her port spreader and was diverting to St Augustine to make repairs. *Rothmans* was the next yacht to head for shelter and repairs, also with rig problems.

As soon as the conditions moderated slightly, Don Wright was hoisted up both of *Steinlager*'s rigs to carry out a thorough check for any signs of problems. In the navigatorium, Quilter had a full-time job analysing both the weather and Gulf Stream maps as they poured out of the weatherfax. There were unpredictable and adverse eddies within the Stream that could catch you out if you weren't extremely vigilant. *F&P* seemed to be doing a better job of playing it for, on a more northerly course, she had stretched out to a 15-mile lead.

By day four the wind had swung back astern once more and lightened, leaving a sloppy seaway that made for slow progress. The *Steinlager* crew was left to fret over the fact that *F&P* might hook into a favourable new weather system and make a really decisive break. The wind freshened slowly throughout the day and they wound back up to respectable speeds, but there were still a lot of relieved Blake people around *Steinlager*'s radio that evening when it became clear that they had at least held their own against their arch-rival.

But later that night their worst fears almost became fact. At 0150 hours, the port mizzen chainplate broke. The standby watch raced on deck to help drop the big red mizzen spinnaker and then the mizzen itself, to unload the rig. The mizzen wasn't the only worry either. The broken chainplate fitting also held the running backstay that supported the main rig. Initially, the titanium fabrication remained attached to the deck, but no sooner had the mizzen spinnaker and main been

223

dropped to the deck than, with a sickening 'bang', the chainplate broke and let go completely. Only Butterworth's instinctive reaction on the helm averted complete disaster. Frantically spinning the wheel, Butterworth threw the boat into a crash gybe. In 20 knots of wind the unsupported mizzen was wobbling around alarmingly as *Steinlarger* rolled in the swells, until Dean Phipps climbed hand-over-hand up the rig to tie a length of rope around the bottom spreaders. This was fed back down to the deck and secured to stabilise the slender spar. Once a few more ropes had been added to further stabilise the rig, Steinlager was safe – at least for the moment.

The possible consequences of the chainplate failure were too scary to contemplate and nobody got any sleep that night. The entire contingent remained on deck creating makeshift chainplates out of padeyes bolted through the deck. After six hours of frantic work, the mizzen was rehoisted and *Steinlager* was back up to full speed again. Throughout the repair, she had been forced to sail downwind on the unfavourable starboard gybe, losing a lot of valuable ground to *Merit* and *F&P*. But she was still in the race with her rigs intact. (The following day *British Defender* was not so lucky. Her mast toppled over the side when a cap stay failed.)

Nevertheless, Blake wasn't entirely happy with the structural integrity of the emergency padeyes and, together with McKay, devised a stronger option. A new chainplate was fabricated from a piece of aluminium cut out of the engine bed and bent into the required shape. Once fitted, the boat could be pushed to its maximum again. It was further decided to keep the events of the night from the rest of the fleet in case Dalton or Fehlmann were prompted to push even harder. The secrecy proved unnecessary, however, as they were to learn later that *F&P* had also gone close to a second mizzen dismasting when their mizzen forestay broke.

On day eight the sea temperature dropped from 18 degrees to 1.2 degrees Celsius in less than two hours. *Steinlager* was out of the Gulf

With the author Alan Sefton on *Ceramco*. Blake and Sefton worked together on three
Whitbread campaigns and a Trophée Jules Verne before forming Team New Zealand for
the America's Cup win in 1995 and successful defence in 2000. They were then, with Scott
Chapman, business partners in blakexpeditions. *Alistair Black, Pickthall Picture Library*

Blake with Pippa, Sarah-Jane and Tom Clark aboard *Lion New Zealand* in 1985.
Clark became a personal friend and campaign mentor.

Lion New Zealand undergoing sea trials in the Hauraki Gulf in 1985. Weight problems – she was too heavy – denied her any chance of major success in the 1985–86 Whitbread.

In the mid-Tasman on *Lion New Zealand*. Like *Ceramco* before her, she was first to finish in the Sydney–Hobart classic (1984) and then did a tour of ports on the New Zealand coast.

Blake and Douglas Myers visiting the America's Cup New Zealand challenge base in Fremantle in 1987. Myers became a main supporter of Blake campaigns, which he saw as good for New Zealand.

The dramatically fast *Steinlager 1* in the 1989 Two-man Round Australia race.

Fractional and masthead – the big ketches *Steinlager 2* (foreground) and *Fisher & Paykel* working up for a Whitbread first and second.

'Big Red' – *Steinlager 2* on the wind in the Hauraki Gulf. Her light airs speed was decisive. *Roger Lean-Vercoe, Pickthall Picture Library*

Steinlager 2 – swooping across the finish line in Southampton, mission completed. *Roger Lean-Vercoe, Pickthall Picture Library*

Game, set and match – the Blakes enjoy Whitbread victory.
Roger Lean-Vercoe, Pickthall Picture Library

Left: Something to smile about – on the helm of the all-conquering *Steinlager 2*. *Below:* Cape Town, 1993 – Blake and Robin Knox-Johnston examine the damage to *ENZA New Zealand*'s starboard hull that ended her first Trophée Jules Verne record attempt. *Barry Pickthall, Pickthall Picture Library*

Pippa Blake prepares the food for *ENZA*'s abortive 1993 Jules Verne attempt – 'How much porridge does one man eat in a sitting?' *Peter Bentley, Pickthall Picture Library*

Blake, Buchanan and McKay prepare to stream the warp and chain bridle astern of *ENZA*. The bite of the chain, in a loop, towed 85 metres (or about one and a half wave lengths) behind the boat, slowed *ENZA* to a controllable 8 to 10 knots and stopped her pitch-poling in a full winter storm as she neared the 1994 Jules Verne finish.

ENZA in the Western Approaches – closing in on the 1994 Jules Verne finish and a world record of 74 days, 22 hours, 17 minutes, 22 seconds for sailing non-stop around the world. *Mark Pepper, Pickthall Picture Library*

With warship escort and the brakes on, *ENZA* in storm-tossed seas off Ushant. *Mark Pepper, Pickthall Picture Library*

Stream and into the freezing waters of the Labrador Current that flows south from the Arctic down the eastern seaboard of North America. The International Ice Patrol reports indicated that *Steinlager*'s chosen course for the Atlantic crossing would take her through an area of 'numerous icebergs' and, having already sighted three very large bergs, Blake decided on a slightly more circuitous course to the south of the heavy ice to reduce the risk of collisions and consequent holings in the dense fog around the Newfoundland Banks. With a lot of time to make up, Dalton continued on the more direct great circle course.

Steinlager and *F&P* led the fleet eastwards and out into the North Atlantic in frustratingly light headwinds, but the other maxis were powering up on them and the biggest improver was *Rothmans*. The weather maps indicated that they could expect an extended period of beating to windward in freshening headwinds behind a slow-moving low-pressure system. In punishing seas, the wear and tear of the long journey began to catch up with *Steinlager* and she started breaking shackles and deck fittings with monotonous regularity, again prompting a consideration of whether to nurse the boat to ensure a finish or to push on at full speed with fingers – and everything else – crossed. The resolution was a compromise – to back off when the sea conditions became lumpy and the boat was slamming, and to go flat out as soon as the sea state allowed it. The middle-ground approach worked for, at dawn on day 12 as *Steinlager* wriggled her way to windward in very light airs, *F&P* was sighted for the first time in 10 days. The previous evening, Dalton had called on the VHF radio to see how *Steinlager* was going; *F&P*, he said, was virtually becalmed under huge black clouds.

By this stage the amount of windward work on this leg was starting to irritate. Tacking on every major shift meant that the off watch, woken each time to shift to windward bunks, was getting little sleep. With four days to go to the Southampton finish, it was time for Blake to put on his lucky fluorescent socks once more, and it came as no surprise when the next day, 400 miles from Land's End, *F&P* was spotted three and a half miles directly to leeward. Almost inevitably, it seemed, another nailbiting finish was in the offing. *Steinlager* and *F&P* were going to slug it out over every last yard of the epic journey.

Off Lizard Point, on the south-western tip of England, the breeze disappeared completely and the two big ketches were becalmed within three boatlengths of one another, the two crews shouting good-natured abuse across the intervening water. Then the gentlest of breezes filled in and *Steinlager* slipped away to a three-mile lead. Then the wind again swung around ahead and freshened, putting the ketches hard on the wind along England's Channel shore. *Merit* had closed in to be 20 miles astern, but with the finish beckoning she was rapidly running out of time.

The final night at sea was mostly spent pushing tide along the southern coast of England, which is notorious for tidal gates around the main headlands that can stop a yacht in its tracks. After a brief park-up off Portland Bill, one such headland, a new south-westerly sea breeze sent *Steinlager* scooting across Poole Bay to the Needles, on the south-western tip of the Isle of Wight, with all reaching sails set. Even *F&P* couldn't handle the cracking pace and she slowly dropped astern. With the tide about to turn in her favour for the final 20 miles up the Solent, there was no catching Blake's big red machine, and she turned it on for the world's press and the hundreds of spectator craft with everything set on her dual rig.

Blake took the helm for the last hour while his crew constantly trimmed the sails and coaxed *Steinlager* along in a faltering breeze. The last miles became a drift until, finally, a puff of breeze filled her light airs spinnaker and nudged her across the finish line, 36 minutes ahead of *F&P*. After 18 years and five campaigns it was game, set and match – and history – for Peter Blake. *Steinlager* and her crew had won

226

all six legs of the race, on line and on handicap – a phenomenal performance given the range of conditions sailed and the quality of the fleet raced.

Blake's people paused in their celebrations to applaud the *F&P* crew as she came into dock. Dalton and his team, with their masthead ketch, had been formidable opponents and had won everyone's respect and admiration – and an emphatic Kiwi '1 and 2' was something to warm the hearts and tickle the pride buds of the folks back home.

Significantly, after nearly nine months at sea and more than 32,000 miles raced through all the world's great oceans, the Blake crew was still very much intact, and in fact was a tighter unit than when they had set sail from Southampton the previous September. They were a special group of highly talented individuals who had raced a special boat – with a very special skipper. Watch leader Glen Sowry observed in the book *Big Red*, which he co-authored with Mike Quilter: 'One of the strengths of the *Steinlager* campaign was the leadership. Blakey always led from up front and he pushed himself harder than anyone else on the boat. It's difficult to grumble about the skipper when he's alongside you on the foredeck helping with a headsail change, getting just as wet and cold as you are. He wasn't afraid to spend money, or ditch something that wasn't performing up to expectations. Blakey never put anyone above anybody else on the boat and allowed for people to have good days and bad days.'

CHAPTER
Ten

'A Cynosure for All Young New Zealanders'

The media reaction to the Whitbread result was huge. Predictably so in New Zealand, where Blake was achieving the level of esteem normally reserved for Everest conqueror Sir Edmund Hillary. Yet more surprisingly so in Britain where the major news outlets seemed to be vying to claim Blake for their own.

The *New Zealand Herald* on 24 May 1990 devoted the back page of its main news section to Whitbread coverage, under the headline: 'Blake's luck turns in double NZ triumph'. Alongside two large photographs, the subheadings included: 'PM salutes skippers'. The then New Zealand Prime Minister Geoffrey Palmer had told the two crews (through the NZ High Commissioner in London, Bryce Harland): 'Your win in the race is the jewel in the crown of New Zealand's outstanding yachting record.'

Britain's mass circulation *Daily Mail* ran a four-column picture of Blake and his family across its front page with the heading: 'Daddy's Home From Conquering The World' and the kicker line: 'World-beating yachtsman Peter Blake savours his finest moment'. The prestigious *Guardian* led its front page with the headline: 'Triumphant Blake Finds the World is His Oyster'. Its coverage was augmented by two five-column photographs of the finish and subsequent celebrations. The similarly influential *Independent* carried a four-column,

231

front-page photograph of Blake spraying his crew with champagne and backed it up with full coverage and more photography in its sports section.

Indeed, a couple of weeks before the finish, the *Independent*'s insightful yachting correspondent Stuart Alexander had led the paper's sports section with a six-column headline declaring 'Kiwi Warrior Heads for the Family Haven', over a story that commenced: 'The odyssey of Peter Blake, 17 frustrating years and nearly 150,000 miles of ocean racing, is coming to an end.'

'No one could accuse the 6 ft 4 in New Zealander of hubris,' continued Alexander, 'and yet the gods may still have a few tricks in store for him. When he arrives in Southampton in just over two weeks, the cheers which should acknowledge his victory in the Whitbread Round the World race will have more than a trace of relief in them . . . to his countrymen he is a kind of warrior-chief in a nation that reveres tough sportsmen [and the] Whitbread Race has dominated his adult life . . . Blake is a complex character. At sea he is a hard taskmaster, meticulous without being fussy, and in the early days he was prone to try and do everything himself. Now, he delegates more, especially as some key colleagues have matured alongside him. Even with the bitter disappointment of coming second in the last Whitbread he was still able to attract a first-rate crew for what has so far been the near perfect campaign in *Steinlager 2*. . . . Away from racing, when he has had enough, he shuts the door and rejoins his family, wife Pippa, daughter Sarah-Jane, 7 this week, son James, 3, and his circle of close friends. It is to that family that Blake, now 41, will return when this Whitbread is over. The worry is what he will do if he is robbed by something like gear failure on the last leg. Could the man who has been so obsessed with victory in such a tough arena walk away as a five-times loser with the spotlight on him?'

Following *Steinlager 2*'s success, on the other side of the world the main *New Zealand Herald* editorial on 24 May redressed the record and called for Blake's achievements to be recognised with a knighthood: 'Peter Blake, a Devonport lad who began a remarkable sailing career in tiny P-class yachts, received what may be the ultimate accolade when he sailed into Southampton at the head of the round-the-world yacht race fleet. Such was the comprehensive hold that he and his fellow New Zealander Grant Dalton took on the Whitbread event that British commentators were scrambling to claim some part of him as their own . . . The sailing world and those who acknowledge great deeds in any pursuit know better . . . It is an extraordinary achievement for two entries from one small nation to lead home an international fleet in what may justifiably rate as the longest and most gruelling competitive event in sport . . . For Peter Blake, the totality of his success in his fifth and final such circumnavigation is particularly sweet. It has been a 17-year commitment, a 150,000-mile blue-water odyssey, and a testament to superb seamanship and managerial ability. With excusable hyperbole, his victory has been likened to a personal Everest. The most fitting reward for such an outstanding ambassador for his country seems no less than that given the first New Zealander to conquer that particular landlubbers' summit.'

Later that year, on 23 November, when commenting on the New Zealand Sportsman of the Year Awards, the *Herald* editorial read: 'Few would have been surprised when Peter Blake was named as Sportsman of the Year. The fact that he was the overwhelming favourite to win the award indicated how broad was support for the determined yachting personality. His emphatic victory in the round-the-world race came after two decades of striving for that goal. In spite of the inevitable hoopla surrounding such international success, the modest and personable Blake remains a cynosure for all young New Zealanders. It was just as fitting that the crew of *Steinlager 2* should win the team-of-the-year award.'

The most telling testimony to Blake's achievement, however, is that of Mike Quilter and Grant Dalton. Quilter recalls: 'The

Steinlager 2 programme was a happy combination of the right people and Blakey in the right place at the right time . . . *Steinlager 2* was just one of those boats in which everything you do turns to gold, everywhere you go turns out to be the right way. Put good people on board and you win – and you expect to win . . . Pete was directly involved in everything, but he had also learned to delegate, which he did in a way which left you in no doubt as to the confidence and faith he had in you . . . It was almost the perfect campaign and it was probably a sign of Pete's campaign maturity – getting all the bits right. Maybe *KZ7* and *Steinlager 2* were the start of a good era in New Zealand yachting – the start of professional yachting. On *Lion*, it was the wrong sort of boat, maybe, and we were unpaid, so we didn't really make a huge splash. On *Steinlager 2*, we were a lot more professional than the rest of them – although Dalts, *Rothmans* and Fehlmann were right up there with us. It was the start of 15 good years I guess, that should still be going.'

Dalton admits: 'My whole view of Blakey was changed by the *Steinlager* campaign . . . The thing that he did on *Steinlager* that I didn't do on *F&P* was that he lived on a philosophy of employing the best people for the job and letting them get on with it . . . I can tell you now that, although *F&P* was second, we weren't even in the hunt. He dicked us good. It was arguably the best Whitbread race ever. On paper, *F&P* probably led for more miles around the world than *Steinlager*. What people have forgotten – and I don't remind them – is that he destroyed everybody on the first leg. So even though people talk about a close race, it wasn't – because he was gone. But if you forget the huge margin he built up on the first leg, after that it was really good stuff. Coming across the Great Australian Bight for instance, when he was surfing up our arse – wow! But basically, he just gave us a lesson. The margin doesn't look that much, but in actual fact there was a chasm between those two campaigns . . . So from then on, and to this day, I have employed what I learned from Pete.

The way he set up and ran the *Steinlager* campaign and the way he went about sponsorship. Hell, he wrote the book on sponsorship, and all we've done is follow the chapters and adapt them to our own ends. My respect for him did not grow until *Steinlager*, but then it was complete.'

Blake's sponsor was impressed too. The Lion Nathan 1990 Annual Report recorded: 'Aided by worldwide publicity from *Steinlager 2*'s Round the World race victory, Steinlager exports rose 22% to again reach record levels. Sales in the United States rose 33% and those in the United Kingdom by 84%.' While the Blake campaign clearly wasn't the only reason behind those impressive increases – the company had, for example, achieved new and improved distribution deals in both the British and US markets – the Whitbread race publicity clearly hadn't hurt, as Douglas Myers attests: 'We didn't have any sales in Australia. So the Around Australia race, while a great thing to do, was really supporting him because he had bent over backwards to be very supportive of us and was doing great things. The *Steinlager 2* campaign was different. I felt that was unfinished business and I thought he could win it. So it was a trade-off of being supportive of someone who had done well and who had done well by you – more than one would have expected. And if that's what turned him on, we could help him. That was a very successful campaign from a corporate perspective . . . The *Steinlager 2* campaign was good stuff, it really was. I think that if he had rested on his laurels after that . . .'

But, typically, resting on his laurels was the furthest thing from Blake's mind. While Lion Nathan changed its mind and did not want to complete the trilogy, Blake's enthusiasm for blasting around the world as fast as possible had only grown.

Recalls Quilter: 'Pete always talked about what ultimately became the Trophée Jules Verne, so maybe the trimaran (*Steinlager 1*) was the precursor to his around-the-world non-stop ambitions. But later on he was always talking about going up the Amazon and going to the

Antarctic. He was always thinking 10 years ahead – it was remarkable just how many of his dream projects that he actually did.'

Pippa Blake adds: 'Peter never was one to just let things lie so he was probably already putting things into place for the Jules Verne. It was obvious that he wasn't just going to retire from yachting. After the *Steinlager* win he said, "Never again – that's it!" But that was "it" in terms of the Whitbread race only. He really felt it was time to leave that. Why try again? Nobody else, probably, is ever going to win all six legs of the race again. They haven't yet, and I don't think they will. But there was still a lot more that Peter wanted to do in sailing, and by this time that meant Trophée Jules Verne.

'The *Steinlager 2* campaign was everything Peter could have hoped it would be. He got enormous satisfaction from it. His huge smiles at the end of the race said it all really – that particular moment, when he lifted the trophy above his head – he'd done it. You often see that photograph and it says it all. He had done the race in the right boat for the first time ever, and nothing had gone wrong. It was a great crew and they did it all pretty magically. He really felt that was the culmination of his whole career. He could put that one under his belt and put it all behind him. I think he thought he could then settle down to normal life. He didn't. He carried on with other things. We always talked about having a normal life, but I never knew what a normal life with Peter was.'

CHAPTER Eleven

Too Little, Too Late

W hile Blake was already focusing on the Trophée Jules Verne as his next great adventure, back in New Zealand and, more particularly, in San Diego, other forces were at work. Sir Michael Fay and the New Zealand challenge were mounting New Zealand's third America's Cup campaign in the space of five years. Dennis Conner and the San Diego Yacht Club would defend the famous trophy in 1992, in a new class of yacht that had emerged from the turmoil created by Fay's 1988 'big boat' challenge, or more particularly, San Diego's amoral 1988 catamaran defence.

The story of that ill-fated but hugely influential saga in Cup history is too long and complex to catalogue in detail here. Essentially, however, Fay and his advisors became frustrated with the long delays in San Diego announcing the timing and venue for its defence of the Cup following *Stars & Stripes'* win in Fremantle in 1987.

Fay's yachting lawyer Andrew Johns used some of the down time researching the history of the Cup, in particular the Deed of Gift that vests ultimate oversight and control of the venerable contest in the New York Supreme Court. Johns' research confirmed something that he had long suspected – that the Cup is in fact challenge driven as opposed to defender controlled. No challenge, no event, and – in the absence of mutual consent on the basic parameters – the challenger dictated crucial elements, such as the size and type of yacht to be used. If someone challenged in a 70-foot waterline ketch, for instance, the defender (at least by tradition and in the interests of fair play in what was officially and legally designated a 'match' race) was obligated to follow suit and defend in a 70-foot waterline ketch.

The yachting world had simply got used to New York Yacht Club defences in 12-metre yachts, and to the club, while still in the process of a defence on the water, announcing that – should it be successful in that defence – it would defend in 12-metres at Newport, Rhode Island, in three years' time. This was presumed to be the legitimate way of things – whereas it was in fact New York's way of controlling the event, right down to the boats to be used and the timing of the next contest. Gambling that San Diego was as ignorant of the real facts as the rest of the sailing world, in August 1987, Fay issued a challenge to race San Diego in 90-foot waterline sloops in May 1988. If San Diego had not received a prior challenge, it was now obligated to defend against Fay in a 90-foot waterline yacht.

San Diego, it transpired, had not received a prior challenge, but instead of accepting Fay's and negotiating from there, sought to have the challenge invalidated by the New York Supreme Court. But the court ruled the challenge legitimate and ordered San Diego to defend or forfeit. So in September 1988, San Diego obeyed the court and defended – but in a state-of-the-art 60-foot catamaran with a winged mast. The 'contest' against New Zealand's 90-foot waterline monohull was, most predictably, one of the biggest mismatches in sport and the cat won the best-of-three series 2–0.

Fay protested the use of a catamaran and the whole affair dragged on through various levels of the US court system until 26 April 1990 when the New York Court of Appeals, on a five to two vote, came down in favour of San Diego with one judge, somewhat remarkably, asking, 'Where in the Deed of Gift does it say that the America's Cup is supposed to be fair?' This despite being told by the New York Yacht

Club, the original trustee and keeper of the Cup for all but four of its 140 years, that San Diego's defence with a catamaran was contrary to everything that the America's Cup represented as a sporting trophy.

Although Fay Richwhite had been one of the sponsors of *Lion New Zealand*, Blake did not know the principals Michael Fay and David Richwhite very well. And while he accepted the legitimacy of the 'big boat' challenge and was appalled by the catamaran defence, Blake found the whole big boat affair and prolonged court proceedings distasteful. They did not sit well with his rather English view of how things were done, and he had little or no time anyway for the America's Cup and all its politics.

Fay and Richwhite, meanwhile, had taken the appalling court ruling manfully and challenged for the next Cup, in San Diego in 1992. They gave that challenge everything at their disposal in terms of resources and support and it would be fair to say that the campaign lacked for nothing in that respect. Nevertheless, it was a campaign that proved to be fatally flawed in its structure, and this became evident when people and boats were moved to San Diego for the final work-up before the contest itself.

It is conventional wisdom in modern Cup competition, proven by hard experience, that you don't hand your campaign over to a skipper, nor to a designer or designers. Uncharacteristically, Fay ignored that wisdom and effectively handed control of the 1992 challenge to the Farr design office. Intermediaries were appointed to oversee the day-to-day operations and provide the Farr office with the interface they would need, but these individuals, highly talented as they were in their specialist fields, were not strong enough and lacked the campaign experience to handle the Farr team or the people problems that emerged.

Ross Blackman, who'd helped secure product and official suppliers for the 'big boat' challenge, worked full time on the subsequent 1992 campaign and witnessed the problems first-hand. He

241

recalls: 'We had a management structure that, in reality, was dysfunctional. Michael had identified that he couldn't manage the campaign himself because he wasn't a yachtie and he didn't have the intuitive answer to things that required an immediate sort of reaction when it came to decision-making. So he put in place David Barnes, John Clinton, Russell Bowler and Bruce Farr as the management team. I was asked to come in and look after the business side. The net result was that Bruce and Russell were so strong that they ran the campaign, and they ran it from Annapolis, on the other side of America.

'We were 18 months in San Diego and it wasn't long into that stay that everybody realised we were short of grunt. It wasn't talked about internally but Michael obviously identified it and he sought advice on what to do. I believe he talked to Tom Clark, Douglas Myers and other people [and] was told that he had to get a one-person-in-charge structure and the one guy who could do the job was Peter Blake.

'Peter was approached, came in, and that turned that campaign around. Not to everyone's pleasure I might add, but certainly to my pleasure. I was delighted that finally we had someone who could and would make decisions. But Peter did not enjoy that campaign. The main thorn in his side – and mine – was the Farr office. We had a lot of really capable people on that team who could make great decisions but were never allowed to.

'The other main problem was that none of the foot soldiers knew who the skipper was going to be and they were basically gambling on who to align with – Rod Davis, David Barnes or Russell Coutts – so we didn't have everyone going in the same direction. When the skipper decision was finally made, there were more problems. That decision was that Davis would be the skipper/helmsman with Russell Coutts his tactician. It was Blake's job to advise everyone, so, late that night, he visited Coutts and told him. According to Blake, Coutts accepted the role he would play. Early the next day, however, Coutts

242

visited Blake in his apartment to tell him that he had changed his mind after talking to someone back in Auckland. He preferred to drive the back-up boat rather than be on the race crew.'

According to Blackman, once Davis was appointed skipper with Barnes his tactician, Coutts and Butterworth, teamed together on the back-up boat, quickly lost interest in the campaign. The only real positives to come out of it, he says, were: 1) that it finished and 2) that Blake experienced in a graphic way how *not* to run an America's Cup campaign . 'Having said all of that,' he adds, 'and bad experience as it was, it was invaluable in terms of 1995. If Peter had not experienced 1992, I don't think he could have gone into 1995 with a lot of the strengths and convictions that he had, because, before that, his campaigns had been much smaller and relatively short compared to trying to hang something like America's Cup 1992 together.'

Blackman found it ironic to be making some of the above observations. He was, nominally, the CEO of New Zealand's disastrous 2003 Cup defence that not only had a multiple management structure but was run by Tom Schnackenberg, who was also the design coordinator. And once again that structure prevented talented and experienced people from making decisions that might have meant a better result.

Tom Clark recalls that he wasn't sure that Blake would accept the San Diego job. He was still winding down after the *Steinlager 2* campaign and relaxing with his family in England. And he wasn't a fan of the Cup anyway. 'I was worried,' he says. 'I was hearing on the grapevine that there was no real excitement about the whole thing. Everybody was doing a job and getting through it as best they could. Then I got the call from Michael and went up there to see for myself. I went with an open mind but I was wary about what I would find. When I got there, I thought, "This thing is going to fly to pieces." So I said to Michael that there was only one guy who can rescue this operation and that's Peter Blake.' Fay asked Clark whether Blake would accept an offer to join the campaign, and Clark told him: 'Give him full control, and I bet he could be talked into it.' Fay answered, 'Right, go and see what you can do.'

'So I said to Peter,' recalls Clark, ' "You get full control." He was wary but I guaranteed it. But I sold him a pup, because he never did get the control he needed. He did his best and things were looking good when we were 4–1 up in the Challenger final. But it wasn't to be, and it was all preordained really.'

Douglas Myers reflects: 'During that period (early 1991), I started saying to Michael Fay, who I didn't know very well, that he wasn't going to win it because it wasn't his thing. Michael wanted to be the operator. He had lots of positives. He had the guts to do it, he had the money, and he had the charisma to create a lot of interest. But then to actually manage the programme, which he was doing . . . I said, "If you want to win it as against creating a lot of publicity for yourself, you've got to get a professional in there. Come on, if you want to win it, talk to Peter." Too late in the day, they did. Peter came in at the end and probably saw enough to know how he wouldn't want to run it. By then he was obviously patently nationalistic enough to be interested in winning in nationalistic sorts of ventures. Because he had been adopted by then, after the *Steinlager* campaign, as a national hero. And what else could he have done?'

The 1992 challenge was the year of 'The Little Red Sled', as New Zealand's NZL 20 was nicknamed. She was light displacement, carried less sail than her rivals and was more dinghy-like than America's Cup-ish. She was even more radical in that she sported a fixed bowsprit and, after the first round robin, a tandem keel. If the rest of the fleet was in the middle or towards the right-hand end of the design spectrum allowed by the new International America's Cup Class (IACC) rule, NZL 20 was at the extreme left. Instead of one keel blade, which was the norm, the tandem keel featured two long and slender fins to which, at the bottom, the 20-ton, torpedo-like keel bulb was attached. This cut down wetted surface (drag) and provided other potentially attractive characteristics. But what wasn't immediately obvious was that the set-up, while technically brilliant and with intriguing potential, would prove to have handling performance boundaries that inhibited speed development. And once the keel was on the boat there was no going back to a conventional set-up – the major structural changes required were too time-consuming in the middle of a regatta.

There were those who viewed the tandem as a step backwards from the highly sophisticated and beautifully engineered, more conventional keel used in round robin 1. They included the Japanese who insisted that *NZL 20* was faster with the conventional than she was with the tandem. But while the tandem may have inhibited speed development, it was the comparatively innocuous-looking bowsprit that proved a more obvious source of New Zealand's eventual undoing. And it was the bowsprit that Peter Blake wanted removed.

As top qualifier for the Louis Vuitton Cup final, in which her opponent would be Italy's *Il Moro di Venezia*, everything started well enough. But *NZL 20*'s bowsprit was about to become the focal point of the regatta. Up to this stage the bowsprit had been only slightly controversial, and in fact had been cleared by the International Jury for the Louis Vuitton Cup. But there was a new jury for the America's Cup match which held different views to the Louis Vuitton Cup jury, and when he made his move, *Il Moro*'s skipper Paul Cayard's timing and strategy were perfect, if a little knife-edged.

NZL 20 was 4–1 up in the best-of-nine series and needed just one more win to clinch matters. She looked the equal of *Il Moro* upwind and was quicker downwind. The margins weren't large, but in America's Cup racing they don't have to be. Also, Rod Davis and his crew, just about error free around the course, were showing Cayard some of the advantages of the tandem keel on the start line.

However, following *NZL 20*'s win from behind in race 5, Cayard protested New Zealand under International Yacht Racing Union (IYRU) Rule 64 which, in part, says: 'No sail shall be sheeted over or through an outrigger . . . An outrigger is any fitting or other device so placed that it could exert outward pressure on a sheet or sail . . .' The hearing of Cayard's protest, with both skippers in attendance, went deep into the night. Eventually, the jury found that, for approximately eight seconds, the tack of *NZL 20*'s gennaker was being controlled by a line from the tack of the gennaker through a block near the end of the bowsprit, which was a violation of Challenger of Record Committee (CORC) Rule 8.9. Instead of disqualifying *NZL 20* and awarding the win to *Il Moro*, however, the jury annulled the race. The score returned to 3–1 for New Zealand. But Cayard wasn't happy, and neither was the *Il Moro* 'owner' Raul Gardini. They wanted victory and Cayard wanted the jury to address Rule 64.

At 8 a.m. the next day, Cayard told a packed press conference: 'First, this jury, in my thinking, is consistently in New Zealand's camp on this issue.' He revealed that New Zealand had made a video of how they used the bowsprit and presented it privately to the CORC jury, who approved its use. This, he said, was highly irregular, as was the fact that a member of the jury that made the decision was the father of a crew member on *NZL 20*. Probably most importantly, Cayard pointed out that the Louis Vuitton Cup was being raced under different rules (relative to New Zealand's use of the bowsprit) than those to be used for the America's Cup match and this called into question the credibility of the entire challenger-selection series.

At this same press conference, Raul Gardini, the somewhat sinister head of the *Il Moro di Venezia* syndicate, told the assembled media: 'New Zealand has been racing in the Louis Vuitton Cup with an unsportsmanlike manner and with the same unsportsmanlike attitude using this bowsprit in this way.' The gloves were off.

Later that day, the Italians won Race 6 by 43 seconds and Cayard filed another protest, based on how New Zealand was carrying its spinnaker when 'straight-line sailing'. The complaint was dismissed, but not before both Cayard and Davis, with their respective teams of advisors, spent another long night in the protest room.

The next day, Dr Stan Reid, the chairman of the Challenger of Record Committee, and the Challenger jury held a press conference at which Dr Reid revealed that, the previous night, CORC Rule 8.9 had been amended again so that it now followed the exact words from a March interpretation by the America's Cup jury. Dr Reid added: 'New Zealand has told me that they will be complying with this amendment in today's race.' Cayard had won, with a telling combination of aggression and smarts.

With only a brief practice session to trial a new system for flying and gybing gennakers, the Kiwis did change the way they used the bowsprit in Race 7 and it was obvious that the crew's job had been made more difficult. More importantly, confidence was eroded and morale was low. Cayard won the start and went on to take the race by 53 seconds, levelling the series at 3–3 with two races still to go.

In a bid to stem the flow of events, New Zealand took the dramatic step of changing both skipper and tactician – Davis and Barnes were dropped leaving Coutts to take over the helm with Butterworth calling the shots. It looked like it might be a winning ploy when Coutts edged the start of Race 8, forced Cayard to tack away and opened up a two-boatlength lead. But the newcomers were short of match practice and small errors of judgement on their part contributed to Cayard's narrow 20-second win. In a dramatic turnaround, *Il Moro* was now just one win away from becoming the challenger.

The final match in the long and contentious series was a disappointment from a New Zealand perspective. *NZL 20* should have been at her best in the 12-knot breeze but it was the still-improving *Il Moro* that looked the more impressive with more new sails and the confidence of being on a roll. And there was nothing that Coutts and Butterworth – or the reinstated Barnes – could do about it. Cayard won the start, led at the first mark by 1 minute, 13 seconds, and remained more than a minute ahead for the rest of the race to win by 1 minute, 33 seconds. They would be the challenger.

Looking back, the bowsprit should never have been allowed to become New Zealand's Armageddon, insists Ross Blackman: 'I recall Peter Blake saying on numerous occasions, "Cut the bowsprit off!" That was Peter in a nutshell. If it wasn't going to work, get it off the boat. The sailors said cut it off too. They didn't need it and would have had it off in a heartbeat. But the bowsprit was a point of principle for the Farr office and totally driven by them. Pete didn't have the power to overrule them, and we lost.'

The bowsprit itself was never illegal. But the way in which New Zealand used it quite clearly could be. And the alarm bells should have been ringing their heads off at the New Zealand dock when, between round robins 2 and 3, the America's Cup jury (as opposed to the Challenger jury) was asked by both the America's Cup Organising Committee and the Challenger of Record Committee, the organisers of the whole regatta, for an opinion. Goran Peterson, the head of the America's Cup jury, said categorically that to use the bowsprit in the manner being employed by New Zealand – attaching the gennaker sheet to the bowsprit – was a violation of IYRU Rule 64. The America's Cup jury had not been empowered at that stage so was merely expressing an opinion. But as they would be in power for the match itself, with Peterson the chairman, one would have thought their views would have been taken very seriously.

In fairness to New Zealand, though, the Louis Vuitton Cup jury refused to be bound by the America's Cup jury's opinion, prompting Peter Blake to comment to the media: 'Here we are contesting the most prestigious sailing regatta in the world, but the referees can't agree on the rules. Where does that leave the competitors?'

Blake wasted no time in getting out of San Diego once his commitments were completed. He was frustrated by his ultimate lack of control and at not having been able to run the campaign his way. Within days, he was on his way back to England – but not before he'd had a wind-up session with Sir Michael to see what lay in the future. Sir Michael was non-committal on whether he and partner David Richwhite would back another challenge. They had much to think about and to discuss. But he did promise Blake every assistance should he decide to pick up the baton. That consideration would have been very low on Blake's priority list at the time. For the moment, he had had enough of the America's Cup, its politics and its protests, and wanted to escape with his family to their home in Emsworth and enjoy the walks on the nearby South Downs.

CHAPTER Twelve

In the Footsteps of Fogg

Mainly through the Whitbread race, a strong bond of friendship and mutual respect has developed between New Zealand and French long-distance ocean racers – each sharing the thrill to be had from challenging the elements and pushing sail boats to the limits in open waters. The French media also gives the sport the same lavish coverage as their counterparts in New Zealand, so the leading figures in French offshore racing are treated as sporting heroes. As a result of this enthusiasm, Peter Blake and his exploits were almost as well known and respected in France as in his native land. Hence it was no surprise that together Blake and the French should arrive at and confront the next step up of their sport.

Catamarans and trimarans were the go-fast machines of sailing and the French, with their record attempts around the North Atlantic, 'owned' the big multihull scene. The mainstream competitive sailing fraternity, meanwhile, remained leery of the big cats and tris because of their propensity to tip over and remain inverted, and only rarely did sailors from across the Channel – like Robin Knox-Johnston, Chay Blyth and the late Rob James (husband of record-breaking solo sailor Dame Naomi James) – seek to challenge Gallic dominance in this arena.

Always seeking new fields to conquer, Peter Blake had been

253

nurturing the concept of blasting non-stop around the world since before the 1985–86 Whitbread race and had had very preliminary discussions with the Farr office about some way-out monohull ideas. He'd also gone as far as to make what he called his 'master blaster', the third component in his sponsorship pitch for what became the Steinlager trilogy, and had challenged his French counterparts to try and beat him around the world in 80 days, following in the footsteps of the imaginary voyage of French author Jules Verne. At that stage, nobody knew whether such a venture was possible or, at that time, achievable. To sail 28,000 miles in 80 days, a yacht would have to average 350 miles a day (or 14.58 knots).

On his return to Britain after the 1992 America's Cup, Blake, together with Knox-Johnston, was appointed to the Whitbread Round the World race committee. As they were walking out of their first committee meeting, at the Whitbread brewery in London, their conversation turned to the developing momentum for what had been named the Trophée Jules Verne, a non-stop journey around the world under sail.

Not surprisingly, the French had taken the bull by the horns and, under the patronage of the French Ministry of Culture, were creating the Association Tour du Monde en 80 Jours, of which Blake would become the founding president. The first edition of the event was tentatively scheduled for January or February 1993 – in just seven or eight months' time.

Knox-Johnston revealed that he was thinking of a Jules Verne entry and Blake intimated that he had had exploratory talks with the Farr office about a long, slim and water-ballasted monohull for the same purpose. Knox-Johnston, who had done a lot of big multihull sailing in the 70-foot *British Oxygen*, the 70-foot *Sea Falcon* and the 60-foot *British Airways* – all catamarans – said he was looking for 'the biggest bloody cat I can lay my hands on', because they were good, stable machines that could be driven. The conversation lasted only about three minutes, at the end of which they agreed to join forces and pool their resources in the search for a sponsor. By this stage Lion Breweries had made it clear that they were no longer interested in part three of the Blake trilogy. Consequently five companies – three in New Zealand and two in Britain – were approached. Two of the Kiwi possibilities responded immediately, expressing interest. Nothing was heard from the other three.

Shortly afterwards I arrived in Emsworth to discuss with Peter the possibility of another America's Cup challenge. More than six weeks had gone by since *NZL 20*'s exit from the 1992 event and both Blakey and I had had plenty of time to sort out our thinking. My case to Pete was straightforward. New Zealand had, in the space of just six years, already challenged for the Cup three times. It had twice reached the challenger final and, on the other occasion, had been the challenger. That was a formidable record when you considered the performance of every other nation that had aspired to win yachting's biggest prize. New Zealand clearly had the talent to win, if we could only get the challenge formula right, I argued. Furthermore the country, through its support for all three Kiwi campaigns to date, had demonstrated that it had a huge appetite for the Cup and, principally through Sir Michael Fay and business partner David Richwhite, had invested too much time and money – and gone too close to succeeding – to let the whole thing drop now.

Nothing had changed either. The biggest attraction of the America's Cup was that if you won it, you took it home with you – event, attendant industry and all. That could mean significant direct and indirect benefits to New Zealand, particularly to its tourism, boat-building and marine support industries. This last element had been of major importance when, in late 1984, Ron Holland and I had initiated the process of interesting Fay in backing a Cup challenge. I was confident it would be a persuasive consideration with Blakey too. Both men were patriots, keen on seeing their country advance (even if there were times when they must have wondered why they bothered, given some of the treatment they later received from sections of the Kiwi media). Sure enough, after several days spent swapping thinking and ideas in our usual fashion, to see whether we were on the same wavelength, it was clear that Peter was keen enough to at least give it a shot. Given his very recent misgivings about the Cup, it was significant progress.

It wouldn't be an easy undertaking, however. Some rough budgeting indicated that we would need around $31 million to do justice to another campaign in San Diego – an awful lot of money – and there would be no safety net like the deep (and generous) pockets of Messrs Fay and Richwhite. We would have to stand on our own feet and the whole enterprise would have to be funded by commercial sponsorship. Could the comparatively small number of major corporates in New Zealand afford the dollars we would be seeking, and would they be supportive?

There was only one way to find out, and that was to ask. So we wound up the Emsworth sessions with the plan that I would return to New Zealand, do the preparatory work and set up meetings, then Pete would fly back early in September for the series of discussions we would need to have with the people whose judgement we respected in terms of the steps we would have to take. They included Douglas Myers, Sir Michael, Brent Harman (the then CEO of Television New Zealand) and Bob Field (the CEO of Toyota New Zealand), all of whom had been involved in the Cup before with the New Zealand challenge, plus senior representatives of Tourism New Zealand and Trade New Zealand.

Through all of this, I tended to turn a deaf ear whenever Peter talked Trophée Jules Verne, which he frequently did. That event seemed a step too far, even by Blakey's extraordinary standards. So you could have knocked me over with a feather when Peter arrived in New Zealand for our scheduled round of meetings and, with a huge grin, calmly revealed that he thought he had a sponsor for a Trophée Jules Verne campaign. I didn't even dare think about how we would put together an America's Cup campaign, with all its myriad demands and complexities, and mount a Trophée Jules Verne bid at the same time, but Pete seemed completely unfazed by the prospect.

Before flying back to New Zealand, he had taken Robin Knox-Johnston to London to meet with Brian Aitken of the New Zealand Apple and Pear Marketing Board, the government-controlled cooperative of New Zealand's apple and pear growers that was responsible for the grading and marketing of the fruit worldwide. The board had been a sponsor of the *NZL 20* campaign in San Diego, where Blake and Aitken had met, but only briefly. It used the San Diego campaign to introduce its cooperative members to ENZA, a new brand-name for its global marketing endeavours, and was now looking for a vehicle with which to launch that brand internationally.

Aitken was the board's General Manager, Fresh Fruit Export, and had just returned to New Zealand after a four-year stint in Britain where he was General Manager, Europe and the Middle East. He was on a flying visit to the UK when Blake and Knox-Johnston called. 'I liked what they had to offer,' he recalled, 'but at first I couldn't see how we would make it work. That night, I caught the flight back to New Zealand and used the time to write a paper for the board which I gave to Joe Pope and Dean Soldera on my arrival.' Pope was the board's CEO while Soldera was General Manager, Processed Products. With Aitken they operated as a troika, and what they recommended the board usually went along with.

'Joe and Dean liked the proposal so we put it to the board,' continued Aitken, 'wheeled Pete in and it was on. Next, we phoned Knox-Johnston in England and had him jump on a plane to Newport (Rhode Island) to buy the catamaran *Tag Heuer*. Time was of the essence if we were to be on the start line in January, and building

257

a new boat – multihull or monohull – clearly wasn't an option.'

Blake had been in discussion with top British multihull designer Nigel Irens and had two big Irens-designed multis under consideration – *Fleury Michon* (a 75-foot trimaran) and *Tag Heuer* (at that stage a 75-foot catamaran). Irens recommended *Tag*, which had the reputation of being a very fast and safe all-round boat. She would need some refinement, but would be more appropriate for the job in hand. Beautifully crafted by Canadian aerospace company Canadair, *Tag*'s construction – all resin pre-impregnated Kevlar – borrowed from the composite aircraft that Canadair was building and was quite unique in boat-building at the time.

Tag started life as the 82-foot long *Formule Tag* but then was shortened to 75 feet to fit the maximum length allowed by the new multihull circuit in France. This was achieved by lopping 7 feet off the twin hulls aft of the main beam. When the Apple and Pear Marketing Board bought her (in September 1992), she had been sitting in Newport for about four years, out of the water and very much neglected. So the first task was to get her to England where she would be brought back up to scratch as a racing boat by the Carbospars yard at the Hamble. Blake, Knox-Johnston and Blake regular Don Wright ('Jaws') flew to America to make the trans-Atlantic delivery.

A big powerful boat, *Tag* was known as a bit of a nose-diver – that is, she had a dangerous tendency to bury her bows when shooting down waves. There had been modifications to try and correct this characteristic by increasing volume in the bow sections. 'Jaws' discovered all of this when using the toilet, which was in the for'ard part of the port hull. *Tag* was pushed quite hard into a wave and he was literally squeezed off the toilet seat. The bow sections were panting in and out to the extent that they were losing displacement as the boat went down waves and the hulls were pressed in. This was clearly contributing to the nose-diving, and lots of broken frames and stringers in the bows bore testimony to the problem.

When the boat arrived at the Hamble, Blake faxed former crewmate (now yacht designer) David Alan-Williams with a drawing of *Tag* and a note that asked: 'What about a trip around the world on this?' Alan-Williams sketched in some modifications, including extended hulls, and faxed it back, saying 'Yes'. 'I always thought that length was the important thing on these things (record-breaking multihulls),' says Alan-Williams. 'It's a game of sustaining high speed averages, and from a naval architectural point of view, long slim hulls are easier to drive and you get the sustained speeds. So I was always keen to make the boat long.'

With *Tag* now out of the water at Carbospars, Irens was on the same wavelength as Alan-Williams and wanted the hulls back to their original 82 feet, with a 'nicer shape'. Alan-Williams wanted to go even longer but Irens was worried about *Tag*'s nose-diving traits and did not want to add further to the volume aft. So they compromised at 85 feet. To help curtail the nose-diving tendency, a new rig was designed with a very extreme rake to bring the centre of effort way aft. If you dropped a halyard straight down from the top of the new mast, it would have hung about four metres back from the base of the rig. Most importantly, the new mast was built of carbon fibre and, with new rigging of the same space-age material, the set-up was approximately 1100 pounds lighter than the original.

Another major change was the construction of a small, central control nacelle between the hulls and just for'ard of the aft beam. This replaced the tiny steering cockpits aft in both hulls that had proved inadequate – and extremely exposed and slightly dangerous – when running with a Force 10 gale during the Atlantic crossing. The nacelle would be the nerve centre of the vessel, housing all the navigation and communications equipment, along with bunks for Blake and Knox-Johnston. It quickly became known as the 'God Pod'.

Blake and Knox-Johnston flew to Paris for the official announcement, at the Yacht Club de France, of the Association Tour du Monde en 80 Jours and of the first Trophée Jules Verne race in January/February 1993. Knox-Johnston recalls: 'Everyone was making announcements and suddenly they remembered that we were sitting there in the corner. I got up and told them that Peter and I were together again, that we had bought *Formule Tag* and that we would be on the start line in January 1993. They suddenly realised that "Whoopsy, this is a bit serious". They were very much aware of Pete's Whitbread record and knew that I had done the multihull circuit, and it dawned on them that this was a serious Anglo-Saxon team.'

The rules for the Trophée Jules Verne were written by the would-be competitors and, in their simplicity, reflected their origins. The event was open to all types of vessels, with no size restrictions or handicap considerations. The safety of boats and crews would be the responsibility of the entrants and no physical outside assistance would be permitted. The start and finish would be an imaginary line across the mouth of the English Channel between the lighthouses on the Lizard (on the English side) and Ushant (on the French side). The course would be east-about around the world, leaving the Capes of Good Hope, Leeuwin and Horn to port and Antarctica to starboard. The timing of attempts would be coordinated between the Association and the World Speed Sailing Record Council.

Work on resurrecting and rebuilding the former *Tag* – now *ENZA New Zealand* – went on through the dark months of the British winter, with hardly a pause for Christmas, and trialling was carried out on an inhospitable Solent through a succession of winter gales. Finally, on Thursday, 28 January, *ENZA* was ready to head to Brest for a Jules Verne start from the French end of the line. Bob Rice, *ENZA*'s American router, had forecast a weather window for a start the following night.

ENZA beat out of the Solent into a freshening south-westerly and headed for Cherbourg before tacking to lay along the French coast, past Alderney and the Channel Islands and on to the north-western tip of France. But the breeze died overnight and Rice had to revise his forecast. The next window of opportunity would be Saturday night. *ENZA* put into Brest where the crew used the time to complete a host of unfinished jobs.

She would have two French multihulls for company – and as rivals – on her record attempt. Both were skippered by men who were household names in France – Bruno Peyron in the 85-foot catamaran *Commodore Explorer* and Olivier de Kersauson in the 90-foot trimaran *Charal*. Blake and Peyron had an agreement that, if possible, they would time their starts together and race around the world as well as chase the record for the circumnavigation under sail. De Kersauson, a local hero in Brest, was a loner and not interested in any such cooperation.

Commodore was berthed nearby when *ENZA* was towed into the magnificent Brest Harbour, and the Blake team grabbed the opportunity to look her over and compare vessels. The decision: of the two, *ENZA* was the right boat for the task. Despite her higher bows *Commdore* would be a wet ride. Her equipment was newer and she was nicely finished but, with narrower hulls, she was cramped below with everything to sustain her crew of five for the long journey.

That night Blake and his crew slept aboard and waited to see whether Rice was correct in his predictions. If he was, they needed to be on the start line off the dramatic Ile d'Ouessant by 0600 hours and then start as soon as there was enough breeze. This waiting for the right weather window was important. The Bay of Biscay can be a nasty place in a winter gale and Rice was looking as far down the course as the Canary Islands, off the coast of North Africa, and the Doldrums as he searched for the right combination of conditions to provide *ENZA* with the slingshot start she would need if she was to achieve her targets.

Commodore Explorer's router obviously did not agree with Rice, for *Commodore* was still tied up at the dock when, at 0551.58 hours GMT on Sunday, 31 January 1993, *ENZA* crossed the line and set out in pursuit of Phileas Fogg. There was no wind in Brest Harbour at the time and *Commodore* would not set out in pursuit of *ENZA* until 1300 hours GMT – some seven hours later.

In a 15-knot north-easterly *ENZA* had to beat briefly to clear Ushant but then set her large, 1.5-ounce spinnaker and set off at 18 to 23 knots. Rice's forecast was correct, almost to the minute, and the record bid was on. It was not the last time that the taciturn American would prove unerringly accurate in his forecasts, or that he would amaze the Blake team with the precision of his weather calls from the attic office in his Vermont home – even for parts of the globe as distant as the Southern Ocean. Rice, who had forecast the weather for Everest ascents and for round-the-world balloon adventures, would prove a real find.

ENZA averaged 19 knots for the first three hours, blasting along with her helmsmen hunting up and down to keep the apparent wind forward as they went for more and more speed. The noise inside the hulls was almost overpowering. After 12 hours she had scorched 227 miles. At that pace, she would clear the Bay of Biscay in the first 24 hours. Cape Finisterre was left astern in the early hours of Monday morning and *ENZA* rushed on to a first day's run of 403 miles, averaging 16.5 knots, even though the wind had freshened and headed her. There was still plenty of scope for improvement though. One of the targets was the world record for a 24-hour run, which was 525 miles.

The second day's run was 381 miles which meant that *ENZA* was 150 miles ahead of where she was projected to be and 100 miles ahead of the record schedule. *Commodore Explorer* was 128 miles astern while

Charal, which had started six days before *ENZA*, was 1800 miles ahead. Testimony to *ENZA*'s dramatic progress south was that it was already getting warmer and the crew were shedding layers of thermals on just the third day at sea. The Straits of Gibraltar were already astern, as the Canaries would be by tomorrow afternoon.

The third day's run was 405 miles at an average of 16.88 knots. *ENZA* had covered 1189.4 miles in those first three days, averaging 16.5 knots. The ride was wild and the big cat's motion violent, but she was gobbling up the miles. Still finding his sea legs on his first major offshore experience, video cameraman George Johns wandered on deck to proclaim: 'And I thought I was here to film Match of the Day.'

Approaching the coast of North Africa, *ENZA* found herself further to the east than planned, only about 60 to 70 miles to seaward of Mauritania, with a forecast of light easterlies for the Cape Verde archipelago, now just ahead. But *Commodore* was still 120 miles (or six hours' sailing) behind and not making any real impression.

By day 5 *ENZA* had passed between the Cape Verde Islands and the west coast of Africa. She had covered 1762 miles, averaging 14.68 knots, and was just ahead of the overall average required. A little further down the Atlantic, *Charal* was reported to be averaging 11 knots and was just south of the Doldrums, which were now dead ahead of *ENZA* at 5 degrees North. The high-speed sailing was exhilarating, with *ENZA* doing a steady 25 knots as she rode the backs of the waves.

The Doldrums in fact moved south ahead of them and were at 2 degrees North, filling the night sky with lightning as *ENZA* approached in very hot and sticky conditions, the wind switching between west and south. Now 300 miles to the west of *ENZA*, *Commodore* did a 470-mile day, and by day 8 was 30 miles further south than her New Zealand rival. The French were getting shore-based meteorological help, raising the question as to whether this was within the 'rules'.

The equator was crossed on day 9, which meant that *ENZA* had covered 3010 miles since leaving Ushant, at an average of just on 14 knots. Following a heavy rain squall at daybreak, the wind finally settled and she was out of the Doldrums and doing 16 knots in the right direction. The next obstacle to overcome was the South Atlantic High which was well south and west of its normal position. That could mean light winds ahead unless the high shifted.

Everything was working well on the boat and everyone was enjoying the fast ride. Blake, as per usual, was more relaxed and talkative with every day at sea. But in the mostly light and changeable conditions since the Cape Verde Islands, *ENZA* was falling behind her required average. She was too close to the South Atlantic High and continued to pay for it until day 16, when the wind started swinging through the west and the water temperature dropped quickly from 28 degrees to 22 degrees Celsius. They were finally around the back of the high.

The weather maps showed a succession of lows passing through at 42 degrees South, so there was no obvious need to go too far south to find the consistent wind they were seeking. Doing a better job of picking her way through the light patches, *Commodore* was already 125 miles further south and slightly east. First into the new breeze, she could be expected to stretch that lead in the short term. The first albatross and Cape pigeon sightings were a reminder that it was time to start making preparations for the Southern Ocean. Thermals and foul weather gear were checked, sails were moved aft and all unnecessary weight was removed from the bows.

On day 17 *ENZA* was back in the high-miles club with a noon-to-noon run of 392 miles. Both Paul Stanbridge and David Alan-Williams topped 28 knots during spells on the wheel and *ENZA* was off across the Southern Ocean, blasting along under full main and No. 1 jib, shaking and shuddering and tossing spray in all directions. *Charal* reported in to say that she was headed for Cape Town after hitting ice and damaging her starboard hull. At 47 degrees South, and with

264

a deep low approaching, she was about to encounter severe conditions and De Kersauson was contemplating seeking assistance from the South African Air Force.

ENZA's high-speed dash under South Africa continued until day 26 when, at 42 degrees 04 minutes South and 50 degrees 42 minutes East, and some 1500 miles out into the Southern Ocean between South Africa and Australia, her journey came to a grinding halt.

Following a particularly loud smack when a small wave broke over the starboard hull amidships, Don Wright came scurrying on deck in thermal underwear, yelling for the helmsman to fly the hull – that is, get it out of the water. It was 2 a.m. and pitch-dark. He'd been off watch, getting some rest, when sea water started lapping into his bunk in the starboard hull.

With an 'all hands call', *ENZA* was luffed up almost head to wind to slow her right down while the crew scurried to find out where the water was coming from. The boat was stern down on the starboard side and there was water in the generator room aft (the generator was half flooded). The front of the hull was dry, but the middle area and aft to the bunk area were 2.5 feet under water. There had been increasing problems with leaking centreboard cases in the preceding week but the crew had thought they had that situation under control.

The skin fittings were checked (and proved all right) while the portable hand bilge pump was put to use and the crew bailed with buckets. Finally, with the introduction of the electrical bilge pump, some headway was made on the water level. Wright, meanwhile, had felt the floor in the starboard hull flexing under his feet. Closer examination revealed a long fore-and-aft split in the bottom of the hull, just off the centreline, and a right-angle rupture up the turn of the bilge. As the water level slowly went down, it could be seen that the crack extended forward along a line of screw fastenings supporting some stowage netting. So long as they kept bailing, ENZA was in no danger of sinking, but her Trophée Jules Verne bid was definitely over – this time around at least. The boat's repair kit was probably just sufficient to control the situation but not to do the substantial renovation that would be required.

The work to stem the flow of water went on through the night, with floorboards chopped up to fabricate patches which were braced in place with sail battens. By dawn, the effort began to show results. The temporary repairs and patching were holding and, even though there was water still coming in at a steady rate, the torrent had been contained. Bleary-eyed and exhausted, everyone gathered in the 'God Pod' for a cup of tea (laced with whisky) and a discussion on the options available. They were few and none. It was clear that ENZA could not continue at full pace, which made it pointless to carry on with the record attempt. With heavy hearts, they turned the boat north towards South Africa and calmer waters. It was going to be a long haul to the South African coast, for ENZA was headed directly into the big high-pressure system that she had been skirting on her dash eastwards and there was little or no breeze in the offing.

The initial thoughts were that ENZA's starboard hull had hit a submerged object – maybe a shipping container floating just below the surface. She had definitely hit something submerged off Brazil during her dash down the Atlantic and her centrecase leaks had started after that collision. An underwater inspection of the damage confirmed what had been seen inside – the outer Kevlar skin of the hull was split longitudinally and there was a big patch of Nomex core material sticking out of the crack. The area affected was about a metre in diameter. There was not much that could be done from the outside, even if they'd had the materials. Also very much in evidence was the starboard centreboard, with a piece broken off its end. Other than that, and a small dent in the skin, there was no obvious outside damage. Perhaps the bit that had broken off the centreboard had hit the hull and nicked the outside laminate, starting a chain reaction that resulted in the cracking that caused the major leaks. Loading and fatigue could have done the rest.

It took 16 days for *ENZA* to limp her way to the southern coast of Africa, pumping every 15 minutes or so to keep the starboard hull dry. She first made the safety of Mossel Bay and then, after taking stock of the situation, moved on to Cape Town where she was lifted from the water for a fuller assessment of the damage.

The great adventure was over – at least for the time being – and Blake was considering his options. *Commodore Explorer* was continuing with her attempt and the initial view was that if she was successful, and broke the 80-day barrier, that would be it. It was important to be first.

I had been in South Africa to communicate with *ENZA* while she was struggling back to safety and to coordinate the shore arrangements for lifting her out of the water and making temporary repairs. On the long flight back to New Zealand, where Blake and I would report personally to the Apple and Pear Marketing Board, we reviewed the situation. If *Commodore* did succeed and set a new mark, would that not mean more unfinished business, rather than an end to Trophée Jules Verne ambitions? After all, the board already owned a vessel that had shown it had the legs to do the job, and the groundwork had been prepared – plus the world's media had displayed a ready appetite for coverage of the adventure. So wouldn't it make more sense to repair and – with the benefit of experience – modify *ENZA*, and go back and finish the job?

By the time we reached Auckland, we had fleshed out a new game plan that involved not only another *ENZA* attempt at the Jules Verne, but would also see the Apple and Pear Marketing Board become a sponsor of New Zealand's next America's Cup challenge.

CHAPTER Thirteen

Fully Fruited

D espite sustaining damage that had skipper Bruno Peyron considering a stop in New Zealand for repairs, *Commodore Explorer* went on to complete the global circumnavigation in 79 days, six hours, 15 minutes, 56 seconds – a new mark for sailing non-stop around the world and breaking the mythical 80-day barrier.

Blake and I, meanwhile, had had a number of meetings with Messrs Pope, Aitken and Soldera, working through a proposal for another Jules Verne attempt, and it was now time to put that proposal to their board. By this stage in his career, Blake had acquired an aura of authority and dependability that were only augmented by his track record for delivering and by his physical presence. He didn't say much in meetings or presentations, leaving the detail to me, but when he did speak, the audience was all attention. To complement that mana, however, he never lost the common touch and was invariably easy and engaging in one-on-one conversation. He simply told the fruit growers and their executives that the Trophée Jules Verne was unfinished business – both for the Board and for him – and that given *Commodore*'s performance and the experience with *ENZA*, a time of 77 or even 75 days was highly achievable in the existing boats. Furthermore, he had changes planned for *ENZA* that would substantially enhance her prospects of success. There were always risks when you went to sea he admitted but, given the right conditions and the touch of luck that all sailors needed, he was confident he could set a Jules Verne mark that would make the trophy *ENZA*'s for some years to come.

Pope and Aitken weighed in with a reaffirmation of the board's sponsorship policy as a means of launching and establishing the ENZA brand internationally. Despite being cut short, the first Trophée Jules Verne attempt had generated an estimated $NZ100 million worth of media coverage for ENZA in key European markets. While this was obviously important from a brand awareness perspective, of equal import was the facility for consumers to associate the ENZA brand with a quality New Zealand product. International yachting sponsorship provided a perfect vehicle for both objectives. Using a range of high-profile, image-compatible sponsorships, they argued, the plan was to establish ENZA as the premium brand of fresh fruit in the international marketplace within five years. They didn't have to add that they saw Blake as a perfect ambassador for those endeavours.

Blakey and I were then asked to wait outside while the Board discussed our proposal. In a very short space of time, Pope came out to advise us that the second Trophée Jules Verne attempt was a 'go'.

ENZA, meanwhile, had been shipped to London where she was 'parked' outside St Catherine's Dock, near the Tower of London, awaiting the board decision on her future. Arrangements were immediately made to ship her to New Zealand where she would undergo a complete refit and be modified at the McMullen & Wing yard before she was shipped back to Europe to be on the Jules Verne start line again in January 1994.

The modifications were substantial, most of them inspired by the experience of the first attempt. Blake gave Alan-Williams carte blanche to go right through the boat and make the changes they felt

272

were required. Another 5 feet was added to the aft end of the hulls, and the bows, which were originally vertical, were drawn out into long overhangs, with reserve buoyancy up high to make ENZA better in waves. The result was that she was 93 feet long in modified form, as opposed to her 85 feet the first time around. New and much better shaped centreboards and rudders would be a significant improvement, while a 60-foot-long false bottom of foam – that started at the bow and faired out just behind the aft beam – was added to the outside of the hulls to clean up the profile of the boat, add more depth and shift the centre of buoyancy forward. This would lift the bow and allow ENZA to sit back on her newly extended stern. The false bottom would also provide protection against collisions. In total, the alteration would provide a 15 per cent increase (1.5 knots) to ENZA's average speed and result in a boat that was much better to sail.

In addition, McMullen & Wing cleaned the boat out from stem to stern and repainted the interior. The pièce de résistance, however, was a complete new external paint job that was all apples and pears – there would be no mistaking who ENZA represented. Blake went a step further by applying the same apple-and-pear theme to crew clothing, foul weather gear and all.

When the 'new' ENZA emerged from the builder's shed towards the end of September for a 10-day tour of New Zealand ports before being shipped back to Britain for final preparations, she was now the biggest and probably the most seaworthy racing catamaran in the world, and she certainly looked the part. 'We've got the equipment and the crew, and we certainly have the will to finish the job,' Brian Aitken told the re-launch gathering.

Her crew for the second attempt would include six of the seven who raced her the first time around. Back for more would be Blake, Knox-Johnston, Alan-Williams, Ed Danby, Don Wright and George Johns. Two newcomers would be Barry McKay (replacing the unavailable Paul Stanbridge) and Angus Buchanan. It was an international line-up of four Kiwis (Blake, Danby, Wright and McKay), three Brits (Knox-Johnston, Alan-Williams and Buchanan) and one Welshman (Johns).

Also key to the programme would be weatherman Bob Rice. It had been decided that shore-based weather routing, as used by *Commodore Explorer* on the first attempt, was permissible, so Rice would be providing much more than situation reports the second time around. Blake had complete faith in Rice's abilities and that faith would be handsomely rewarded in the months ahead.

Everything would, of course, depend on the weather. All things being equal, however, the Blake/Knox-Johnston game plan involved a slingshot start and a dash through the north-east trades to the equator. Swift passages through the Doldrums (both going south and, later, coming north again) would be one of the keys to success. Heading further south, *ENZA* would follow the old clipper ship route, skirting around the back (to the west) of the South Atlantic high-pressure system and passing close to Tristan da Cunha, before flattening out on a course through the Southern Ocean that would take her past the southern tips of Tasmania and New Zealand on her way to Cape Horn. She would not dip down to latitude 56 degrees South to round the Horn until the last few days of her Southern Ocean traverse, and once around the Cape would quickly arc north-east into the South Atlantic again for the long haul back to the Western Approaches and the finish in the English Channel.

The projected mileages were conservative, but would make a mockery of normal passage times. *ENZA* would, for instance, reach the equator within 10 days of leaving the start and in another 10 days would be south of Tristan da Cunha and levelling out for her dash across the Southern Ocean. Thirty-seven or 38 days after leaving England, she would be passing just to the south of New Zealand and 12 days later would be rounding Cape Horn. From there it would be

274

a 25-day gallop to the finish, recrossing the Doldrums in the process.

With her greater speed potential, *ENZA* would not dig as deep into the Southern Ocean as Whitbread race fleets, which went down as far as 60 degrees South, chasing gale-force tailwinds and reduced distances to be sailed as the earth tucks in towards the pole. She would, instead, ride the systems as deep as 50 degrees South, and this was where Blake saw the big cat covering the high daily mileages that would be essential to achieving the target. In the approximately 30 days she would spend in the Southern Ocean, she would need to cover 12,800 miles, averaging better than 400 miles a day, to stay on schedule.

Overall, *ENZA*'s projected route and target times called for her to sail 27,500 miles in 77 days or less, and to do that she would need to average better than 350 miles a day (an average speed of just under 15 knots). 'That's a big ask,' Blake observed. 'But if the objective was easy, we wouldn't be attempting it, and the improvements we have made to the vessel are all designed to give us the best chance of succeeding.'

Back in Emsworth and making final preparations, Blake was getting ready to leave his family yet again, and he was finding that the process was getting harder each time, particularly with two growing children with whom he had a very special relationship. He would later write: 'Anything I have ever done, right from the beginning of our relationship, has been a joint effort between Pippa and me. She is the person I count on most and has always helped enormously.'

Despite the growing complexity and increasing professionalism of his ventures, Blake still involved the family as much as he could and, as usual, they were very much in evidence in those final weeks of the *ENZA* build-up, hard to miss in their apple-and-pear crew gear. It was again Pippa's job to prepare the menus and do the provisioning, and with weight so critical to *ENZA*'s performance, the process produced its moments, as she recalls: 'We'd be sitting in bed in the middle of the night talking about the food and working out amounts. Suddenly we'd wonder: "How much porridge does one man eat in a sitting?" Then we'd rush downstairs and pour a bowl of porridge, weigh it and zip back to bed to do the sums.' Finally, the food for eight men for 77 days was spread out in her parents' dining room, to be carefully sorted and packed into watertight bins. Three meals for eight people for 77 days equalled three bins a week for 11 weeks – 33 bins to be packed and stowed in total.

By 1700 hours on Friday, 14 January Blake decided there was nothing more to be done – *ENZA* was ready. Just after 2100 hours, the lines were slipped and *ENZA* disappeared into a black night, short-tacking down the West Solent and headed for the English Channel. Late the following afternoon, she was in the Chanal du Four off Ushant and picking up a tow into Brest Harbour where she tied up alongside de Kersauson's 90-foot trimaran *Charal* (now renamed *La Lyonnaise des Eaux Dumez*). Blake and the French skipper had agreed to a duel around the world and there were forecasts to be checked and a projected start time to review. Rice was predicting a perfect weather window early the following afternoon.

The two big multihulls slipped their lines shortly after 8 a.m. on a still-dark and windy Sunday morning and headed out into the main Brest Harbour and then for the start line off Ile d'Ouessant. After a wet and bumpy – but fast – reach out to the start area, they were finally ready to go and, at 1300.05 hours GMT on 16 January 1994, *ENZA* crossed the line and was off in a 35-knot north-easterly and very steep seas. *La Lyonnaise* beat her to the punch and was eight minutes ahead. This would not matter in terms of the record as their respective voyages would be individually timed, but rankled the racing instincts on the New Zealand boat nevertheless.

Rice had got it right again and *ENZA* bore away on starboard gybe to soon be averaging 20 knots as she chased after her French rival,

SIR PETER BLAKE

under complete control and already showing some of the benefits of her modifications, with considerably less water over the deck and a more bearable noise level inside the hulls. By the next morning, she was doing long bursts of 25 to 27 knots with a top speed of 29.2 knots. On the first go-round, she had struggled to better 25 knots and it wasn't until the Southern Ocean that 29 knots had been achieved. The first day's run was 411 miles, so the forecast 15 per cent gain in speed through the modifications was already being achieved. So too was the media coverage anticipated by the Apple and Pear Marketing Board. Five minutes of the start from Ushant was shown on prime-time television in France and there was a similar response back in New Zealand.

With Rice providing the overall picture from nearly 3000 miles away in Vermont, Blake and Knox-Johnston threaded ENZA down a corridor of wind off the coast of Spain and Portugal. The latitude of Lisbon was left astern early in the morning of day 2 and Madeira was coming up fast. Rice's advice was to carry on down the same course line, which would take them between 150 and 200 miles to the west of the Canaries, all the way to the equator, and was predicting 10- to 15-knot easterlies even that far south.

ENZA's runs started to build. On day 3 she did 457 miles, then 465 on day 4, 490 on day 5 and a whopping 517 on day 6. By now she was already south of the Cape Verde Islands, had just sailed more than 1000 miles in two days, and was claiming a world record for her 517-mile noon-to-noon run (which, by 1400 hours, became 520 miles in 24 hours). Alan-Williams recorded in his log: 'During the morning it turned out we have been going too low and wide of the Cape Verde Islands. So it is down spinnaker. The genoa and full main are set in 25 knots of wind. To keep things under control, Peter has set a speed limit of 28 knots. Now life is just one big speeding ticket as the 28 knots speed limit siren rings again and again. We started to really blast and were having a great ride, sitting on 28.5 with bursts of 30 knots. Barry (McKay) is decidedly uncomfortable and has the main sheet to hand. Time to ease up. Just as Pete pops his head up to also suggest slowing down, the boat sets off down a wave at 32.7 knots. Fortunately Robin and Barry had their heads down under the cabin top whilst talking to Pete, so he didn't see the speedo.'

ENZA passed through the ITCZ without dropping boat speed below 10 knots and was into a fresh south-easterly as she crossed the equator into the Southern hemisphere. Her time from Ushant to the equator was 7 days, 4 hours and she was already three days ahead of projected progress for a 77-day record. Bob Rice was giving Blake a three-degree-wide corridor, between 30 degrees and 33 degrees West, to sail down the South Atlantic, and advising that ENZA should get south as quickly as possible without straying to the left or right of that corridor. There was little or no wind to the right (the west) and the South Atlantic High was out to the left (the east). His forecast for midnight Sunday, 30 January (day 14) was for 5 knots at 260 degrees. He was wrong. It came 45 minutes late.

Such was the remarkable degree of accuracy in Rice's forecasting that Blake and Knox-Johnston followed his advice to the letter and kept ENZA tracking south down her private corridor of breeze for the next week. It was painful at times as her daily runs dropped to as low as 112 miles in the 24 hours to noon on day 14. But it was the only game in town as the South Atlantic High drifted slowly west and threatened to engulf them. Some 350 miles astern, La Lyonnaise had already tacked onto the lay-line to the Cape of Good Hope and was stuck in the high that ENZA was wriggling around, albeit painfully. But late that night came an abrupt change in the sea and wind conditions. ENZA was officially into the Roaring Forties and on her way again. The Blake team didn't need any urging to speed their escape from the clutches of the high, as Rice was warning that where they had been the previous evening, the centre of the high would be tomorrow.

ENZA continued to 43 degrees South before gybing over for her dash through the Southern Ocean. Behind her and falling ever further behind, *La Lyonnaise* skipper de Kersauson was reported to have radioed ashore with the comment: 'La merde sur la tete de le routier' ('Shit on the head of the router').

With Cape Horn not too far astern, *ENZA* had started her 12,800-mile mini-circumnavigation of the globe through the Southern Ocean. She would need to complete that part of the journey in approximately 30 days if she was to keep to schedule. By day 18 she was at 45 degrees 24.37 minutes South, 01 degree 48.18 minutes East, some 1400 miles to the south and east of Madagascar, while *La Lyonnaise*, still struggling to escape the grip of the South Atlantic High, was more than 900 miles astern and between Tristan Da Cunha and Cape Agulhas. *ENZA* was making nearly 10 degrees of longitude a day – which meant 17 days to New Zealand at that latitude and speed. Rice, tracking a 'bowling alley' between 43 degrees and 48 degrees South, was warning Blake to stay out of the left (northern) gutter as there were lighter winds up there.

On past the Prince Edward and Marion Islands and then the Iles Crozet, *ENZA* maintained a steady average of more than 440 miles a day. They were easy miles with little strain on boat or crew – until day 24, that is, when, in gusts of up to 55 knots and with Buchanan on the wheel, *ENZA* went down the mine, charging down a particularly steep wave and burying her bows deep into the valley at the bottom. Alan-Williams describes the plunge: 'The seas were building and it was getting quite exciting on the deck. Angus was driving and, although he hadn't been down there (the Southern Ocean) before, he was doing a good job. It was just one of those situations, but you could feel it coming. You kind of know after a while that something is in the air. The Southern Ocean is a strange situation. Everyone thinks you are always on this kind of big roller. Whereas the seas are more confused than anything you would get in, say, the Hauraki Gulf –

279

because you are living in the wave pattern of the storm that has been, you are living in the wave pattern of the storm you are in now, and you are living in the wave pattern of the storm that's coming. So you get these very confused seas and, every so often, these cycles of a big build-up. After several Whitbreads, it gets so that you can almost time it, to about every 45 minutes, and normally it's fun because you end up with a good surf. But on this occasion it was a tricky balance and the boat was starting to get a bit edgy. Robin was already on deck and Pete, working in the "God Pod", could feel it too. You could see him coming up through the hatch just when we buried the boat – bows under and ENZA grinding from 25 knots to a 6-knot stop. We could see it and could brace but Peter couldn't. He was shot forward the whole length of the God Pod to slam backwards into the edge of the chart table, severely hurt. It was a potential pull-out-and-abandon-the-race situation – divert to Western Australia or Tasmania.'

The irony of the mishap was that ENZA was in almost precisely the same position as when she was holed and had to abandon her first Jules Verne attempt.

Buchanan's penance was that as the yacht's medic he had to take care of his badly injured skipper. Blake was given Bufferin for his injuries, removed from the watch system and confined to his bunk with suspected broken ribs and a badly bruised back and pelvis. However, while the severe bruising was obvious and cracked or broken ribs – although extremely painful – can be dealt with, Blake's pain was much worse than that and the worry was that there might be internal damage. A bunk in a catamaran dashing through the Southern Ocean was not exactly the place to be with such injuries, either. Alan-Williams aptly described it as: 'Crash and bash all day long, like running on four square wheels all out of phase with one another.'

Blake was stuck in his bunk for a week with the crew running a

280

'meals on wheels' service, feeding him and helping him get his strength back. For the first couple of days he didn't want to know about anything, and then he began to get very agitated because he was incapacitated and couldn't get up and do things. Knox-Johnston and the rest of the crew examined their options, the most obvious of which was to divert to Perth or Tasmania where Blake could be properly treated. But that recourse was more than a week ahead and, anyway, the unanimous decision was that Blake was the spirit of the boat and, if you started together, you finished together. *ENZA* would continue at best-possible speed while the skipper's condition was continually monitored.

None of this information was communicated to the shore, but there were indications that all was not as it should be aboard the big cat. Back in New Zealand, in Blake's absence, the formation of the team to mount the next America's Cup challenge was continuing and early design decisions were being taken. It was one of my jobs to keep Blake in the loop with regular heads-of-department updates which were telexed to the yacht. When one of the departments repeatedly failed to deliver, Blake started to get angry and he finally, and uncharacteristically, vented some of that anger on me via a very terse telex message. Working 18-hour days to maintain *ENZA*'s twice-daily media communications while also putting in full days helping to organise the America's Cup team, I was on a short fuse myself. After a second extremely terse telex, I sent Blakey an equally abrupt missive to say he could stick it where the sun didn't shine. I'd had enough and there were better ways to live one's life. Almost immediately he came back with a brief note that read: 'Oh, come on Alan. You are getting as bad as me!!' Knox-Johnston had heard and seen some of this very unusual exchange between the two of us and decided that it was time I knew what had transpired. It wasn't until Blake finally came ashore that it was discovered that he not only had cracked ribs but had also cracked his pelvis.

While Blake gradually recovered, *ENZA* maintained her charge towards New Zealand, continuing to clock up 450- to 470-mile days without much effort, even though her crew eased back a bit to make life a little more bearable for their stricken skipper. 'We could have added probably another 20 miles a day,' says Alan-Williams, 'but eased up a bit, mainly because we'd get these great bellows from down in the God Pod telling us to "Stop jumping the boat around!" We'd look at each other sheepishly and mutter something like, "Sorry, boss".'

By day 29, Monday, 14 February, Blake was beginning to get back into it. Alan-Williams noted in his log: 'P. J. Blake is a happier chappy today, after a shave, and is now on the radio telephone to all and sundry who are at home to answer the call.' *ENZA* was approaching the Great Australian Bight on a great circle course to Stewart Island at the southern tip of New Zealand, with Rice telling Blake to head south-east to avoid a high that was spreading across her more direct route.

The following day Blake managed a couple of half-hour stints on the wheel in 18- to 25-knot winds. He was obviously itching to rejoin the fray, but it would be the end of the week before he was stable enough. (In Wellington, Apple and Pear Marketing Board chairman Joe Pope, in a meeting with New Zealand Prime Minister Jim Bolger, had advised him that Blake was eager to get back among it. Bolger had replied: 'I tried out his bunk when the boat was in Wellington. I wouldn't want to stay in it for long either.')

That morning *ENZA* passed the meridian of Cape Leeuwen, on the south-west corner of Australia. It was the second 'mark of the course' and she was now claiming world-record times from Ushant to the Cape of Good Hope and from Ushant to Leeuwen. To celebrate, there was tea and fruit cake all round. At the same time *La Lyonnaise* was passing the Kerguelen Islands at approximately 50 degrees South in the Southern Ocean and about halfway between South Africa and Australia. She was 1400 miles behind. Two days later, she was running under bare poles in 50 knots of wind, with a lot more forecast. She had run into a significant low which the French media were describing as a cyclone.

On day 32 *ENZA* was at 47 degrees South, passing below Tasmania. She was averaging 19 knots, 1500 miles ahead of where *Commodore Explorer* was on the same day and 3.5 days ahead of *La Lyonnaise*. But there were problems ahead. Rice was insistent that they had to go down to 57 degrees South – and quickly – to get underneath a ridge of high pressure with light winds that was stretching the length of New Zealand and blocking their path.

Blake ordered a more southerly angle with a reduction in speed to control the pounding that *ENZA* was taking in difficult seas. She headed south-south-east out of the Tasman on a course that would take her between Macquarie Island and the Auckland Islands, and south of Campbell Island. But the high-pressure system chased her south and east and it was a race to get down to 60 degrees South where Rice reckoned it would be safe to level out and head east again. While *ENZA* was making this almost right-angle turn, *La Lyonnaise* closed the gap on her by nearly 400 miles. It was significantly colder on deck when *ENZA* gybed on to a due east heading and set off along the 60 degrees South parallel at 20 knots, with her crew scrambling to unpack their thick thermals and gloves.

In the afternoon of day 36 (Monday, 21 February) an Orion from the Royal New Zealand Air Force's search-and-rescue base at Whenuapai, in Auckland, found *ENZA* at 59 degrees 46 minutes South, 175 degrees 53.5 minutes East. The Orion's (unofficial) mission on this occasion was not rescue, however. It was to receive George Johns' video footage, beamed up from *ENZA* by microwave link, for dissemination to television stations around the world. The *ENZA* shore organisation had perfected this technique and had already achieved superb footage off the Canary Islands and off the coast of Brazil as well as from south of Cape Town.

While *ENZA* was transiting the Great Australian Bight, the plan had been to collect new footage using private charter flights from the New Zealand mainland. But when *ENZA* made her dive south, the shore team ran out of land-based options. Only an aircraft such as the Orion could safely reach her.

The RNZAF was approached and, while keen and enthusiastic at operational level – finding sailing vessels in the open ocean was about the best exercise of search skills that they could get – there was sensitivity about being perceived to be using taxpayers' money to assist a private yachting venture. Some Air Force bigwig had just been exposed for spending $NZ800,000 of Air Force money on upgrades to his (Air Force) house. A completely different scenario to that in Cape Town, where the South African Air Force had been only too keen to send out a Hercules to receive the *ENZA* footage. The Orion ultimately flew a decoy mission almost to the Antarctic ice and 'just happened' to over-fly *ENZA* on her return journey to New Zealand. After circling the big cat above the cloud base, the Orion set off home with nearly two hours of Johns' footage that included live interviews with *ENZA* crew.

The high-pressure system not only chased *ENZA* south, it also moved east with her, so that she would spend the next 12 days at around 60 degrees South, threading her way through a most unusual weather pattern in the loneliest stretch of ocean in the world, with the sea temperature down to 1 degree Celsius and the Antarctic ice not too far to her south. With skipper Blake now getting about more, the meals on wheels service to the God Pod had ceased. Behind *ENZA*, *La Lyonnaise* was enjoying a much better run and had closed the gap to 742 miles, and was gaining at the rate of 100 miles a day. One consolation was that *ENZA* crossed the dateline 3 days, 20 hours and 11 minutes faster than *Commodore*'s 40 days, 6 hours.

On day 47, after nearly two weeks of slow progress, icebergs, and even calms at around 60 degrees South (and down as far as 62.5

degrees South), *ENZA* was at 58 degrees 22.1 minutes South, 75 degrees 12.5 minutes West and entering Drake Passage on an approach that none of her crew had experienced before. She was in a full storm, all sails down and hove to in 55-knot headwinds and 17- to 18-metre breaking seas in the most feared stretch of water in the world.

The boat was handling the conditions well, but Blake was clearly concerned. At the height of the storm, he managed to get a clear link through Portishead Radio in England. It was a beautifully sunny March day in Auckland when he made contact with *ENZA*'s position update. Then, soon afterwards, he came on again to ask me to stand by phone and computer. *ENZA* was being forced south and didn't have too much sea room between her and the Antarctic Peninsula as she was being swept along by the Drake Passage 'greybeards'. This was the first and only time in our 14 years of similar communications on his various adventures that Blake had asked me to stand by, or even hinted at potentially serious problems.

Alan-Williams described *ENZA*'s predicament: 'On this occasion, Cape Horn and Drake Passage lived up to their reputations. We had an horrendous time. The wind and seas built up rapidly and we were forced to heave to three times in a day and a half. It's always hard to measure waves but they were *big*. I go more on when one breaks, how big an area of destruction there is behind it. In this case, it was the size of a rugby pitch – just white water. They were 17- to 18-metre "Greybeards" and when they broke, you wondered if you would survive. It was like walking through a minefield and we were fortunate that we didn't get hit by a big one. We had a little bit of steerage on to manoeuvre around them, but there was not much else we could do. The north-easterly headwinds were slowly driving us south-west into the Antarctic Peninsula. It lasted about 36 hours overall. We'd heave to for about four to five hours at a time, with the centreboards up so that the boat could slip sideways and not trip up over them. Then it would ease off and we would get going again. We couldn't just keep drifting further because there was land not far away to leeward. All we could do was minimise the losses and survive it. We got everything ready to drop warps over the back in preparation for running downwind if we had to – all the rope and chain we could lay our hands on. We didn't actually deploy it in the end but it was good practice for later on.'

At last, on day 48, the wind moderated. The staysail replaced the tiny storm sail that had provided minimum steerage during the blow, then a triple-reefed main was hoisted. One reef was shaken out but immediately the wind gusted more than 35 knots and it was back to three reefs again – and then to the storm staysail as it gusted up to 40 knots. That was, however, a final front passing through. The wind went north-west and the sea began to settle. *ENZA*'s log noted: '*Lyonnaise* has caught up to within 367 miles behind. We have lost a 1000-mile lead while crossing the Southern Pacific. In the last four days, we covered what we normally do in less than two.'

As *ENZA* finally passed the longitude of Cape Horn, which was 100 miles to the north across Drake Passage, a small aircraft appeared overhead with the *ENZA* film crew and New Zealand yachting commentator Peter Montgomery aboard. They'd flown from Puerto Williams in the Beagle Canal and – because *ENZA* was so far south in the Drake – were carrying extra cans of aviation fuel in the cabin to pump into the wing tanks. (Montgomery still has nightmares about that trip, with vivid recollections of the pilot casually smoking cigarettes in a cabin that reeked of aviation gas fumes.)

ENZA's time to the famous Cape, from Ushant, was another record. She had covered the 18,000 miles in 48 days, 2 hours, 32 minutes, which was 5 days, 4 hours, 10 minutes faster than *Commodore Explorer*'s time. But the second half of the Southern Ocean and Drake Passage had cost her dearly. She would now have to do some smart sailing and weather routing to achieve her real objectives.

The Drake experience had also set her up badly for the journey up the South Atlantic. She had been pushed south and east so that she was clearing the Cape area in a very wide arc out to the east, akin to the old clipper ship route, as opposed to cutting in close to Statten Island and inside the Falkland Islands, as *La Lyonnaise* was doing astern of her.

There were other hazards too, as her course took her just north of the Weddell Sea out of which the huge icebergs calving off the Antarctic ice pack start their long journey to gradual extinction in the warmer waters of the Southern Ocean. The ice report warned of bergs as big as the Isle of Wight in *ENZA*'s vicinity. These create their own micro weather patterns and *ENZA* found herself relying heavily on radar as she headed east in thick, berg-generated fog.

She now had just under 22 days to sail the projected 8000 miles to the finish and much of that looked like it would be windward work and light airs sailing, which weren't her forte. *Commodore Explorer* had taken 26 days for the same journey. For the moment, Blake had *ENZA* aiming for a waypoint of 40 degrees South, 20 degrees West, which was near Tristan da Cunha, in order to skirt around the eastern side of the South Atlantic High. That waypoint soon became 50 degrees South, 41 degrees West as Rice forecast that the high would become more stable and not move east.

It was day 52 before *ENZA* started to get a wriggle on again. Alan-Williams noted in his log: 'Some fast and furious night sailing, with intermittent flashes of lightning piercing the thick fog. Lumps of phosphorescence are flying up in bright sparks, like off the wheels of a locomotive in the darkness. The boat is rattling along at 20 knots with only a boat's-length of visibility. The odd wave is raking the boat with spray for good measure. Good, steady miles all day long.

'The water temperature leapt from 4 to 11 degrees Celsius as the fog cleared away and for the first time in weeks one could drive the bus without hats, gloves or balaclava. It is possible we have just passed through a region of iceberg country, without seeing anything. But it is very wet with occasional dousings in the cockpit at 20-plus knots.

'These are the first big miles in nine days and only the third 400-plus mile day since Tasmania. We did 40 miles more than *Lyonnaise*. The French are claiming they are only 90 miles behind, which may be the case in a straight line to Recife but, from Bob Rice's latest forecast, they are driving straight into the high and an area of less wind.'

Two days later *ENZA* sailed out of the breeze and parked in balmy conditions at 35 degrees 17.2 minutes South, 25 degrees 25.4 minutes West. The crew set to work on the long job list before enjoying their first wash and shampoo in nearly four weeks.

Holding up to the east in order to clear a high-pressure ridge, *ENZA* continued to struggle upwind in light airs and by day 56 was only just ahead of the projected mileage to complete the voyage in 75 days. *Lyonnaise* was out to the west, making similarly slow progress on the other side of the ridge. The French were being forced in towards the coast of Brazil off Recife, which was where *Commodore Explorer* got stuck in light winds for three days in 1993. Who had got it right? The outcome of this particular tactical duel would almost certainly decide which of them reached the finish first.

They got the answer on day 60. *ENZA*'s 24-hour run was 383 miles compared with *La Lyonnaise*'s 202 miles. The apple-and-pear boat was 468 miles north and 300 miles east of her rival, having gained a day on them in the last three. This was the jump that Blake and his team needed heading into the Doldrums.

ENZA spent day 61 threading her way through massive rain squalls under towering cumulus clouds, but averaging more than 15 knots. She was now 556 miles further north than *Lyonnaise* which was closing in on the shore off Recife. Late in the day, there was a distinctive change to the clouds, which cleared away to leave just high cirrus. Rice came through by telex to say the ITCZ had jumped south. As she prepared to recross the equator, this time heading north, it looked like *ENZA* was through the Doldrums with her French rival nicely under control on the coast of Brazil. *Commodore* had crossed the equator on day 67 and taken another 12 days to finish. But as it turned out, Rice's Doldrums prediction was a little premature. It took *ENZA* another two days of waffle to fully clear the ITCZ into the north-east trade winds of the North Atlantic. The next hurdle to clear would be the Azores High.

By day 65 the *ENZA* crew were noting a series of lows that were crossing the North Atlantic ahead of them and that might provide the prospect of a slick last three days run in from the Azores. *Lyonnaise* had gone quiet, not giving out her position, which might mean that the French had problems with the weather, or boat, or both. There was another high developing in the West Atlantic and Rice's advice was to head due north as quickly as possible to get through a gate between this new system and the normal Azores High. Blake had *ENZA* aiming for a position 40 degrees North, 30 degrees West, before turning east for a three-day run in to Ushant.

By day 69 *ENZA* was sailing in a big, awkward swell and being headed, so that she was making course just north of east. That was spot on for the finish, but Rice was now urging strongly that they head north, or even west of north, to make best time to another weather system crossing the Atlantic.

Lyonnaise finally broke her radio silence on day 70 to reveal that she was 600 miles astern of *ENZA*. There were big smiles all around on the New Zealand boat, particularly on the face of Blake. As the wind started to build ahead of another front due that night, the crew set about a check of the rig and all other gear in readiness for what would hopefully be a fast finish. There were still 1620 miles to go but spirits were high because *ENZA* was 1200 miles ahead of *Commodore*'s time.

ENZA was heading north on port gybe in building seas. The starboard gybe was more favoured in terms of heading straight for the finish, but Rice wanted them to get to 42 degrees North before gybing over. The forecast front eventually arrived within 30 minutes of Rice's prediction – once again, amazingly accurate forecasting – and brought rain and a wind swing to the west of north. Blake immediately phoned Rice. For once, he and Knox-Johnston would overrule their trusty weatherman. There was no need to keep plodding north for another two degrees of latitude. It was time to gybe.

With less than 1350 miles to go, *ENZA* had passed to the north of the Azores and had, hopefully, turned the last corner in the track. She was on target to break the 75-day barrier, but there were more trials in store and she would nearly come unstuck and lose all with the finish line virtually in sight.

The wind continued to build through day 72, and by day 73 was a constant 40 then 55 knots. Sail on *ENZA* was progressively reduced until she was running square under bare poles, the main boom out to one side and windage on the hulls providing more than enough horsepower. She was making 11 to 15 knots with bursts of 20 knots, the howling wind whipping the tops off the waves and sending white spume everywhere, when – without warning – she went down the mine and nearly pitch-poled. Alan-Williams recorded in his log: 'The finish is less than a day away, but the opera most definitely isn't over until the fat lady sings, and you are not safe until you've left the auditorium, gone home and closed your front door. With "The Boss" at the wheel, the bows tipped down a big steep hole and we buried the hulls back to the main beam. The off-watch crew were shot out

290

of their bunks (the reason for always sleeping feet forward). The biscuit container in the galley was thrown forward three metres and exploded its contents everywhere, and the breakfast porridge, soaking in a closed pot, leapt up a metre and forward two metres to land on top of the food bins.

'We hurriedly reduced sail down to a triple-reefed main only. Then, as the nerves recovered, went gradually back up to a winged-out staysail and double-reefed main. The forecast now is for storm Force 10 winds later today or tonight, so it will be no easy finish. Just over 300 miles to go at 0700 hours. It could just as well be 3000. Ed (Danby) and Angus (Buchanan) are preparing the chains and warps to stream behind like a big bridle, if the forecast is correct and we have to run under bare poles (the same set-up that Danby and Knox-Johnston prepared at the height of the storm in Drake Passage, but wasn't used). A hurricane-force wind has passed just to the north of us, at 50 degrees North, which is not that far away.'

Late that afternoon, with the sea state getting up again, Don Wright was the next to go mining, sliding ENZA down a wave at 20-knots plus. The big cat did a handbrake stop at the bottom of the trough as she again impaled her bows in a solid wall of water, hurling her crew everywhere. That was enough for Blake. The staysail (the only sail set) was quickly dropped and ENZA continued under bare poles again. But she was still travelling too fast in 45 knots of wind and awkward seas. So, with all hands on deck, the chain and warp bridle was deployed in a loop from each transom, so that the bite of the chain in the loop was towed 85 metres, or about one and a half wave lengths, behind the boat. The effect was immediate. ENZA slowed to a controllable 8 to 10 knots – and just in time too. The wind quickly built again to 55 knots and there was another front due that evening.

ENZA was only 175 miles from Ushant, within touching distance of all her objectives, but her crew was being made to work for every last mile of the long journey. Ahead of them, all ferry activity in the English Channel had been cancelled and the French Maritime Authority had closed Brest Harbour to all shipping movements. On hearing that, Blake retorted: 'They can close the harbour if they like, but after sailing around the world we're coming in.'

The final night at sea, in a full North Atlantic winter storm, was as dark and wild as any in the whole trip. Great flurries of wind and spray whistled across the boat's deck, but the warps and chains did their job, keeping boat speed down to 8 to 10 knots and preventing the big cat charging down any more steep valleys. They could have gone faster, but there was too much at stake at this very late stage.

ENZA was still under bare poles and still towing her warps and chain when, in the early hours of Friday, 1 April, she was met by a French Navy pocket cruiser that took up station and escorted her to the finish. Aboard were Blake's French contemporaries on the Association Tour du Monde en 80 Jours – Florence Arthaud, Bruno Peyron and Titouan Lamazou – plus New Zealander Peter Cornes who had been delegated to represent the Apple and Pear Marketing Board while Brian Aitken got a closer view of events from the wildly pitching decks of a French lifeboat.

A large search-and-rescue helicopter loomed overhead and the grinning face of a Pippa Blake was spotted through its windows. Between the squalls, the warmth of the sunshine contrasted starkly with the wild seascape and the *ENZA* crew strained to spot Ushant light which would mark the end of their marathon.

Finally, *ENZA* was surrounded by low-flying media helicopters, cameramen hanging out their doors, as Blake took his big cat across the finish line to claim the Trophée Jules Verne with a world-record time of 74 days, 22 hours, 17 minutes and 22 seconds. And she did so still towing warps and chain from her sterns to slow her down.

CHAPTER
Fourteen

Team Game

The reception ashore in Brest was moving and memorable. It was Good Friday in a Catholic country, which traditionally means a quiet, family day, and the vessel coming in was the non-French contender. But the people – old and young – were out in force and lining the high headland that protects the Moulin Blanc Marina where *ENZA* was bound. And it was clear that they fully appreciated the significance of what they were witnessing.

Brest is an historic sea port and naval base, strategically positioned on the edge of the mighty Atlantic Ocean, at the entrance to the English Channel and the busiest sea lanes in the world. Its inhabitants have seen it all – storms, gales and invaders – and they've sent their men to sea for centuries and seen them come back and, sometimes, not return. So it didn't matter to them that the strangers, dressed in apples and pears and struggling to find their land legs on the marina below, came from the other side of the world and from across the English Channel. They were seafarers who had just sailed the world's great oceans and returned safely – and triumphant. They deserved the utmost respect for what they had done.

The applause was polite to begin with, but the deferential reserve was quickly replaced by genuine warmth and admiration as the *ENZA* crew and shore team made their way through the crowds and up the steep paths from the marina, headed by a tall figure of a man, clearly their leader, who had a young boy on his shoulders and his wife and daughter on his arms. Pippa Blake asked her physically drained husband whether he was 'going to do this sort of thing again'. The response was an emphatic 'No way'. Someone shouted out to ask whether he was happy to see his family again. He just smiled that famous smile that said it all.

Then he was congratulated by French contemporary and *Commodore Explorer* skipper Bruno Peyron. The pair just looked at each other, and Blake commented later: 'His eyes clearly said that he had seen what we had seen out there. We shared the privileged experience of having sailed around the world in under 80 days – one of our century's last great adventures.' This was a defining moment in Blake's life and a fitting climax to his career as probably the outstanding blue-water ocean racer of his generation.

Alan-Williams summed up their enthusiastic reception when he observed: 'We could not have finished in a better country, or been received in a better city by better people. They really knew and appreciated what it was all about.' The response by Blake and his crew was just as spontaneous. Immediately the arrival press conference was over, they threw open the doors to the venue to let in the public and then sat there for hours, sipping beer and chatting to total strangers.

Pippa Blake observes: 'Peter felt that (the *ENZA* voyage) was special, one of the best things he'd ever done. The children feel the same too. They really remember going to meet him in Brest as one of the highlights of our lives together. That was a pinnacle – a very moving experience. I know *Steinlager*'s win was a huge achievement, but Peter felt that *ENZA*'s was bigger. It was probably the most challenging thing he had ever undertaken and, therefore, the most rewarding. He'd done what he really, really loved, which was to challenge and be with the elements, relying on good seamanship. He'd seen Drake Passage at its worst and beaten it. That's what he felt he was all about – good seamanship. He didn't really have much time for people who weren't good at managing boats, at which he excelled.'

Blake himself wrote later: 'The jubilation aboard was amazing – the total thrill of knowing that not only had we made it around the world and broken the record of all sailing records (by 4 days, 7 hours, 58 minutes, 34 seconds), but that we were home again with our families and friends. No more drenching waves, no more dehydrated food, no more seawater washing, no more sleeping in damp bunks. We were extremely tired mentally, and physically exhausted, but this took nothing away from the exhilaration of what we had just achieved.'

Of the fact that *ENZA* crossed the finish line still towing warps and chain, Blake told an estimated 300 international journalists at the dockside: 'We probably could have taken it (the bridle) in before we got to the line, but it was still very choppy and there was too much nervousness.' And of the trials of the final few days, he remarked: 'It wasn't as punishing or as potentially dangerous as *ENZA*'s struggle around Cape Horn. It's true that we buried her on two occasions and came close to pitch-poling. We were in the Western Approaches, close to land, and the seas were shorter and sharper – the sort you can trip over. Off the Horn, however, the seas were the ones that would just pick you up and cartwheel you. If one of those broke on top of you, you would just go down and someone else would pick up the pieces afterwards. *ENZA* handled them well, but it was knife-edge sailing and we weren't certain if we would see the sun come up the next morning. It was a fantastic learning curve in seamanship.' (This from the man with seven circumnavigations and more than 400,000 ocean-racing and cruising miles under his belt!)

ENZA broke 11 world sailing records in the course of her journey. The big two were the new mark for sailing non-stop around the world and the best 24-hour run under sail. Her overall time around the world – 74 days, 22 hours, 17 minutes, 22 seconds – was 4 days, 7 hours,

58 minutes, 34 seconds faster than the previous best, recorded by *Commodore Explorer* in 1993. Her best 24-hour run was 520.9 miles on 21–22 January while heading south down the Atlantic off the coast of Mauritania. This was accurately corroborated by satellite positioning, whereas the unofficial mark – *Jet Services'* 522.7 miles – was interpolated from a recorded 514 miles in 23 hours, 36 minutes.

The other nine records were:

- Ushant to the equator: 7 days, 4 hours, 24 minutes (1 day, 15 hours, 2 minutes faster than *Commodore*).
- Ushant to the Cape of Good Hope: 19 days, 17 hours, 53 minutes, 9 seconds (1 day, 18 hours, 54 minutes faster than *Commodore*).
- Ushant to Cape Leeuwin: 29 days, 16 hours, 1 minute, 45 seconds (3 days, 15 hours, 46 minutes faster than *Commodore*).
- Ushant to Cape Horn: 48 days, 2 hours, 32 minutes (5 days, 4 hours, 10 minutes faster than *Commodore*).
- Ushant to the Equator (travelling north): 61 days, 11 hours, 35 minutes (5 days, 1 hour, 40 minutes faster than *Commodore*).
- The equator to the Cape of Good Hope: 12 days, 13 hours, 29 minutes, 15 seconds (3 hours, 52 minutes, 45 seconds faster than *Commodore*).
- Cape of Good Hope to Cape Leeuwin: 9 days, 22 hours, 8 minutes, 30 seconds (1 day, 20 hours, 51 minutes, 30 seconds faster than *Commodore*).
- Ushant to the 180 degree meridian: 36 days, 9 hours, 49 minutes (3 days, 20 hours faster than *Commodore*).
- Equator to equator: 54 days, seven hours, 11 minutes (3 days, 10 hours, 38 minutes faster than *Commodore*).

Equally as impressive were her best 10-days run (4347.5 miles averaging 18.11 knots) and her best 20-days run (8482 miles averaging 17.67 knots).

Two days later, when they returned to the Moulin Blanc to welcome Olivier de Kersauson and *La Lyonnaise*, the *ENZA* crew were

SIR PETER BLAKE

still coming to grips with their achievement. Messages of congratulation had been pouring in from all around the globe, and the media reaction – particularly in France, where top yachties are feted as heroes – had been nothing short of staggering. *ENZA*'s record-breaking voyage was the lead item on television and radio, and dominated the front pages of the country's major dailies. But Blake's thoughts were already turning to what would prove another date with destiny – the 1995 America's Cup.

In our round of exploratory meetings with selected business leaders, the consensus of the advice received was that a New Zealand challenge funded by sponsorship money only was do-able, but the most we could expect to raise in New Zealand was $NZ30 million – not a large sum in Cup terms, even in those days. The already tight budgets were trimmed to match that figure and we pressed on with the next steps in the process, which were securing a club through which to challenge, lodging an entry, forming a team and seeking sponsorships.

We had no money until we could generate sponsorship income, so Blake agreed to pay the entry fee of $US75,000 while I funded the day-to-day running costs, which were mainly telephone and facsimile charges. However, we needed not only money to submit an entry. We also had to have a club and a name. Moreover, it was vital to have a strong point of difference between the new entity and Sir Michael Fay's New Zealand Challenge. While I'd always considered Team Dennis Conner – the name under which the famous American skipper mounted his campaigns – to be more than a little pretentious, Team New Zealand had just the ring of patriotism that we were seeking. I put it forward, nobody had any objections, and so what would become one of the strongest brands in New Zealand sporting history was born.

Securing a club was a little more complex. We wanted to challenge through the Royal New Zealand Yacht Squadron. We were both members, the club had been the challenge entity for two of Sir Michael's campaigns, and we considered the Squadron's standing – both in the community and in international yachting – to be important to the sponsorship quest. The only problem was that the Squadron had already been approached by Chris Dickson, who was also planning a challenge, and an element of internal lobbying was already evident. The Squadron would have to make a choice.

As the deadline for challenges approached, we had not yet received a decision from the club, so we moved to line up an alternative. Peter was the patron of the relatively recently formed Gulf Harbour Yacht Club, based in the new harbour and marina development on the Whangaparaoa Peninsula, some 12 miles (by sea) north of Auckland. We explained the situation to the Gulf Harbour flag officers, who were most understanding and accommodating, and they agreed to be our club of challenge if the Royal New Zealand Yacht Squadron decided to go with Dickson.

The Squadron finally made its call, which was to back Blake and Team New Zealand. So, on 24 October 1992, the then commodore Brian Maples signed the entry forms and we shifted office into the 'Crow's Nest' library at the top of the Royal New Zealand Yacht Squadron's premises in Westhaven, in which there was barely enough room to swing a cat. The forms were then faxed and couriered to the San Diego Yacht Club commodore, Fred Delaney III, who welcomed the entry with the comments: 'We know the standing of the Squadron and of Peter Blake, and have good reason to respect the Kiwis. Their challenge is icing on the cake as far as I am concerned. A Cup regatta would not be the same without New Zealand.'

There was still the matter of the $US75,000 entry fee to resolve. Blake, at this moment in time, was in the middle of the Atlantic delivering *ENZA New Zealand* to the Hamble in England. When I advised him that all other items were in place and we were ready to enter, he phoned Pippa in Emsworth and asked her to visit their bank manager the next day to organise a wire transfer to San Diego. The media would construe this action as the Blakes mortgaging their house to pay the entry fee. While it wasn't quite that severe, the payment did make a very big dent in their life savings.

Peter Blake had come a long way from the disenchanted man who could not get out of San Diego quickly enough after the 1992 New Zealand challenge. He would later observe: 'Whilst the Jules Verne Trophy was the most exciting and personally rewarding sailing experience of my life, the America's Cup sits on a pedestal all by itself. It is unique. In the past, it has been full of mystique and dirty tricks, of political manoeuvring and espionage. I agreed to lead what became Team New Zealand because I really do believe in New Zealand's yachting industry and expertise. Peel away the cloak-and-dagger stuff and the America's Cup is just another yacht race with similar needs to any other long-term campaign that must have the right people if it is to succeed.'

A lot of thought, time and effort certainly went into ensuring that Team New Zealand had the right people, and the net had to be cast wider than the small but growing army of 'Blake's people', many of whom would play key roles in the events that would enfold over the next two and a half years. To begin with, Team New Zealand comprised just Blake, myself and then Ross Blackman, who came on board at the outset as business manager. The first recruit to the line-up was Russell Coutts and he was quickly followed by Tom Schnackenberg.

The Coutts decision was pivotal. We were determined not to make the same structural mistakes as the 1992 campaign was perceived to have done and, among other departures, would name

301

the skipper early so that he was a key part of all important decision-making. But there were other potential contenders and Coutts, in the view of some, came with baggage. He was very much his own person and could be difficult to handle. The truth of it was, however, that he was smart, inspired loyalty (albeit in a different way to Blake), was a ruthless competitor and – if you were going in the same direction as Russell, and if he agreed with what you were doing and why you were doing it – you couldn't have a better man on your side. The fact that he also had an engineering background that enabled him to understand, and become an important part of, the design process turned out to be a bonus of some significance.

We still did our homework though, canvassing the opinions of many of the top people in New Zealand sailing, some of whom were Coutts contemporaries and others his competitors with not a lot of reason to like him. The outcome was a unanimous vote that Coutts was the best man for the job. Blake immediately dispatched Ross Blackman, who had the best relationship with Coutts, to tell him he was the designated skipper and make him an offer. Blackman couldn't find Coutts anywhere in Auckland and finally tracked him down to the family bach north of Auckland. It transpired that Coutts was planning to work for the Nippon syndicate from Japan, who would also be challenging in 1995, but as Blackman recalls, it didn't take much to sway his mind: 'We talked for a while and then I put Blakey's offer to him. It was generous by Team New Zealand standards but probably was a lot less than the Japanese would pay him. Obviously, along with Blake's job description, it was impressive enough, because he accepted. Blakey had pitched it just right and we had our skipper.'

The choice of Schnackenberg was a lot easier. He had been around the America's Cup for a long time, was highly experienced in the game, and was a genuine intellectual who was well versed in the design processes required. Additionally, he was one of the

302

world's leading sail designers and a racing navigator who was completely at ease with all the electronic gadgetry that was now a pivotal part of that role. Most importantly, he had Coutts' confidence and got on well with the new skipper. One hitch was that Schnackenberg was planning to rejoin the Australians, with whom he had a long Cup relationship, going right back to Alan Bond's challenges in the early 1980s. Also, he didn't know Peter Blake very well. So he agreed to help with the early planning and see how the campaign developed.

The next additions to the cause came from close to the 'family' – Coutts' match-racing regulars Brad Butterworth and Simon Daubney, Blake's trusted sailing lieutenant Mike Quilter, and sailmaker Mike Spanhake. Thereafter, it was an unwritten rule that anyone brought on board would have to get the nod of the already incumbent. At this stage, nobody was being paid, nor would they be for some time. They simply bought into a campaign that would be run the Blake way – with lots of emphasis on compatibility, loyalty, personal commitment and accountability – and they had the confidence that the money needed to mount the campaign would somehow be raised.

A lot of emphasis was placed on good communication within the growing group, which would be essential given that Blake would be busy with *ENZA New Zealand*'s first Trophée Jules Verne attempt in the early months of 1993 and Coutts, who was living in San Diego, and his match-racing crew had commitments on the international circuit. If decisions had to be made, Blake would make them – he had never been shy in that department – but he preferred, and encouraged, the consensus process that quickly emerged in a team of people who collectively had an impressive range of skills and experience and also had the utmost confidence in one another.

One of the first tasks that Coutts undertook, and at his own expense, was an assessment of what design talent and data were – within the strict nationality rules of the Cup – available to Team New

Zealand in other countries, particularly the United States. Bill Koch's winning *America³* campaign had reportedly spent $US60 million on research and development to win the Cup in 1992. With its much more modest budget, Team New Zealand had to be open-minded and innovative if it wanted to close the technology gap and, if possible, achieve a winning edge. The Coutts exercise would prove highly productive in the critical months ahead as Team New Zealand developed its campaign philosophies and assembled a research and design group that was capable of winning the America's Cup.

In hindsight, *ENZA's* demise in the 1993 Jules Verne attempt was a blessing in disguise. It brought Peter Blake back to New Zealand in late March 1993, at a critical time in the formative process, and, even though we couldn't announce the fact until much later, led to Team New Zealand's first sponsorship.

As we prepared to report to the Apple and Pear Marketing Board on *ENZA's* Jules Verne failure, we decided to take the bull by the horns and not only recommend that the board should mount another Jules Verne attempt, but it should also become a sponsor of Team New Zealand. We floated our ideas with Messrs Pope, Aitken and Soldera and they were supportive. In their view, the 1995 Cup campaign would provide a logical extension to their promotional and marketing plans for the ENZA brand. So it was that we flew to Dunedin in April to meet with the board who were gathered for the opening of a new cold store in the South Island port city. We must have been persuasive, and no doubt the Pope, Aitken and Soldera troika had already done its work behind the scenes, for it didn't take the board long to give our two-tiered proposal the green light. The only condition on their approval was that we could not say anything of the arrangement until the apple and pear growers had been properly advised. It wasn't yet lunchtime, but we found the closest bar in which to toast the courage and vision of the nation's fruit growers – and with something a little stronger than apple juice, I might add.

Given that our $NZ30 million budget was too rich for any one company in New Zealand, we had decided to target a 'family' of five sponsors through which to generate a net $NZ16 million. We would then have a supporters' club to sell and other fundraising opportunities to pursue in order to reach our target. A vital element in our sponsorship packages was a Television New Zealand media component that Grant Dalton and Julian Mounter, then CEO of TVNZ, had developed for Dalton's 1993–94 Whitbread Round the World race in *Endeavour*. While developing those packages and finalising the media component we received a lot of help from TVNZ's marketing team, headed by Des Brennan, and from the country's two top advertising agencies, Saatchi & Saatchi (James Hall) and Colenso (Roger MacDonnell). That component involved bonus advertising for an agreed level of incremental spend with TVNZ and provided in itself a sound commercial basis for sponsorship investment. It also had the added attraction of locking a media partner into the campaign, guaranteeing a quantifiable level of media exposure. The packages, costing at $NZ6.5 million, would still be a hard sell in the economy of the time, but were decidedly more attractive because of the media element.

Still without being able to disclose our success with the Apple and Pear Marketing Board, we started in on our short list of potentials and, given the size of the marketplace, it was decidedly short. Time was not on our side either, as the Cup's nationality deadline was swiftly approaching, by which date we had to have enough sponsorship signed in order to guarantee any commitments made in terms of people or services recruited overseas. (Any non-New Zealanders working for, or contributing to, the campaign had to have New Zealand residency two years in advance of the first race of the America's Cup match, which meant by 6 May 1993.)

Russell Coutts, meanwhile, was continuing his assessment of what was available, and what was desirable, offshore. In the process, he learnt that Bill Koch wanted the Cup out of San Diego and, to achieve that objective, was prepared to sit out the next event and then, hopefully, be a challenger in the one to follow. In the interim, he needed to keep his research and design team on the pace with developments, and to do this, he was prepared to allow extensive access by a challenger to his people and technology. This suited Team New Zealand's needs admirably, and while Coutts focused on who and what we needed, or might like, from the *America³* portfolio, Blake met with Koch in Paris to lodge Team New Zealand's interest and establish its credentials.

Coutts' initial efforts kept leading him towards Professor Jerry Milgram, of the renowned Massachusetts Institute of Technology (MIT), who received a lot of the credit for Koch's technology. Milgram was already in discussion with the French, but was more than interested in what Team New Zealand had to offer, and agreed to fly to Auckland to meet with Schnackenberg and the rest of the group. But with a lot of names and reputations to sort and sift through, Coutts was still striving to identify who in fact was responsible for what in the *America³* design effort.

Another who was high on the Team New Zealand 'wanted' list was Californian Doug Peterson, generally regarded as one of America's leading yacht designers. From the outside looking in, he appeared to be the principal marine architect in the Koch set-up. He had already been contacted by both Blake and Blackman, but had made a verbal commitment to join the would-be Italian syndicate headed by Paul Cayard. On 12 April Schnackenberg faxed Blake to brief him on a series of conversations he'd had over Easter with potential design assets in America, including Peterson, telling him: 'We are pretty keen to get Doug who really enjoyed talking to you. He likes [you] and also David Alan-Williams, and gave PJB a good

306

write-up – this is a big factor. One of the keys in getting him to decide on Team New Zealand instead of Cayard and the Italians will be these personal relationships. They are going to pay him three times what he asked of us – assuming they get the financing. There is no suggestion that we pay him more – he understands our budget constraints. However, I think another phone call from you plus our efforts to get him down here to get a stamp on his passport could be very beneficial.'

In the midst of these negotiations, and with the residency clock ticking, Coutts met with Peterson in San Diego and phoned Blake and Schnackenberg to say he had finally met the individual from Koch's group who, he felt, had not only been a significant influence in the design of *America³*, but who understood Koch's complete design programme and could explain it to others.

Blake didn't waste any time. He and Blackman jumped on the phone to Peterson in San Diego, but they appeared to be too late. Peterson had decided to join Cayard and was about to fly to Italy to finalise the deal and kick-start his Italian residency. 'OK,' said Blake, 'fly to Rome, but do so via Auckland on a Team New Zealand round-the-world business-class ticket.' Peterson agreed and jetted south instead of east, on a round-about route to Italy. The courtship continued with a meeting in the Squadron's Crow's Nest.

Peterson's position hadn't changed though. While he felt the campaign being put together by Team New Zealand would have the greater chance of succeeding, the Italian offer, in financial terms, was too good to turn down. Not to be deterred, Blake asked: 'What if we were to offer you the same money as the Italians. Would you say "Yes"?' Peterson replied that he would, and before he could change his mind they shook hands and the deal was done.

Blackman, while delighted to have secured Peterson, was also dismayed. What represented a hefty portion of Team New Zealand's all-up design budget had just been committed in one deal. Where would the extra money come from? Blake simply shrugged and said: 'We'll find it. We have to.'

As it turned out, we didn't have to. Peterson would do what he considered to be the right thing by Team New Zealand. Fully aware of our small and extremely tight budget, he ventured that if Italy failed to raise the money to challenge, he would work for Team New Zealand on the terms originally discussed.

To his eternal credit, on the day that late entries closed and Italy was not in the final line-up, Peterson walked into Blackman's office to shake hands on the terms of our initial offer – a handshake that cost him hundreds of thousands of dollars.

Team New Zealand had now committed its two principal yacht designers – Peterson and highly successful Kiwi naval architect Laurie Davidson. They would form a formidable duo with different, but complementary, design philosophies and talents, who would work with a group of top people, mostly New Zealand in origin, in a genuine design team.

A major departure from previous challenges, particularly the 1992 campaign, was the attitude that the ultimate 'customer' of the design group was the sailing team, headed by Coutts. In 1992 the sailing team was subordinate – in effect, contracted by the designers (the Farr office) to sail the boats – and had little influence on the design approach. For 1995, however, the old adage 'The customer is always right' would be very much front of mind.

Schnackenberg would coordinate the total design effort and, in a bullet-point briefing paper prepared for a full review meeting towards the end of March 1993, he outlined the thinking that had emerged from the months of examination and discussion of the challenge ahead. In the light of Team New Zealand's dismal performance in the 2003 defence, some of the details of that briefing paper make particularly interesting reading.

Under the heading 'Design Team Philosophy', Schnackenberg wrote:

1: We don't want to win the designers' award – just the Cup.

2: We don't want any big weaknesses – a good all-round boat that is conservative with respect to the opposition [is the goal].

3: We need good quality control of the research – i.e. check, check and recheck.

4: We need a wide variety of input attacking the design problem from different angles to arrive at the correct solution.

5: This starts as a design contest and ends as a campaign contest.

Under the heading 'Strategy', he wrote:

1. Source best candidates for design team, accumulate reports and info.

2. Evaluate accurately where we are.

3. Evaluate from all perspectives what was important tactically last time – including prediction of what will be important next time.

4. Develop a full set of design tools – [ones] that work!

5. Cover the existing gaps – in particular, buy some *A3* people and other experienced outsiders.

6. Take our time developing a plan – revise all information and budgets.

7. Define programmes.

And in a summary of Team New Zealand's assets and position, he noted:

Strengths:

- General experience and knowledge in campaigning
- Engineering

- Sailing ability and big boat talent
- Rigs and hardware talent
- Ahead in tandem technology
- Boat construction ability
- Yachting community/public support
- Large pool of full-size data

Weaknesses:
- No data from 1992 – tank-testing data etc
- No design tools or VPPs
- Likely to be trying to develop a different weight of boat
- Behind in conventional appendage development
- Behind in mast stiffness technology
- Possibly behind in sea-keeping
- Behind in aerodynamics and facilities (Boeing etc.)
- No base of IACC experienced yacht designers
- Limited number of research people in NZ

The 'weaknesses' column highlights difficulties that Team New Zealand was experiencing in sourcing pertinent design information from the 1992 campaign from the Farr office, even though Sir Michael Fay had given his consent for that data to be handed over. It was an obvious starting point for the 1995 campaign, particularly as *NZL 20* – the 'bowsprit boat' – would be the trial horse for the first yacht built by Team New Zealand.

The Farr office still featured on Team New Zealand's 'wanted' list whenever design assets were assessed, and Blake communicated this desire to Bruce Farr and Russell Bowler in Annapolis at the outset – even though there were those within his own camp with serious doubts whether the Farr organisation would fit with the design team approach that Team New Zealand was pursuing.

As the residency deadline approached, and non-resident assets were being secured, the Farr office still featured in the 'ideal world' option, in a design team with Peterson, Davidson and possibly Milgram, along with a group of wind tunnel, towing tank and construction experts.

At the end of March 1993, I sent out a position paper to would-be sponsors that outlined progress made. It read: 'Team New Zealand's 1995 challenge for the America's Cup has been described as the same old syndicate in changed guise. Nothing could be farther from the truth. Different leadership, personnel and philosophies are being employed to ensure that New Zealand's fourth challenge for the Cup has the most realistic chance yet of succeeding . . . The team leader is Peter Blake, who needs no introduction as one of the sport's great campaigners. The skipper is world match-racing champion and Olympic gold medallist Russell Coutts . . . The team they have assembled knows how to win where it matters – on the water.'

Both Peter and myself wanted to stress to potential sponsors that the most important departure to date from previous campaign methods was in the Team New Zealand approach to boat and sail design. Given that America's successful defence in 1992 was the result of a massive technological effort by the world's most technologically advanced country, a New Zealand challenge would need to be smart about closing the technology gap and even stepping around the world leaders while remaining within budgetary constraints. To do so, it was putting together a design and development team that would be as powerful as any yet assembled and which, with the approval of Bill Koch, would include key elements and people from *America*³.

After outlining the Koch people being considered by Team New Zealand – research scientist Professor Jerry Milgram and naval architect Doug Peterson – I argued that they would considerably augment New Zealand's traditional strengths in this critical area of the campaign, working with Kiwi designers, computer flow analysts, wind tunnel and tank-testing technicians and sail designers, and bring with them the vital design tools currently the best in the world. This combination of talents would have obvious short- and medium-term benefits to Team New Zealand, while the longer-term benefits to the New Zealand marine industry and technological community would be just as significant because the whole of this effort would be driven from New Zealand, in the process exposing a large number of our own scientists and technicians to a wide-ranging research and development effort which would normally be beyond this country's means or capabilities.

'This major pool of talent will be directly responsible to Blake and Coutts,' I emphasised, 'but will be controlled day to day by Tom Schnackenberg in the role of design coordinator . . . The approach to determining a racing team has been just as thorough as that which has gone into the design and development line-up. Coutts will skipper New Zealand's challenger . . . Around him he will have the very best that New Zealand can offer – and [his] crew will be named very early in the piece so that everyone can concentrate on how to get the most out of the boat they will finally be given to campaign . . . The enthusiasm to be on board is typified by Craig Monk, New Zealand's Finn bronze medal winner at the 1992 Olympics. [A] world-class helmsman and skipper in his own right, [Monk] is more than prepared to work as a grinder while also contributing to speed and tactics. It would be safe to say that no other country could assemble such talent in such depth. The key to all of the above is, of course, funding and Team New Zealand is now at the stage where it has to have up-front commitment from major sponsors in order to secure the people it needs before the 6 May 1993 nationality deadline. The campaign budget is $NZ32 million. This is less than two-thirds the amount invested in the 1992 campaign but, given the association with Koch, is completely adequate for the task without compromising the objective of winning.'

312

Having made our pitch, now we would just have to wait – and hope.

In the interim, for a variety of reasons – some clear and others not – dealings with the Farr office were not going well, even though Coutts twice visited Annapolis in late 1992. And matters weren't helped when Bowler faxed Blake on 15 December saying: 'If I was a lecturer in management I would be giving you a D for the work so far. It may be the NZ way, and maybe I've been here too long but it is not the way to win the campaign . . .' Nor by a Bowler fax to Coutts following their 24 December meeting, referring to a suggested follow-up meeting in February, in which he wrote: 'We see little value in an off-the-cuff, rambling, shoot-the-breeze style of meeting, much as we would enjoy it and the company of yourself and Tom [Schnackenberg]. If you still want to do this we suggest that it be done in a long evening or two with a few very good bottles of wine so that at least it is enjoyable. If you got any high-quality decisions from a meeting like that it would be a fluke. Any more of these and the D management rating handed out last week will drop to an E . . . Could you both please get the act together.'

Eventually, dealings with the Farr office lapsed into a negotiation over use of design and testing data from the 1992 campaign, and how much accessing the data would cost. Even that process ceased when Blackman calculated what it would cost: 'We couldn't afford the catalogue of data that would be made available, let alone the data itself. There was no point going any further.'

On the afternoon of Friday, 5 May it was crunch time in the Crow's Nest. We had agreed that we needed three sponsors on board to have enough confidence to press the button and make the financial

313

commitments that went with securing non-resident assets, and the deadline was now little more than 24 hours away. But we only had two on board – the Apple and Pear Board, and Toyota New Zealand.

Blake phoned the CEOs of those two organisations to brief them, then headed off to the Lion Nathan head offices where he met with Douglas Myers and some of his sponsorship team. It was a protracted session, with Blake phoning the Crow's Nest every now and then to check facts and update the small but anxiously waiting start-up group. Finally, the phone stopped ringing and the worst was feared. Then, well after 6 p.m., Blake came through the door armed with a Lion Breweries promise of the advance of enough interim funding to allow us to make the impending residency-related commitments.

It wasn't, however, a commitment to sponsor. That would be a decision for the Lion board the following Friday. So, we were still one sponsor shy of the target that we'd set as a minimum requirement to proceed. Did we push the button or pull the plug? In his habitually optimistic way, and confident of Myers' continuing support, Blake summed up the situation: 'We've got the Apple and Pear Board and Toyota. That's two. We've got Steinlager helping us and Doug Myers to count on. That's at least two and a half. Let's call it three. We'll do it.'

The phone calls were made and, with the Farr office situation still to be resolved (no residency issues there), Team New Zealand was committed to an on-board design group comprising principal designers Laurie Davidson (from New Zealand) and Doug Peterson (from the United States), theoretical fluid dynamicist Professor Peter Jackson (from New Zealand), practical fluid dynamicist Richard Karn (from New Zealand), and rig designers Steve Wilson and Chris Mitchell (both from New Zealand), along with structural experts High Modulus and sail design experts from the North Sails loft in Auckland, all of whom would work under design coordinator Schnackenberg as an integral part of the bigger team.

314

As things turned out, Bowler's 'D for management so far' would prove somewhat pre-emptive and the lack of Farr office participation would not affect the final outcome.

CHAPTER
Fifteen

Black Magic

The Blake management style, which had evolved and matured through five Whitbread campaigns (three of them his own), an unsuccessful and frustrating America's Cup, and an abortive then successful Trophée Jules Verne, was progressing still further.

There had been plenty of evidence of a more mature and informed approach in the *Steinlager 2* programme. He'd surrounded himself with people that he trusted and in whom he had confidence, delegated responsibilities and then concentrated on managing the total programme and getting the best out of his team. However, he was unable to adopt or extend that approach in the 1992 America's Cup programme. The people had been chosen and the structures put in place long before he got to San Diego with the last 12 months of the programme to run. If the San Diego 1992 programme taught him anything, it was how not to structure and run an America's Cup.

The *ENZA New Zealand* campaign, on the other hand, came naturally – a small, hand-picked and fully motivated team tackling an exciting challenge on tight time frames. But Blake wasn't so naïve as to think that America's Cup 1995 with Team New Zealand would be the same. An America's Cup campaign is one of the most complex and demanding undertakings around. Proof of that is the list of people who have got it wrong. That list is long and distinguished, and includes many powerful and successful businessmen with international reputations.

Although a decision-maker by instinct, Blake always put a lot of effort into seeking other opinions on his proposed activities – what he used to refer to as 'my one-man surveys'. Typical of this trait was his phoning and faxing the Farr design office in June 1992, seeking the views of Bruce Farr and Russell Bowler on the prospects of another New Zealand campaign for the Cup. Although they had sometimes had their differences, Blake had the utmost respect for the talents and experience of the Farr office principals. The reply he got from Bowler contained a most astute summary of Cup campaigning, which Blake most certainly would have taken on board as he organised his thinking and his own views.

Bowler wrote: 'Firstly, there is only one (or perhaps two people) that could successfully get both NZ corporate and NZ people support for the sort of fiscal contributions required for a challenge. That would be your role. Secondly, you do not belong in a role of campaign manager or leader (by campaign I mean boat, sails, research, design, keels, masts, sailors, rules). I don't believe anybody can lead the campaign. Some perceive there is a role where the right single person will provide the direction and leadership. I think this is a dream. Such a role and such a person do not exist because no one has sufficient technical knowledge in all areas to effectively lead. Also, if a leader is put in place, a large part of the accountability stops with that leader when it should stop at department heads. The campaign (as defined above) will be successful if competent, committed, communicating, experienced people are placed in accountable leadership positions in each area of activity. Some coordination may be required but leadership will come from that group of leaders. You should be involved in or even lead the setup . . .'

Blake faxed back to say: 'Thanks for your America's Cup fax . . .

and . . . for being honest about what you think. As it happens, your ideas are very similar to mine in many ways. This is very much the way I ran the Steinlager campaign and that worked out well . . .'

And that, in fact, was the way in which the structure of Team New Zealand evolved – policy and strategy decided group-fashion by the department heads whose job it then was to achieve the agreed objectives in the agreed way, and within budget, with Blake maintaining a complete overview and keeping the whole show on track. Those department heads were Ross Blackman (administration), Russell Coutts (sailing), Tim Gurr (boat-building and shore team), Tom Schnackenberg (design and testing), Alan Sefton (communications) and Steve Wilson (rigs).

A high degree of cross-team communication was vital and this process was augmented by weekly full-team update sessions. These were stand-up jobs, with each head of department giving all team members a brief summary of activity and progress last week and an overview of what was planned for the week ahead. Then there were the regular 'full family' sessions when sponsors and outside contractors would be invited in for a complete review and update. One of Blake's ploys in these meetings would be to remind everyone that there was no pecking order of importance in Team New Zealand. The sailors might get to race the boat and so be in the public eye, but they were no more essential to the total programme than the receptionist, Michelle Hebditch, who just happened to be a school leaver in her first job.

A highly useful addition to the team in the context of this collaborative environment was lecturer in management studies Peter Mazany, introduced to the programme in April 1993 by Schnackenberg, through his Auckland University connections. Schackenberg commented at the time: 'I have watched a number of America's Cup challenges, and in this one so far have attended several meetings, listening to the conflicting opinions, all voiced by earnest believers. When you add in the impressions from all the experts, it becomes obvious that we need to employ the latest techniques and experience in both team management and project planning. I have brought Peter Mazany up to speed a little with the history of the America's Cup challenges and Peter Blake's approach to this challenge. It seems we have a natural fit in that the ideas Pete Mazany talks about are exactly what we have been talking about ourselves. So, I am hoping that what he can do is add a bit of "method to our madness", and help us to achieve just what we are after.'

Mazany, in an unobtrusive way, did just that, encouraging cross-team communication and the link between sailors and designers and researchers. While he had nothing earth-shattering to add to the mix – in fact, a lot of what he preached was already, or was becoming, team practice – he helped smooth out the wrinkles in the processes with constructive comment, encouragement and suggestions of different and highly pragmatic approaches to problems and solutions.

With Mazany's help, at the outset of his involvement, we developed the Mission and Vision Statements that became the team's 'bibles'. With their emphasis on the purpose of the individual within the group, and the larger responsibility of the team to the nation – in this case, New Zealand – these statements of intent were in many respects a distillation of the Blake campaign management philosophy.

The Mission Statement read:

Team New Zealand's 1995 challenge for the America's Cup is a statement about the ambition and resolve of a country.

It would be easy, after three previous challenges, to retire from the fray and content ourselves that we have given the oldest trophy in sport our best shot. But that is not the New Zealand way.

322

Nobody, perhaps, expects us to challenge again. But they certainly will respect us for doing so.

The Cup is, for New Zealand, unfinished business – a sporting Everest that can and will be climbed.

This challenge will become synonymous with and, in significant ways, could be a catalyst in New Zealand's fight back to economic and social wellbeing.

The Vision Statement read:

For the Team New Zealand America's Cup Challenge, our aim is to build a challenge that can win for New Zealand and that we can be proud of – to succeed in all aspects.

We want a small, informed and fully motivated team that:

- Works in an environment which encourages every member to make a meaningful contribution

- Has a high degree of personal integrity and group honesty

- Recognises personal goals but not hidden agendas

- Continuously monitors and improves its performance

- Is fun to be in

After the Cup had been won, Mazany would write: 'Team New Zealand was widely considered to be a very highly motivated team exhibiting great loyalty to one another and to Peter Blake in particular. Why was this so? Because a high degree of trust had been built up – not a blind trust that "all will work out well in the end", but a well-reasoned organisational trust that was built by people acting consistently with their words and delivering on their promises. It was built up slowly but steadily by the consistent application of the fundamental rules and norms that the team had set for itself. These were embodied in the vision and ground rules of the Team.'

In his summary of the win, Mazany stated that Team New Zealand had succeeded because it developed great vision and rules of operation, chose the right people, developed highly responsive systems that resulted in great motivation, had a wealth of experience within the team, focused and used common sense, had good project management, was very good at everything and the best at a few, and had high-quality design–sailor–construction interactions. In Peter Blake, he said, Team New Zealand had a leader and figurehead with a very high degree of credibility – within both the team and the country at large – and one who embodied New Zealand's ideas of fair play and established high standards of integrity, respect and trust within the team.

Mazany added: 'One of the things that comes across most strongly in the public interviews and private discussions with team members is their tremendous loyalty to Blake, because of the trust that he built up with members over the duration of the challenge and, in many cases, over many years. In addition, Blake had the expertise to maintain discipline in the critical decisions. That is not to say he made or had to make all of these decisions but, since he was involved and had knowledge of all key aspects of the challenge – the business and sponsorship side, the sailing side, the design and the building side – he was able to provide a stabilising influence when different agendas in those areas came to the fore. Finally, he had a management team all of whom were able and willing to exert significant leadership in their areas.'

Interestingly, Team New Zealand's extremely tight budget was a major factor in achieving the cross-team communication objectives. There was absolutely no fat in that budget, and a system that Ross Blackman called 'budget raiding by consensus' quickly evolved.

If, for instance, Blake and the group agreed on four rudders for the programme, and further down the track the sailors and the design group found that we needed a fifth, it would be Schnackenberg's job

324

to go around and argue his case with the other department heads and try to get them to make savings in their departments to free up the money to build another rudder. This type of situation occurred with reasonable frequency, and in probably every instance the money was found. The process had the added benefit of ensuring that all department heads – and Blake – were fully aware of progress and developments in the other departments.

Blackman commented: 'It was a brilliant idea – "we're going to need $200,000 so everyone's going to have to chip in" – it worked really well.' He added: 'What we have learned subsequently is that that sort of decision-making process requires the very best people in all areas of the campaign. If you have weaknesses in the campaign, then those people will get run over and you might not get the right decision for the right reasons. The sailors in 1995 were strong, capable and experienced. They knew what they wanted, and that system works if you have that quality of people and the buy-in to the process.'

The fact that we were 'on the bones of our arse' all the way through made us think smart. We could not afford to make bad decisions, and that was when Blake's management style came to the fore. He had a disarming way of saying: 'Absolutely, a great idea, sounds perfect to me. Going to cost $100,000? Not a problem. Just go and talk to everyone else. Get it out of their budget and you can do it.' That meant there was a wonderful filtering system for decision-making because you had to go and sell everyone else on your idea. If you were successful, it probably was a great idea. If you couldn't sell them, it was probably a wrong idea.

Blackman recalls: 'Doug Peterson was always great at going around the design team to Blakey saying, "Peter, they're messing it up. We've really got to do this." Blakey would say, "Listen, if you're asking me to make a design decision, we're in big trouble. You designers make a decision and I'll back you up. But don't ask me to make that decision." He never did, and that was the strength of the decision-making in the team.'

The tight budget impacted in other areas too, such as the decision to work-up in Auckland until the last minute before shifting to San Diego just before the event. There was certainly a strong element of better-quality test results in this call, but in the final analysis it was driven by the hard fact that we couldn't afford to be in San Diego for longer than six months – to the day. If we were, the campaign would be subject to a different – and more costly – set of Californian tax laws. As a result, most of the team flew to San Diego exactly six months before the scheduled date for the final race in the 1995 Cup match, and left California with three or four days to spare before the tax deadline.

For the record, that budget was $NZ29.9 million with a contingency of $NZ3 million. We never raised (and so did not spend) the contingency, and the final total cost of the campaign was $NZ27 million. One thing we did not budget for was a victory party at the end. That would have been tempting fate. As it turned out, our sponsor group was more than happy to come to that particular party.

Peter Mazany would later observe: 'New Zealand is a small country with limited resources when compared with many others. This means that New Zealanders must "work smarter" than their competitors to succeed. We do not have the luxury of being able to throw lots of money at a project, make lots of mistakes and to do it all again.

'As a consequence, it seems as though New Zealanders have developed a big degree of common sense. In cases where we have succeeded we have been forced to be creative and even ingenious, and often applied a "do-it-yourself" approach to the problem at hand – whether it be our forces in the great wars, the development of the Hamilton Jet or the John Britten Superbike. So focus has always been a necessity and has always worked to New Zealand's advantage.

326

'The Team New Zealand experience was no different in these respects. There was a good common-sense use of the technology, since the limited budget meant that money could not be thrown at every idea. Cost/benefit trade-off had to be thought through and this meant that money was put only into areas that really mattered. Where there was an alternative method that would give 95 per cent of the benefit at 10 per cent of the cost, it was always taken. This also resulted in greater overall focus, since scarce resources tend to make one focus only on the most important issues.'

Two different examples of Team New Zealand's 'creative' and 'even ingenious' approach to its budgetry constraints were in computer resources and the manufacture of the wings on the torpedo-like keel bulb that added lift upwind.

Computer 'grunt' is a prerequisite in any yacht design programme. It takes a lot of computer muscle to grind through the endless permutations available in, say, the shape of keel wings and where they should be positioned on the bulb. Team New Zealand was singularly short of this grunt as the design group got serious about the appendage programme, and at one stage resorted to begging time on the new Lotteries Commission computer in Wellington.

Peterson had introduced to the team a New Zealand computer whizz, David Eagan, who was familiar with the sorts of codes and programs to be used. Eagan, in turn, introduced Team New Zealand to Jim Clarke, founder of the Califonia-based computer company Silicon Graphics, which had made a name for itself designing and building the computers that were enabling the new-age special effects in a lot of the big movies coming out of Hollywood. And it just so happened that Jim Clarke, who was also a keen sailor, would soon be visiting Auckland in his cruising yacht.

A Clarke/Blake dinner was organised at which Blake took the opportunity to discuss Team New Zealand's computer needs. Clarke was invited to visit the team's design offices to see what we had in terms of computer hardware. He took one look and exclaimed: 'Goddam it, I've got more computer horsepower in the nav station on my boat!' – and he did.

Clarke straight away organised for his nav station computers to be delivered to Team New Zealand and then facilitated an 'official supplier' arrangement that saw Team New Zealand with the Silicon Graphics equivalent of 1.4 super-computers working 24 hours a day, seven days a week in the design room of the San Diego base. This technology proved invaluable in the constant search for more boat speed.

The wing development programme, however, looked like it had hit the wall almost before it got started. The first wings on *NZL 32* were milled from stainless steel, and they cost in the region of $US30,000 a pair. That meant we could afford probably two sets. Then Tim Gurr and his boat builders had a look at the situation and made up a set in timber and carbon fibre which cost a mere $US300 a pair. They worked perfectly and the wing programme was back in business.

Probably the two most pivotal decisions in the campaign were to build two boats and to put Blake in the race crew.

It was always the plan to build two boats, but when it came time to commit to Boat No. 2, there wasn't enough money, and if we started the second boat there might not be enough left to complete Boat No. 1.

Blake presented the pros and cons to our directors in the boardroom of the Shortland Street premises that we were now 'borrowing' from Lion Nathan. The emerging consensus was that we had to be responsible and cut our cloth to suit our purse – in other words, build only one new boat, even though that would be to the detriment of the campaign.

328

Sir Tom Clark, who had mostly just listened to the arguments for and against, finally slammed the table and said: 'For fuck's sake. We can't win the America's Cup with only one boat. We've got to have two. We'll build two and worry about it later. I might have to make some phone calls.'

Blake then moved in quickly to say: 'Right, everyone agreed? Meeting finished.'

As it turned out, in terms of performance, we could have won the Cup with just the first boat built, the legendary *NZL 32*, or *Black Magic 1*, but we would have been taking a huge risk. Boat No. 2 – her near-sister ship *NZL 38* (*Black Magic 2*) – was vital to the continuing test programme in San Diego, where development of performance continued right to the end, and she gave us protection in the event of catastrophic damage to *NZL 32*. Also, as it also turned out, having the second boat allowed some very productive tactical and psychological game plans.

NZL 32 was designed and built to win the regatta. She was the best that we could do, the ultimate product of the collective brain power and creative abilities of the design group and sailors, and beautifully built by Tim Gurr with the McMullen & Wing yard on the Tamaki River.

When she hit the water in September 1993, later than originally planned because some exciting developments in the towing tanks in Britain had produced some late results that could not be ignored, *NZL 32* was – for all the world to see – very narrow. Laurie Davidson had been arguing for narrow for some months and the late test results supported his contention. Even so, the black hull of *NZL 32* looked extremely skinny compared with the 1992 fleet, and particularly in comparison with the dinghy-like *NZL 20*. Media tongues immediately started to wag. Had Team New Zealand hunted the corners of the rule and taken a punt?

There was more conjecture soon afterwards when *NZL 32* lined up for her first test against trial horse *NZL 20*. The encounter was on a shifty day in the entrance to Rangitoto Channel and in full view of the waterfront. The first couple of line-ups were inconclusive, then the two boats positioned themselves for a gate start to a short race to one of the channel markers.

NZL 20 was first out of the gate, didn't appear to have too much trouble with the trailing *NZL 32*, and rounded the channel marker narrowly but comfortably ahead. The news spread quickly – Team New Zealand had got it wrong. Their new boat was 'a dog', couldn't even beat last time's loser, and the word went out internationally.

What the shoreside watchers didn't know was that the trim tab and genoa sheeting hydraulics on *NZL 32* weren't working. Nor had they noticed a couple of big wind shifts in *NZL 20*'s favour that would have seen a lesser yacht than *NZL 32* behind by a considerably bigger margin. And, in their haste to spread the news, they didn't hang around long enough to see the rocket ship that emerged when *NZL 32*'s trim tab and genoa sheeting system were made fully operational.

Rather than try to correct the rumours that quickly emerged, Team New Zealand actually encouraged them and even helped muddy the waters further by starting a rumour of their own – that *NZL 32* didn't measure under the IACC rule. As a result, the yachting world – and the America's Cup community in particular – took its eye off the black boat, beguiled into believing it wasn't quick, and this was still the general perception when the America's Cup regatta started.

Team New Zealand's second new boat – *NZL 38* – was launched some three months after *NZL 32* and was shipped straight to San Diego. Conscious that *NZL 32*, in her narrowness, was off to one side of the design band, Team New Zealand deliberately designed *NZL 38* closer to where they felt the rest of the fleet would be in the design spectrum. Among other variations to the *NZL 32* approach, she was beamier.

In the short work-up period in San Diego, there wasn't much between the two boats. While *NZL 38* appeared to have an edge

SIR PETER BLAKE

upwind in breezier conditions, which you would expect from a beamier, more powerful hull, the view was that *NZL 32* was definitely the faster all-round boat. The reality though was that both were fast, and Team New Zealand took advantage of this fact with probably the masterstroke of psychological gamesmanship in the regatta.

When, on the eve of the first race, the teams had to announce which boat they would use in round robin 1 of the challenger series, Blake calmly announced: 'We will be using our new boat.' That meant *NZL 38*, lending more credence to the view that *NZL 32* was slow – certainly the slower of the two black boats.

NZL 38 went through the first four round robins of the regatta unbeaten on the water in 24 races. She had one win reversed in the protest room when John Bertrand's *oneAustralia* syndicate, in round robin 2, protested Team New Zealand's practice of hauling one of its tacticians, Murray Jones, up the rig to look for wind up the track.

The Australians protested under IACC Rule 41.2, which states that 'no crew member shall station any part of his torso outside a vertical line through the sheerline in a heeled or level condition except when necessary to perform a task, and then only temporarily'. The rule was originally written to stop crew hiking or trapezing off halyards in order to increase stability and didn't seem applicable in this case. If anything, having Jones near the top of the rig would have decreased stability. But the jury ruled in oneAustralia's favour. *NZL 38*'s win was deducted and gifted to the Aussies.

Imagine, then, the reaction at the pre-semi-finals press conference when Blake was asked which boat we would use and responded with: 'We're using the old boat.' *NZL 38* was being retired undefeated. It was time for *NZL 32* to make her racing debut. The media scrambled for the exits. The view still persisted that *NZL 32* was the slower of the New Zealand boats. Why else would the Kiwis use their newer boat, and wasn't it undefeated on the water in 24 starts?

The opposition must have been confused too. *NZL 38* had been an impressive all-round performer and didn't appear to have any weaknesses. But the Kiwis weren't stupid. They wouldn't take a chance with a slower boat – not in the semis. What the hell were they up to? Their confusion would have quickly turned into trepidation if they'd known that *NZL 38* had raced the round robins using second-best sails and equipment. Again because of the tight budget, all of what yachties call 'the real fruit' was being saved for *NZL 32*, to be used when the results really mattered. This, of course, was a closely guarded secret in the Team New Zealand camp.

The decision to have Blake in the race crew was another masterstroke in its own right.

In the final weeks before the start of the Louis Vuittton Cup, Butterworth came into my office, closed the door, and enquired: 'What do you think Pete's reaction would be if we invited him to be on the crew?' I told him it was a great idea and that I felt Blake would be flattered.

Blackman recalls: 'My understanding is that it (inviting Blake into the crew) was probably Brad's suggestion to Russell, because Brad knew Blakey well and had sailed with him a lot. I think he told Coutts: "Hey mate, if you need another sail, or if you need another keel, or if you need something, it's going to be much better for you if Blakey's on the boat and sees the need for himself, rather than you having to go back and sell it to him."'

Blake jumped at the opportunity and was given the jobs of trimming the mainsheet traveller and grinding the mainsheet, which meant he was in the back of the boat, privy to and part of all the major decision-making. If it was needed – and it probably wasn't, given the structure of Team New Zealand – the move bridged the gap between race crew and shore management that has been the undoing of many a Cup campaign.

From that day on there was an extra spring in Blake's step. Like most competitors, he wasn't the best of spectators and probably wasn't relishing the prospect of sending out a race boat and crew every day and not being in the thick of the action himself.

If the move was good for Blake's morale, it had a less beneficial effect, however, on his elbows. He developed tendonitis and needed constant treatment to keep him in the starting line-up. Fortunately, we had recruited the services of the All Blacks' physiotherapist David Abercrombie who, on race days, would set up his treatment table in the main room of the Team New Zealand base compound and await customers from the race track. Usually, Blake and mid-bowman Joe Allen, who spent much of his race days diving down below in the boat to organise sails for the next leg or repack sails from the last leg, were first on the table. Allen's job was highly demanding physically, and he too developed problems with knees and elbows that required constant attention by the physio. We even had a decompression chamber – loaned to us by a Canadian company with whom Laurie Davidson had contacts – parked in our compound to assist the treatment processes.

There was another spin-off from Blake being on the crew – one which would provide a much needed boost for the campaign's fast-disappearing funds and also a national symbol for support of the campaign back home in New Zealand. As was tradition in the Blake household before every big event, Pippa presented Peter with a pair of new socks on Christmas Eve, 1994. On this occasion, they were red. Blake wore them for race one, which *NZL 38* won. So he wore them for race two, and every race after that. And *NZL 38* and later *NZL 32* kept on winning – until race four of the Louis Vuitton Cup final against *oneAustralia*.

The problems that day surfaced first of all in the pre-start sequence when suddenly the boat's hydraulics and performance electronics went down in quick succession. One such equipment failure would have been unusual on the superbly maintained Kiwi race boats, but two at once!

NZL 32's performance was immediately impaired and the Australians took full advantage, leading off the line and controlling the first beat to windward. Coutts and his crew threw everything at their rivals but Rod Davis, on the helm of the Aussie boat this time around, sailed one of the races of his life and denied his former New Zealand team mates a way past – *oneAustralia* won, but by only 15 seconds.

It was Team New Zealand's first defeat in the regatta – and it didn't take long for the folks back home to realise that it was also the first race that Blake, with his perceived 'Lucky Red Socks', had missed. His elbows weren't up to it on this occasion and he had to watch instead of sail.

The Sunday following – we'd now seen off the Aussies 5–1 and were through to the match, in which we'd race our favourite 'enemy' Dennis Conner – I got a call from TVNZ boss Brent Harman. He had his marketing team and a group of top advertising industry people in his office (it was Monday in New Zealand) and they were discussing how they could help us. The word was out in New Zealand that we were struggling financially. The New Zealand public, and particularly our sponsor group, knew that we were running on vapour in terms of funds and were still seeking financial support from wherever we could get it. Would we have a problem if they used Blake's 'Lucky Red Socks' in a nationwide fundraiser, Harman asked. 'Hell no, go for it,' was the instant reply.

The idea had apparently come from a young member of Harman's staff while TVNZ – like the rest of the nation – was celebrating Team New Zealand's finals win over *oneAustralia*. 'Why doesn't the whole country wear Blake's red socks and give real

SIR PETER BLAKE

meaning to their support,' he'd asked. Harman immediately saw the potential and organised the Monday meeting to work the idea through to a proposition for us to consider.

However, not even Harman and his conceptual group could have predicted the phenomenal success of their brainchild. New Zealand seized on Blake's 'Lucky Red Socks' as its way of identifying with and supporting the campaign in San Diego. Everyone, from the Governor-General and Prime Minister on down to the elephant in Auckland Zoo, was wearing them, and the nation's knitting mills struggled to meet demand.

The injection of $100,000 in proceeds into Team New Zealand's coffers, that by now were decidedly bare, was much needed as the team struggled to refurbish *NZL 32*'s sail wardrobe and equipment for one last round of racing. Just as important was the realisation generated in the camp that there really was a whole nation riding on the black boat.

In the event, *Black Magic* didn't just beat Conner's *Young America* in the best-of-nine match, she hammered her 5–0 in a fitting climax to what veteran Cup commentators would describe as the most comprehensive campaign in the Cup's long history. Her winning margins – 2 minutes 45 seconds, 4 minutes 14 seconds, 1 minute 51 seconds, 3 minutes 57 seconds and 1 minute 50 seconds – fully supported that view. The reaction back home is now part of New Zealand history.

The final race was sailed on Saturday, 13 May 1995. Across the date line, that was Sunday, 14 May in New Zealand, which is Mother's Day. If they weren't up early, a lot of mums must have missed out on this occasion, for by the time *Black Magic* crossed the finish line at around 10.45 a.m. New Zealand time, the whole country was in party mode.

The team knew, from the thousands of faxes and emails sent to the dock, and from the many hundreds of Kiwis who jetted in just for the match, that their exploits were being closely followed, and with some enthusiasm, back in New Zealand. Even so, they weren't ready for what awaited them when they finally arrived home. The nation was in the grip of Cup euphoria and Blake and his Team New Zealand were the toast of Aotearoa (Land of the Long White Cloud). There were huge turnouts for the welcome-home parades in the main centres – Auckland, Wellington, Christchurch and Dunedin – and the team could have spent the next three months travelling the country if all the other invites to visit had been accepted.

As Blake put it, when the first television microphone was thrust into his face on the stern of *Black Magic*, 'Little old New Zealand' had most definitely won the America's Cup. He wrote later: 'Nothing in all the world could have prepared us for the reception we received. Sailing for us is like baseball in America or football in Europe. It was really very moving to see so many people, young and old, with tears in their eyes, as New Zealand gave us the most memorable days of our lives. Pippa was still finding ticker tape in my pockets weeks later!'

On the victory itself, Blake reflected: 'Experience and compatibility were vital in this, but the will to win was paramount. The entire team, whether on the boat or shore-based, were all highly skilled and motivated. And they all knew that victory at this level depended on a total effort. There were no small jobs; they were all important. A second's gain in a mile over the 20-mile course was enough to win.

'I believe we caught the Americans at a time when they were confident that they would win purely because the Cup had only been taken away from them once in 144 years. But they hadn't taken into consideration the expertise and the enormous will to win that exists in New Zealand, as well as the vast amount of experience acquired in all types of competitive sailing over the years.

'I don't think I have ever seen so many really happy people, so many cameras pointed our way, or so many helicopters filming just one scene, or so much champagne. Corks were exploding all around us and the streams of bubbly were criss-crossing like firemen's hoses, dousing cameras, journalists and every bit of our clothing. We could hardly believe it. We had done it.

'For my parents, it must have seemed a long way from the lemonade christening of my little dinghy *Pee Bee* that they'd built for me 40 years earlier and I know that they, in their own quiet way, were getting as much pleasure and excitement out of this as we all were.'

In the middle of all the tours and receptions, Blake received a call from Internal Affairs to advise him that he was going to be knighted for his services to New Zealand yachting in the Queen's Birthday Honours List.

Pippa Blake recalls: 'He was sitting in the bath in a hotel in Wellington when the news came through. To this day, I don't know how they tracked us down, but it probably wasn't too difficult. He was tickled pink. It didn't affect him as a person. I know, though, that he was very proud from a family perspective, but in a nice sort of way. He sort of thought "I've done all right". The children were more excited than he was – very proud of their dad, as I was. It was a big honour to have and I think Pete utterly deserved it.'

The 1995 campaign wasn't just the Peter Blake show of course, just as it wasn't the Russell Coutts show. It was a complete team performance. Although they had to lead from the front, they, like everyone else in the 66-strong group in San Diego, were consummate team players and, again just like everyone else, lived by the team's vision and mission statements.

As yachting commentator Peter Montgomery wrote in his foreword to the 'Black Magic' souvenir, published to coincide with the arrival home: 'This time, Team New Zealand really was a team.'

Pippa Blake recalls: 'Teamwork was what Peter really loved – the banter and the rapport he had with other people, the humour and the fun. There was lots of that in '95. That was a great campaign.

337

He also got a huge kick out of winning the Cup for New Zealand and found the whole Red Socks thing overwhelming. He couldn't get over the adulation that ensued and would never have forgotten those street parades. It was a magic time.'

Blackman reflects: 'That campaign was a culmination of all the lessons that came out of the campaigns that Michael Fay and David Richwhite had paid for – in '87, '88 and '92. It was also a culmination of everything that Peter had learned in his Whitbread campaigns, particularly *Ceramco*, *Lion* and *Steinlager 2*, because by now "Blake's people" had essentially become the backbone and the heart of New Zealand yachting. With a few notable exceptions, like Coutts, Daubney and Fleury, Team New Zealand was, in effect, the extended Blake family.

'So, it was all the lessons that we had learnt at Michael's expense allied to everything that Peter had learned in his own campaigns. And Peter had the personal experience of campaigning as a yachtsman, and the leadership skills, to put it all together and hold it together. In that campaign, we saw Blake at his absolute best.'

On a personal note I have been in and around sporting teams all of my life, including playing soccer for New Zealand, managing New Zealand yachting teams and getting close to some of the biggest names in team and individual sport through my profession, journalism. And I can say without fear of contradiction that being a part of Team New Zealand, and working again with Peter Blake in that team, was the most pleasurable and personally rewarding experience of my career.

It was hard work though. The team was so small and the budgets so tight that there was always a lot of sharing of needs and loads. But the only cross words I can remember came when Coutts called in the chase boat and stepped off *NZL 32* in the early work-up days in San

338

Diego. He wasn't happy with the effort he was getting and he let the sailing team know. But that was as much tactical as it was necessary. He was simply reminding everyone of what was required of them.

By the end of the campaign, the whole group in San Diego was so closely knit and united in its task that, from the outside looking in, it must have appeared impenetrable and invulnerable. In this instance, appearances were not deceiving.

With the campaign motto 'Deeds not Words', Team New Zealand had gone resolutely about its business, fully focused on results where they counted – on the water. It was a campaign philosophy and approach that reflected Blake's personality and that got the full support of everyone in the organisation.

CHAPTER
Sixteen
The Vexing Years

New Zealand was now only the second country in 144 years of competition to take the Cup off the Americans (our Tasman neighbours had been the first with *Australia II's* historic victory in 1983). Team New Zealand now had the new challenge of hosting the next regatta, as well as mounting a defence campaign.

First, however, Blake had to be persuaded to remain in charge. He'd about run his race in competitive sailing and could have been asking himself: 'What else is there to win?' He also wanted to be around his family more. The children were growing up fast and neither they nor his wife knew what having a normal life was.

'Peter said afterwards that he wished he'd got out in 1995,' recalls Pippa. 'There was no point in going back. He'd been at it enough. He'd had the experiences of two America's Cups, culminating in the success of 1995, and I think he felt he'd done it all and why not get out while at the top. It certainly would have been easier on us as a family. But the importance of defending for New Zealand was quite an attraction, as was the fact that the Cup had not been successfully defended before, except by the Americans.'

In the end, Blake remembered Team New Zealand's promises to the country – of the benefits that would ensue if we won the Cup

– and the commitments that had been made to the sponsors who, to varying degrees, had backed Blake and his reputation for delivering, as much as supported a team that looked as though it might be able to win.

He met with the sponsor group, all but one of which were ready to back Team New Zealand again, and made the commitment to lead the defence. He also made it clear that, after the defence, he was off. He was keen to move on to something else that was close to his heart – caring for the world's oceans and exploring remote parts of the planet, like the Antarctic, that to date he'd only glimpsed while rushing by in a race boat.

The other piece of housekeeping to be taken care of related to the fateful decision to commit to two boats for the 1995 campaign. It proved to be an unpleasant experience and was definitely something we didn't need, let alone deserve.

When the board voted in favour of two boats, it did so on the understanding that the New Zealand government would support the campaign as the equivalent of a fifth paying sponsor (our deal with 'Family of Five' member TVNZ was in kind, not in cash). Prime Minister Jim Bolger's communications advisor Richard Griffin had put a lot of time into riding the proposal through, intimating to me that it was '98 per cent assured' – information that I passed on to the board.

Then, in a complete about-face – and to Griffin's horror as much as ours – the Government changed its mind and wouldn't back us financially despite the fact that its trade and tourism people were in favour of it doing so. Even the support of Prime Minister Bolger himself didn't help us prevail.

We hadn't forgotten all of this when Minister for Sport John Banks, deputising for the Prime Minister at the welcome-home ceremony in Auckland's Aotea Square, began extolling the virtues of Team New Zealand and what its achievements meant to the

344

country. Blackman whispered to Blake: 'I think I'm going to throw up.' Blake whispered back: 'I'll be first.'

The Government's eleventh-hour pull-out had left us with a $NZ4 million hole in our fundraising. We had a problem – and it was serious. We had no replacement lined up, we had a team, including Peter Blake, and one boat already in San Diego and another on its way there by ship, and the regatta was scheduled to start in a little over a month's time. There were no alternatives – we had to advise our sponsors that, at least temporarily, we needed more funding from them. We did that by phone, then Richard Green, our chairman, and I flew to Wellington to meet with the sponsor group.

I felt reasonably confident going into that meeting. One of the sponsor CEOs had told me: 'Everything will be all right – leave it to me.' However, that confidence began to fade when Richard and I were left to cool our heels for quite a while in reception while the sponsor group continued talking in the boardroom. It evaporated completely when the same CEO who had been so comforting emerged with an odd smile on his face to say: 'Things aren't going quite the way I planned.'

When Richard and I were finally admitted to the boardroom, it was clear that the sponsors, understandably, were not happy, but they agreed to commit to another $NZ1 million each, with the non-cash sponsor Television New Zealand providing the equivalent on-screen value in bonus advertising.

The quid pro quo, however, was that the sponsors would have certain options that they could exercise in terms of the future. Those options, effectively, amounted to ownership of Team New Zealand and any rights, such as those to a defence, it might possess.

No wonder my reassuring CEO had had a strange little smile on his face when he came out to see us in reception. There were clearly new forces at work in what, until then, had been a focused and supportive group, and those forces were driven by personal ambition.

Green and I had no options. Given the time frames and the fact that the team was already in San Diego, it was, for us, the only game in town. We would have to sort out the ramifications at a later date.

Those personal ambitions revealed themselves again in San Diego when, between the challenger final and the match, we started to draft the protocol for the next Cup. Some of the sponsor group who'd flown in for the match (most of whom had been at the Wellington meeting) got their noses out of joint because they weren't consulted.

Then, when we got back to New Zealand, we had to fight tooth and nail to preserve the Team New Zealand entity that we had created and, by winning the Cup, had apparently made so attractive. We had to convince those who wanted to go again (the Apple and Pear Board would not be there and TVNZ wanted a different role next time) of the obvious – that their 'owning' Team New Zealand would be tantamount to commercial suicide.

In 2000 we would not only have to replace ENZA and TVNZ for the defence, we would also have to find another group of sponsors for the event. Who, we asked, would be prepared to invest the millions of dollars we needed once they knew that we were 'owned' by other commercial enterprises, some of which might even be competitors?

Thankfully, common sense and sanity prevailed over the personal goals of a minority among our sponsors. Team New Zealand remained the entity that everyone knew, operating as a charitable trust. We weren't to know it at the time, but those personal ambitions that we had just had to subdue would later cause us more grief.

The charitable trust structure for a major yachting campaign dated back to the *Steinlager 2* campaign and Sir Michael Fay's 1992 challenge, as Richard Green explains: 'We used a corporate trustee structure that provided completely viable options in terms of the law and in terms of running these campaigns. For 1995, the Team New Zealand Trust was established, the trustee of which was Team New

Zealand Trustee Ltd. The entity that carried out the sailing campaign, Team New Zealand Ltd, was owned by the trust.

'The corporate trustee layer provided a level of liability protection, which is quite important when you are dealing with a commercial yachting campaign, and equally it was a structure which was intended from day one, if it was successful, to benefit nominated maritime educational charities. That ultimately proved to be the case both after the winning campaign in San Diego and more substantially after the success in 2000.'

The five directors of Team New Zealand Trustee Ltd were also directors of Team New Zealand Ltd. They were chairman Richard Green (a respected tax lawyer and partner in the Russell McVeigh law firm), Jim Hoare (of the Fay Richwhite merchant bank), John Lusk (an expert in corporate law and also a partner in Russell McVeigh), Roger France (a respected financial accountant and the then managing partner in Coopers and Lybrand, Auckland), and Sir Tom Clark (retired business leader and a mentor of Sir Peter Blake).

In 1995, after we'd won the Cup, the structure was changed to accommodate the new circumstances. AC2000 Ltd was introduced as a subsidiary of Team New Zealand Ltd, with the responsibility of staging the event. The executives of both Team New Zealand Ltd and AC2000 Ltd were Blake, myself and Scott Chapman, the latter being a qualified accountant who, while working for Fay Richwhite, had been invaluable to Sir Michael in the 1988 and 1992 challenges and who also helped Team New Zealand in the early days of the 1995 campaign.

Even after the cash-strapped 1995 campaign, the Team New Zealand Trust was able to meet its charitable objectives, donating $100,000 to the Spirit of Adventure Trust, which provides sail training experiences for young people from all around New Zealand. After the successful defence in 2000, it donated another $500,000 to the Spirit of Adventure Trust, and $500,000 to be split between the New

Zealand Coastguard and Auckland Coastguard organisations. It also set up a new trust with Yachting New Zealand to fund a development programme for young sailors. Still another sum was also destined to go into youth yachting.

During the 2000 defence campaign, some private agendas got out of control and the media was led to believe that there was something sinister about the trust structure, that it was being abused for the personal benefit of the directors. Nothing could have been further from the truth. That structure enabled us to optimise the use of the sponsorship money raised, and the organisations named above were the only beneficiaries of the Team New Zealand Trust.

'It was a completely straightforward and logical business structure,' insists Richard Green. 'Why the media could not understand it is beyond me. They seemed to suspect that the trust was a private trust in some way, because the shareholders of the trustee company were the five directors, which was simply a structural thing. They seemed to think there was personal or private benefit. Of course there was none. The trust could only spend its money on charitable purposes, which certainly did not include the directors, and the trustee company itself had unpaid share capital at the end of the day.'

Green added that, apart from ordinary fees received by some for professional services to the campaigns, the directors went unrewarded for the considerable time and effort they put in, not to mention the responsibility they shouldered.

The defence of the Cup, while demanding in organisational terms and daunting in its funding needs, should have been relatively straightforward for a team that had just achieved the impossible in the most convincing manner – and had done so on a shoestring budget by America's Cup standards. But it was far from that, and led to the unhappiest campaign experience in Blake's long career.

The situation that developed was quite simply a power play by Coutts and Butterworth and, somehow, Schnackenberg got involved in their schemes.

They wanted control of the future and weren't prepared to wait until the end of the 2000 campaign, when Blake, Sefton and Chapman would be leaving, to see whether there was in fact a future for the team. Nor were they happy, if there was a second defence, about having to honour Team New Zealand's on-going commitments to the sponsors that had not only funded the 1995 challenge, and so made everything possible, but had also continued to support by sponsoring the 2000 campaign.

Some of those sponsors, like Steinlager, TVNZ, Telecom and Toyota, had been around New Zealand's Cup challenges since before Team New Zealand was even formed. This disdain of loyalty went against everything that Blake believed in.

They openly challenged and undermined Blake's authority and responsibility for the 2000 campaign and event, and made life so difficult for him that, in his preparatory notes for a meeting with the trio on 14 April, 1999, he asked: 'Can you tell me what I have to do to get this situation to improve, apart from shooting myself?'

The problems surfaced early and got progressively worse. Coutts balked at signing a contract for the defence unless the terms included commitments for the future. Because of its structure and contractual arrangements with various sponsors, Team New Zealand could not make those commitments.

Team New Zealand was a campaign entity, formed and structured to mount one campaign at a time. All of its contractual arrangements were entered into on that basis, including those of the sponsors, even though they built into their contracts first rights of refusal to being involved should Team New Zealand campaign again – a perfectly normal scenario.

Also, Blake leading the team was a prerequisite to most of the sponsorships achieved and the sponsors would want, at least, to review their position if that was no longer the case and Blake wasn't there.

The situation degenerated into one of barely concealed hostility and defiance of team rules. Coutts and Butterworth, with some of their established afterguard, formed Team Magic New Zealand and borrowed from Team New Zealand's logo and livery to an extent that the marketplace could be confused into thinking that Team Magic was a part of Team New Zealand. They opened a Team Magic bar in downtown Auckland, which was set up and operated as though it was the official 'watering hole' of the team.

Then advertisements began to appear in which Coutts, over the Team Magic New Zealand logo, endorsed a brand of sunglasses. The advertisements made it abundantly clear that the endorser was the skipper of Team New Zealand's America's Cup winner *Black Magic*. Not surprisingly, the Team New Zealand sponsors started to ask what was going on.

As the situation got progressively worse, Blake endeavoured to manage through the problems, working to the same rules established for the 1995 campaign when, with the full support of Coutts and the sailing team, there was no planning for 'next time' until it was clear that there *was* a 'next time'.

On 19 March 1998, Blake wrote to Coutts in an effort to dampen things down. Although not in a position to do so contractually, he effectively 'anointed' Coutts as the leader of any future Team New Zealand campaign. Some of the phrasing in that letter reflects the difficulties he was having in getting Coutts to toe team lines. He wrote:

'Following the discussions we have been having over the last few months, I thought it best to set out the basic principles of your engagement by Team New Zealand as skipper and head of the Sailing Team for our defence of the America's Cup 2000 . . .

'I believe that it is critical to our chances of successfully defending the Cup for us to operate as a very cohesive team – 'team' meaning all aspects of the campaign from office staff through to the bowman on the race yacht. Any internal problems that we can't control will only diminish our chances.

'The following outline sets out the basis of your engagement and recognises your very important and central role in the previous and present campaigns – and also your aspirations for the future.

'Ultimate authority rests with me as the Chief Executive Officer of Team New Zealand appointed with approval of the principal sponsor CEOs.

'You, as head of the Sailing Team, account and report to me. You are a key member of the Co-ordination Group, which has the responsibility for supervising the design and sailing operations within the overall budgets set and agreed to.

'You and your crew are free to participate in match racing and international regatta events that you feel are applicable as long as these do not, in the opinion of the Co-ordination Group, disrupt Team New Zealand's operations.

'It would be appreciated if you, together with other designated senior management, would attend the regular board meetings as observers. This will be very helpful to the overall running of Team New Zealand.

'So long as you carry out your obligations to Team New Zealand, and subject to the rights of Sponsors and the Royal New Zealand Yacht Squadron, you will have the right of first refusal to acquire the assets of Team New Zealand after the conclusion of the America's Cup match in 2000 for a further defence / challenge of the next America's Cup.

'The price of the assets will be determined having regard to all

351

of the circumstances including the obligations of Team New Zealand and the Trustee of the Team New Zealand Trust, and the nature of any alternative structure that you may use to pursue any defence / challenge and in particular whether it is for the ultimate benefit of charity or not. The directors of Team New Zealand and the Trustee of the Team New Zealand Trust will confirm your rights to acquire the assets on this basis.

'You will be intimately involved in all decisions of importance relating to the choice of any future challenger of record, the terms of the protocol and all other decisions affecting the conduct of an ensuing defence. You will also be provided, when appropriate, with such information as is necessary to enable you to plan the next defence / challenge.

'As a member of the Team New Zealand team, you will from time to time be expected to assist Team New Zealand and its principal sponsors in the promotion of their sponsorship, but you are not required to give your own personal or individual endorsement to any product. For its part, Team New Zealand will not allow its sponsors to exploit your individual personality without your approval.

'You have indicated that you understand the need for you to wear Team New Zealand clothing while on Team New Zealand business, and not Team Magic or other clothing.

'You are free to enter into new sponsorship or endorsement contracts that do not place your involvement with Team New Zealand or the America's Cup at the forefront of any advertising. However, it is a requirement that you obtain my consent to any such new activity to avoid conflicts with existing sponsors. Such consent will not be unnecessarily withheld.

'In order to avoid possible confusion with Team New Zealand, the words "New Zealand" will not be used in connection with the Team Magic logo in New Zealand and will not be included in any registered mark of Team Magic in New Zealand.

'Black Magic' – *NZL 32* powers upwind in the 1995 America's Cup. She was always viewed as faster all-round than *NZL 38* – but there wasn't a lot in it. *Carlo Borlenghi, Pickthall Picture Library*

The torpedo-like bulb on the bottom of *NZL 32*'s keel. *Kaoru Soehata, Pickthall Picture Library*

The 1995 'Black Magic' in control of *Young America* and on the way to what Cup veterans determined was the most comprehensive win in Cup history. *David Hallett, Fotopress*

San Diego, 1995 – time to celebrate winning the 'Auld Mug' after a clean-sweep 5–0 win over Dennis Conner's *Young America. Kaoru Soehata, Pickthall Picture Library*

'Little ol' New Zealand's just won the America's Cup.' *Bob Grieser, Pickthall Picture Library*

Above: Proud as punch – Blake with America's Cup, winner's medal and a celebratory glass of champagne. He would soon add a knighthood to his collection. *Luciano Borsari, Pickthall Picture Library*

Opposite: More 'Black Magic' in the 2000 match, *NZL 60* dominates Italy's *Prada* on the way to another 5–0 America's Cup win. Team New Zealand became the first non-American to successfully defend the Cup. It was 'men against boys' on the Hauraki Gulf. *Fotopress*

Jubilant scenes in Auckland's rebuilt Viaduct Harbour
following the 2000 America's Cup win. *Fotopress*

Massive ice sculptures dwarf *Seamaster* in Antarctica. The huge bergs calf off the Antarctic
ice shelf in the Weddell Sea to begin their journey to slow extinction in warmer waters
of the Southern Ocean. *Don Robertson, blakexpeditions*

Left: Seamaster in Amazon mode. Her heavily insulated hull was as effective against Amazon heat as Antarctic cold, but she still needed to shade her aluminium deck against the tropical sun. *Frank Socha, blakexpeditions*
Below: Peter and Pippa Blake against a giant kapok tree near Velho Airoa in the Amazon. *Don Robertson, blakexpeditions*

Cast a giant shadow – Peter Blake just before his tragic death
in December 2001. *Don Robertson, blakexpeditions*

'Russell, the above sets out what I consider is a very fair deal between you and Team New Zealand. I think it vital, for the good of the overall programme, and to have the best chances of a win, that we keep everything on a really firm and friendly footing. Any disharmony will only lessen such chances.'

The points made in Blake's letter would later become the basis of what became known as 'the handover'. But the letter had little apparent effect.

Matters started to come to a head in April 1999 when Blake met with Coutts, Butterworth and Schnackenberg to again try to sort things out. As was his practice, he made preparatory notes of the issues that needed to be discussed. Those notes read:

'The team isn't one right now. It is very split. This situation must improve.

'If we continue like this, we won't win. Not because of the shape of the yacht, or the sails, or the sailors' expertise – but because we are imploding.

'Split in TNZ, between admin and sailors – rumours are rife around town. This needs to stop NOW or life will get quite tough.

'You are tearing apart the image that we have all spent years building up, and I don't know why.

'The people you are bagging and the people with whom you are at pains to be at odds (and that includes me) are working very hard to make sure that you have everything you need to win.

'Can you tell me what I have to do to get this situation to improve, apart from shooting myself?

'If I decide to leave, you can forget the funding. Life will get very difficult indeed. But, unless it does improve . . . I am giving it until the middle of the year – then I will be away.'

By this time, in an effort to enforce better communications, Blake had moved his office into the dock compound where Coutts and company could not avoid him. But it didn't help and he would wander across the road to where the syndicate's administration was based, and ask: 'What have we done to deserve this?'

On more than one occasion he was so distressed by it all that he offered to resign, and had to be persuaded to continue. In his first letter of resignation, written on 5 October 1997, he said:

'When I was asked by the FOF Sponsors to again be part of Team New Zealand for the Defence of the America's Cup in 2000, I was actually quite excited about the prospect. Not so much from the sailing point of view, but because of what such a win would mean to New Zealand and all New Zealanders. A win would be a great legacy to leave the country, something that not many other events can remotely offer.

'I also feel very strongly that this event should be as fair a sporting event as possible, and I know that the work done on the rules and protocol reflect this, to everyone's very real credit.

'For me, the quality and enthusiasm of the people and the organisation necessary to achieve this win is what will make or break this campaign. We definitely have the ability to win, there is no question about that. Harmony within a Team has always been a very strong factor in anything I do – it is also very important that all of the Team 'buy into' the overall concept and work towards the one goal – with no hidden agendas.

'It has become obvious in recent weeks (and months) that a very real clash of personalities has developed within Team New Zealand. It has become obvious that there are significant "hidden agendas" that are working against everything I believe in.

'For three of our very key sailors, Russell Coutts, Brad Butterworth and Tom Schnackenberg, their egos are seemingly out of control. And there is not much doubt that they don't trust me any more. Their recent actions speak for themselves. I feel that Russell, Brad and Tom are vital to the winning of the Defence of the America's Cup for New Zealand. We could do well without them, but a win would be much less assured. They also have the complete confidence and respect of all of the sailing and design team which, for this project, is very necessary. And, to lose Russell, Brad and Tom, would possibly mean losing other very key players at the same time.

'But I have decided that I am personally not prepared to put up with their attitude towards me any further. I don't know what I have done for them to behave this way. I don't know what else I can do to get them to understand what it is that I require if I am to be head of Team New Zealand. I am exceedingly disappointed that people I thought of as good friends could have so little allegiance and respect . . .

'I would like to remain with Team New Zealand, particularly to repay the debts that we all owe to the Directors and Sponsors of Team New Zealand – but am finding it very difficult to think positively at the moment.

'Therefore, I would like to tender my resignation as CEO of Team New Zealand, to take effect immediately.

'The last letter I ever thought I would get around to writing is this one. But enough is enough.

'My sincere apologies to those of you who have backed me for so long in my career. I won't forget.

Kindest regards
Sir Peter Blake KBE

The alternative solution was to fire Coutts and Butterworth. The directors, on two separate occasions when this was discussed at board level, made it clear that if this was Blake's decision, they would support him. It was, however, his call. But Blake wouldn't do that. Coutts and Butterworth were the best in the world at what they did in preparing and racing an America's Cup yacht, and Team New Zealand could be the loser if he dumped them. Better to try and manage things through, no matter what that might entail.

For Blake, one of the almost-final straws was Coutts and company holding pre-launches of the two new race yachts without consulting with, or inviting, the management team, including Blake. The other was being told that the crews trialling the yachts had been instructed, by Coutts, that under no circumstances were they to acknowledge the yacht *Archangel* which was out on the America's Cup course every day, often with Blake aboard, as mother ship to the campaign's extensive weather programme.

By June that year, the sponsor group was fully aware of the problems within the camp and a meeting was called to discuss this. A 'transition committee' was set up in an endeavour to convince and satisfy Coutts and his people that they would inherit Team New Zealand and also help them take some initial steps to prepare for this.

The meeting was attended by David Bale (the CEO of Lotto), Blake, Butterworth, Coutts, Bob Field (the CEO of Toyota New Zealand), Richard Green, Douglas Myers (the CEO of Lion Nathan), Schnackenberg and myself. All of us signed a pledge to 'work together in an open and cooperative manner to achieve the above objectives, to personally commit ourselves to respect each other's role in achieving these objectives and to support the extra processes to maintain mutual understanding'.

The 'above objectives' were listed in a Memorandum of Mutual Understanding and included the setting up of a transition committee 'to cooperatively plan for a smooth transition to the new trust structure after June 2000', by which time Team New Zealand 2000's activities would be wound up. Butterworth later described this memorandum as not worth the paper it was written on.

356

On 29 November, Blake wrote a personal letter to the CEOs in which he said:

'I understand that some of you will be meeting on Wednesday 1st December, followed by a Transition Committee meeting to discuss the latest Protocol, when Richard Green, Alan Sefton, Russell Coutts, Brad Butterworth, Tom Schnackenberg and I will join in.

'In your discussions during the morning, I would appreciate it if you would please consider my following concerns. I have enclosed a letter (written) back in June of this year when the idea of a Transition Committee was being formalised. My views now are no different to then. And my views when I wrote this note are totally in line with various formal views expressed during the latter stages of our challenge in San Diego in 1995 – when no one was encouraged to discuss "next time" at all. In fact, they were all actively discouraged, which was, in my mind, totally necessary to achieve the focus required for the win.

'I consider the latest Protocol items as being important to be formalised now – and this is close to being achieved. Sincere thanks to all involved.

'But my very real concern is that there seems to be a move to carry on and organise much more of "next time" than just the Protocol items. I am advised that the Royal New Zealand Yacht Squadron has been approached, that more than one sponsor has been approached, and that potential new trustees of Team New Zealand are now requesting meetings with the existing trustees . . .

'I have given the matter of "next time" considerable thought over a number of days, and weeks, and months and years. And I am convinced that this is NOT the way to go ahead. We stand the chance of falling like the All Blacks if we think we have this America's Cup won. We don't.

'I believe we stand a good chance of losing unless the FOF help us by keeping to the guidelines that I have requested since day one of last time's challenge.

'Overall, I have the greatest respect for the way that the sailing team, design team, shore team and others have handled the job of developing the fastest yachts possible. I am sure that the yacht and crew that we finally race will have the best chance we are ever going to have of winning.

'But only if the focus stays in place.

'I need you to help me by agreeing to discuss and work through the Protocol items only, with everything else being put on hold until we have a result – i.e. in March of next year.

'If we win, then all the advice in the world will be welcome. But until then, I consider such well-meant "help" will have the exact opposite effect.

'I have not written this letter lightly. I am adamant that this is the way it must be, until we know the result of the racing. I would really appreciate your backing on this one.'

For some time prior to the signing of the Memorandum of Mutual Understanding, Coutts and Butterworth, through their legal advisor, had been requesting the unconditional right to take over Team New Zealand at the conclusion of the 2000 defence. In the meantime they wanted to have sole responsibility for all matters that related to a subsequent defence. They refused to accept that this was not possible even though it was explained to them on numerous occasions that the sponsors for the 2000 defence had contractual rights in relation to any subsequent defence, including the right of renewal, the right to require Team New Zealand to defend the Cup again, if it were successful in 2000, and rights in relation to the appointment of the CEO.

These were absolutely acceptable concessions when the 2000 contracts were negotiated because it was seen as advantageous to have a sponsor group committed, at least in principle, to going again should there be another defence. But having the existing sponsors on board didn't necessarily fit with the Coutts/Butterworth plan either.

358

They appeared to have their sights firmly set on much bigger budgets than those to which the existing Team New Zealand and its sponsors were accustomed.

By this stage the Louis Vuitton Cup elimination series to find a challenger was reaching the serious stage. The 11 contenders, from seven countries, were into their third round robin of racing and the main contenders appeared to be the two United States syndicates, AmericaOne and America True, along with Italy's Prada and Japan's Nippon Challenge.

An uneasy peace settled over the defender camp as the New Year dawned. The Transition Committee was doing its work and there was the sailing campaign to concentrate on.

While the finishing touches were applied to the Team New Zealand programme, the challengers raced a six-boat semi-finals series in January and then a two-boat final that ran into February, to determine who would meet the defender.

Paul Cayard's *AmericaOne* was the first boat to make the final. New Zealand's bitter rival from the 1992 and 1995 Cup campaigns was looking strong and could afford to relax as he watched the fate of his main adversary, Italy's *Prada*, decided in the very last race of the semis, between the fast-finishing Dennis Conner in *Stars & Stripes*, and Dawn Riley's slightly undernourished *America True* campaign.

The odds had to be with the hugely experienced Cup legend Conner, but *America True* gained big-time from an early wind shift and sailed on for a comfortable win. Conner was out, and *AmericaOne* would race *Prada* in a best-of-nine final.

Back on Syndicate Row in Auckland's Viaduct Harbour, the subterfuge continued at Team New Zealand. Coutts, Butterworth and Schnackenberg had nominated their own trustees to negotiate with the soon-to-be outgoing Team New Zealand Trust directors and, on 1 February 2000, John Risley, a wealthy Canadian businessman who was one of those nominated by them to be a trustee of the new set-up, sent a memo to the trio and fellow trust nominee Peter Menzies, an Auckland businessman.

In the memo Risley said: 'We need to convert the "implied" acquiesence to a change of control into a clear, widely understood and accepted principle. Our ability to effect this has maximium leverage in the run-up to the Cup. We simply can not wait till after the event and hope all will go smoothly.

'The more we try and take charge of post-this-Cup issues now, the more apparent it will become as to whether there are pockets of resistance to the change of control. We should therefore seize every opportunity to convey to the outside world (from the Mayor's office to anyone of importance having an interest in the next event) that decisions in respect of the next Defence are the property of the new guard.

'That is not to say Blake should be kept in the dark as to our messaging. In fact, to the contrary, he should be told what we are saying and to whom, so as to both cement in his mind where the authority lies and to ensure he does not say anything inconsistent or that would prove embarrassing (to him). In the event we do encounter resistance we are able to identify the source of the problem and marshal resources around dealing with it.

'. . . All of this is predicated on a successful defence and, to a very large extent, it is unfair that RC/BB/TS should have their focus on this diluted by these sorts of issues . . .'

In the meantime *AmericaOne* and *Prada* had raced one of the great America's Cup series. New Zealand wasn't involved – it was waiting to meet the winner – but the nation was on the edge of its seat as Cayard and Italy's Francesco de Angelis slugged it out in the nine-race final.

The clash went all the way to the wire, the score 4–4 with just

360

the final race to go. The unpredictable Italians had, however, saved the best till last. De Angelis sailed a flawless final race to win by just 49 seconds and *Prada* became a popular challenger for Team New Zealand in the America's Cup 2000 match.

From the perspective of anyone who wasn't a Kiwi, the match was anything but that. Team New Zealand demolished *Prada* in a completely one-sided affair. Doing what they do best, Coutts and Butterworth led a superbly prepared defender to another clean-sweep 5–0 win. It was really men against boys on the Hauraki Gulf racetrack with the Italians completely outclassed in all facets of the game – from design to tactics to sailing.

Again the nation celebrated with abandon while Auckland basked in its now international image as truly 'The City of Sails', with a completely redeveloped waterfront and downtown structure for which Team New Zealand's achievements in San Diego had been the catalyst, and which had been driven through the usual complex consent processes with a lot of persuasion, input and help from Team New Zealand's management.

For many in the Team, however, it was a victory tinged with regrets. There was a large element of 'Blake's people' in the ranks and they were greatly saddened by what he had been put through. And, like him, they struggled to come to terms with what it had been all about and why it had all been necessary.

In the immediate post-match period the process of handing over the organisation to the 'new guard' was quickly finalised – but not, as it would transpire, to the satisfaction of Coutts and Butterworth, even though Butterworth went on record on 31 March to say that the deal was done and accepted.

If Team New Zealand had managed to keep a lid on things thus far, that lid really came right off the pot when the 'new guard' started feeding the media all sorts of unseemly rumours and allegations. Unable or unwilling to work it out for themselves, the press grabbed at the easy headlines so thoughtfully provided.

There was the allegation that Blake and his management team (which really meant Blake, myself and Scott Chapman) were siphoning off money and paying ourselves huge sums, to the detriment of the sailing programme. How anyone believed this, given (in particular) Blake's reputation and integrity, together with the make-up of the Team New Zealand board and the operational structure of the programme, was, and still is, beyond me. But believe it a lot of people did.

The simple truth was that Blake, and rightly so, was the highest-paid person in the campaign, his salary package negotiated with, and approved by, the sponsor group. The second highest-paid, and again quite rightly so, was Coutts, followed by a couple of the design team. Chapman and myself slipped into the top five only because we earned a 1.5 per cent incentive payment on any new sponsorships achieved (not including the 'Family of Five'). Otherwise, our salary was the same as that of the campaign's shore boss.

While Blake's name and image were absolutely vital to the funding process, he made it clear from the outset that he would not do the selling this time around. That was the task of myself and Chapman, along with our other campaign responsibilities.

Then there was the allegation, driven particularly by Butterworth, that Team New Zealand was owned by the five trustees/directors and the sponsors. Even the most cursory of examinations of this charge would have shown it, at the very least, to be a mischievous red herring. Team New Zealand was a properly constituted charitable trust with appropriate charitable obligations and, as such, it was subject to the scrutiny of the Inland Revenue Department.

Almost certainly as a consequence of all the misinformation being fed to the media, Team New Zealand was subjected to a full

362

examination by Inland Revenue and received a completely clean bill of health. Not one cent was unaccounted for and everything was as it should be.

But perhaps the nastiest move in the Coutts/Butterworth media campaign was the claim that Team New Zealand owned the private home in which Blake lived in Auckland's Bayswater suburb. This absolutely unsustainable allegation first surfaced in the form of a totally unrelated question from television personality Paul Holmes in a live interview with Blake on his highly-rated nightly current affairs programme. Completely out of the blue, Holmes asked Blake: 'Is it true that the Team New Zealand Trust owns your home?' Slightly taken aback, Blake said it was absolutely not true. The house in New Zealand was owned by a family trust, probably as was Holmes' residence.

The following morning, I asked Holmes: 'Where on earth did that question come from?'

'From the other side [i.e. Coutts and Butterworth],' he replied, 'they wanted me to ask it.'

The house referred to by Holmes *was* owned by a family trust. Richard Green, chairman of directors of the trustee of the Team New Zealand Trust, was, as a personal friend, a trustee of a Blake family trust. Someone in the 'new guard' decided to make 1 + 1 = 3, and Holmes was used to perpetuate another totally unfounded rumour on national television.

As a journalist myself, it still staggers me that a national television presenter of Holmes' reputation, with the depth of investigative resources at his disposal, could and would be used to plant an inference that his researchers could have quickly dispelled as untrue. Having said that, I was also dismayed by how other supposedly responsible news organisations, such as the *New Zealand Herald* and the *National Business Review*, could be similarly duped by the orchestrated Coutts/Butterworth media campaign.

363

Another example of the lack of investigative rigour was a *Herald* editorial on 25 January 2003 which said: 'There remain unanswered questions, of course . . . How alienated Coutts became from Sir Peter Blake, especially after becoming aware that Sir Peter and three other executives were paying themselves vastly more than him.' In hindsight, the media bias was strong evidence of the fact that the 'tall poppy' syndrome was still very much alive in New Zealand and that even favourite sons such as Blake weren't safe from lazy and irresponsible journalism.

All of this took a heavy personal toll on Blake, as witnessed by Richard Green: 'It was a very difficult time for Peter. It affected him badly and it required a lot of reinforcement and careful managing through.'

It affected Blake so badly because he was very strong on loyalty, which was an integral part of his management style. Also, having 'anointed' Coutts as his successor, in the letter dated 19 March 1998, he still couldn't work out a reason for all the animosity he was being subjected to by the 'new guard'.

Pippa Blake recalls this painful period in her husband's life: 'I wasn't aware that things were not going as they should have been until quite late on really. Peter tended to keep his work to himself, didn't really like bringing his work home, and the America's Cup was different to the Whitbread. It was more of a business, more of an office job, and Peter wasn't very fond of office jobs. So he wanted to come home and leave it all behind him and do things for the children, or switch off and go for a walk.

'Then it became very evident that Peter, for the first time since I had known him, was stressed up – and he wasn't someone who got stressed very easily. He was so optimistic that stress was not something that was an issue with him.

'We didn't really talk about it but I knew that Russell and Brad were causing him problems, that it wasn't really a harmonious team.

'I thought at one point that he wasn't in great health, but he was fine.

'He would get quite grumpy, and we all used to joke about it – "Oh, Blakey's getting a bit grumpy". But the great thing about Peter was that if there was something he wasn't happy with, he'd get grumpy then he'd come right. He never held grievances. He'd just get on with it and leave it all behind him. He never harboured a grudge against anyone.

'I know he offered to resign on at least a couple of occasions when the stress of it all was really getting to him. He really did want to leave. But it was for *New Zealand* and he didn't want to let anyone down. He would see it through – even though he struggled to comprehend the levels that the pettiness reached.

'He protected us from most of it, didn't really want to bring that baggage home. He would rather help James with his homework or we'd all go for a walk. He had a kayak and would go paddling in that, or go and have a cup of tea with his mum and forget about it.

'When it was all over, his attitude was to put it all behind him – "We have, after all, achieved another magnificent win, let's not forget that." But then he couldn't put it behind him because all the other rubbish started coming out in the media – about management stealing money and the Team New Zealand Trust owning the house.'

The transition process complete, Coutts, Butterworth and Schnackenberg were now in control of Team New Zealand and could officially start preparing for the announced defence of the Cup in 2003. But on 19 May 2000, New Zealand was rocked by the news that Coutts and Butterworth had quit and were going to challenge with Swiss billionaire Ernesto Bertarelli instead.

This announcement fuelled a new round of accusations. Coutts and Butterworth claimed that the difficulties and delays they had experienced in the handover process, and the terms and conditions of the arrangement, had made it impossible for them to carry on. The 'old guard' of Team New Zealand refuted this claim, pointing out that the delays in achieving a handover deal – once the Cup had been retained and a deal could be done – had been caused by Coutts and Butterworth, and that the terms and conditions of the arrangement (apparently agreed, if Butterworth's media response on 31 March was to be believed) closely mirrored those outlined by Blake in his letter to Coutts as far back as March 1998.

The tragedy of it all was that, in the process of the huge and public squabble that ensued, the fact that Team New Zealand had won, and won so well, was quickly overshadowed. So was the reality that the problems encountered on the way through the campaign, while serious, involved but relatively few individuals out of what, as a whole, was a highly dedicated and committed team that had again done its country proud.

CHAPTER
Seventeen

Making a Difference

C aring for the oceans from which he derived so much pleasure had been in Peter Blake's future plan for a long time. He often told the story of first becoming aware that all was not as it should be when he realised during Whitbread races that albatross numbers were diminishing in the Southern Ocean. Then there was the increasing pollution in even the remotest and most environmentally sensitive places on the earth – places such as Antarctica, the ongoing health of which is vital to the future of the planet.

When Blake read and researched more, he found that whole species of animal and marine life were being decimated as a result of mankind's uncaring greed and ignorance of the delicate balance of nature, and that vital ecosystems such as those of the Antarctic and the Amazon were being severely stressed.

There was ample scientific testimony backing up his first-hand observations, and lots of well-qualified and well-intentioned people around the world providing the evidence of how dangerously high the levels of exploitation and pollution were. But the message that humankind had to change its ways and care more for the environment, before it was too late, wasn't getting through.

Something needed to be done about that and, typically, Blake decided to put up his hand. He had an international name and

369

reputation that would attract attention and command a hearing. If he could use his standing to get the message across to a global audience, he might just help make a difference.

His thoughts on how to go about doing that began to crystallise in the spring of 1997 when he was contacted by the Cousteau organisation. The legendary Jacques-Yves Cousteau, whose ground-breaking television programmes on under-sea exploration and expeditions to the remote corners of the world had inspired Blake's generation, and others to follow, was advanced in years and in failing health. He was looking for a successor to continue his work with the Cousteau Society and Blake, it would appear, was an obvious choice.

The prospect 'flattered and excited' Peter, recalls Pippa. 'It was a natural and logical course for him to take after the America's Cup, something he could do for ever.'

The two, Cousteau and Blake, had never met, so arrangements were made for them to get together. Before that could happen, however, Cousteau died suddenly and responsibility for the running of his organisation transferred to his wife Francine.

Madame Cousteau pursued her late husband's choice of successor and in September 1998 Blake took a short break from the America's Cup to lead a joint UNESCO–Cousteau expedition to the Caspian Sea to investigate, among other issues, the alarming depletion of sturgeon fish stocks (the source of the much sought-after – and expensive – delicacy caviar, the export of which is highly important to the economies of communities and countries around the shores of the land-locked water). It transpired that a combination of over-fishing, pollution, industrial development and rising water levels was taking a heavy toll on the spawning grounds of the sturgeon from which the caviar is extracted.

To get to the Caspian, Blake joined the Cousteau team aboard the expedition vessel *Alcyone* in the Turkish city of Istanbul. From there it was across the Black Sea to the Russian port of Novorossiysk followed by several hundred miles of inland waterway travel through the Sea of Azov, the Don River, Volvodansk Lake and the Volga River – a vital economic route, consisting of complex and historical canal locks, connecting the Black and Caspian seas. *Alcyone* was reported to be the first foreign vessel permitted to travel these waterways in more than 50 years. From the lower delta of the Volga River, it was then south to Baku, the oil-rich capital of Azerbaijan, where Blake left the expedition to return to New Zealand and the America's Cup defence.

In his continuing talks with Madame Cousteau, it was identified that the Cousteau Society needed more than one vessel. Blake was keen to navigate the North West Passage, the sea route through the Arctic to the north of Canada that links the Atlantic and Pacific oceans. The 31.1 metre-long (103 feet) *Alcyone* wasn't the boat for that journey so Blake cast around to find a vessel that was.

His search took him to the Atlantic coast of France, to the old French port town of Camaret, where a vessel called *Antarctica* had recently returned from a charter to Iceland. Prior to that she had been languishing in Camaret for three years. It was almost a case of love at first sight.

Antarctica was very different – a 36-metre-long schooner, designed by Luc Bouvet and Olivier Petit, and built specifically for polar sea exploration by French adventurer/explorer Dr Jean-Louis Etienne. Her reinforced aluminium hull (1.6–2.5 cm plate, heavier and further reinforced in the bow area, for ice-breaking) enabled her to shoulder her way through sea ice approximately one metre thick.

If caught in the ice, her hull design (rounded sections) meant she would pop out on top rather than be crushed. With special insulation and heating she could withstand being 'frozen-in' and be self-sufficient, even in outside temperatures of minus 40 degrees Celsius. Shallow draught, retractable centreboards and rudders, and tunnel-mounted propellers enabled her to operate successfully in minimum depths of water – in ice, close to shorelines, or even among the sandbanks of the Amazon River, another projected Blake destination.

Blake first became aware of *Antarctica* in 1994 when carving across the bottom of the world at 60-plus degrees South in the catamaran *ENZA New Zealand*. While the big cat was skirting the Antarctic Circle, Jean-Louis Etienne and *Antarctica* were heading north from the Ross Sea after an expedition to ascend Mt Erebus and carry out a seismic study of its crater lake. The two vessels crossed paths and attempted a mid-polar ocean rendezvous, but only got close enough to exchange pleasantries by radio.

Antarctica was ideal for the journeys that Blake had in mind and, as soon as he learned that she was available, he moved to buy her. According to Pippa Blake: 'Peter was inspired by Jean-Louis Etienne, who'd walked to both poles and had climbed Mt Everest, and he thought that *Antarctica* was perfect for what he was planning for after the America's Cup. He really loved her. She was his kind of boat – not exactly pretty but well thought through and absolutely purpose-ful. Peter was never swayed by luxury. Give him functional every time.'

Antarctica was immediately made ready and provisioned for the long delivery trip to New Zealand where she would undergo a major refit before starting life sailing under the Cousteau flag. She arrived at Opua in the Bay of Islands shortly after New Year's 2000, and moored but a stone's throw away from where Captain Thomas Wing had first anchored in the *Fortitude* nearly 170 years earlier.

If he had been watching, Captain Wing would have appreciated his great-great-grandson's choice of vessel. With her purposeful ice-breaker bow, bare aluminium hull and solarium-style coach house streaked with salt, she was clearly a workhorse, designed and built to cross major oceans and to go where most vessels would feel threatened.

Blake was there to meet her, accompanied by a team of hull

372

signage specialists. *Antarctica* would be renamed *Antarctic Explorer* before she completed the last 180 miles of her journey and entered the inner basin of Auckland's newly built Viaduct Harbour which now bristled with a large number of the world's biggest and most glamorous private yachts, gathered in the City of Sails for the final stages of the America's Cup regatta.

Among that opulent assembly, and to the eye of the uninitiated, *Antarctic Explorer* looked more like a leftover from the latest *Mad Max* movie and stood out like the proverbial ugly duckling, but she soon became the focal point for those who understood where she would be going and who appreciated the purpose for which she had been built.

By now Madame Cousteau was due in Auckland, with Cousteau Society executive Bob Steele, to establish the structure of the organisation and review a new business plan for when Blake left behind the America's Cup and stepped full-time into the shoes of the society's celebrated founder.

Blake, Scott Chapman and I were keen to complete this handing over process. There had been increasing signs that Madame maybe wasn't comfortable with what Blake understood were her late husband's intentions.

Working closely with James Hall and his team at Saatchi & Saatchi in Wellington, we had carried out extensive research on the status of the Cousteau brand and its potential in the current marketplace. The brand was still powerful. Cousteau still had a legion of devotees out there who had grown up with his fascinating and inspirational television programmes, but the brand was tired and needed rejuvenating.

In the process of this rebranding exercise, the message that Blake wanted to convey was filtered down to the strong reminder that:

'Earth is a water planet on which quality of water defines quality of life. Good water, good life. Poor water, poor life. No water, no life.

'Man is fishing to extinction species that are vital to earth's food chain. He is polluting, to a frightening degree, most if not all of the great rivers, lakes, seas and oceans. He is devastating rainforests that are essential keys to the earth's unique and delicate environmental balance.

'If this beautiful water planet on which we live is to survive as we know it, something has to be done, and we are determined to help make a difference.'

To complement this standpoint, the Saatchi creative people had produced a Cousteau rebranding theme that was as brilliant in its simplicity as it was surprising in its obviousness. They had played around with the name Cousteau and, with simple graphics treatment, had emphasised the 'eau' – the French word for water. Who we were and what we were all about was encapsulated in that one clever action.

It was, in fact, so simple and so obvious that the Saatchi creative team leader seemed reluctant to present it to us. When he did, Blake looked at Chapman and myself and we nodded in unison. 'Right on the mark, fantastic,' was Blake's emphatic response.

The approved concept was incorporated into storyboard examples of its application, and off we went for our meeting with Madame Cousteau, excited by what we had to present as the fresh image and branding for the Cousteau Society and a new way forward in terms of funding its operations.

To our dismay, Madame seemed to be singularly unimpressed. Her only comment was: 'Those aren't Cousteau divers' – pointing to the fact that the scuba divers used to illustrate the new treatment of the name Cousteau on wet suits had bent legs. Cousteau divers, it seemed, swam with stiff legs. We weren't off to a very good start, and the meeting went downhill from there.

Ultimately, it was clear that Madame was reluctant to rejuvenate the Cousteau image, had strong reservations about changing the way the Cousteau Society raised its money, and certainly didn't see Blake becoming the Society's new leader – that was *her* role.

Somewhat disenchanted, we regrouped with Saatchis to consider our options. We'd had enough of politics and in-fighting in the America's Cup and wanted to embark on the new direction with everyone on the same page and singing the same song. Equally, our research had shown unequivocally that the Cousteau brand, while still strong, really did need a makeover, and our concerns that the way in which the Cousteau Society funded its operations wasn't a viable or sustainable business option, were serious.

Could we, instead, achieve our objectives under the 'Blake' banner?

More thought and research were required but, ultimately, the answer was 'Yes'. It would be a considerably more challenging path to follow, but Blake's name and image were strong enough internationally to make it fly.

Thus 'blakexpeditions' was born. We could pursue our goals, uninhibited by someone else's history, tradition and agendas, and we could do so under the New Zealand flag.

By now America's Cup 2000 was over. Team New Zealand had despatched the Italians 5–0 and, while the directors dealt with the hand-over to Coutts, Butterworth and Schnackenberg, Chapman and I got on with the task of winding up the Team's business affairs and shutting down the whole 2000 campaign.

Even though the media was still taking misinformed shots, we could feel more than a little pleased with the outcome. Despite all the trials and tribulations, Team New Zealand had still triumphed where it mattered most – on the water – and had done so in the most convincing fashion. As a result, New Zealand could look forward to a second defence of the Cup in 2003 and Auckland could plan for another international sporting event utilising the completely rebuilt and reshaped waterfront that was another direct legacy of the Team's endeavours.

Blake, meanwhile, had returned with his family to Britain where he could escape the Cup completely and focus properly on the new challenges ahead.

'Finishing it all and being able to return to Emsworth was a big relief,' remembers Pippa. 'He enjoyed coming back. He was sad to leave Auckland behind but he had a lot to look forward to. He liked popping up to the village for his paper without being stopped – a nice contrast to NZ where he could not walk anywhere without being recognised. It was a lot quieter in Emsworth and he could be himself.

'He got on very well with my father. Whenever he'd come back from overseas, almost the first thing he would do is go and have a cup of tea with my parents. He was very fond of them, and they of him.

'Since the early Whitbread days, they'd become a central part of any crew's visit to England. It was always known that there would be a barbecue at the Glanville house. My father would get out the croquet kits and set up the tennis court for these sporting tournaments – usually New Zealand against England.'

When the Blakes contemplated organising their lives around the 2000 defence in New Zealand, they had the children's education to consider, particularly Sarah-Jane's. She was very settled at Canford boarding school in Dorset and was approaching GCSE stage. It was felt that she should not be uprooted and she was happy to stay in school in England.

James was in his last two years of prep school and his leaving for New Zealand was not such an issue, so in 1998 he joined Peter in Auckland where, in 1999, he attended Kings Prep School.

376

Pippa explains their arrangement: 'We decided to move James out to Auckland and give him the chance of the outdoor lifestyle that New Zealand offers. Most importantly, though, he would be with Peter.

'Peter loved the garden of the house in which we lived in Auckland. The native bush was very much New Zealand with all sorts of trees – kauri, pohutakawa and so on. It was already there but he did a lot to it and loved it. He'd never shown green fingers before but I know that, later on in life, while still carrying on with expeditions, one day we would have a property with lots of space.

'Peter talked about the west coast of England, or of going up to Scotland. I think he rather saw himself on a big estate with lots of land and lots to do, and he always talked about having a river running through the property.'

The 'five-year' plan that emerged for blakexpeditions was that we would journey to environmentally sensitive parts of the planet to study and report on the effects of global warming, pollution and exploitation.

First up would be Antarctica, by way of Patagonia, and an attempt to reach 70 degrees South in George VI Sound off the Bellingshausen Sea. This would allow us to report on any retreat by the Antarctic ice shelf.

Then we would head for Brazil and Venezuela where we would journey 1400 miles up the Amazon and Negro rivers to look at the effects of changing weather patterns, increased population, over-fishing and deforestation.

From there it would be through the North-West Passage (probably east to west), down the Pacific to the Galapagos Islands, then across to the Yangtze River and the coral reefs of Japan before heading for Australia's Great Barrier Reef.

After that, it would be a circumnavigation of Antarctica prior to expeditions to the Mediterranean and up the Nile and Ganges rivers.

But first we had to secure initial funding to keep us going until we could get fully organised with the new entity and plan in the sponsorship market. Blake called on the watch company Omega in Switzerland. They had been with Team New Zealand for both the 1995 America's Cup challenge and the 2000 defence and were more than satisfied with the experience. Also, the company had been a pioneer of underwater watches, and its 'Seamaster' range included top-class diving and sailing timepieces.

Omega was familiar with the Blake approach to servicing sponsorships and signed up almost immediately, which resulted in another name change for the former *Antarctica*, which now became *Seamaster*.

On Saturday, 11 November 2000 the completely refurbished *Seamaster* set sail for Cape Horn and Ushuaia, at the southern tip of Argentina, with a delivery crew of 10 aboard. She was laden with all the equipment for the Antarctic expedition plus food for 15 people for a minimum of nine months, including several hundred steaks and thousands of sausages, along with chicken, lamb, ham and turkey (the last for Christmas).

Blake wrote for the *Seamaster* log on the blakexpeditions.com website: 'We will follow the route we often took in the Whitbread Round the World Race, when getting south quickly was to have the best chance of being first into the favourable westerly winds of the Roaring Forties before turning left for Cape Horn.

'We are slower than normal due to the ice grids installed over the propeller tunnels, to protect the blades from Antarctic ice. But we are prepared to trade speed now for the extra security they will offer then. Fitting the grids on arrival in Ushuaia would have been difficult.'

Then he readily lapsed into his usual descriptions of the ocean and of bird and sea life: 'At the moment, there is a black-browed albatross circling *Seamaster* (it has been with us since soon after dawn) and dolphins alongside.

378

'There is rain all around, but we are paralleling the rugged coast north of Gisborne, only a few miles offshore, with the land standing out stark and clear in the background. Shafts of watery sunlight starting to blow holes in the clouds from time to time . . . it is south once more into the loneliest expanse of ocean on the planet.'

Ten days later, with *Seamaster* tasting her first Southern Ocean gale under new ownership, Blake wrote: 'The seas quickly became quite large, with breaking crests. Much of the day was spent with only a reefed foresail and headsail set. *Seamaster* marched south-eastwards at 9 to 10 knots – not fast but, under the conditions, about right. Compared to the race yachts that I have been on down here in the Roaring Forties, being on *Seamaster* is like being on an aircraft carrier. At times she was right on the top of a crest of breaking, foaming white water and it seemed as though the bow of our vessel was in the air on one side of the crest, while the stern was in the air on the other. Most times, however, the waves went harmlessly underneath.

'There are albatross with us. They seem to go away during the midday period (off for lunch maybe) and return in numbers in the evenings. There were two Sooty, or Light-mantled, albatross circling us a while ago – probably the prettiest of all sea birds, with various shades of chocolate colouring and very delicate features. They are nowhere near as mighty as the Wanderers or the Royals, but they certainly look the part. The type we most often see are the Royal Albatross – the biggest variety of sea bird there is with a wing span that can get to 3.5 metres. Most of the ones we have seen to date are probably not much more than two metres across, but they are still large birds. This is their home, not ours, and they are the most graceful flyers imaginable. They can travel extremely fast or almost hover in one place, all without flapping their wings.

'They use the up-currents of air from the waves and swells of the ocean to give them "lift". When turning at low level, they bank over so that one wingtip is just brushing the surface of the sea. Quite often,

379

they land nearby and watch us sail past – very buoyant and quite at ease on the surface of the sea, even with breaking waves about them.

'Over the next few months, we are looking forward to having a closer look at the bird, sea and animal life that abounds in the waters ahead . . .

'All of this life feeds from the sea and, so, is completely dependent on the quality of life in the sea. Until recent times, that has been a given and all the [various] species . . . have thrived. Travelling again through these southern waters, across many thousands of miles of lonely ocean towards one of the most unique and precious places on earth, one wonders why that isn't still the case.'

The answer, Blake realised all too well, was that many of the species which *Seamaster* encountered were under threat, even endangered, by the influences of man who was 'still ravaging and polluting their environment as though there was no tomorrow'.

On 20 November Blake wrote: 'The early morning light showed the seas to be starting to streak with foam ahead of the squalls that developed very quickly . . . The wind went to 56 knots in gusts, the surface of the sea turning white with spume blowing down the faces of the huge, breaking seas. We are still running before these seas which have built in size to be quite awe-inspiring – probably up to 10 metres high with the crests breaking and rolling down their faces. One wave came roaring aboard over the stern whilst we were working in the mid-part of the yacht tidying up the mess from the morning . . . The barograph has risen 20 mbs in the past eight hours – an extraordinary rise that makes the gale and vicious squalls easier to understand . . . what we are going through has made everyone onboard realise what a fantastic vessel *Seamaster* is. She has handled everything with ease, even in extreme conditions.'

Sailing across an ocean probably means different things to different people. 'Generally, though,' wrote Blake, 'it makes people appreciate how large the oceans are, how much water there is, but

SIR PETER BLAKE

also how much life there is. It isn't just a great, empty expanse of only wind and waves.'

This was Blake truly in his element, crossing one of the world's great oceans in a well-found yacht and completely at home amid the wind, the waves and the wildlife. Captain Thomas Wing would surely have empathised with his feelings.

'Peter changed in personality 24 hours off the dock,' said Pippa. 'He loved the ocean and was so at home on a boat. It was his biggest way of relaxing – cast off the lines and all the troubles would just float away.'

As a reminder of the real purpose of the journey, Blake added: 'There are seven large albatross with us this morning. Ollie fed them leftover strips of potato and they all landed and sat in the water in a tight ring, squabbling over the feast and obviously enjoying the different fare.'

What alarmed Blake was that magnificent birds like these were likely to disappear from the planet if something wasn't done immediately to curb the actions of long-line fishermen. It is estimated that 40,000 albatross are caught every year by long-liners and in drift nets, which is completely unsustainable. However, the evidence was that the message was not getting through. For Blake, the issue boiled down to the simple fact that 'while man is the cause of most if not all of the problems [affecting the natural world], he has the choice whether to influence environmental matters, for good or for bad. He has the ability and the technology to make immediate and quick changes that will go a long way to alleviating the problems he is causing. But has he the will?'

On 9 December, *Seamaster* was off Cape Horn and Blake wrote: 'It wasn't just Cape Horn that had us captivated, even though, I must admit, I have never seen it with a snow topping before, or looking so menacing in the early morning light. The bonus was the background of other islands, other more distant and jagged mountains covered in white, that continued to unveil themselves as we turned left and headed north towards the Beagle Canal.

'We all feel we have accomplished something. As a destination, after 5000 miles at sea through the Southern Ocean, you can probably guess that we are not displeased. For me, after racing past so many times, to now be able to stop and look at what I have only seen fleetingly through binoculars, fills a void.

Seamaster spent the next month exploring the Beagle Canal and Tierra del Fuego with their snow-capped mountains, glaciers, fjords and extraordinary wildlife. The Blake family and others flew in for the Christmas/New Year holidays and it was a time to completely relax in some of the most glorious cruising waters in the world.

'Peter was in his element and he just loved having us there,' recalls Pippa. 'He made sure it was interesting for the children and was great company, totally relaxed and lots of fun.'

To the Blakes, the troublesome world of the America's Cup must have seemed a million miles away.

Come 10 January 2001 *Seamaster* pointed her bows south across The Drake and headed for the great frozen continent of Antarctica. Her ultimate destination would depend on how far the ice shelf had receded, but the target was a point on the chart further south in George VI Sound than any vessel had been before.

On 6 February, at 69.15 degrees South, Blake wrote: 'George VI Sound beckons. We want to see what has happened to the George VI ice shelf that fills the channel (the Sound) between Alexander Island and the mainland at the base of the Antarctic Peninsula. Indications are that it has receded dramatically, especially over the past eight to 10 years. We probably won't make it to the face of the ice shelf itself. It is dropping so much old ice into the sea as it recedes and the channel is full of it. We are, however, going to give it a go.

'We are in the middle of Marguerite Bay as I write this – heading south and about to turn to starboard to round the Flyspot Islands. The calm sea that we are motoring in is normally a mass of fast ice, but not this year. For the first time that anyone can remember, it is totally ice free.'

For Blake and the crew of the *Seamaster*, the very favourableness of the conditions through which they were travelling was an ominous sign.

The following day, the log read: '7 February, 2001. Latitude: 69.52 S. Longitude: 68.48.5 W. Location: Moored alongside the edge of the sea ice in George VI Sound.

Visibility: Unlimited with a blue haze over distance. Conditions: Amazing.

'All we can see now to the south is snow and ice – miles and miles of it. To the west and east as I look from the pilot house is more ice, plus distant high mountains and glaciers. To the north, behind *Seamaster*, are patches of sea – full of icebergs.

'We are 7.6 miles short of latitude 70 degrees. This is as far south as we can get. No vessel could go further, not this year. Probably no vessel has ever been as far south in this arm of George VI Sound. In previous years, where we are now would have been frozen solid. So would the rest of the Sound through which we have just passed with comparative ease.'

In 1974 the permanent ice shelf was where *Seamaster* was now moored. The shelf had, however, receded at approximately one sea mile per year for the past 26 years or so. So, this year, that shelf was at least another 25 miles further south through the ever thickening and permanent sea ice that fronts it.

The next day, with *Seamaster* still moored to the sea ice, Blake was involved in a satellite telephone link with the United Nations Environment Programme (UNEP) headquarters in Nairobi where environment ministers from more than 80 countries were gathered to talk through the problems of global warming and other ecological issues.

He told the gathering: 'To describe what we have found over the past few days and weeks, to be here on *Seamaster* on a piece of sea that no one has ever been on before (because it is normally frozen) really brings home what is actually happening to the ice in this part of the world. It is now going to be, more and more, up to individuals who will accept nothing less than what is needed to enable nature to accommodate our presence on the planet.

'That is the reason for blakexpeditions and what we are doing. We want to educate and encourage as many people as possible to want to make a difference, and we are using all of the modern communications technologies to do so. To be part of what UNEP is doing, and have them officially on board with us, is a constant reminder that while we are only a few individuals with certain ideals there are others who also think the same way. And, between us, we can all help to bring about worthwhile change.'

Seamaster remained tethered to her chilly 'marina' until 14 February when the pack ice started to break up all around her. As she started to thread her way back out of George VI Sound, Blake noted: 'The summer is definitely going. On the east coast of the Peninsula, in the Weddell Sea, the pancake ice is starting to reform already – a prelude to the coming freeze. So we have good reason to keep moving north. In a few short weeks' time, no more movement will be possible by a vessel such as ours. The biggest natural happening on our planet is under way. Antarctica will, in the winter months, double in size – as it does every year.'

To Blake, the Antarctic Peninsula was an extraordinary place and one of critical importance to the wellbeing of the rest of the planet. To be there, even for a brief time, he believed, made you 'suddenly realise that you are part of something far greater, more magnificent and intricate, and more fragile than you ever imagined. You suddenly

384

understand that the environment must be appreciated and nurtured for all the right reasons, that it is what makes this planet of ours different to anything else in the known solar system.'

As he navigated *Seamaster* northwards up the Antarctic Peninsula, Blake was clearly more and more in his element and growing into his new mission in life. His seamanship, as usual, was impeccable, even though the circumstances were novel – even for him. His daily website offerings on environmental issues became more authoritative and his descriptions of the wildlife and the rugged and potentially dangerous environment in which he was operating, more passionate and perceptive.

His energy seemed boundless and his attention to detail in the running of the vessel infinite. Even so, he would regularly be found fast asleep over his computer in *Seamaster*'s communications cabin, his latest log-offering half finished on the screen in front of him.

By 15 March 2001 *Seamaster* was anchored near Yankee Harbour on Greenwich Island in the South Shetlands, and it was definitely time to be leaving the Antarctic Peninsula or risk getting iced in for the winter. A few days earlier, while on the way from Trinity Island to Discovery Bay on Greenwich Island, *Seamaster* had been caught in a full gale in the Bransfield Strait, at night and in heavy ice conditions. Blake sparely wrote: 'It was not the place you would have wanted to be.'

As evening approached, a large patch of packed brash ice, sea ice and icebergs appeared dead ahead of *Seamaster*, blocking her path. There were four hours of daylight (or twilight) left and only 35 miles to go, so Blake decided to press on, skirt around the ice reef ahead, and still reach Discovery Bay in time for dinner.

Seamaster headed north-east for nearly three hours to try and get around the ice but there was no way through. The 'patch' extended as far as the eye could see from the deck and it was too rough to have a man go up to the crow's-nest to check further. The wind rose as the evening progressed until it was blowing 35 to 40 knots from the east with driving sleet.

The decks gradually became sheets of ice and the spray from the bow wave turned to ice crystals as it blew over the boat. There was so much ice in the water that *Seamaster* was taking constant avoiding action with forward visibility reduced to less than 100 metres.

'So, there we were – trying to find a way through floating ice of all sizes, in a gale, with driving sleet, in the middle of the night,' Blake wrote. 'We didn't find "the corner" until much later and, rather than the escape we were seeking, it proved to be the start of a narrow lane in a much bigger sheet of broken ice than we could ever have imagined. At times the floes pinched in on both sides so that we had to slow right down and squeeze through the narrowest of gaps, not exactly sure how or if we were going to make it until the very last moment.

'By midnight, however, we had finally cleared the last funnel between the two sheets of compacted ice, and passed to leeward of an enormous berg that was only just discernible in the driving sleet, even though it was only a few hundred metres to windward.'

Blake and his crew hadn't intended to be at sea in these kinds of conditions but knew that, at some stage, it would be an inevitability and so were prepared for it. Even so, Blake wrote: 'I have raced through the Southern Oceans a number of times and had near misses with ice as well as seen many bergs. But I have never had a night like that one. It will certainly be recalled as one of the highlights of our journey, but one that I will be pleased not to repeat too often. We are very fortunate to be in such a strong, well-found vessel. *Seamaster* really came into her own. Only equivalent ice-breakers would have attempted such a passage.'

Early on 18 March *Seamaster* cleared McFarlane Strait – 'a narrow, winding and turbulent channel with a 3-knot current against us' – and met again the Southern Ocean swells in Drake Passage. Cape Horn was 250 miles ahead and her destination, Ushuaia, another 100 miles beyond that.

Two days later Blake's log read: 'We are presently sailing in a very fresh wind with white caps everywhere. This follows a night of near gale-force conditions and rough seas. *Seamaster* was jumping around like a small dinghy at times, but making good speed even though our sails were well reefed.

'The islands north of Cape Horn are off to port as we head towards the eastern entrance to the Beagle Canal, with Puerto Williams planned as our first stop back in South America. We left here two and a half months ago. Since then we have had a most extraordinary and rewarding time "down south".

'When we set out on this, the first voyage in a five-year programme of expeditions to some of the most remote locations on the planet, we really weren't sure of the outcome. Now that we have had time to look, to learn, to listen and, most importantly, to think, we have gained an appreciation that perhaps we didn't have before. And we are even more fascinated by what we find around us. The natural world, the environment that means so much to all of us, is truly a wondrous place.

'The most important objective for this and future expeditions we undertake is to help "make a difference" to how we all perceive the environment, to explain why it matters and to outline the reasons that change is necessary in a number of vitally important areas. I think we've made a good start. Next stop – the Amazon.'

CHAPTER
Eighteen
A Date with Destiny

Seamaster entered the mighty River Amazon on 28 September 2001, through the southern entrance that leads immediately to the river city of Belem, 70 miles inside the mouth.

The approximately 4000-mile journey north from the Beagle Canal, via Buenos Aires and Rio de Janeiro, had taken the best part of five months, including a survey and refit and the conversion of *Seamaster* from polar exploration mode to something more appropriate for a vessel about to make a near 3000-mile voyage that would roughly parallel the equator up and back down the Amazon and Negro rivers.

Seamaster was designed and built primarily to operate in extremely cold climates. She could safely withstand minus 40 degrees Celsius temperatures, and could winter over, completely self-sufficient, should she become 'frozen in' when exploring the ice regions of the planet.

The huge amount of insulation incorporated into her construction, however, also meant that she should be a good vessel in the intense heat of the tropics, so long as her metal decks were protected from the sun and the below-decks ventilation throughout was upgraded.

Awnings were made to cover almost the entire deck, new extractor fans would provide a gentle breeze throughout the interior, and specially-made scoops, incorporating insect netting, would enable the deck hatches to be kept open even in driving rain. The ice grids that protected the propellers in Antarctica wouldn't be needed for this part of the journey and were removed in Ushuaia.

Extra refrigeration was installed in the divers' shower area aft, to keep the salad and vegetables fresh, and a special water purification system, custom-designed and built, would provide safely drinkable water from the rivers when tropical downpours weren't enough to top up the tanks.

Blake used the five-month refit and delivery time to return to New Zealand where, in July 2001, the executive director of the United Nations Environment Programme, Dr Klaus Toepfer, made him a UNEP special envoy. Then it was on to England to help finish two one-hour television documentaries of *Seamaster*'s Antarctic expedition.

He rejoined *Seamaster*, with daughter Sarah-Jane, for the Buenos Aires to Rio de Janeiro delivery, which included some special film work for Omega, and then, with Sarah-Jane, returned to Britain to help finalise arrangements for documentary coverage of the Amazon and Negro expedition, before flying back to rejoin the boat at Belem.

In his first log from the Amazon he wrote: 'The Antarctic Expedition was the most memorable experience of my career to date. It has, and will continue to have, a lasting effect. I have to go back.

'The Amazon and Orinoco Rivers will produce other feelings – maybe. To again be able to go to one of the most critical environmental areas of the planet and become part of it, even for just a little while, will be very rewarding.

'We feel very fortunate to have the opportunity, especially as our crew, through our television documentaries and our website activity, will be millions – not just the 15 that are manning the watches at the moment.'

The plan was for *Seamaster* to make her way 1000 miles (1600 kilometres) upstream in the Amazon to the large and modern city of Manaus, which is at the hub of Brazil's massive river system. Here, *Seamaster* would branch right into the Rio Negro, another of the world's great waterways, and forge her way north-west upstream to San Gabriel, near the Venezuelan border and about as far as she could expect to proceed before the river became unnavigable.

The *Seamaster* crew would then split into two. A 'jungle team' would continue on in a shallow-draught river boat, through the Canal Casiquiare, the web of natural waterways that links the Amazon river system with that of the Orinoco, and then down the Orinoco to the Caribbean. *Seamaster*, meanwhile, would retrace her course back down the Amazon and then head north and west to the mouth of the Orinoco, to pick up the other half of her crew.

Blake's first Amazon log asked: 'Why are we doing this?' and then continued: 'The reasons are similar to those that took us to 70 degrees South on the Antarctic Peninsula.

'It is part of our mission to visit the "pulse points" of the planet and report on what we see, on what we find, and on what we learn through our adventures on this very special vessel of ours. Rather than reading about it, we want to "see for ourselves", form our own opinions, and share our experiences with as many people as possible.

'Is the ice melting in Antarctica? Are the forests of Amazonia being destroyed and, if so, what will be the outcome of such destruction? How will it affect you and me, and our children, and their children?

'It has taken me a long time to even start to understand the term "global warming". The more I have got to grips with it and have come to understand and appreciate what it means, the greater has become my concern about what we are doing to this planet of ours.'

Blake added some facts and figures to provide a perspective on the great river that he and his crew were about to navigate, bringing

393

to bear the same meticulous attention to detail that had gone into all his exploits on the water over the years.

The Amazon is the world's largest river in volume of water and second longest (after the Nile). From its source, 5168 metres (17,000 feet) high in the Peruvian Andes and less than 125 miles (200 kilometres) from the Pacific Ocean, the main stream collects water from more than 1100 tributaries as it travels the 4030 miles (6448 kilometres) to the Atlantic. With its tributaries, it holds an estimated 20 per cent of the world's liquid fresh water. The river is navigable by oceangoing ships for 2414 miles (3885 kilometres) upstream, as far as Iquitos in Peru.

The Amazon Basin is the earth's biggest freshwater ecosystem and reservoir, draining an area of more than 7 million square kilometres (more than half the South American continent and equivalent to three-quarters the size of the continental United States). Its equatorial rainforest is the largest in the world, occupying approximately 42 per cent of the total area of Brazil and representing 30 per cent of the remaining forest in the world (an area larger than the whole of Western Europe). It comprises one-tenth of the planet's entire plant and animal species and produces one-fifth of the world's oxygen. At the river's mouth, water flows into the Atlantic Ocean at 160,000–200,000 cubic metres per second – a flow greater than the world's next eight biggest rivers added together, or 10 times that of the Mississippi.

The Portuguese and then the Spanish were, in the fifteenth century, the first to explore the Amazon. The latter made two trips down the river after plundering the Incas in the Andes. The former were the first to travel the river upstream. The lure of gold was the first attraction. When that proved fruitless, the 'green hell' of the conquistador became the 'paradise' of the naturalist.

The next great explorers came in the eighteenth century – Charles Marie de la Condamine and Baron Alexander von Humboldt – and the attraction now was intellectual enlightenment and immense botanical riches. De la Condamine planned to be in the Amazon for two years, but stayed 10. Von Humboldt catalogued more than 12,000 plant species, most of which were new to science. He also entered the natural canal system that links the Amazon and Orinoco river systems (the Casiquiare) and, in a very arduous journey, tracked it for 200 miles (322 kilometres).

These scientific explorers gave a changing Europe more than just catalogues of plant and insect life, however. When de la Condamine returned to France in 1745, he took with him the first example of latex sap from a rubber tree, an important element at the beginning of the Industrial Revolution.

Then there was a remedy used by the native Indians for malaria – a bitter-tasting alkaloid called quinine, obtained from the red bark tree that is a native of Peru and Ecuador. An Englishman took seeds of the tree to India, where they flourished, and quinine became a worldwide treatment for malaria. The drug was made into a tonic, to which the colonials added gin (to mask quinine's inherent bitterness) and the world-famous G&T (gin & tonic) was born. Hardwoods, including mahogany and teak, were also exported in large quantities.

Chocolate made from the seeds of the 'cacao' tree became a popular drink among teetotallers, notably Quakers such as the Cadbury family.

Nothing, however, prepared the Amazon for the follow-on effects of de la Condamine's introduction of latex to Europe. Its value in the newly industrial world was huge, and it was tightly controlled by government and private companies who maintained a tight rein on exports, to control prices, while also exploiting a completely unprepared and hapless local workforce. The native Indians were forced to tap the raw latex from the trees and prepare it for shipping, under fear of torture and death. Their lives were incidental to the ever-increasing lust for profits.

395

Rubber ruled supreme for 30 years, between 1880 and 1910, until rubber plants were eventually smuggled out of the Amazon to British colonies around the world and the monopoly held by the rubber barons was broken.

The exploitation of its rich natural resources poses an even greater threat to the Amazon today, as modern felling and milling practices devastate the rainforest and open-mining techniques scour the landscape and pollute the river and its tributaries. Then there's the massive shift in population in economically struggling Brazil, with people moving to the milling and mining areas (i.e. the rainforest) to find work. Their needs to survive – food and wood for cooking – have imposed a new strain on the forests and led to wholesale slaughter of the animal life and overfishing of the rivers and streams.

A voracious reader and researcher, it didn't take Blake long to get to grips with the bigger picture and to come to the realisation that another of the world's vital ecosystems was under severe threat and on a one-way course to extinction unless humankind changed its ways.

He wrote in his daily log: 'Here in the Amazon, the timber, minerals and fossil fuel sources are not the only easily-available "resources" to be exploited. Most of the bigger animals here are already gone – or nearly so. Many others are following the same fate. The world market for endangered species, be it jaguar pelts or boa constrictor skins or live parrots, is increasing.

'Making a quick dollar is generally the motive behind the deforestation, the mining, the stripping, the cutting down, the shooting, the capturing – and so on. But because this is happening to some faraway forest, jungle, ice shelf, whale, jaguar, life in the sea or in a river, and because it doesn't directly affect us on a daily basis, we choose perhaps not to care enough.

'We should. This Amazon basin in its present form, for instance, is vital to all of us. For every five breaths that we take, no matter where we are in the world, the oxygen for one of those breaths comes from here – i.e. one-fifth of all the world's oxygen is produced by the plant life in the Amazon.'

Blake's research had informed him that the Amazon jungle also regulates climate, smoothes out water flows after heavy rain, and contains more biodiversity – plants, animals, insects, birds, all life – than any other single place on the planet. He was not alone in realising that cutting down the rainforest for short-term financial gain would be foolhardy in the extreme, but there was a plan afoot to do just that – the government-sponsored 'Advance Brazil' scheme – which would mean the loss of 40 per cent of the jungle.

Blake wrote: 'The results will not just be the loss of a large part of the "lungs of the planet" and the destruction of a unique and vital ecosystem, the flow-on effects will be huge. Cut down the jungle or forests and water quality drops away as the natural filtering process disappears. Erosion sets in. The climate changes. Desertification begins. If we keep taking from nature in the way we are, be it from the forests or from life in the sea, then the not-so-long-term effects will be catastrophic.'

Seamaster began her long river journey from Belem on 2 October 2001. Eighteen days and 1000 miles later, she left behind the muddy-brown waters of the Amazon and crossed into the clear-black waters of the Rio Negro, the fourth-largest river in the world and the Amazon's second-biggest tributary. The sprawling city of Manaus, with its population of two million people, was off to starboard.

Blake would briefly leave *Seamaster* here to make a quick trip to Rio de Janeiro, where he would meet with Dr Toepfer and attend a UNEP-sponsored meeting of the environment ministers of all the Latin American and Caribbean countries. In his log, he noted: 'The ministers that I spoke to were all very aware of the need to manage the Amazon and its resources with extreme caution, in a very sustainable way. But there are many other pressures being brought to bear and the solutions to saving the Amazon from catastrophic exploitation on a grand scale will not be easily found.

'It's a complex problem that revolves around what the forest is worth in its present state – to a country that is struggling to cope with an ever-increasing population, massive debt, a ruined economy and high levels of poverty among its people, and to all mankind, now and away into the future.

'I am fast coming to the conclusion that the rest of the world is going to have to act if the Amazon is to be saved. The world as a whole is going to have to invest in preserving this rainforest which is so essential to the global climate, as a carbon sink, and as a "lung" that generates one-fifth of the world's oxygen . . .

'The fate of the Amazon, then, is a global challenge that will be a severe but crucial test of man's ability to come to terms with the fact that he can, in environmental terms, very definitely influence the future. The big question is whether he will choose to influence for the good or for the bad.'

On rejoining *Seamaster*, progress up the Rio Negro slowed as she zigzagged her way through sandbars, rocks and islands with sometimes only the barest minimum of water between her raised centreboards and rudders and the riverbed. The river level was lower than the locals could ever remember. *Seamaster* was nearing the end of her trek westwards and it would soon be time to bid au revoir to the 'jungle team' and turn back to the Amazon.

On 5 November Pippa Blake joined her husband and crew for a month, jetting from London to Manaus and then catching a float plane to find *Seamaster* still plugging upstream on the Rio Negro between Manaus and Barcelos. It was a long and difficult journey and, with Christmas and the children's school holidays so close, Pippa had several times thought of not making it. But the prospect of being with her husband for a month on a river that had

SIR PETER BLAKE

always fascinated her won out. That was to be a fateful decision.

Three days later, with *Seamaster* now at Ilha Cuando, Blake was as far from his beloved oceans as he has ever been in his life. He wrote in his log: 'We are midway between the Atlantic and Pacific – right in the centre of the Amazon Basin. This is as far as *Seamaster* will get up the Rio Negro this year.

'We have made it to 1245 miles (1992 kilometres) from the sea against a stiff current, doing so at the "low-river" and experiencing to the maximum the beauty of the scenery, the friendliness of the people and the unknowns that we have had to deal with. *Seamaster* has only just scraped through at times – with the bottom of our vessel millimetres from the sand.

'As *Seamaster* turns back down the Amazon to the Atlantic Ocean, the "jungle team" will continue on up the Negro, aboard a shallow-draught ferry, to San Gabriel. The river will be extremely low at that point so they will pick up trucks and journey overland to the Venezuelan border – a ride of about six hours of dirt road. Then, as *Seamaster* heads for the Atlantic swells, the salt air and trade winds once more, and turns left towards the Caribbean, the "jungle team" will be using three bongos (local river craft), and one of our inflatable dinghies to traverse the Casiquiare Canal.

'They will spend time living with a Yanomami Indian tribe and they will be putting up with the privations of river travel at its most basic. The insects will be far more numerous and voracious than anything we have experienced so far.

'There are many miles yet to cover, on both rivers and on the ocean. The Orinoco lies ahead for both groups – but a long way ahead at the moment.'

On 15 November 2001 *Seamaster* sent the jungle team on its continuing journey upstream and turned back for the Amazon. The return trip downstream was twice as fast as that going up, river current adding considerably to their speed over the bottom. By

399

30 November she was back at Manaus, and by 4 December nearing Macapa, the seaport in the northern entrance to the Amazon where she would pause to complete immigration and border clearance before heading out into the Atlantic.

Blake wrote in his log: '4 December 2001, nearing Macapa.

'Dusk has turned the surface of the river into a greasy grey – the sky quickly darkening after the sun's orange and golds have gone. We always hope for a clear night, and tonight the moon will be up soon after 9 p.m. – two and a half hours of real blackness before then.

'There are flashes of lightning up ahead and the radar is showing a band of rain stretching out either side of our course. There are lights of ships, barge traffic, ferries and small towns; and the flaming floating pots marking the extremities of the fishing nets that have to be avoided.

'A cool breeze blows out of the lightning cloud and the as-yet unfelt rain. The moon is up but soon disappears behind the arriving ragged cloud. A few cold drops are felt but that passes, leaving us in clearing conditions, the only breeze provided by our forward speed. The rain has fallen before reaching our position and we are left with air full of the smells of damp earth and warm vegetation.

'The river tonight is flat calm, then briefly choppy in puffs of wind from the clouds, then calm once more. At times the swirls and small waves are caused by the current flowing over the very uneven river bed – 40 metres at times with sheer cliffs to 20 metres, then deep again. Sand waves up to 12 metres high beneath us show on the depth sounder – as regular as a geometric design – the sand marching slowly to the Atlantic on a journey that began thousands of miles away, driven onward by this vast amount of moving fresh water.

'There is a crew member on lookout duty on the bow of *Seamaster*. The main obstacles to our progress are large logs, patches of floating weed, or fishing boats without lights. He has the big searchlight with which to check from time to time. It can be quite

400

SIR PETER BLAKE

cold up front – the temperature down to 26 degrees Celsius or so –
and thermal clothing is occasionally needed. How strange to be in
the Amazon with polar-fleece jacket and trousers on.

'The lookout is in continuous communication with the pilot house
– the crew there monitoring engine gauges, making hourly checks of
the engine room, pumping fuel, marking our progress on the chart,
and keeping an eye on the radar and depth sounder – our two
most useful instruments for river travel. Hardly more than a few
minutes go by without a change of course to keep in the deepest
section, or avoid a sandbar, or pass an island. There is not much time
to relax.'

In a poignant counterpoint to *Seamaster*'s ecological mission,
Blake noted bands of smoke – thick smoke – pouring out of some
of the inlets and out of the forest, making walls right across the river.
The smell of the burning forest filled the air and also the boat's cabins.
Strong wafts of the aroma of piles of Brazil nuts added to the tang
of the smoke.

He was prompted once again to ask himself what they were
doing there: 'What has been the point of leaving Antarctica in March,
refitting in Buenos Aires over the southern winter, then undertaking
the long haul north to spend some time in the Amazon? Why is part
of our team off in the jungles of Venezuela?

'We want to restart people caring for the environment as it must
be cared for, and we want to do this through adventure, through participation, through education and through enjoyment. Technology gives
us the ability to bring our experiences into homes, offices and class-
rooms around the world on an almost immediate basis, through the
Internet and our website . . .

'Our aim, using all this technology, is to have as many "crew" as
possible travel with us and share our experiences. Those people may
then gain a better appreciation of the reasonably remote parts of the
world that we visit. And, even more importantly, begin to understand

401

the reasons why we must all start appreciating what we have before it is too late.

'We could have come here by commercial plane, stayed a few weeks and left. But that wouldn't have given us the essence of the Amazon. To travel by *Seamaster* means we appreciate the immensity of this water region and, in turn, have a real feeling for it. Exploring isn't about "getting there" as fast as possible. It is about the logistics, the planning, the research, the operation of our vessel, the crew, the meals, our equipment, the bureaucracy involved in taking all of us and *Seamaster* where yachts rarely venture . . .

'The environmental messages that we have become quite passionate about apply all over the planet – not just the Amazon. The quality of water and the quality of life, in all its infinite forms, are critical parts of the overall ongoing health of this planet of ours – not just here in the Amazon, but everywhere. With nearly 50 per cent of all of the peoples of the world now living in towns or cities, we wanted to begin the process of bringing back the appreciation of nature that may be missing from many daily lives . . .'

After briefly describing the upcoming television documentaries on *Seamaster*'s Antarctic leg and filming in progress on their Amazon journey, Blake concluded: 'The top of the environmental awareness mountain that we are endeavouring to climb may be out of sight through the clouds right now. But to win you first have to believe you can do it. You have to be passionate about it. You have to really "want" the result – even if this means years of work.

'The hardest part of any big project is to begin.

'We have begun. We are under way. We have a passion. We want to make a difference.'

That was the last log that Sir Peter Blake ever wrote. Twenty-four hours later he was dead, shot twice in the back while defending his boat and crew against river pirates.

On arriving at Macapa, Blake first anchored *Seamaster* off the main township. After starting the clearance process, and on local advice, he moved his boat several miles downstream to anchor a couple of hundred metres off a village called Fazendinha where she would be less conspicuous. Macapa had a reputation for 'river rats' – local gangs who raided visiting 'luxury' vessels. *Seamaster*, a big yacht by anyone's standards, fitted the bill.

Three of the crew – Don Robertson, Geoff Bullock and Rodger Moore – and visiting journalist Mark Scott, went ashore at approximately 4.30 p.m., to have a beer while they made telephone calls home to New Zealand (at a much cheaper rate than if they used *Seamaster*'s satellite phone link).

Blake joined them ashore when Robertson radioed the boat and asked for his camera to be brought in, leaving the yacht's delivery skipper Rob Warring, along with Leon Sefton and Robin Allen, aboard to take care of the boat and maintain security.

Robertson was, among other things, the blakexpeditions photographer, and most of the pictures from the Antarctic and the Amazon that appeared on the official website were his digital images.

The skipper was in high spirits as he relaxed in the company of his crew and talked of the future: blakexpeditions was off to a fine start with its first two voyages almost completed and two television documentaries going to air around the world, with another two almost ready for post-production; the blakexpeditions.com website had a growing and global audience with schools in a number of countries accessing the site to research environmental projects.

To Blake, though, that was literally only the start. With that familiar 'over the horizon' look in his eyes, he enthused about his vision of blakexpeditions having at least two or three eco-friendly vessels based at convenient locations around the world, positioned to respond quickly to major environmental events. He had already carried out substantial research into the design and equipping of these vessels, which would

403

be driven by hydrogen-powered motors for minimum emissions.

He was excited by the prospect of having the BBC come aboard as a media partner, with investigative journalist and presenter Donal MacIntyre 'fronting' future television programmes. And he was ambitious to expand in his role as a UNEP special envoy. But probably most of all, he was fully energised by the prospect of being at sea again in the trusty *Seamaster* after more than two months of being constrained in rivers – albeit it very big ones.

He and the rest of those ashore returned to the boat at sunset (approximately 6.30 p.m.) and relaxed with a beer in the large cockpit area while *Seamaster*'s Brazilian chef Paulo prepared dinner in the galley below. The night was pitch dark, with no moon, but the company and the music on the stereo system were good.

Some time between 10.15 p.m. and 10.30 p.m., *Seamaster* was boarded by eight armed intruders wearing balaclavas or motor-cycle helmets. They had pulled up under the boat's stern completely undetected, the sound of their approach in a 30-foot river craft masked by the stereo and by the ever-present onboard background noise of generator and extractor fan.

The *Seamaster* crew was taken completely by surprise when the intruders emerged, two at a time, from behind a shower curtain that had been rigged on the aft deck, some with one firearm and others with two.

Events then moved very quickly.

Blake moved swiftly towards *Seamaster*'s pilot house and the stairway leading below decks. As he raced past Bullock, he said: 'This is for real.'

Moore, who was closest to the aft deck when *Seamaster* was boarded confronted the first intruder and squirted a can of beer in his face. The intruder responded by hitting Moore in the face with a pistol, rendering him semi-conscious.

The rest of the *Seamaster* crew were then herded to the starboard side deck and, at gunpoint, were ordered to hand over their watches and money.

One bandit held a gun to Robertson's head and ordered him to lie down on the deck. Robertson resisted and had to be constrained by crewmates who feared for his life.

Paulo, the boat's chef, had meanwhile raced below to the communications room and was trying in vain to summon assistance.

Also down below, Blake had gone straight to his cabin where two .308 rifles were stored securely behind the door. These firearms were on board in case of problems with polar bears on the next leg of *Seamaster*'s voyage schedule – through the North-West Passage in the Arctic.

In his cabin opposite Blake's, Leon Sefton had been reading and then sleeping but was woken by the scuffle on deck. As he emerged to go topsides, he saw Blake entering his cabin and closing the door behind him.

Sefton went through the main saloon area and was about to enter the companionway aft when he was confronted by one of the intruders who ordered him back into the main cabin at gunpoint.

When Blake eventually emerged from his cabin, rifle in hand, the first thing he would have seen was Sefton with a masked intruder's gun aimed at his head.

Blake didn't hesitate. He advanced on the gunman, shouting at him to 'Get off my fucking boat'. Even though Blake's rifle was still at his side, the gunman retreated down the companionway aft, with the angry *Seamaster* skipper in pursuit.

Still in the main saloon, the next thing Sefton heard was an exchange of gunshots which sent him diving for cover in Blake's cabin. When that exchange stopped, he moved forward, spare ammunition in hand, to see whether Blake needed help. The skipper was banging the butt of his rifle on the deck, as though to clear a jammed cartridge. He instructed Sefton to go for'ard and turn off

405

the hatch fan in the forepeak, to clear an escape route to the main deck.

While doing so, Sefton heard another exchange of gunfire aft. As he made his way back through the main saloon, he heard several more shots before the gunfire stopped.

It would later become clear from police evidence that Blake had hit the intruder twice in the first exchange of fire – once in the gun hand (smashing the handle of the intruder's pistol), and once in the arm. He was Isael Pantoja da Costa, a 27-year-old on home detention for an earlier robbery.

As da Costa retreated to the cockpit area on deck, a second gunman, Ricardo Colares Tavares, a 23-year-old on bail also for an earlier robbery, ducked his head into the pilot-house area for a quick look down the stairway leading below. He would have seen Blake apparently attempting to clear a jammed rifle.

Tavares ducked out of the pilot-house area and then stepped straight back in to fire two shots down the stairway.

At the bottom of the stairs, Blake was hit twice – once in the back, near his left shoulder blade, and once in the right side of his chest.

The intruders then retreated in unison, using one of *Seamaster*'s inflatable tenders to make their escape. As they left, they loosed off at least three shots at the *Seamaster* crew, one of which creased Bullock's shoulder blades, opening up a wound that would require 14 stitches.

Desperate attempts to resuscitate the fallen skipper began and continued for more than an hour until an emergency crew that belatedly responded to *Seamaster*'s distress calls declared him dead. It later transpired that Blake's wounds were such that he would have died instantly from a ruptured aorta. The resuscitation attempts were in vain.

While a shocked world struggled to come to terms with his senseless loss, Blake's body was flown back to England for burial.

With heavy hearts, the jungle team completed its journey down the Orinoco River to rejoin *Seamaster* in Grenada. They felt that that's what their skipper would have wanted.

Sir Peter Blake KBE was buried in the St Thomas à Becket Church, near his home in Emsworth on the south coast of England, on 14 December 2001. More than a thousand people, including representatives of the British Royal Family, of the United Nations Environment Programme, and of the New Zealand and British governments, attended the service. Fittingly, the coffin was carried from church to grave by six of 'Blake's people' – former Blake crew who had flown from New Zealand to bid a last farewell to their beloved skipper.

On 23 December 2001, in his native New Zealand, a memorial service to Sir Peter was held in the Auckland Domain overlooking the city and the harbour where, and upon which, he grew up. More than 30,000 people gathered to celebrate his extraordinary life and to hear tributes from such dignitaries as New Zealand's Governor-General, Her Excellency The Honourable Dame Silvia Cartwright, New Zealand's Prime Minister, the Right Honourable Helen Clark, a kaumatua of the Ngati Whatua tribe, Sir Hugh Kawharu, and Brazil's National Secretary of Sports, Mr Lars Grael, representing His Excellency, President Fernando Henrique Cardoso.

The service was broadcast live on nationwide television and, later in the day, an estimated 8000 boats took part in a moving sail-past on Auckland Harbour as New Zealand's yachties said 'bon voyage' to their favourite son.

Eight men were ultimately brought to trial in Macapa and found guilty on charges relating to Sir Peter's murder: Ricardo Colares

Tavares, the 23-year-old who confessed to shooting Sir Peter in what he described as self-defence, was sentenced to 36 years and 9 months; and Isael Pantoja da Costa, the 27-year-old who first exchanged shots with Sir Peter, got 35 years. The six other intruders were sentenced to a total of 122 years with prison terms ranging from four months to 32 years, eight months.

The judge disallowed defence claims that the ringleader Tavares was mentally ill at the time of the incident. He also refuted the claim by some of the accused that Sir Peter fired the first shot. He based his ruling on evidence from the crime scene and the sequence of events apparent in court testimony.

The judge further affirmed that given the nature of the armed invasion of the *Seamaster* there was no scope under Brazilian criminal law for the accused to claim 'self-defence' in the face of the crew reaction. It was 'absolutely impossible' to characterise Sir Peter's reaction to the situation as 'unfair' when faced with an 'arbitrary and illicit' attack. Sir Peter, he said, could claim 'legitimate defence of himself and his companions'. Defence suggestions that Sir Peter would not have been killed if he had not reacted as he did were 'absolutely unacceptable, pure conjecture and vain speculation', in his opinion.

On appeal, Ricardo Colares Tavares' sentence was reduced to 32 years, two months, four days, and Isael Pantoja da Costa's to 30 years, seven months. Similarly the sentences of the other four main culprits were reduced by an average of three years.

An appeal by the prosecutor to impose stiffer sentences on the grounds that the shots fired by the bandits as they fled were tantamount to attempted murder, was dismissed. A further appeal by the prosecutor to increase the sentences of two of the accessories to the crime was also disallowed.

New Zealand Prime Minister Helen Clark welcomed the decision to uphold the original sentencing, even though the sentences themselves had been slightly reduced on appeal.

'This brings finality to a tragic episode for both the Blake family and New Zealand,' Clark said in a media statement. 'The Brazilian court system acted swiftly to bring Peter Blake's murderers to justice. The final sentence for these young men reflects the severity of the crimes they committed and I am satisfied that justice has been done in this case.'

Clark added that Sir Peter would always be remembered and honoured in New Zealand, both for his sportsmanship and for the huge profile he brought the country through his yachting conquests.

The British inquest into Sir Peter's death recorded a verdict of unlawful killing, with the Deputy Coroner for Portsmouth and Southeast Hampshire, Peter Latham, observing: 'On that night he (Sir Peter Blake) showed outstanding bravery in trying to protect his colleagues and the ship in what must have been for everyone terrifying circumstances. He was a great man.' A sentiment few would dispute.

Epilogue

What was it that made Peter Blake almost instinctively reach for a gun on that ill-fated night in Macapa?

Blake wasn't what one might consider 'a gun person'. In fact, in many ways he was a shy and gentle soul who disliked personal confrontation and was invariably considerate of others. He loved to laugh – hands on hips, head back, big frame shaking. Probably as a result of being brought up on boats in a different era, Peter liked nothing better than playing board games – be it Monopoly with his children, as a preferred option to television on a night at home, or Scrabble with his wife, to while away the hours on a long aeroplane flight. He cherished family time and struggled increasingly to justify to himself the lengthy periods for which his chosen profession and way of life took him away from that family.

He adored children and their uncomplicated perspective on life, and kids loved being with him. In many ways, he identified more readily with youngsters and their joy in growing up than he did with adult company or concerns. Similarly, when visiting friends, he would make a beeline for their pets and animals, often in preference to adult conversation.

On family cruises, he would instigate kite building or model-boatmaking contests, or organise sail-boat races, and would always be the keenest competitor. On a beach, he would dig deep holes or build sand castles – always intent on ensuring that his children, or anyone else's in the vicinity, had the best possible time.

411

In his quieter moments, and usually only when family or close friends were around, he played piano, and did so well, with a good ear and beautiful touch. This was almost a contradiction of his personal taste in music to take on a long sea voyage, which usually scaled the audio heights only as far as a Willie Nelson tape.

Yet on that fateful night when bandits boarded his boat, he didn't hesitate. Immediately telling one of his crew, Geoff Bullock, 'This is for real', he hastened below to get a firearm. Then, when confronted by the sight of another of his crew, Leon Sefton, with a masked thug's gun at his head he was instantly outraged and drove the intruder back by pure force of presence and will, his rifle not even presented or pointed but still at his side.

There was one aboard *Seamaster* that night, journalist Mark Scott, who had made the journey down the Amazon in order to research an article for *New Zealand Geographic* magazine, who would later opine that Blake and his crew should not have resisted the intruders. That they should have submitted and handed over their valuables, and all would have ended well. That the 'river rats' would have taken their loot and fled into the night.

But that lone view was not consistent with the *Seamaster* team's briefings on piracy in the Amazon, or the not-too-far-away Caribbean, which warned that, in some extreme instances, whole crews had been robbed and then shot.

Blake would have been furious that his boat was being invaded and his crew threatened and assaulted. Given the man he was – always the skipper – his immediate reaction would have been to protect those for whom he was responsible, including Scott.

It probably never even entered his head that he might have to use the weapon that he went below to get, but there is an old saying that there's no point taking a knife to a gunfight, and Blake's instincts would have been to meet force with force, show them that you've got a gun too, and scare them off.

The Brazilian judge who sentenced Blake's murderer and accomplices dismissed as 'absolutely unacceptable, pure conjecture and vain speculation' the suggestion that Blake would not have been killed if he had not reacted as he did.

Probably most of us have wondered how we ourselves would react in circumstances later described by the coroner in England as 'terrifying'. Hopefully, we will never have to find out.

But probably very pertinent on this awful occasion was the thought that flashed into Leon Sefton's mind as his skipper drove back an armed intruder by sheer force of will: 'You're a brave bastard, Pete.'

Douglas Myers remembers: 'Pete wasn't an aggressive personality at all, but he had a tenacious aggressiveness in terms of what he wanted to do. He had all the internal drive and desires, but this wasn't translated in a destructively egotistical sort of way.

'There was, if you like, a hidden side of him. He was a very quiet, manly person vis-à-vis women or vis-à-vis men. Most of us were in his protection – not lesser in a silly way, but more like he was at a different level.

'When you look back at everything he was and everything he did, it all looks like it was preordained. You couldn't imagine that it could have been anything other than it was. But that's not the way the world is. So what was it in his character that resulted in the outcome being as it was?

'That, you've got to say, is 120 per cent due to what he had. He was a remarkable human being. Like all of us, he had great deficiencies, but in his case the deficiencies were quite attractive ones. He wasn't aggressive, in that way. He wasn't egotistical, in that way. He didn't have many hang-ups.

'I read an article on what makes entrepreneurs entrepreneurial. A lot of them didn't do well and weren't all that well liked at school, a lot of them were dyslexic, and then they either did it for reasons of power, status or revenge. Driven by power, they wanted to get revenge on those who perpetrated the crap on them, to show them that they should have been head boy or whatever. But where was Peter? Not in [any of] those three [categories] . . .

'Look at his last log exhortation – you've got to keep on keeping on. That's not a normal Kiwi trait and it is probably not a normal human trait. But he had it, and he didn't have it for negative reasons because he had to get back at people.

'He liked being a hero but he wasn't driven by public acclamation. In many ways it probably annoyed him. That wasn't the driver. And nor was status.

'So, there was an inner demon that required him, on behalf of New Zealand, mankind, his family and so forth, to keep on going . . . He was successful in a range of things. He had a round-the-world racing career, then he was the promoter, manager and organiser of a highly complex contest that he wasn't that good at himself (the America's Cup challenge in 1995 and defence in 2000), and then he translated it all into the third phase of his career (with blakexpeditions).

'That sort of thing is maybe what I sensed when I first met him – he was unusual in that he operated in another dimension to most people.'

Blake occasionally visited Myers on his farm in Northland, and Myers recalls that his guest would habitually get up early, go for long walks by himself, and then have a cup of tea. Then he would always have a cup of tea last thing at night.

'We talked very easily but you were always conscious that there was this other dimension to him that I doubt he shared with anyone,' says Myers. 'He may have been incapable of articulating what it was, and that was the demonstrable side of the fact that he had what adventurers and heroes have. I haven't experienced that with anyone else.

'That's what made him attractive and that's probably what killed

414

him – that other dimension, that instinct that he had to protect others. I doubt that many people would have done what he did in Macapa. He probably felt a sense of indignation, that he was the captain and that a certain reaction was required of him – "I'm the captain, I'm in charge, I'm responsible."'

The last time Pippa Blake saw her husband alive, they enjoyed a cup of coffee and a long chat at Manaus airport while she waited to catch a flight back to London after nearly a month in the Amazon aboard *Seamaster*.

He was relaxed and talkative. The Amazon/Negro expedition was nearly completed and he was looking forward to Pippa, Sarah-Jane and James joining *Seamaster* for a cruise in the Caribbean before she headed up the eastern seaboard of the North American coast to Baffin Island and the North-West Passage.

Although neither talked about it, the trials of the 2000 America's Cup had put a strain on their marriage, but now they had discovered that they could share the new direction in Peter's career. It would be just like the pre-America's Cup days again with the whole Blake family an integral part of Peter's team.

'My time with Peter up the Amazon was magical,' remembers Pippa. 'The America's Cup wasn't really something that we could do together as a husband-and-wife team – apart from the social functions and me hopefully being supportive. So I had started painting and Peter was sort of doing his own thing.

'But suddenly it became evident that here was something that we could really take part in together again. I was able to continue my passion, painting, and express my view of the river and incredible scenery, with Peter enjoying showing me the wildlife and telling me about some of his adventures. I was part of the expedition, part of the team, and that was wonderful.

'Peter was very keen that there might, later, be a role in blakexpeditions for James, provided he got himself a degree in marine biology or some similar qualification. That, I suppose, is another part of the tragedy of what happened in Macapa.'

Whenever Pippa thinks about her husband, which she does frequently, the image in her mind is one of him with his head back, laughing. He did that a lot and it was a sight to enjoy. She is not unmindful, however, of the impact that he had on the lives of others and on the world around him:

'He was a pretty special guy, by anyone's standards. He had a major impact on the destiny of the Whitbread Round the World race and he had a major impact on the destiny of sailing in New Zealand. A lot of people would not be where they are today without his pioneering. That's what he probably would like to be remembered for.

'But he was also a really good husband and father, a good family man. He was a genuinely decent person who knew the difference between right and wrong and had the right values in life. I'd like to think that he passed all that on to the children.

'One of the bigger tragedies of his loss was that blakexpeditions was just starting to get some real traction. I believe he would have moved some mountains with blakexpeditions. It would have achieved its objective – to make a difference.'

When Douglas Myers reflects on Blake's life, there is an almost inevitable reference to New Zealand's other great adventurer son – Sir Edmund Hillary:

'Probably Blake and Hillary would be the two names to come forward if you asked people to think about New Zealand. They both achieved great things for their country.

'I wouldn't want to have to compare the two, [but] Hillary conquering Everest was probably more visible at the time on a world

416

basis, and he's been a great ambassador for the country. [Whereas] Peter's legacy is showing New Zealanders that they are capable of being successful internationally in complex undertakings, of winning with complexity. The impact of that on New Zealanders, and the resulting benefits to the country, might be the greater.

'He showed us that if you are tenacious and extraordinarily hard-working, and have self-belief, you can pull something together for New Zealand.

'Pete's legacy is that for 20 years he served up a menu of nothing but good news. That's why I was so outraged by all that crap at the end [of the America's Cup defence], because he had such a clean record of excellence – as a human being, as a generous person, as a leader, as a winner.'

While Blake's death shocked and distressed his old friend Martin Foster, the fact that Blake had gone for a gun to drive the intruders away did not surprise him: 'I can't imagine Peter just sitting there and allowing bandits on the boat. I can, however, imagine him getting a gun and ordering them off his boat, which, under normal circumstances would probably have frightened them off, but in this case . . .

'At 53, he'd accomplished so much. There was so much more to do, but he had achieved one hell of a lot.'

So from where did Blake acquire his almost legendary leadership skills?

You can't teach yourself to be an inspirational leader. You either are one, or you are not. But few are simply born great leaders. The ability lies latent in them but they have to work hard to realise the potential. Blake, it would appear, was one of the latter kinds of leader.

There can be no doubt that leadership qualities were in his genes. His great-great-grandfather Captain Thomas Wing had them and so,

417

to a degree, did his father Brian who skippered gunboats in World War II. But to quote Simon Gundry: 'Blakey evidently didn't rattle too many dags at Takapuna Grammar, did he? He wasn't a great First XV player. He just got on and did his own thing. My sister was in the same sixth-form year with him and can hardly remember him.' Martin Foster also recalls that 'Pete's leadership skills were not really in evidence when he was a teenager'.

So his development as an inspirational leader of men probably started when, as a 19-year-old in 1967, he built the JOG racer *Bandit* and got to skipper his own boat and (albeit small) crew of brother Tony and family friend Crawford Duncan. He always had plenty to contribute on how a boat should be sailed, however – evidence his verbal tussles with father Brian on *Ladybird* and his chiding the crew on *Red Feather* for over-indulging in the gin-spiked oranges on the way to Suva in 1969.

The development curve would have steepened appreciably in 1970 when, as a 22-year-old, he joined Les Williams on *Ocean Spirit*, and even more so when, the following year, Williams made him a watch captain for the Cape Town–Rio race. That same year, he made his first blue-water trip as skipper when he was in command of the 70-foot *Ocean Spirit* for the delivery back to Britain from Rio de Janeiro.

The inaugural Whitbread race in 1973–74, when he was watch leader on *Burton Cutter*, would have been another big step in the right direction, as would have been the 1977–78 Whitbread as watch leader on the maxi *Heath's Condor*.

By the time he had skippered *Condor of Bermuda* on the maxi circuit and in the 1979 Fastnet Classic, he was ready to lead his own Whitbread campaign, and his burning ambition to do the race with an all-New Zealand boat and crew became reality in 1981–82 with *Ceramco New Zealand*. That was the campaign that launched the 'Blake family' of racing crew which was to become the backbone of New

418

Zealand yachting for the next 20 years, the family growing in numbers as Blake continued to mature and hone his people skills through two more Whitbreads in 1985–86 and 1989–90.

By the time he got through the America's Cup campaign in 1992 and the *ENZA New Zealand* voyages in 1993 and 1994, he was nearing the top of his game, and he left nobody in any doubt as to his formidable leadership abilities with the celebrated Team New Zealand and its 1995 America's Cup win.

Choosing the right people was always the key element in the Blake approach to putting crews together. He was then always completely loyal to those crews, as they were to him, and he had the precious ability to instil people with great self-belief and the ethic to always be accountable.

Peter Blake always led by example and got the best out of the chosen group around him. Offshore, no matter what the circumstances, he radiated an aura of confidence in his own seamanship and ability that made others feel secure. Witness the comment by Gundry that, if Blake asked him to sail around the moon with him, he'd jump at the chance, knowing that his skipper would get him back safely; or the Ed Danby remark that, no matter how bad conditions were for the catamaran *ENZA* in her two Trophée Jules Verne attempts – and they got pretty hairy on a number of occasions – 'whenever Blakey came on deck, you always felt safe'.

Blake didn't inspire just his crews either. He worked very hard at ensuring that his sponsors felt an integral part of what he was doing, and always went the extra yard to ensure that they got value for money if they backed him. This certainly impressed brewery chief Myers and, behind him, the decision-makers at the New Zealand Apple and Pear Marketing Board, Toyota New Zealand, Telecom New Zealand, the New Zealand Lotteries Commission and Television New Zealand, all of whom came back for more – some for more and more – after being exposed to the Blake approach.

In the process of this drive to engage with others, he became a consummate communicator, always radioing his position and circumstances to the media ashore to ensure valuable television, radio and newspaper coverage. This was ground-breaking stuff in the 70s and 80s, and he went a step further in the *ENZA* campaign with the pioneering use of microwave equipment to transmit television images and audio to waiting aircraft at strategic points of the big cat's journey.

There were, of course, other sides to the Blake character and personality. In many ways he was the quintessential, self-reliant Kiwi yachtsman, a product of his upbringing on and around the water. But he was also what New Zealanders perceive to be 'very British' in his quiet reserve and respect for others – attributes he obviously inherited from his parents who were of British origin and who were both delightfully reserved and respectful of others.

He would often use his six-foot four-inch height to advantage, peering down at the less vertically endowed. He didn't readily suffer fools either (shades of Captain Wing?) and he was something of a disciplinarian. Martin Foster recounted two examples of this aspect of Blake's personality.

The first was when he told a *Condor* delivery crew that he would throw overboard anything that he found lying around in the cockpit. Somebody made the mistake of leaving their prized transistor radio on deck, and over the side it went.

The other was in the inaugural Two-man Round the North Island race when he and Foster, as the race organisers, were approached by one skipper who had a problem with a piece of navigational kit that was, in fact, a forerunner to the highly sophisticated GPS equipment of today. It was broken and he wanted a time allowance in order to get it repaired before starting on the next leg of the race. Blake just looked at him and said: 'You've got a sextant – use it.'

Of the fact that Peter Blake was one of the greatest long-distance ocean-racing campaigners of his generation, there is little doubt. His contemporaries agree, and his record – including *Steinlager 2*'s all-encompassing Whitbread win and *ENZA New Zealand*'s mark for sailing non-stop around the world – speaks for itself.

The fact that he also twice led New Zealand to victory in the America's Cup, building Team New Zealand and then leading it through two highly complex and successful campaigns (crewing on the race boat in one of them), puts him in a unique position to claim a special place in the annals of international yacht racing.

But Blake was much more than a racing yachtsman. He was, in every sense of the word, a seaman and he had a seaman's love of, and respect for, nature. In the latter part of his extraordinary life he was endeavouring to use the fame and esteem that he had created for himself to inspire people to take better care of the natural world, and he was doing so in a realistic and inclusive way that was a lot more likely to hit the target than the exclusionist 'greenie' approach.

He wanted to show everyone that you can be a conservationist and still live in the world and want to be part of it. His message was one of 'Go and see for yourselves how unique and beautiful it is, then you'll fall in love and want to take better care of it' as opposed to one of 'It's precious (because we're telling you it is), don't go there, don't touch it'.

It's not surprising, given the scope of his many achievements plus his image and reputation abroad, that some of the more objective assessments of Blake's career as a yachtsman come from overseas.

Sir Robin Knox-Johnston observes: 'Hillary probably made New Zealanders think they were a nation of natural mountaineers. Some 40 years later, Peter made the nation think they were all natural sailors. And look at where they are today, look where New Zealanders have got to in sailing. Peter was the one who led the charge.

'He has left behind, for us all, a standard of professionalism in all aspects of the game, and not just because he could sail. Peter was a great sailor, but he wasn't the world's greatest sailor, and he never claimed to be. But when he put a package together he was a world-beater.'

Journalist Bob Fisher recalls the very moving experience when *ENZA New Zealand* finished her successful 1994 Trophée Jules Verne attempt in Brest: 'The welcome to a non-Frenchman was so emotional. That was because Blakey actually captured French hearts, something that is bloody difficult to do if you are not French.

'I was in France some weeks after Peter's death and they were still in shock – six weeks to two months later. He was definitely one of their heroes – they could identify with him.'

Of Blake's accomplishments, Fisher says: 'There may never be a man so consummately good. To have won the Whitbread, to have held the Trophée Jules Verne and to win the America's Cup – all at the same time – that's really something. For the majority of people, just competing in a Fastnet or a Hobart is a personal Everest, but they were mere foothills for Peter, the starting blocks on the way to much loftier peaks.

'His achievements were second to none. Nobody has achieved what he did and nor are they likely to do so in the future. He was a 100 per cent, flat-out racer, but he was also a seaman. Being a seaman is so important. There are times when the chips are firmly down, when there are racers and there are seamen, and the seamen are the ones who come out on top. Blakey was the best. Nobody else could compare. He was a complete yachtsman who appreciated the total game better than anyone, and he was inspirational.'

Back in New Zealand, Simon Gundry, who did two Whitbread campaigns with Blake, says: 'You can never take away from someone the fact that they sailed around the world with Peter Blake. You can't say the glue in that was winning because, although we did our share of that, most of us didn't win the big one.

'So, the glue had to be Peter and his way of keeping everything together. He gave you a lot of confidence in him plus faith in yourself. Nobody ever left Peter's boat and told him to stick it up his bum. I'm probably the only person that left his crew, and I did that because of personal things with my family.

'He always had a wonderful sense of humour, telling us that we were there to enjoy ourselves. If we weren't enjoying ourselves, then we may as well not do it. And he was always so polite. I can remember Roy Mason and me walking up the marina at the Hamble, in England, one morning after we'd finished the Channel Race in *Lion New Zealand*. We were following Peter and Pippa and heading back to the crew house for breakfast. Peter turned around and asked if it would be all right for he and Pippa to come back to the crew house for a cup of tea.

'I mean – it was his deal, his house, and we were his crew. He could have just told us he was coming back for a cuppa. But he had enough politeness to recognise that the crew house was our space and he was considerate enough to ask whether it was all right for him to intrude. Humbling, absolutely humbling. He was a unique individual.'

Mike Quilter, who did two Whitbreads and the Round Australia race with Blake, and was also part of his 1995 and 2000 America's Cup campaigns, observes : 'For 15 years, maybe 20, New Zealand led the world in sailing, and that was largely thanks to Blakey. With his whole approach to campaigns, particularly to sponsorship, he opened the door to professional sailing for a whole generation of Kiwis and they grabbed the opportunity with both hands. He was 20 years ahead of his time.

'It was not so much a Blakey training ground. It was, and still is, a family. If anyone sailed with Blake, they became part of that family. There is a special bond between anyone who sailed with him. It's hard to put your finger on why, but it is a fact and it had a lot to do with the man himself. When you look at what members of the family have achieved, you realise that he was pretty good at picking people.

'I've sailed around the world with Blake and Dalts (Grant Dalton) and there's really never been a bad word spoken. Perhaps people who sail around the world are a unique bunch of individuals anyway, but Pete's guys were probably special among them.

'The world is poorer without him. He was a statesman. I always thought he would have made a good Governor-General because he was such a statesman.

'What a waste. He had already achieved so much, but there was so much more that he could and would have done . . .'

Sir Peter Blake – A Life

Born:	1 October 1948, Auckland, New Zealand	
Died:	6 December 2001, at the mouth of the Amazon River	
Education:	Takapuna Grammar School	
	Auckland Institute of Technology (1966–69)	
Profession:	Engineer/Yachtsman/Adventurer	
Wife:	Pippa, Lady Blake	
Children:	Sarah-Jane, James	
Honours:	1983	MBE, for services to yachting
	1991	OBE, for services to yachting
	1995	KBE (Knight Commander of the Civil Division of the Most Excellent Order of the British Empire), for services to yachting
	1995	Life Member of the Royal New Zealand Yacht Squadron
	1995	Honorary Member of the Royal Yacht Squadron
	1995	Inducted into the America's Cup Hall of Fame
	1996	Fellow of the Royal Geographic Society
	1999	D Com, Massey University
	2000	Honorary doctorate, Auckland University
	2001	Appointed a Special Envoy for the United Nations Environment Programme (UNEP)

| 2002 | Olympic Order (from the International Olympic Committee) 'to pay tribute to Sir Peter Blake's outstanding sailing career and to his genuine passion for sport and adventure' |

Positions held:	President of the Jules Verne Association
	Patron of Devonport Yacht Club (New Zealand)
	Patron of Gulf Harbour Yacht Club (New Zealand)
	Patron of Essex Yacht Club (England)
	Vice-president of Royal Port Nicholson Yacht Club (New Zealand)
	Trustee of New Zealand International Yachting Trust
	Life member of West Mersea Yacht Club (England)
	Honorary member of Royal Southern Yacht Club (England)
	Honorary member of Royal Southampton Yacht Club (England)
	Member of the Emsworth Sailing Club (England)
	Member of the Ocean Cruising Club (England)
	Member of the Association of Cape Horners

Awards:	1982	New Zealand Yachtsman of the Year
	1989	New Zealand Sports Personality of the Year
	1989–90	Communicator of the Whitbread Round the World race

1989–90	New Zealand Yachtsman of the Year (with *Steinlager 2* crew)
1990	New Zealand Sporting Team of the Year (with *Steinlager 2* crew)
1990	ABC 'Wide World of Sport' Athlete of the Week (in May)
1990	Public Relations Institute of New Zealand Communicator of the Year
1990	Yachting Magazine (USA) Yachtsman of the Year
1994	International Yacht Racing Union World Sailor of the Year (with Robin Knox-Johnston)
1994	Hobson Medal for excellence in New Zealand Maritime Endeavours
1995	New Zealand Sportsman of the Year (with Team New Zealand)
1995	New Zealand Sports Team of the Year Award (with Team New Zealand)
1995	New Zealand Outstanding Management and Marketing Achievement Award
1995	Royal Yacht Squadron Sir Francis Chichester Trophy (with Robin Knox-Johnston)
1995	British Yachtsman of the Year, 1994 (with Robin Knox-Johnston)
2002	International SeaKeepers Society SeaKeeper Award for 'extraordinary dedication and leadership in the cause of marine conservation'
2002	Ocean Stewardship Award from the United Nations Environment Programme

Yacht-racing milestones

1967–68   Won New Zealand Junior Offshore Group (JOG) Championship (in *Bandit*)

1971   Line honours in the inaugural Cape Town–Rio de Janeiro race (watch leader on *Ocean Spirit*)

1973–74   Contested the inaugural Whitbread Round the World race (watch leader on *Burton Cutter*)

1974   First monohull in Two-man Round Britain race (on *Burton Cutter* with Robin Knox-Johnston)

1977   Line honours in inaugural Two-man Round the North Island race (of New Zealand) (on *Gerontius* with Graeme Eder)

1977–78   Contested the second Whitbread Round the World Race (watch leader on *Heath's Condor*)

1979   Line honours in Miami–Montego Bay race (skipper of *Condor*)
Line honours and race record in Antigua–Bermuda race (skipper of *Condor*)
Line honours and race record in Fastnet race (skipper of *Condor*)

1980   Line and handicap double in Sydney–Hobart race (skipper of *Ceramco*)

1981–82   Handicap wins in legs two and four of the third Whitbread Round the World race (skipper/navigator of *Ceramco*)
Roaring Forties Trophy for best corrected time performance in legs two and three (the Southern Ocean legs) of the Whitbread Round the World race (skipper/navigator of *Ceramco*)

1983   Contested Admiral's Cup challenge (skipper/team captain of *Lady B*)

1984	Line honours in Sydney–Hobart race (skipper/navigator of *Lion*)
1985–86	Contested fourth Whitbread Round the World race (skipper/navigator of *Lion*)
1988	Line hours in inaugural Two-Man Round Australia race (on the trimaran *Steinlager 1* with Mike Quilter)
1989–90	Line honours in the English Channel Race (skipper of *Steinlager 2*)
	Line honours in Fastnet Race (skipper of *Steinlager 2*)
	Line and handicap honours in all six legs of the Whitbread Round the World race (skipper of *Steinlager 2*)
	Overall line and handicap honours in Whitbread Round the World race (skipper of *Steinlager 2*)
	Roaring Forties Trophy for best corrected time performance in legs two and three (the Southern Ocean legs) of the Whitbread Round the World race
1991–92	Manager of New Zealand's America's Cup challenge in San Diego (New Zealand lost to Italy in the challenger final)
1993	Contested the inaugural Trophée Jules Verne attempt (skipper of the catamaran *ENZA*)
1994	Won Trophée Jules Verne with a record 74 days, 22 hours, 17 minutes, 22 seconds circumnavigation (skipper of the catamaran *ENZA*)
1992–95	Founded (with Alan Sefton) and was syndicate head of Team New Zealand
1995	Won the America's Cup (syndicate head of Team New Zealand and crew on the match winner *NZL 32 Black Magic*)
1995–2000	Syndicate head of Team New Zealand

2000	Successfully defended the America's Cup – the first non-American to do so (syndicate head of Team New Zealand)
	Founded (with Alan Sefton and Scott Chapman) and was head of blakexpeditions
2001	Undertook inaugural blakexpeditions voyage of exploration – to the Antarctic Peninsula (reaching 70 degrees South in George VI Sound)
	Undertook second blakexpeditions voyage of exploration 1400 miles up the Amazon and Negro rivers in Brazil

Acknowledgements

There are those without whose help this book would not have been possible. For their input and candidness, I would like to thank: Pippa Blake, Brian Aitken, David Alan-Williams, Ross Blackman, Tony Blake, Neil Burgess, Sir Tom Clark, Grant Dalton, Bob Fisher, Martin Foster, Simon Gundry, Sir Robin Knox-Johnston, Roy Mason, Douglas Myers, Ollie Olphert, Barry Pickthall, Mike Quilter, Don Robertson, Leon Sefton, Janet and Les Stokes, and Les Williams. For their patience, understanding and support: the team at Penguin Books New Zealand, in particular Geoff Walker, Rebecca Lal and Mike Wagg. Then there are my family (Kel, Leon and Justine) and the Chapmans (Scott, Marea, Bennett and Roni) who were always there when I needed them.

The quotes and extracts in Chapter One are from T. B. Byrne's wonderfully researched book *Wing of the Manukau: Capt. Thomas Wing: His Life and Harbour –1810–1888*. The early history of Brian Blake's side of Sir Peter's family was sourced from *Eighty Years Around the World – An Autobiography Covering Most of the Century* by Don Blake. Some of the other extracts and quotes covering Sir Peter's Whitbread career were sourced from *Blake's Odyssey –The Round the World Race with* Ceramco New Zealand by Peter Blake and Alan Sefton; *Lion – The around the World Race with* Lion New Zealand by Peter Blake and Alan Sefton; *Big Red – Round The World Race On Board* Steinlager2 by Mike Quilter and Glen Sowry; Sir Peter's own logs and David Alan-Williams' *ENZA New Zealand* logs. The Peter Mazany extracts are from his book *Team Think*. The publisher and author have made every reasonable effort to locate the copyright holder of the poem on page 11 of this book. If you have any information regarding the identity of this author please contact the publisher.

SIR PETER BLAKE

Index

442

443